COMMUNITY
PSYCHOLOGY

COMMUNITY PSYCHOLOGY

Karen Grover Duffy

State University of New York at Geneseo

Frank Y. Wong

Boston University School of Public Health and
South Cove Community Health Center
in Boston, Massachusetts

Allyn and Bacon
Boston • London • Toronto • Sydney • Tokyo • Singapore

Vice-President, Publisher: Susan Badger
Series Editor: Mylan Jaixen
Editorial Assistant: Susan Hutchinson
Executive Marketing Manager: Joyce Nilsen
Production Administrator: Annette Joseph
Production Coordinator: Susan Freese
Editorial-Production Service: TKM Productions
Manufacturing Buyer: Megan Cochran
Cover Administrator: Linda Knowles
Cover Designer: Suzanne Harbison

Copyright © 1996 by Allyn & Bacon
A Simon & Schuster Company
Needham Heights, Mass. 02194

Library of Congress Cataloging-in-Publication Data

Duffy, Karen Grover.
    Community psychology / Karen Grover Duffy, Frank Y. Wong.
        p.   cm.
    Includes bibliographical references and indexes.
    ISBN 0-205-13696-6
    1. Community psychology.   I. Title.
    RA790.55.D84   1995
    362.2--dc20   94-42725
                                                                                  CIP

Printed in the United States of America

10 9 8 7 6 5 4 3   00 99 98 97

BRIEF CONTENTS

CONTENTS

PREFACE

Welcome to the field of community psychology. We trust that you will find our book to be a scholarly, complete, yet engaging and interesting introduction to community psychology. This text presents a general overview of the concepts, theories, and research in the field of community psychology. The extensive scope of this book showcases more than community mental health issues. We believe that the field of community psychology has long outgrown its mental health image and is ready for a new text that goes beyond that focus.

Using our book, you, the reader, will develop an appreciation for community psychology. This text will foster an understanding of and a respect for the values of community psychology that often go beyond those of traditional psychology to which most of you have already been exposed. Although *Community Psychology* is designed for upper-division psychology students, including master's candidates, it is suitable for all perceptive students who have a rudimentary background in psychology. We hope the book promotes in you a respect for the cultural diversity of this country's communities. Wherever we can, we highlight research on cultural diversity or profile diverse individuals working in the community.

Community Psychology is comprised of five parts with a total of 12 chapters. The first 2 chapters (Part I) are introductory and will educate you about the purpose, history, philosophy, and research methods in community psychology. Part II pertains to social change. In the first chapter of Part II, you will discover what social change is and why it is important. Chapter 4 discusses the implementation of community and social change.

The chapters that follow systematically examine various community settings, interventions, and populations of interest to community psychologists. We examine in each chapter a few of the traditional approaches to serving the affected groups and settings and then review some of the alternative approaches as developed within community psychology. We do so first for the classic area in community psychology—mental health. Two chapters (Chapters 5 and 6) are dedicated to mental health because it is still a prominent theme in the field. These two chapters constitute Part III.

Part IV features areas into which community psychology has expanded. Chapters 7 through 11 focus on social and human services, schools and education, law and society, health care, and community organizations. Again, in each of these chapters, we first explore past approaches to relevant issues and then discuss alternatives offered by community psychologists. Finally, we conclude the text with Chapter 12, which summarizes the field and forecasts future trends for community psychology (Part V).

Every chapter contains special interest features that we believe will engage you, our student readers. Each chapter presents Profiles of people working in the community and Cases in Point to illustrate an important or interesting concept, as well as informative tables and figures throughout various chapters. The Profiles sometimes describe the work of a prominent community psychologist, typically an individual who has been honored by Division 27 of the American Psychological Association. We occasionally profile an individual who is doing work in a community agency, such as someone who arranges stress-management workshops in an organizational setting. These individuals, of course, are less well known. Both types of Profiles are designed to make the person, the community setting, and the work more real for you, the reader.

The Cases in Point are also designed to make the issue or topic practical and to stimulate critical thinking. In the typical Case in Point, a topic such as homelessness or community conflict is discussed in two ways: The issues related to the topic are examined and the relevant research is reviewed.

The chapters also contain several pedagogical aids. Each chapter commences with a chapter outline and an opening vignette. The vignettes are alluded to throughout the chapters and are used to crystallize the material at various points in your reading. We have done something with these vignettes that might be highly controversial for some adopters. The vignettes start with a case history, a very clinical and therefore a debatable approach. We did so in recognition of the fact that *more than half of the graduate community psychology programs* are clinical-community programs. For instructors trained in this tradition, the opening vignette will assist them in moving their students from a clinical point of reference (in which the individual in the vignette is the "figure") to a community (or "background") orientation by the end of the chapter. For those instructors oriented exclusively to community psychology, the Cases in Point are constructed to be more purely based on community psychology. Instructors will want to emphasize the approach and pedagogical aid that best suits their needs. In addition, key terms that are important in the field of community psychology are boldfaced in all chapters. Each chapter then concludes with a summary.

By critically examining the field, its issues, and its research, we hope that you will be inspired to become involved in your community in meaningful ways, such as in community volunteer work, research, or political activism. We also hope that you will think about pursuing a career in the exciting field of community psychology.

ACKNOWLEDGMENTS

We would be remiss if we did not thank the many people involved in this project. We owe sincere gratitude to the individuals who encouraged us in this undertaking and whose remarks on earlier drafts were extremely helpful: Norweeta Milburn, Ana Marie Cauce, John Morigutsu, Joe Ferrari, Ann D'Ercole, and Anthony Jackson. We also appreciate Toshi Sasao's early interest in and willingness to test earlier drafts of this manuscript in his classroom.

We also wish to thank our reviewers, whose critical appraisals of the book often helped us reframe issues and add material that resulted in a better product. These reviewers include James Dalton, Bloomsburg University; Joseph F. Ferrari, DePaul University; Janet F. Gillespie, State University of New York at Brockport; Steve Godin, East Stroudsburg University; Kelly Hazel, University of Alaska–Fairbanks; Jean Hill, New Mexico Highlands University; Patricia O'Connor, The Sage Colleges, Troy, New York; and Toshiaki Sasao, University of California, Los Angeles.

We are grateful to the many individuals at Allyn and Bacon for their patience, gentle prodding, and insights. Thanks to Bill Barke and Susan Badger for having initial faith in this project. Our thanks also go to Mylan Jaixen for his very professional and knowledgeable advice and steady guidance.

Our families, friends, and colleagues also demonstrated immense kindness and patience while we pounded away on our computers and spent long hours in library stacks searching for materials. Special gratitude is extended to Karen Duffy's students who graciously consented to having their contributions included and to her many students who studied from and stumbled through earlier rough drafts, pencil marks and all. Our sincerest thanks to everyone.

K. G. D.
F. Y. W.

ABOUT THE AUTHORS

Karen Grover Duffy received her Bachelor of Science degree in psychology with honors from St. Lawrence University and her doctoral degree in social/personality psychology from Michigan State University in 1973. Since then, she has been a professor of psychology at the State University of New York at Geneseo, where she teaches general, community, organizational, and social psychology.

Duffy serves on the Executive Board for the New York State Employee Assistance Program (EAP). She served as the primary instructor for the New York State EAP Institute for almost a decade. She also serves on the advisory board for the Center for Dispute Settlement, one of the oldest community mediation programs in the country. Duffy won the Gold Mediator award for her service as a board member and as a certified family and community mediator. She has also served on the Board of Directors of Chances and Changes, a shelter for victims of domestic violence.

In 1994, Duffy won a Fulbright Fellowship to teach community psychology and community mediation at St. Petersburg University, St. Petersburg, Russia. She also is the recipient of the Harry Van Arsdale Community Service Award from the AFL-CIO of New York State.

Frank Y. Wong received his doctoral degree in social psychology with a minor in management from Texas A&M University. He has interests in community-based research, focusing on issues related to maternal and child health and alcohol and other drug abuse, especially among racial/ethnic minorities. Wong has served as consultant to state and federal agencies on these issues. He is presently on the faculty of the Boston University School of Public Health and is also affiliated with South Cove Community Health Center in Boston, Massachusetts.

COMMUNITY PSYCHOLOGY

1

INTRODUCTION TO COMMUNITY PSYCHOLOGY

Introduction

Brief Historical Background
◆ *PROFILE 1.1 Seymour Sarason*

Philosophy and Goals of Community Psychology
❖ *CASE IN POINT 1.1 Social Psychology, Community Psychology, and*
   Homelessness
   Prevention Rather than Treatment
   Emphasis on Strengths and Competencies
   Importance of the Ecological Perspective
   Respect for Diversity
   Empowerment
   Choice among Alternatives
   Action Research
   Social Change
   Collaboration with Other Disciplines
   A Sense of Community

Community Psychology Today: Progress in the Field

Community Psychology Today: What's in It for You?
   Undergraduate Education
   Advanced Training in Community Psychology

Plan of the Book

Summary

Social progress makes the well-being of all more and more the business of each; it binds all closer and closer together in bonds from which none escape.

◆ *HENRY GEORGE, 1884*

Dory was born Doreen Snyder. While her mother was pregnant, Dory's father abandoned them. Dory's mother did not want to go on public assistance, so she worked two different jobs. From 7 A.M. to 4 P.M., Mrs. Snyder worked at a budget hotel as a housekeeper. From 6 P.M. to 11 P.M., she worked as a short-order cook in a local bar. Dory's mother was just able to make enough to pay for the rent, food, and Dory's child care with an older woman who also cared for four other children. The truth is that the Snyders lived in poverty.

When Dory was 3 years old, her caregiver remarked to Mrs. Synder that Dory was "odd" compared to the other children. By odd, the woman meant that Dory did not laugh and giggle or play with the other children. When Dory entered school, her mother was very proud and also relieved, since the child-care cost would be reduced. However, Mrs. Synder was soon confronted with the same news about Dory's strange behavior. Dory did not interact with the other children and seemed aloof when the teacher tried to engage her in conversation or in the learning process.

The school recommended an evaluation, which showed that Dory did have some "personality problems," as the psychologist called them, and that Dory's speech was delayed. The psychologist suggested a special class for Dory. Dory seemed to do well in this special class until the school was faced with declining enrollments, at which point the school closed. Dory was transferred to a bigger school where she seemed to get lost in the shuffle. She did not make much progress in her learning or her social skills from then on.

One day when Dory was about 16 years old, her mother received a call from the school saying that Dory had been truant for several days. When her mother confronted Dory about this, Dory flew into a rage, ran out the door, and disappeared onto the streets of the city. At first, Dory's mother searched for her and filed a missing person's report. After several days, when her mother had given up hope of finding her runaway daughter, Dory returned home.

The cycle of Mrs. Synder's confronting Dory about attending school or obtaining a job and Dory fleeing in anger was to be repeated several times. Each time Dory left her mother's small, dingy apartment, her disappearance grew longer and longer. When Dory was about 19 years old, she disappeared onto the streets for the final time. She became one of America's homeless.

On the streets, Dory eventually established a small territory that she considered hers in which she routinely wandered and foraged each day. She knew that Mrs. Fisher at the bakery would give her day-old cookies late each afternoon. She also visited Randy's Diner late at night for whatever was left over. Sundays were particularly hard on Dory, as neither the diner nor the bakery was open. At night, Dory slept in an alley under her big coat, which she had been given by a local shelter for the homeless. Dory often frequented this same shelter in inclement weather. Dory had no other relatives in the big, cold city who could take her in.

Dory knew she was a bit odd and could feel other people's discomfort in her presence, so she became a loner. This is probably why no one missed her for several days. Mrs. Fisher at the bakery finally became concerned that Dory had not appeared for several afternoons. The weather had been particularly harsh, too, with temperatures below zero. Mrs. Fisher called the shelter she knew Dory frequented only to find that the shelter manager had not seen Dory either. Mrs. Fisher's worst fears were realized when she heard from another homeless man that Dory's body had been found under some newspapers in an alley not far from the bakery. Dory had frozen to death.

INTRODUCTION

Pressing community problems such as acquired immune deficiency syndrome (AIDS), homelessness, school failure, teenage pregnancy, chemical dependency, violent crime, and the "isms" (ageism, racism, and sexism) require interdependent and long-lasting interventions. Unfortunately, single approaches to intervention usually seem to dominate in our society (Kelly, 1990). Which discipline asserts that addressing these problems in a multifocused fashion is its goal? **Community psychology**—the focus of this book.

This chapter will examine the history and growth, philosophy and goals, and current status of community psychology. It will also explore theory as it relates to research and practice in the field. This background should provide you with ample knowledge as well as encouragement to explore the rest of this book.

BRIEF HISTORICAL BACKGROUND

In colonial times, the United States was not without social problems. However, the close-knit, agrarian communities that existed often cared for needy individuals, and such care was generally provided without special places to house these individuals (Rappaport, 1977). As cities grew and became industrialized, a trend developed to institutionalize various populations: people who were mentally ill, indigent, and otherwise powerless. Perhaps from an abnormal psychology or other class, you know what these early institutions were like. They were often dank, crowded places where treatment ranged from restraint to cruel punishment.

It was not until the 1700s that Philip Pinel, followed somewhat later by Dorothea Dix and others, attempted to reform institutions by removing the restraints and establishing more positive attempts at changing behavior. However, these more "moral" treatments were sometimes limited to people of financial means (Rappaport, 1977). Nonetheless, institutions, especially the public ones, continued to grow and to house lower-class as well as powerless and other less privileged members of society. As waves of early immigrants entered the United States, many were often mistakenly diagnosed as mentally incompetent and found themselves in the same overpopulated institutions.

In the late 1800s, Sigmund Freud developed a keen interest in mental illness and its then current treatment. You are probably already familiar with his method of treatment, **psychoanalysis**, and his other contributions to psychology and psychiatry. Freud's basic premise was that emotional disturbance was due to intrapsychic forces within the individual and caused by past experiences. These disturbances could be treated by individual therapy and by attention to the unconscious. Freud gave us a legacy of intervention aimed at the individual (rather than the societal) level. Likewise, Freud conferred on the profession the strong tendency to divest individuals of the power to heal themselves; the physician, or expert, knew more about psychic healing than did the patient. Freud also oriented professional healers to examine an individual's past rather than current circumstances as the cause of disturbance and to view anxiety and underlying disturbance as endemic to everyday life. Freud certainly concentrated on an individual's weaknesses rather than strengths.

With regard to Dory Snyder, the young woman you met in the chapter opening, Freud probably would have maintained that her so-called personality problem stemmed from her father's absence and her mother's passing her off to another caregiver. He would have focused on Dory's problems rather than on any competencies she might have. Many other forms of therapy today are based on the assumption that individuals can be treated out of context—that is, without regard to their situation—and that professionals possess the most expert knowledge and therefore ought to design the treatment. Such philosophies fly in the face of community psychology.

World War II commenced around the time of Freud's death. Because of the war, there was an influx of immigrants to the United States. At the same time, large numbers of civilians with emotional problems were also being turned away from the armed services. These situations, in part, fostered the growth of professional psychology as society sought more healers for its disturbed masses.

At about the same time, President Franklin Roosevelt proclaimed his New Deal era. Specifically, heeding the lessons of the Great Depression of the 1920s and 1930s, he proposed a two-prong approach for attacking poverty: income transfers and employment programs. Both led to the development of the social security system, unemployment and disability benefits, and a variety of work relief programs. President Roosevelt's programs seemed more employment based than anything; at the time, there were no broad-based programs to attack poverty (Gottschalk & Gottschalk, 1988). For example, many women did not work. They could not benefit from these programs, however, even though they may have been living in poverty. On the other hand, the idea that poverty (at least as caused by unemployment) can be rectified with social programs had been planted in the American psyche.

Another important point in the history of the development of community psychology occurred in 1946 when Congress passed the National Mental Health Act. This act gave the United States Public Health Service broad authority to combat mental illness and to promote mental health. With the passage of this act and the interest in mental illness generated by the war, clinical psychology began to thrive. Shortly thereafter, the National Institute of Mental Health was established; this organization made significant federal funds available for research and training in mental health issues (Strother, 1987).

At the time, clinical psychologists were battling with psychiatrists to expand their domain from testing, which had been their primary thrust, to psychotherapy (Walsh, 1987). Today, **clinical psychology** is the field within psychology that deals with the diagnosis, measurement, and treatment of mental illness. It differs from **psychiatry**, in part, in that psychiatrists have a medical degree and can prescribe medication. Psychiatrists, then, might have medicated Dory Snyder so that she would have fit into her school environment better. On the other hand, clinical psychologists hold doctorates or Ph.D.s in psychology, which are considered to be research degrees. The battle between the two fields continues today, as some psychologists seek the right to administer and prescribe medications and to obtain privileges at the balance of the hospitals that do not yet allow them to practice (Buie, 1989a, 1989b).

Another aspect of history related to both world wars is that when formerly healthy veterans of the wars returned home, some returned as psychiatric casualties (Rappaport, 1977; Strother, 1987). What had intervened to change the soldiers' mental status? The wars. The terror of war forced psychologists to recognize the role the environment plays in an individual's mental health. Consider Dory, for instance. Perhaps Dory's placement in a large, less caring school or her family's poverty rather than something inherent in Dory's character or in her family background promoted further decline in her learning and social skills. In Profile 1.1, you will meet an individual who was one of the first to recognize how important the school environment is.

In 1949, the United States Public Health Service sponsored a conference in Boulder, Colorado. At this conference, the participants fashioned a model for the training of clinical psychologists that would guide training for years to come (Rappaport, 1977). The model emphasized education in science *and* in the practice of testing and therapy. Psychologists sometimes credit this event with the ability of psychology to further divorce itself from psychiatry, or the field of human medicine.

The 1950s brought significant change to the treatment of mental illness. One of the most influential developments was the discovery of pharmacologic agents that could be used to treat psychosis and other forms of mental illness. Various antipsychotics, tranquilizers, antidepressants, and other medications created ex-

◆ *PROFILE 1.1*
Seymour Sarason

No one who knows of or has worked with Seymour Sarason is surprised that he has been bestowed with so many honors, including the Distinguished Contributions to Community Psychology and Community Mental Health Award from the Division of Community Psychology of the American Psychological Association (APA), the Distinguished Contributions Award from the Division of Clinical Psychology of APA *and* from the American Association on Mental Deficiency, APA's Award for Distinguished Contributions to the Public Interest, as well as the Lifetime Contribution to Education Award from the American Federation of Teachers.

Sarason's distinguished career began at Rutgers University and Clark University, from which he received his doctorate. He recently retired from a long career at Yale University, where he founded the Psycho-Educational Clinic, an early clinic that spawned many of the ideas of community psychology. Although Sarason is a critic of what he sees in today's communities, his desire to go beyond criticism, to offer positive contributions to one's thinking, has made him a well-respected psychologist, as is obvious from his many awards. For instance, in one of his seminal papers for the field, "Community Psychology, Networks, and Mr. Everyman," Sarason (1976) openly challenged the strong field of clinical psychology by stating that it was a field that could not provide an understanding of "coming to grips with the complexity of a community." In fact, he issued a challenge to divorce community psychology from clinical psychology. In clinical psychology, he said, "the individual tends to be figure and all else ground, and we are not even aware that there is a ground" (p. 320). Does this sound as if Sarason was an early proponent of the ecological perspective so cherished in community psychology? Indeed, it does.

We will highlight here only his pioneering work in educational settings. When Sarason started his work, most consultants who ventured into the schools went there to "fix" the people in the schools. Worse than that, other consultants let their educational clients come to them rather than the consultants going to the natural settings of the clients. This was not so with Sarason. At the Psycho-Educational Clinic, the staff would go to the community to be helpful in regard to problems in the setting. In other words, the clinic's staff would be "participant observer-helpers."

Sarason saw the school as a *social setting* in which human capacity could be fostered *or* diminished. For instance, he observed that there is little in classroom life that values curiosity about and respect for diversity in children. In fact, he noted that children often showed more curiosity and learned faster *outside* the classroom. At the time Sarason was making his observations, he noted that teachers played the role of diagnosticians, yet there was nothing else in their role that supported this function— nothing, for example, like case conferences.

Sarason was one of the first to articulate the importance of educational settings in shaping children's development. Beyond that, he did not just make these observations; he offered suggestions for reform. Schools, he argued, needed to acknowledge their role in shaping attitudes toward society and culture; their goals needed to be broadened. School psychologists needed to expand their roles beyond testing to interface with the home and the community. School principals, he reasoned, could be more than piecemeal tinkerers with their schools; they could become long-range planners and designers.

These ideas and others may not seem new to you, but they were revolutionary at the time Sarason proposed them. We have only briefly highlighted his contributions to education here, and we urge you to become more familiar with this man and his distinguished career.

Source: Adapted from "Seymour Sarason: A Celebration of the Man and His Ideas," June 1990, *American Journal of Community Psychology, 18* (3), pages 341–382.

tensive change in the institutions, the major change being that patients became more tractable, or docile. The use of these drugs proliferated despite their major side effects.

In 1952, a pioneering article was published. Hans Eysenck, Sr., a renowned British scientist, launched an attack on the practice of psychotherapy (Eysenck, 1952, 1961). By reviewing the literature on psychotherapy, Eysenck was able to demonstrate that no treatment—in fact, the mere passage of time—was often as effective as professional treatment. Other mental health professionals followed suit and leveled criticisms at other psychological practices such as psychological testing (Meehl, 1954, 1960) and the whole concept, or "myth," of mental illness (Szasz, 1961). These criticisms, of course, have not gone unrebutted; we will review these issues further in the chapters on mental illness. If intervention were not useful, as Eysenck maintained, individuals like Dory Snyder would be left to roam the streets because they would be given little hope by the helping professions, especially if communities and helping systems remained uncaring.

The 1960s witnessed further, sometimes sweeping, reforms. The Civil Rights movement of the 1950s carried over to the 1960s. Minorities, women, and other less privileged members of society cried out for equal rights. At the same time, foreign economic competition, the threat of nuclear confrontation with the former Soviet Union, and the space race forced U.S. citizens to adopt more outward-looking viewpoints. Psychologists were therefore encouraged to "do something to participate in society as psychologists" (Walsh, 1987, p. 524). Those issues, coupled with our increasing moral outrage over the Vietnam War, fueled excitement about citizen involvement in social reform and generated understanding about the interdependence of social movements (Kelly, 1990).

With the election of John Kennedy as president came an invigorated concern about institutionalization, mental health, and the general availability of human services. Kennedy's own mentally retarded sister may have augmented his interest in these issues. Kennedy also was elected on his platform of social change. Social conditions and poverty, he reasoned, were responsible in large part for negative psychological conditions (Heller, Price, Reinharz, Riger, & Wandersman, 1984). Kennedy helped secure the passage of the Community Mental Health Centers Act of 1963, which authorized funds for *local* mental health centers. The centers were to provide outpatient, emergency, and educational services, among others. Although not without problems and not necessarily revolutionary, this act recognized the need for immediate, local intervention in the form of emergency services as well as the need for prevention through education. Such centers meant that individuals like Dory Snyder could seek immediate assistance right in their own neighborhoods.

After Kennedy's assassination, President Lyndon Johnson appeared to be moving the country toward "the Great Society." For the first time, a president issued a blueprint for the War on Poverty in his State of the Union address. The 1964 annual report of the President's Council of Economic Advisors stated:

> *Conquest of poverty is well within our power. About $11 billion a year would bring all poor families up to the $3,000 income level we have taken to be the minimum for a decent life. The majority of the Nation could simply tax themselves enough to provide the necessary income supplements to their less fortunate citizens. . . . But this "solution" would have untouched most of the roots of poverty. Americans want to* earn *the American standard of living by their own efforts and contributions. It will be far better, even if more difficult, to equip and to permit the poor of the Nation to produce and to earn the additonal $11 billion, and more.*

These statements strongly indicate that former President Johnson and his advisors wanted to find ways or mechanisms that could empower people who were less fortunate, to assist them to become productive citizens. Programs such as **Head Start** (addressed in Chapter 8) and other federally funded early childhood enhancement programs for the disadvantaged were conceived within this ideology. Also, many of the prototypes of social and human services were developed around this time. (The social history of the United States will be discussed in other parts of this book.)

Although less important to social history, very important to the history of community psychology was a conference held in Swampscott, Massachusetts, in May of 1965. This conference is usually cited as the official birth date of community psychology (Heller et al., 1984; Hersch, 1969; Rappaport, 1977). This first conference was attended by clinical psychologists concerned with the inadequacies of their field and oriented to creating social and political change. As a result of their small-group discussions, the Swampscott participants agreed to move from treatment to prevention and to the inclusion of an ecological perspective (loosely, a "person-environment fit") in their work (Bennett et al., 1966). This perspective is from Kurt Lewin (1951), the father of social psychology, another area of psychology much akin to community psychology.

The Swampscott Conference was followed by other conferences. Today, research conferences are planned nearly every year. Community psychology is a recognized division of the American Psychological Association (Division 27). Several journals (the *Journal of Community Psychology*, the *American Journal of Community Psychology*, the *Journal of Rural Community Psychology*, and *Journal of Community and Applied Social Psychology*) represent the field, along with many other related journals on social change, community mental health, and other relevant areas (Kelly, 1990).

Contemporary community psychologists have long enjoyed intellectual and research exchanges with colleagues in other academic disciplines such as political science, anthropology, and sociology, as well as other areas of psychology such as social psychology (Altman, 1987). Case in Point 1.1 demonstrates the relationship between social and community psychology. Some are calling for renewed inter-disciplinary efforts (Linney, 1990) with other community professionals, too, such as substance abuse counselors, enforcement agencies, school psychologists, and human services professionals, among others. In addition, community psychologists have proposed further expansion. For example, Shinn (1987), following the lead of Heller and others (1984), suggested that community psychology has and should expand beyond community mental health to schools, work sites, religious settings, voluntary associations, and governments. Other authors in the field have also expounded on the virtues and utility of community psychology outside of urbanized United States. For example, Heyman (1986) recognized the need for community psychology in rural America, Levine (1989) reported that community psychology has much to offer diverse Asian countries, and Bernal and Marin (1985) reported on community psychology in Cuba.

Given this legacy of reform and expansion within and outside the field of psychology, what are the current goals and values of community psychology today?

PHILOSOPHY AND GOALS OF COMMUNITY PSYCHOLOGY

Before beginning this section, the definition of *community psychology* is in order. Singular agreement on a definition for the field does not exist, but the following are among popular definitions:

> *Community psychology...has evolved to study the effects of social and environmental factors on behavior as it occurs at individual, group, organizational, and societal levels. (Heller et al., 1984, p. 18)*

> *Community psychology is, in part, an attempt to find other alternatives for dealing with deviance from societal-based norms....Community psychology viewed in this way is an attempt to support every person's right to be different without risk of suffering material and psychological sanctions. (Rappaport, 1977, p. 1)*

> *Community psychology is regarded as an approach to human behavior problems that emphasizes contributions to their development made by environmental forces as well as the potential contributions to be made toward their alleviation by the use of such forces. (Zax & Specter, 1974, p. 3)*

These definitions from earlier books in the field are all useful and capture the thrust of community psychology. Our definition will complement and embellish

❖ CASE IN POINT 1.1

Social Psychology, Community Psychology, and Homelessness

You have learned in this chapter that community psychologists have issued a clarion call for collaboration with other disciplines both within and outside of psychology. In response to that, we agree that community psychologists and social psychologists have much that they can learn from each other (Serrano-Garcia, Lopez, & Rivera-Medena, 1987).

Social psychologists, psychologists who study social phenomena as they impact on an individual, may have the answer as to why the media, the public, and other psychologists blame an individual's homelessness on the individual (i. e., usually either the person's mental illness or alcoholism.) Social psychologists have developed **attribution theory**, which explains how people infer causes of or make attributions about other's behaviors (Kelly, 1973). Research on attribution has clearly demonstrated that we are likely to place emphasis on characteristics of the individual or use trait explanations for another's shortcomings (Jones & Nisbett, 1971). That is, when explaining the behavior of others—especially other's problems—people are less likely to attend to the situation and more likely to make person-centered attributions.

Does this theory apply to homelessness? Can this theory explain why the media and the public often blame the victim, the homeless person, for his or her problem? *Victim blaming* is a term that describes the tendency to attribute the cause of an indivudal's problems to that individual rather than to the situation the person is in. In other words, the victim is blamed for what happened to him or her. Social psychologists believe that blaming the victim is a means of self-defense (e.g., if a bad thing can happen to her, then it can happen to me). In the case of Dory, did her personality create her homeless situation? Did something in Dory's environment contribute to it? The average person who blames the victim would blame Dory for contributing to her homelessness.

Shinn, a prominent community psychologist, recently concluded a review of research on homelessness as well as conducted a monumental and well-designed study on the issue (Shinn & Gillespie, 1993). She concluded that person-centered explanations of homelessness, although popular, are not as valid as situational and structural explanations of homelessness. Specifically, Shinn suggested that the researched explanations for homelessness are bifurcated—that is, person centered and environmental. She reviewed the literature on each and concluded that person-centered or deficit explanations for homelessness are less appropriate than environmental or situational explanations.

Shinn found studies that suggest that structural problems offer some of the most plausible explanations of homelessness. For example, Rossi (1989) found that between 1969 and 1987, the number of single adults (some with children) with incomes under $4,000 a year increased from 3.1 to 7.2 million. Similarly, Leonard Dolbeare, and Lazere (1989) found that for the 5.4 million low-income renters, there were only 2.1 million units of affordable housing according to the Department of Housing and Urban Development standards. Poverty and lack of affordable housing seem to be far better explanations for today's homelessness than person-centered explanations. Solarz and Bogat (1990) would add to these environmental explanations of homelessness the lack of social support by friends and family of the homeless.

What is important about Shinn's review is not so much that it illustrates that the public and the media may indeed suffer from **fundamental attribution error**—the tendency to blame the person and not the situation—but rather that Shinn offers these data so community psychologists can act on them. Public policy makers need to understand that situations and structural problems produce homelessness. Psychologists and community leaders need to be convinced that providing temporary solutions such as soup kitchens are merely bandages on the gaping wound of the homeless. Furthermore, shelter managers and others have to understand that moving the homeless from one shelter to another does little for them. Families and children, not just the stereotypical old alcoholic men, are part of the "new" homeless (Rossi, 1990). Being in different shelters and therefore different school systems has negative effects on children's academic performance and self-esteem (Rafferty & Shinn, 1991); homeless children lose their childhoods to homelessness (Landers, 1989).

Something must be done about the permanent housing situation in this country. On this point, both community and social psychologists would concur.

on these to reflect changes in the field. *Community psychology* focuses on social issues, social institutions, and other settings that influence groups and organizations (and therefore the individuals in them). The goal is to optimize the well-being of communities and individuals with innovative and alternate interventions designed in collaboration with affected community members and with other related disciplines inside and outside of psychology.

With that definition in mind, we will turn to more specific goals and philosophies that have guided the field over the years. Remember that community psychology today is not what it was at the Swampscott Conference when participants had a decided interest in community mental health. Community psychology has shed its "mental health only" image. Also keep in mind that the community psychology you read about today will probably not be the community psychology of the next decade as the field outgrows its adolescence and matures. Each of the themes presented next is elaborated upon in depth with research and examples in other chapters. Here, the intent is merely to introduce you to each concept.

Prevention Rather than Treatment

The philosophy of **prevention** rather than treatment was inspired at the Swampscott Conference and more broadly by the public health movement (Caplan, 1964; Heller et al., 1984; Kelly, 1990). The underlying theme is that treatment comes too late in the intervention process; it is usually provided long after the individual has developed the problem, so is often ineffective. Noted psychologist Emory Cowen (1980) stated, "We became increasingly, indeed alarmingly, aware of (a) the frustration and pessimism of trying to undo psychological damage once it had passed a certain critical point; (b) the costly, time-consuming, culture-bound nature of mental health's basic approaches, and their unavailability to, and effectiveness with, large segments of society in great need" (p. 259).

On the other hand, prevention could counter any trauma before it began, thus saving the individual and even the whole community from developing a problem. In this regard, community psychology takes a proactive rather than reactive role. Stated another way, if we treat individuals as at-risk populations, they can benefit from the preventive interventions of community psychology (Kelly, 1990). For example, it is possible that sex education before adolescence, teamed with new social policy, can reduce the teenage pregnancy rate that is considered epidemic today (Reppucci, 1987). In other words, perhaps if Dory's mother had been provided with better education about prenatal development and child rearing *before* she gave birth to Dory, Dory would have had a better start on life. In the following chapters, you will read about a variety of techniques in prevention: education, altering the environment, development of alternate facilities, public policy changes, and so on (Long, 1992).

In community psychology, there are distinctions between levels of preventive intervention. **Primary prevention** attempts to prevent a problem from occurring altogether. It refers most generally to activities that can be undertaken with a healthy population to maintain or enhance its health, physical or emotional (Bloom & Hodges, 1988). **Secondary prevention** attempts to treat a problem at the earliest possible moment before it becomes severe or persistent. **Tertiary prevention**, which belongs more in the realm of clinical psychology and is therefore not a focus in this book, attempts to reduce the severity of a problem once it has persistently occurred. Although you might believe that the terms *prevention*, *early treatment*, and *treatment* are better than *primary prevention*, *secondary prevention*, and *tertiary prevention*, the latter terms are preferred (Albee & Gullotta, 1986).

The case of Dory Snyder can be used to illustrate these concepts. In the case of Dory, early psychological testing or early knowledge of her family's poverty may have determined that she was at risk for running away. Had an intervention occurred early and prevented her homelessness, it would be an example of primary prevention. When Dory was first truant from school, had assistance been provided to her mother in dealing with her daughter, her mother would have been provided with secondary prevention. Finally, once Dory was on the streets, anyone attempting to change her situation would have been providing tertiary prevention. As you can well imagine, primary prevention is the most desirable of the preventive levels.

A second example directly from the community psychology research might prove fruitful. The community psychology literature on primary prevention contains a succinct study that pertains to children about to be immunized against rubella. Klingman (1985) trained groups of children to practice skills related to coping with their fear of injections. Compared to control groups, the trained children showed less anxiety and more cooperation when they were inoculated. Thus, the study illustrates primary prevention, as it altogether prevented the problems of anxiety and uncooperativeness in the trained children.

Prevention measures do not always work, but a complete critique of prevention strategies is beyond the scope of this first chapter. Throughout this book, you will read about the utilities and failures of preventive programs in various settings in which psychologists work, whether they be industrial settings, law enforcement agencies, mental health agencies, or sports programs in communities. It is incumbent on psychologists, no matter where they work, to be knowledgeable about appropriate ameliorative interventions and appropriate prevention techniques (Price, Cowen, Lorion, & Ramos-McKay, 1988).

Emphasis on Strengths and Competencies

The field of psychology has historically focused on individuals' weaknesses and problems. Freud planted the seed that was cultivated by later clinicians. However, in 1959, Robert White wrote about **competence**, by which he meant a sense of mastery when interacting with the environment; competence is a basic desire to feel capable. White's notion offered a conceptual change for psychologists concerned that clinical psychology was mired in negative human behavior.

As individuals, none of us likes to feel incompetent; we like instead to feel a sense of strength that comes from mastering some part of our environment. Perhaps you recall your joy when you first passed your driver's test or your exhilaration when speaking a newly mastered foreign language for the first time to a native speaker. The joy of mastery is the result of competence.

The concept of competence was quickly embraced by early community psychologists. First, it had ecological, or environmental, implications. Ecological settings could be altered to maximize an individual's competence in them. Second, competence aligned nicely with the concept of prevention. If strengths were enhanced early in life, problems might be avoided more easily in the future.

Importance of the Ecological Perspective

We have just stated that ecological settings can be altered; settings, then, are important to community psychology. More correctly stated, the **person-environment fit** (Pargament, 1986) is important in community psychology. Exactly what does this mean? Rappaport (1977) explained this term well. The **ecological perspective** means an examination of the relationship between persons and their environments (both social and physical) and establishing the optimal match between the person and the setting. In other words, controlling the environment to control the individuals in it is not useful, nor is labeling the person who does not fit the setting as a "misfit." Rather, the ecological perspective recognizes the transactional nature that people and environments have. Individuals influence the settings in which they find themselves; settings influence the individuals in them (Seidman, 1990). If something is awry with the individual, *both* the environment and the person can be examined and perhaps changed.

A specific example of the importance of the person-environment transaction might help. Dory Snyder's earliest teachers reported to her mother that Dory seemed to have problems attending to educational and social stimuli. However, in the special class at the smaller school, Dory seemed to fare quite well. Sent to another school, with similarly trained teachers, Dory nonetheless did not flourish. The second school was larger, and for some reason Dory did not thrive there. For Dory, the smaller school seemed better. Another student with learning problems similar to Dory's but more socially engaging than Dory might have felt more comfortable in the large school and smothered in the small school. Individuals are unique and so are settings. Finding the right combination is one of the goals of community psychology.

Respect for Diversity

Dory's schools probably wished all their students were alike. How much easier the schools' jobs would be if students were homogeneous! Each individual, though, is unique. People come in all shapes and sizes, from different ethnic backgrounds, with different likes and dislikes, and with various attitudes and prejudices. Individual differences emerge by virtue of each person's unique developmental history. As people mature, they diversify; thus, people merely mimic as individuals what occurs in their communities. Often, as communities mature, they too diversify. The world is a more interesting place because of diversity, but it is a more complex world, too.

There is an appreciation for diversity in community psychology. People have the right to be *different*, and different does not mean *inferior*. If difference is accepted as a fact of life, resources ought then to be equitably distributed to all of these different people. These beliefs are not just noble rhetoric. From a belief in the diversity of people also comes a recognition of the distinctive styles of living, world views, and social arrangements that are not part of mainstream society but that characterize our society's diversity. Moreover, a recognition of these distinctions results in the ability to avoid comparing diverse populations with mainstream cultural standards and therefore labeling these different others as "deficient" or "deviant" (Snowden, 1987), as well as the ability to design interventions that are culturally appropriate (e.g., Marin, 1993).

In a recent examination of the community psychology literature, the reviewers found that about 11% of the articles in community psychology journals pertain to people from ethnic minorities. The authors concluded that progress toward understanding the diverse population is being made but that more needs to be done (Loo, Fong, & Iwamasca, 1988). A second examination of the literature suggests that community psychology has had some success in improving mental health services to minorities (Snowden, 1987). However, other authors have decried the fact that there is no general framework for relating significant social-psychological markers such as gender and race to theory, reasearch, and action in community psychology. Such a framework is hopefully emerging now (Watts, 1992).

Empowerment

If people recognize that everyone is unique and that individuals differ from one another, it would be presumptuous to think that professionals are more expert than are clients at designing environments for the clients. A crucial concept in community psychology is **empowerment**, the process of enhancing the possibility that people can more actively control their own lives (Rappaport, 1981). Empowerment is a process by which individuals not only gain control and mastery over their own lives but over democratic participation in their community as well (Zimmerman & Rappaport, 1988). Julian Rappaport (1987), a leading proponent of empowerment, says that empowerment conveys a sense of personal control or influence and involves an individual's determination over his or her own life.

Empowerment is also a multilevel construct; it is applicable beyond the individual and community levels. Empowerment adapts well to groups and whole organizations. For instance, in Chapter 11, you will learn about the many ways avant-garde organizations, whether they be community nonprofits or large industrial organizations, are enhancing member participation in the design and change of the organization and the tasks its members accomplish.

Empowerment, then, means *doing* (Swift & Levin, 1987); however, it does not mean that community psychologists do things for others. Rather, in the roles of researchers-reporters, collaborators-educators, or advocates-activists, others are empowered so that they can *do* for themselves.

The concept of empowerment has not gone without criticism. Riger (1993) argued that empowerment often leads to individualism and therefore competition and conflict. Similarly, she criticized the construct for being traditionally masculine, in that it involves power and control, rather than feminine, which concerns communion and cooperation. Riger issued a challenge to community psychologists to develop a vision that incorporates both empowerment and community, despite what she construed as the paradoxical nature of the two phenomena.

Related to empowerment is citizen participation in researching community problems, developing solutions, and evaluating the outcomes of community change. Also, citizen self-help and mutual support groups such as Alcoholics Anonymous are means for individuals in the community to assist each other without benefit of professional help. These topics are addressed in detail in Chapter 3.

Choice among Alternatives

Given a respect for the uniqueness of each individual, respect should lead to an understanding that a single human services setting is not optimal for everyone. Furthermore, a variety of alternative community settings and services would best serve the community's diverse population. Likewise, individuals need the power to participate in the design of the services and then select the one best suited to them (Salem, 1990). Providing *choices* in community services is a revered value of community psychology. In several chapters in this book, you will read about the variety of innovative services that community psychologists have promoted or designed as alternatives to traditional ones. Perhaps if a variety of services rather than only one overcrowded shelter had been available to Dory, she would have survived.

Another important aspect of choice among services is accessibility. *Accessibility* means that services should be taken to the people. People should not have to go to services, especially if access is difficult. For example, if mental health services are in the suburbs but people in the inner city most need them, the services will probably be underutilized by those most in need.

Action Research

If a variety of services are optimal for both individual and community well-being and the fit between the individual and the service is crucial, then the best way to ascertain which services and which individuals match is by means of science. Research and science grounded in theory and directed toward resolving social problems is called **action research**. The next chapter discusses in detail how action research is conducted. At this point, it is important to remember that social problems are difficult to resolve, research or not, and that research in community settings is complex. For instance, if one wanted to change a human services agency so that it better addresses community needs, one would probably have to research the whole agency plus the people involved, including clients, staff and their subgroups, as well as all of their interrelationships. Community research is indeed complex.

Social Change

Armed with research, one of the goals of community psychology is to induce social change. Planned social change is such an important part of community psychology that two chapters in this book are dedicated to it. Here, the term will be defined and differentiated from unplanned change. **Unplanned social change** occurs spontaneously. No one planned it; the change just happened. An example of this is the influx of the homeless, such as Dory, onto our city streets. No one purposely decided that we should have more homeless people! On the other hand, **planned social change** is defined as intentionally creating social change. In planned change, what is to be changed is targeted in advance, is directed toward enhancing the community, and provides for a role in the design of change by those affected by the change. In community psychology, planned change is often very innovative, too.

Collaboration with Other Disciplines

Creating social change is a monumental task. Community psychologists would have to be quite audacious to suggest that they can create change by themselves. Collaboration with sister disciplines is a means to producing more sweeping and well-reasoned change (Strother, 1987). In fact, given recent and unfortunate trends in U.S. society, social change agents need, more than ever, to confer with other professionals. Kelly (1990) suggested that **collaboration** with others gives new awareness of how other disciplines experience a phenomenon. A benefit of consultation with others such as historians, economists, environmentalists, biologists, sociologists, anthropologists, and policy scientists is that perspectives can be expanded and new perspectives adopted.

A Sense of Community

Because this concept, a sense of community, comes last does not mean it is less significant than the preceding concepts. In fact, the sense of community is one of the most important concepts for community psychology (Sarason, 1974). The topic was saved until last because here it best fits our scheme for unfolding the philosophy of community psychology.

If environments and individuals are well matched, a more optimal community as well as a community with a sense of spirit and a sense of "we-ness" can be created. Research has demonstrated that a sense of community, or what is sometimes called *community spirit* or sense of belonging in the community, is positively related to the subjective sense of well-being (Davidson & Cotter, 1991). In an optimal community, members probably will be more open to changes that will further improve their community.

Empirical research has demonstrated that a sense of community is positively related to community activism in the form of voting, working on public policies, and contacting public officials (Davidson & Cotter, 1989). Interestingly, recent research has demonstrated that happiness and the sense of satisfaction with one's community is not found exclusively in the suburbs. People living in the suburbs are no more likely to express satsifaction with their neighborhoods than people living in the city (Adams, 1992). Many laypeople and psychologists believe that residents of the inner city are at risk for a myriad of problems. However, recent research has found that there are some very resilient individuals located in the most stressful parts of our cities (Work, Cowen, Parker, & Wyman, 1990).

Community has traditionally meant a locality or place such as a neighborhood. It has also come to mean a relational interaction or social ties that draw people together (Heller, 1989). To these definitions could be added the one of community as a collective political power.

If those are the definitions for *community*, what is the sense of community? **Sense of community** is the feeling of the relationship an individual holds for his or her community (Heller et al., 1984) or the personal knowledge that one has about belonging to a collective of others (Newbrough & Chavis, 1986). More specifically, it is "the perception of similarity to others, an acknowledged interdependence with others, a willingness to maintain this interdependence by giving to or doing for others what one expects from them, the feeling that one is part of a larger dependable and stable structure" (Sarason, 1974, p. 157). If people sense community in their neighborhood, they then feel that they belong to or fit into the neighborhood. Community members sense that they can influence what happens in the community, share the values of the neighborhood, and feel emotionally connected to it (Heller et al., 1984).

A sense of community is specifically thought to include four elements: membership, influence, integration, and a sense of emotional connection.

1. *Membership* means that people experience feelings of belonging in their community.
2. *Influence* signifies that people feel they can make a difference in their communities.
3. *Integration*, or fulfillment of needs, suggests that members of the community believe that their needs will be met by resources available in the community.
4. *Emotional connection* implies that community members have and will share history, time, places, and experiences (McMillan & Chavis, 1986).

A concept related to sense of community is **neighboring**, which is a person's emotional, cognitive, and social attachment to a neighborhood that makes him or her more likely to participate in neighborhood organizations (Unger & Wandersman, 1985a).

A sense of community need not be experienced only in a whole community. People can develop a sense of community in a group, an organization, or for almost any other aggregate of individuals. A relatively new and promising scale has been developed to measure the sense of community (Buckner, 1988). This scale, which is designed to measure neighborhood cohesion or fellowship, seems psychometrically sound and asks reactions to statements such as, "I believe my neighbors would help me in an emergency."

COMMUNITY PSYCHOLOGY TODAY: PROGRESS IN THE FIELD

Where is the field of community psychology today? Has it achieved some of its lofty goals? Fortunately, there is research assessing historical changes in the field to determine whether community psychology is making any progress.

Some in the field feel the ardor, zeal, optimism, and commitment that once characterized community psychology have faded (Linney, 1990). Do data bear out that community psychology is progressing or backsliding? We hope to provide a lengthy answer throughout this book. For our purposes, another way to look more briefly at this question is to compare early and later research in the field. A historical overview will enable us to understand changes in the discipline.

Speer and his fellow researchers (1992) examined the topics, the populations studied, and the sophistication of the measures and methodologies utilized in community psychology research. Fortunately for them, previous research conducted by Lounsbury, Leader, Meares, and Cook (1980) from approximately a decade earlier was available for comparison purposes. Speer and colleagues reviewed 235 *empirical* studies (defined as reporting the results of research investigations) in the top two journals of community psychology from 1984 to 1988 and compared their findings to those of Lounsbury and associates. Here is what they found.

In community psychology, the number of **experiments** where variables were actively manipulated decreased over the decade, whereas the number of **field studies** where no variables were actively manipulated increased. The use of **control groups** or comparison groups also decreased as one might expect because experimental manipulations had decreased.

Participants with identified psychological problems were less likely to appear in the more recent studies than the older studies. Over the years, the reporting of participant gender and ethnic origin increased. Articles categorized as dealing with mental health services decreased with time, but the number of articles categorized by the authors as problem specific increased, particularly in the areas of social support and prevention.

What conclusions can be made about the direction of community psychology from this archival review? First, the authors of this research suggest that just because there was a shift from experimental research to correlational research does not mean the field is less sophisticated. Rather, they argue, psychology as a whole recently experienced more sympathy for qualitative research, and thus the research in community psychology may be a mere reflection of this circumstance. Or, as Speer and associates propose, perhaps the change in methodology indicates that community psychologists select methods based on the concepts they are studying rather than what is "right" at the moment in the whole of psychology.

Second, there are now fewer studies of people who are chronically mentally ill. Instead, examination of larger portions of participants from the community at large demonstrates that recent research is being conducted in settings *as* and *where* social problems occur, which is one of the goals of community psychology. Likewise, the data indicate that the field is acquiring more information about diverse populations in more recent studies—another of its goals.

The disappointing news is that many of the recent dependent measures still focus on the individual level of analysis. Although it is true that today there are more studies on person-environment variables such as **social support** (where individuals assist one another with coping), the literature still very much retains an individual-based, adjustment orientation. Perhaps a study a decade from now will find yet another shift away from this feature of the present research. Based on this literature analysis, we tentatively agree that community psychology is on its way toward fulfilling the goals outlined earlier.

COMMUNITY PSYCHOLOGY TODAY: WHAT'S IN IT FOR YOU?

Undergraduate Education

Many psychology departments now offer community psychology courses. Others offer courses in community mental health or clinical psychology, where the professor prefers to adopt a community orientation. However, the training of-fered to undergraduates may only be a course or two. Another way undergradu-ates can learn more about the community is to become involved in the local college community or the students' hometown. Thousands of community agencies solicit volunteers, but, of course, many of these agencies do not adopt a community psychology orientation. For example, many supply treatment and therefore do not focus on prevention. Volunteers are the lifeblood of many community agencies that run on limited budgets. College personnel may be able to give you the names and phone numbers of local agencies. If you do choose to volunteer, try to determine whether the agency promotes the goals of community psychology and if not, why not. For example, perhaps the agency at which you volunteer would like to conduct educational workshops to prevent community problems, but its budget prohibits it from taking this proactive stance.

Stein (1992) reported a unique collaborative learning project that involved college students and mental health clients. Instead of the usual helper-helpee role that most students play when they volunteer to aid mental health clients, Stein developed a collaborative learning program in which both the undergraduates and mental health clients became "students" participating in a psychoeducational program.

In the program, each student first developed a detailed assessment of his or her social problem-solving strategies and of available resource networks or available supports in the community. Next, all students set personal goals and became involved in skill enhancement to meet those goals. Finally, all students applied these new skills to their network relationships. The program was designed to build skills in both sets of participants as well as facilitate understanding and collaboration between the undergraduates and the mental health clients. Davidson and Redner (1988) also reported research on the effectiveness of community volunteers in preventing yet another social problem: delinquency. Their efforts will be discussed in more detail in Chapter 9.

We, too, encourage our students to become involved in the community to foster understanding of communities and their diverse populations as well as to assist the local agencies. Our students often volunteer in the community as part of their course experience, and many continue the experience after the community psychology course ends. Volunteers are indeed special people in terms of their commitment and identification with the organizations for which they work (Koslowsky, Caspy, & Lazar, 1988). Likewise, by working for someone else's benefit rather than for self-interest, volunteers show selflessness (O'Neill, Duffy, Enman, Blackmer, & Goodwin, 1988). Here are some comments from our volunteer students:

> Today was the first day of my volunteer work at the Hospitality Center, a shelter designed to teach independent living skills and offer long-term transitional services to the homeless. This shelter was designed to stop the cycle of homeless men who go from shelter to shelter and from missionary to missionary....After I left the shelter, I felt really weird. I sort of felt guilty because I was going back to my home. I don't think I ever really fully realized the injustices of the world as much as I did in the car ride back to my home.
>
> Stacey Fishbein, Class of 1993

As I said before, my first day was not the most thrilling experience in the world, at least task-wise. However, it was constantly on my mind that "excitement" or "entertainment" is not the point of doing volunteer work. It felt really good knowing that, no matter how trivial or boring my task, I was doing my little bit to help those who are combating a killer disease [cancer] that has affected millions of people. That feeling is what makes volunteering worth one's while.

Rodney Corry, Class of 1992

Snyder and Omoto (1992) researched AIDS volunteers and their motives for volunteering. Over 80% of the vounteers approached their organizations on their own initiative. Moreover, the volunteerism represented a substantial commitment; volunteers in the sample averaged four hours per week over a period of one and one-half years. Using their new inventory that measures motivation for volunteering, Snyder and Omoto found no differences between volunteer quitters and stayers in reported satisfaction with their service commitments. However, the quitters reported that volunteering was taking too much time and, more importantly, that volunteering for AIDS organizations was stigmatizing them. The initial motivation for volunteering also differentiated quitters from stayers. The stayers reported higher levels of self-satisfaction, learning, and skill acquisition compared to quitters. Interestingly, the volunteers who remained committed did not necessarily report noble motives, such as helping society or humanitarianism, as their primary motives. Snyder and Omoto recommended that volunteer agencies regularly remind volunteers of the personal gains of volunteering.

Internships in community psychology are another vehicle by which undergraduates and graduate students can experience and assist in their communities. Internships often provide students with opportunities to learn about program planning, networking, constraints on service delivery and funding, and other factors that affect community agencies. In addition, internships provide a better gateway for undergraduates hoping to enter programs in community psychology and offset the influence of traditional psychology programs that seem to create students determined to help people only on a one-to-one basis (Elias, 1987). Volunteer experiences and internships at the undergraduate level can often help students find postgraduation employment in human services and feel more positive overall about their educational experience (McVeigh, Davidson, & Redner, 1984).

Advanced Training in Community Psychology

Concentrated training programs in community psychology tend to be master's or Ph.D. programs. The discipline is still rather new compared to other areas of psychology, but some preliminary research does exist on graduate training in community psychology. Sandler and Keller (1984), in a review of graduate programs in community psychology, found that most programs utilize a *scientific practitioner* model. The students are trained to conduct research but also to act on the research or to practice the discipline based on its scientific foundations. Some community psychology programs are freestanding; others are clinical-community programs (combinations of clinical and community psychology). Courses generally include program evaluation, a community psychology seminar, and interdisciplinary courses. The content relates to several areas of community psychology, including, but not limited to, systems change, individual change, prevention, and the psychology of particular settings.

Walfish, Polifka, and Stenmark (1984) surveyed graduates of these programs who reported feeling most competent in program evaluation and needs assessments, moderately competent in intervention skills, and in need of more training in empowerment processes and in mental health interventions in industrial settings. Murray (1984) has explained that traditional training is not always appropriate for every community psychologist—for example, those working in rural settings. Hoffnung, Morris, and Jex (1986) surveyed graduates of master's programs. Their respondents reported high employment rates (90%), with the majority employed in human services (75%). Most graduates (94%) also reported moderate to high job satisfaction.

Walfish, Polifka, and Stenmark (1986) also conducted a survey of job-search outcomes among recent doctoral students in community psychology. The doctoral students had little difficulty finding positions; in fact, 84% reported that it was easy or very easy to find a job. Some 83% reported obtaining the job at their *first-choice* agency. The major employment settings for the doctoral graduates were universities, community mental health centers, medical schools, research and consulting firms, and health care facilities. Table 1.1 lists sample universities with doctoral programs in community psychology.

PLAN OF THE BOOK

Now that you are on your way to understanding community psychology, we would like to tell you what the rest of your journey will be like. In the remainder of Part I, which is the introductory portion of the book, we will introduce you to theory and research in community settings. Researchers in community psychology employ some of the venerated methods used by other psychologists as well as some techniques that are fairly unique to community psychology.

You will next move to Part II, which consists of two chapters on social change. The first chapter outlines why social change is important yet so difficult. The second chapter discusses strategies for creating and maintaining social change.

The third part of the book focuses on the mental health foundations of community psychology. Mental health issues will be discussed first for a very good reason. Although community psychology is shedding its mental health image, mental health still represents the largest portion of the published literature to date.

Part IV will examine settings into which community psychology has expanded. From mental health settings and issues, community psychologists easily

TABLE 1.1   Sample Doctoral Programs in Community or Clinical/Community Psychology

Arizona State University	Michigan State University
Claremont Graduate School	University of Missouri-Kansas City
George Peabody College of Vanderbilt University	New York University
University of Georgia	North Carolina State University
Georgia State University	University of Notre Dame
University of Hawaii	The Pennsylvania State University
University of Illinois at Chicago	Rutgers University
University of Illinois at Urbana-Champaign	University of Texas at Austin
University of Maryland	University of Vermont
	University of Virginia

moved into social and human services, school systems, criminal justice, health care, and community organizational settings and issues. Part V, the final chapter of the book, looks ahead at what the future holds for the field of community psychology.

We will reify each chapter by profiling a community psychologist or another community activist. Not all individuals practicing community psychology are trained in the discipline. In fact, some citizens do not even realize that they are fostering the principles of community psychology. We will also present one or two Cases in Point to engage you more actively with the material or to exemplify or illucidate a particular point. Unlike the vignettes, which will be somewhat clinical in nature, as explained in the Preface, the Cases in Point will be more purely oriented to community psychology.

SUMMARY

Community psychology's early history closely parallels the history of clinical psychology and psychiatry. Sigmund Freud's legacy of treating the individual rather than the setting and focusing on the expertise of the professional is intertwined with traditional treatment plans in clinical psychology and psychiatry. Both world wars assisted psychologists in realizing the effect the environment plays in people's behavior. The 1950s brought the development of psychoactive drugs and landmark research that questioned the traditions of psychology, including psychotherapy.

Both the Civil Rights movements of the 1960s and the Swampscott Conference spawned the birth of community psychology. The rights movements focused psychologists on empowerment, whereas the conference shifted psychologists' attention from individuals to settings and from treatment to prevention.

The goals of community psychology are interrelated and include prevention and empowerment as well as an emphasis on competencies and ecology, respect for diversity, choice among community settings, action research, planned social change, interdisciplinary efforts, and a sense of community.

Recent research indicates that community psychology is making some headway on its goals. A comparison of literature reviews from the 1970s and 1980s demonstrates the recent emphasis on diverse populations and on refocusing efforts away from mental health.

Students of community psychology, particularly undergraduates, are encouraged to volunteer in their communities to develop a better understanding of the community. Graduate programs, especially doctoral programs, have great success in placing their graduates who, when placed, report that they are usually employed in their first-choice settings.

2

SCIENTIFIC RESEARCH METHODS

The connection between cause and effect has no beginning and can have no end.

◆ *LEO TOLSTOY, WAR AND PEACE*

Sharon was a 16-year-old high school dropout when she learned she was pregnant. She quit school because she found it boring. She couldn't find work, so she hung out on the streets. That is where she met Tony, the father of her child. Tony worked hard all day as a mechanic, so he had some extra spending money. Sharon moved in with Tony and soon discovered how Tony dealt with his mundane existence and stress from a day's work—marijuana. Tony quickly had Sharon hooked on "grass" as a way of life. Sharon believed Tony when he said, "Dope takes the edge off."

After four months of living with Tony, Sharon began to think she was allergic to grass. After a night of smoking it, she awoke sick. Tony jokingly teased her that she had morning sickness. Little did Tony realize how true his joke was. Sharon was pregnant. She had learned in school that drugs affect the unborn. She now had to choose between her baby and "taking the edge off."

INTRODUCTION

In the past 10 years, there has been a dramatic increase in drug abuse among pregnant women in this country. Recently, several state governments have taken actions to prosecute these women or remove their children from them. However, most scientists—community psychologists in particular—disagree with the use of these heavy-handed, legal actions. When no substance-abuse prevention or treatment programs are available for these women, they are likely to be repeat offenders (Weber, 1992). If prevention programs are available, the goal of these programs should be to empower pregnant women such as Sharon. Not only is it important that they understand the danger drugs pose to them and their fetuses (e.g., fetal alcohol syndromes) or newly born babies (e.g., crack babies with congenital neurological disorders) but they must also understand the importance of the general quality of life for the mother and the child.

Past research (Chasnoff, Landress, & Barrett, 1990) indicates that about 14% of pregnant women abuse some form of drugs at some point during pregnancy. Also, such drug abuse is equally likely among rich and poor women, as well as those with high school and college educations. Several years ago, one of us (Wong) was a member of a research team investigating drug abuse among pregnant women as part of a larger study. One of the team's objectives was to replicate these findings using a larger, more representative sample.

The team was given permission by six hospitals with large obstetrical/gynecological services to study potential drug abuse among pregnant women. The women's participation in this study was entirely voluntary, and anonymity and confidentiality were guaranteed. Umbilical cord blood specimens were taken from a sample of women immediately upon delivery during a specified 12-day period. Self-report questionnaires were also administered to these women. Consistent with past research, based on the blood specimens, the research team found that a large number of women abused some form of drugs at any given time during pregnancy. Interestingly, using the self-report questionnaires, only a small percent of these women acknowledged drug abuse during pregnancy (Blakely, 1991).

THE ESSENCE OF SCIENTIFIC RESEARCH

The preceding research study presents a scenario all too familiar to community psychologists. The two scientific research techniques (umbilical cord blood specimens and self-report questionnaires) *did not produce the same results*. Furthermore, some scientific research techniques are insensitive or inappropriate to investigate certain issues, especially those that may jeopardize the well-being of the participants. It should come as no surprise that many women were not telling the truth about their drug use during pregnancy, because the general attitude in this country leans toward criminalizing rather than helping those who exhibit such behavior. Speaking the truth would not only likely put these women at risk with the legal system but also may have meant that their newly born babies might be taken away from them.

This example also intimates that research in the field of community psychology is often conducted with a sense of urgency not seen in other fields of psychology. That is, the issues examined by community psychologists are often important, pressing social issues of the day. Before discussing some of the issues (e.g., confidentiality and cultural sensitivity) related to this urgency, we will present some definitions and the reasons for engaging in scientific research. The dicussion will be followed with a review of the various types of scientific research methods utilized by community psychologists—both traditional and nontraditional psychological research methods.

Why Do Scientific Research?

As you may recall from Chapter 1, a major principle of the field of community psychology is to create or engage in some form of social change so that individuals and communities may benefit. In order to distinguish the effective from the less effective changes, psychologists need a way to help understand and assess these changes. Scientific research provides that mechanism.

For example, how can researchers be sure that decreases in drug abuse during pregnancy are solely due to women's participation in some form of prevention or treatment programs? If Sharon had the opportunity to participate in such a program, how could someone determine whether her participation reduced her likelihood of drug use during pregnancy rather than other factors—such as Sharon's breaking up with Tony? Although one might find that women who enroll in such programs (a social change) are less likely to abuse drugs during pregnancy compared to those who do not, a further analysis of the data might indicate that it is those women with spouses who are nonsubstance abusers who most benefit from the programs. That is, for many women such as Sharon, enrollment in a prevention or treatment program is not sufficient to deter drug abuse during pregnancy *unless* they can go back to a home environment or community with some social support (the ecological perspective). However, the validity of this assumption can only be verified using some form of scientific research.

What Is Scientific Research?

On a daily basis, people observe and make attributions about many things. For example, you may have some hunches as to why women abuse drugs during pregnancy. However, to scientists, research is more than hunches. In other words, when scientists conduct research, they utilize a set of related assumptions and activities. Figure 2.1 depicts the process of scientific research.

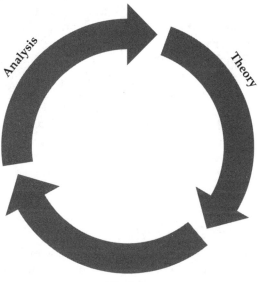

FIGURE 2.1   The Process of Scientific Research

Theory and theory-based research are an integral part of all scientific disciplines (Kuhn, 1970), and the field of community psychology is no exception. Before we begin discussing theory, however, we would like to explicate three theoretical terms that often confuse scientists and laypersons alike.

At one time or another, you probably have heard some people use the terms *theory*, *model*, and *paradigm*. The terms are often used interchangeably, but they are not quite synonymous. A **theory** is a systematic attempt to explain observable events relating to an issue such as homelessness or alcoholism. More exactly, a theory is a "set of interrelated constructs (concepts), definitions, and propositions that present a systematic view of phenomena by specifying relations among variables, with the purpose of explaining or predicting the phenomena" (Kerlinger, 1973, p. 9). The goal of a theory is to allow researchers to describe, predict, and control for *why* and *how* a variable or variables relate to observable events pertaining to an issue. For example, did the presence of Tony or boredom with school really cause in whole or in part Sharon's drug use?

Bear in mind that social science theories best serve as guideposts for studying observable events. In other words, description and prediction of, as well as control for, these events are based on suggested *rules* rather than *absolute laws* such as what is more often found in the physical sciences (Kuhn, 1970).

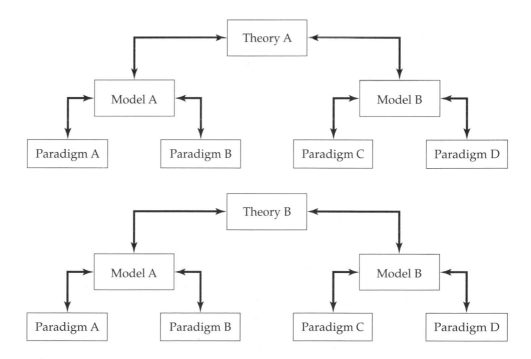

FIGURE 2.2 The Relationship among Theories, Models, and Paradigms

On the other hand, a **model** is a working blueprint of a theory. A **paradigm** is a yet smaller framework that guides researchers to conceptualize events in a consistent fashion. Figure 2.2 depicts these relationships.

A theory may consist of more than one model or blueprint. These models guide the understanding of the different observable events pertaining to an issue. A well-developed theory is likely to be made up of two or more compatible models, which are likely to be conceptualized using similar paradigms or frameworks. In the case of an undeveloped theory, different paradigms may lead to the formulation of different models. It is plausible, then, for observable events relating to an issue to be explained by more than one theory.

A more concrete example will help you understand these terms. For decades, researchers investigating alcoholism or alcohol abuse (*the issue*) have conceptualized excessive drinking (*the observable event*) as a consequence of a genetic predisposition—a medical explanation of alcoholism as a disease (*the theoretical perspective*). This theory helped to shape the development of various models about alcohol abuse. For example, one model promoted the identification of the gene or genes responsible for the disease of alcoholism. Another model allowed for the comparison of alcohol use in identical twins versus genetically unrelated individuals.

In recent years, some researchers have begun to challenge the genetic disease theory of alcoholism. Instead, they argue that some aspects of excessive alcohol use (again, *the observable event*) may be a consequence of something in the environment, such as stress from losing one's home, a difficult life on the streets, prolonged unemployment, or some other traumatic life event. Thus, a new theory emerges—the distress or disorder theory of alcoholism. This *paradigm shift* or refocusing of thinking or conceptualizing from genetics to environment again leads to the development of models. One model specifies that socioeconomic status influences alcoholism. Another model suggests that the stress of minority ethnic status plays a role in alcoholism. In other words, this theory allows for the description and prediction of differential alcohol use for individuals with different environmental stressors. On the other hand, the first theory—the disease theory—offers description and prediction of individual differences based on genetics.

These two examples illustrate the dynamic nature of or ever-evolving aspect of the development of scientific theories. Kuhn (1970) argued that major scientific development is not linear, not a step-by-step accumulation of fact. Such is the case of theory and research in the field of community psychology. Within a scientific discipline, a crisis may cause a shift in thinking; this paradigm shift may shape the development of a new theory. You will recall that just such a "crisis" (discouragement with traditional methods of treatment of mental illness) gave birth to the field of community psychology, which developed new methods and theories about community problems. Kuhn argued that a paradigm serves as a *guide* rather than an absolute theoretical standard for scientific interpretation.

Theories, models, and paradigms in the field of community psychology serve this function as guides. When a theory does not work, it needs fine-tuning or abandonment. You will read about many of the current theories, models, and

❖ *CASE IN POINT 2.1*

A Theory of Drug Abuse That Incorporates the Principles of the Field of Community Psychology

There are over 40 theories for studying drug abuse (cf. Lettieri, Sayers, & Pearson, 1984). Some of these theories are person centered, such as the medical or genetic theory of alcoholism; other theories are environmental, such as the stress or disorder theory.

Flay and Petraitis (1991) identified a number of determinants of drug abuse on the basis of 24 different studies. They concluded that the determinants of abuse are some combination of the social environment; social bonding of the individual to the family, peers, and community organizations such as schools; social learning or learning from others; intrapsychic factors such as self-esteem; and the individuals's own knowledge of, attitudes toward, and behaviors related to alcohol. Flay and Petraitis argued that a majority of the theories only address one of these domains. For the field to advance, an effort needs to be made to integrate more of these domains into one coherent theory. Community psychologists would heartily agree.

Responding to this challenge, D'Ercole, Milburn, Wong, and Beatty (1992) proposed an integrative theory for studying drug abuse among African American adults. This population was singled out because, compared to Whites, a smaller proportion of African Americans are believed to seek treatment. Perhaps in part this is because most substance abuse and prevention programs have been designed for White males (cf. Trimble, Bolek, & Niemcryk, 1992).

D'Ercole and colleagues recognized that client characteristics such as minority status play a large role in drug abuse among African American adults. Research suggests that lower socioeconomic status, which often describes minorities' income, acts as a barrier to treatment effectiveness. Other research investigating social bonding and social environments provided an additional feature in D'Ercole and associates' theory of drug abuse. Work on social networks indicates that networks serve as buffers against the impact of stressful life events and may facilitate coping. On the other hand, negative social interactions (criticism) and stigmatization (social rejection or prejudice) may cause damage to self-esteem and exclusion from social networks. The social situation of each African American could well influence his or her sobriety or recovery.

An important third aspect of D'Ercole and associates' theory of drug abuse was drug treatment programs themselves. That is, it is important to specify the treatment ingredients that are effective, such as program staffing and employment opportunities for those in recovery. Such ingredients have an important effect on the process of abstinence or recovery (Moos, Finney, & Cronkite, 1990). Figure 2.3 depicts D'Ercole and colleagues' (1992) theory of drug abuse in detail.

The theory is to be applauded as it moves from a single-domain explanation—as in person-centered explanations (e.g., genes) or environmental (e.g., societal stress in the form of prejudice) explanations of alcohol abuse—to the combination of these two *in addition to* features of the alcohol treatment programs and other ecological factors.

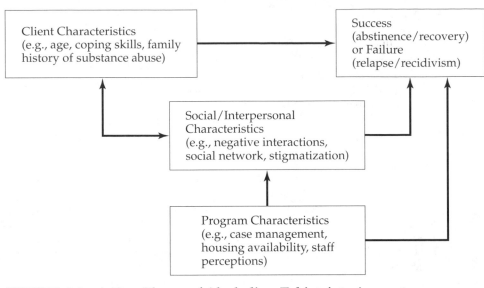

**FIGURE 2.3   A New Theory of Alcoholism Taking into Account
Multiple Causes**

paradigms in the field of community psychology in other chapters of this text. You will also be introduced to the research related to each theory; it is through research that one makes judgments about theories. Case in Point 2.1 introduces a new theory of drug abuse.

A special category of theory in the field of community psychology is systems theory. **Systems theories** are theories that presume that systems underlie the process, behavior, or issue being discussed. A **system** can be thought of as objects that relate together. More precisely, a system is an organized, unified whole that is made up of parts, components, or subsystems that are interdependent such that the whole is recognizable as a whole.

Another concrete example might be useful. A school is a system. It is comprised of its various rooms: the classrooms, cafeteria, gymnasium, and administrative offices. However, to be a system, in the sense that community psychologists use the term, the people, their roles, their interpersonal relationships, the informal and formal rules by which they operate, and other less tangible aspects must also be taken into account because all of these are interdependent on each other. Systems theories in the field of community psychology help capture the complexities of the world as well as the transactional nature between settings and the individuals in them so as to better understand them.

Given the fact that a theory is a global conceptualization of a set of related features pertaining to an issue, to measure or test features, or to do both, we must be specific. That is, we must first operationally define some features of the theory. An **operational definition** specifies how a construct will be measured, describing specifically the operations or steps that will be conducted to obtain the measurement. For example, D'Ercole and associates (1992) postulated that some client characteristics (e.g., coping skills) may be related to success (abstinence or recovery) or failure (relapse or recidivism) of individuals in primary and secondary drug-abuse prevention and treatment programs. Coping skills can be operationalized using the Drinking Profile, a scale designed to measure the circumstances under which people consume alcohol (Marlatt & Gordon, 1985).

Not all operational definitions share the same function. Some are meant to be used as independent variables; others are meant to be used as dependent variables. An **independent variable** is a presumed cause of an effect known as the **dependent variable**. Again, a concrete example is needed. Suppose you wanted to determine whether school climate in a drug or alcohol user's life influences or causes an individual to begin consuming drugs, much as Sharon did. In your study, the absence or presence of a positive school climate (i.e., an ecological factor) would be the independent variable. Consumption of drugs by your target individuals or study participants would be the dependent variable.

The decision of which operational definition of an independent or dependent variable to use is often dictated by the theory under study. For example, using D'Ercole and associates' (1992) theory of drug abuse, independent variables might include levels of coping skills, self-esteem, school climate and pregnancy status of study participants. Nonpregnant women might be presumed to use or abuse drugs more than those who are pregnant, thus making Sharon an exception to your theory. Upon testing the theory, you cannot ethically manipulate or control women's pregnancy status, but you might be able to assign nonpregnant and pregnant substance abusers to different primary and secondary prevention and treatment programs. Two dependent variables that could be specified are the number of days of sobriety and the number of meetings attended of Alcoholics Anonymous or other support group.

Having decided on some operational definitions for a particular theory, one begins to engage in activities pertaining to design and measurement. A **design** is a systematic plan to test out a hypothesis, including the quantification, or **measurement**, of the independent and dependent variables. For example, using D'Ercole and colleagues' (1992) theory of drug abuse, you might interview nonpregnant and pregnant women concerning their substance use. To achieve this, some form of sampling strategies need to be used. **Sampling strategies** are the procedures used to select participants in a study. You may want to be sure that all pregnant women have an equal statistical opportunity, or are drawn from a random sample to participate in the study. A **random sample** is a sample in which every member of a population has an equal chance of being selected. On the other hand, a **convenience sample** is one chosen for no other reason than that it is available. College students often represent a convenience sample in much psychological research, as the students are readily available to participate in research conducted in psychology departments in colleges and universities. A **purposive sample** is one chosen for a specific reason. In a test of drug use among pregnant women, only pregnant women would be chosen to be assessed; therefore, they would represent a purposive sample. Random samples are the revered form of sampling in psychology. However, a true random sample is not always possible, as in the case of a design where the independent variable can be totally manipulated or controlled. In such cases, it is important to determine that participants are **randomly assigned** to different conditions so that all in the sample are equally likely to be exposed to any condition.

As just mentioned, random sampling and random assignment are not possible for all designs. For example, using D'Ercole and colleagues' (1992) theory of drug abuse, one may think there is a random sample of nonpregnant and pregnant substance abusers participating in some form of primary and secondary substance-abuse prevention or treatment program, but research indicates that substance abusers are likely to have come from economically disadvantaged backgrounds (e.g., homeless). Thus, a random sample does not exist because the groups differ in their economic backgrounds. However, even when a random sample of the two groups is secured, one cannot always randomly assign some participants to primary and secondary substance-abuse prevention or treatment programs that promise to be more effective than others, because federal guidelines dictate that no individual should be denied access to the best possible program. Ethical guidelines stand in the way.

All of these related assumptions and activities are implemented by way of a process known as **hypothesis testing**. For example, using D'Ercole and associates' (1992) theory of drug abuse, one could postulate or hypothesize that there is no statistical differences (the null hypothesis) in substance use/abuse, as measured by self-reported drug use (dependent variable), between nonpregnant and pregnant women (independent variable). Psychologists do not usually predict the null hypothesis, however. They generally predict the **alternative hypothesis** or hypothesize differences between groups. When results indicate that there *are* statistical differences between the groups, the alternative hypothesis is confirmed. In other words, the use of hypothesis testing in science means that one can only *disprove* certain features (e.g., null hypothesis or no statistical differences between nonpregnant and pregnant women in substance abuse) not pertaining to a theory. Rarely can one *prove* features (the alternative hypothesis or statistical differences between the two groups) pertaining to the theory (cf. Popper, 1968).

Having implemented some form of hypothesis testing using our research design, we are ready for **analysis**. There are various levels of analysis (e.g., choice of statistics) but all must match the theory. D'Ercole and associates' (1992) theory of drug abuse will once again be used as an example. If the hypothesis is that client characteristics (e.g., pregnancy status) are related to success (abstinence and recovery) or failure (relapse and recidivism) of individuals in primary and secondary drug-abuse prevention or treatment programs, the unit of analysis should be the individual. The individual level of analysis is not the primary one community psychologists hope to achieve. If the hypothesis is that program characteristics (e.g., infrastructure of an organization or type of treatment program) are important, the unit of analysis should be the programs. Communities could also be used as the level of analysis when research is conducted on how various communities differ.

Taken together, the three sets of defining features of scientific research (theory, design, and analysis) are multidimensional in nature. That is, theoretically speaking, there is an infinite number of operational definitions, independent and dependent variables, designs, levels of measurement, and so forth. Pragmatically, only a small fragment of a theory can be investigated. It is possible that two different types of measurement (e.g., umbilical cord blood specimens and self-reported drug abuse) investigating the same dependent variable (e.g., drug abuse during pregnancy) lead to two different conclusions. Even in the case when the **null hypothesis** is rejected (meaning that there *is* a statistical difference in the observations), there still exists an infinite number of other plausible or possible alternative hypotheses.

Profile 2.1 introduces Karl Popper, a philosopher who suggested that science can inform humans but cannot necessarily prove the "truth" with certainty.

The Fidelity of Scientific Research

Ethics, reliability, internal validity, and external validity are the four sets of related issues that speak to the fidelity of research. Each of these needs to be examined in more detail.

A major principle of scientific research is that the well being of research participants must be ensured (American Psychological Association, 1985). In other words, participation in research should not endanger people in any physical, psychological, or social way. All participants must be informed about the purpose of the research as much as possible (without jeopardizing the integrity of the research) and the use of deception must be minimized because it is **ethically** undesirable (cf. Christensen, 1988). In many research institutions and universities, before research can be initiated, approval from an **institutional review board** must first be secured, demonstrating that all ethical guidelines (e.g., participants must be fully debriefed about the purpose of the study) have been met.

Reliability refers to the extent that concrete or measurable features, or both, of a theory are replicable. For example, using D'Ercole and colleagues' (1992) theory of drug abuse, pregnancy status (a client characteristic or the independent variable) is said to be reliable if it consistently predicts the number of days of sobriety and the number of Alcoholics Anonymous meetings attended (the results or dependent variable) of women participating in primary and secondary substance-abuse prevention or treatment programs.

Internal validity refers to the degree to which an independent variable is responsible for any observed changes in an dependent variable. In other words, research is said to have high internal validity when confounding effects are at a minimum. **Confounding effects**, or variables, are extraneous variables that influ-

◆ *PROFILE 2.1*
Karl R. Popper

Karl R. Popper (or Sir Karl,—as he was knighted in 1965) is probably the most influential philosopher of science. He is well known for his assertion that scientific theories can *never* be proved via experimental tests but only disproved or "falsified."

Popper grew up in an intellectual family in the early 1900s in Vienna, Austria. His father was a professor of law and his mother was an accomplished musician. Until his seventeenth birthday, Popper was drawn to Marxism. However, growing disgusted by the dogmatism of Marxism, he soon found intellectual challenge and satisfaction in science upon learning that Albert Einstein's theory of gravity could be used to predict a solar eclipse.

At the time, the philosophy of science was dominated by **logical positivism**—the belief that most things are knowable. Popper agreed with this premise, but he rejected the contention that one can ever *know* the truth. Popper argued that sciences can inform people about their world with some level of certainty, which is inherently subjective. This subjectivity is consistent with an emerging subfield of physics now generally known as *quantum mechanics* (the manifestation of an event is not absolute but dictated by probability), which eventually has led to many great discoveries and inventions (e.g., microwaves).

Popper was catapulted in the world stage of sciences when he published the now classic book entitled *The Logic of Scientific Discovery* in 1934. At the time, he was teaching high school. He was soon offered a philosophy professionship at Canterbury University College in New Zealand. After World War II, Popper joined the London School of Economics and Political Science.

Source: From "Profile: Karl R. Popper: The Intellectual Warrior" by J. Horgan, 1992, *Scientific American, 267*, pages 38, 40, 42, 44.

ence the dependent variable or results and invalidate the conclusions drawn from the research. For example, using D'Ercole and associates' (1992) theory of drug abuse, pregnancy status (a client characteristic) is said to have high internal validity if it is related to the number of days of sobriety (the results) of women participating in primary and secondary substance-abuse prevention/treatment programs. On the other hand, pregnancy status might not be related to sobriety, because some other factor (e.g., brain size, school climate, or the presence of friends who use drugs) is. Researchers would then acknowledge that pregnancy status is not internally valid.

External validity refers to the generalizablity of results from one study to other studies or to settings other than the researched one. Again, using D'Ercole and colleagues' (1992) theory of drug abuse, one may find that women in New York City who enroll in primary and secondary substance-abuse prevention or treatment programs are less likely to abuse drugs during pregnancy compared to those who do not. Until these results are replicated with similar samples in other cities or settings, the results must be interpreted as norms only for New York City women.

A number of factors may also influence the fidelity of research. If it is important for a study to have a random sample, one must be certain that there is no **selection bias**. That is, all potential participants should have a statistically equal opportunity to be selected into a study. For example, using D'Ercole and associates' (1992) theory of drug abuse, one could investigate people's reactions to two different primary and secondary substance-abuse prevention and treatment programs, although those who are not selected to participate in the program that they desire may work harder, or **compensate**, for their participation in the program where they belong. Even when compensation (not to be confused with a monetary reward) is at a minimum, it is possible that those who enroll in different programs communicate with each other.

A consequence is **diffusion of treatment**, meaning that it would be difficult to draw definitive conclusions about the respective efficiency and effectiveness of each program because neither program is now pure. The effects of one treatment have spilled over into the other. Participants of such programs are also likely to have other problems (e.g., to be homeless) in addition to substance abuse, which make them vulnerable to discontinued participation. When participants drop out, it is known as **experimental mortality**. Enrollment in such programs is no guarantee that participants' subsequent abstinence or recovery is solely due to some components of the programs. It is possible that certain client characteristics (e.g., less physical tolerance of the drug) lead to abstinence or recovery naturally over time. In other words, it is due to some form of **maturation**. Certain historical events (e.g., Nancy Reagan's campaign to "Just Say No" to drugs) may intentionally or inadvertently encourage participants' enthusiasm about such programs.

Community Researchers as Consultants

When community psychologists conduct research, they often do so in the role of consultant. A **consultant** is someone who engages in collaborative problem solving with one or more persons (the **consultees**) who are often responsible for providing some form of assistance to another third individual (the **client**; Mowbray, 1979). Because consultants *collaborate with* the consultees, those who participate in the research, including the consultees and their clients, are not called *subjects*, as they are in other psychological research, but rather are called *participants*.

Consultants work in a variety of community settings: educational, industrial, human services (especially mental health related), governmental, and others. Some consultants conduct research for the government. A number of universities have developed or are developing public policy research laboratories to assist in public and private sector research. Other consultants evaluate programs or conduct needs assessments, and still others lend their expertise to solving social problems by designing preventive education programs or by helping to change aspects of agencies and communities. In other words, consultants appear in many different settings and work on a variety of problems, most of them related to research.

Many of you may perhaps dream of being a highly paid consultant, but the life of a consultant is not always easy. There are a variety of complex issues facing most community consultants. Consultants often enter a situation not knowing what the real problem is that they are being asked to help solve. In a business setting, for instance, a consultant might be hired by management because productivity is low. However, the real underlying problem might be that the management style is so unwelcomed that employee productivity has declined. Would you want to be the consultant who delivers the news to the management team who hired you that management is the problem? Given the nature of the problems for which they are asked to intervene, community psychologists acting as consultants need to weigh the ethical considerations of to whom they are responsible and for what (O'Neill, 1989).

A consultant is also faced with what methods of investigation and change to utilize (Heller, 1990). For instance, the consultant might recommend educational or research services. Similarly, he or she might choose some mix of **outcome** or **process measures**. Outcome measures address what happens *after* the change occurred (i.e., did the change work?). Process research addresses the transactions or processes that took place *during* the change (Kazden, 1980). Processes often underlie outcome. An example of an outcome measure might be that there are fewer pregnant drug users, such as Sharon, in a community after instituting a prevention program for them. Higher self-esteem and satisfaction with their pregnancies would be processes that underlie the success of the prevention program.

Consultants also need to ask, Are the methods, research and otherwise, affordable, workable, and understandable for this set of clients? Furthermore, ethical consultants work *with* not *for* those who hire them (Benviente, 1989; Christensen & Robinson, 1989). In fact, all consultants need to ensure **constituent validity**, which means that those participating in the research or change are not considered subjects to be acted upon, but rather participants whose perspective *must* be taken into account in planning and other related activities in order for the activities to be valid (Keys & Frank, 1987). Consultants need to *empower* the population with whom they are working to create and sustain the change initiated by the presence of the consultant. This means that the consultant needs to find a good way to "wean" the clients or participants, lest they become too dependent on the expert consultant.

Professional change agents or consultants also need to assess the prevailing culture as well as the trust and the respect held for them in a particular setting. Such assessment will help consultants determine how visible they should be. Consultants also need to evaluate their own personal values and communicate them openly *before* the consultation or research begins in order to avoid ethical dilemmas after the collaboration process has commenced (Heller, 1989). Finally, consultants must evaluate their work with their clients; they need to ask the question, Did I improve the community by my presence? It is through research that this question can best be answered. Without evaluation, how would a change agent know if the change worked and whether it ought to be repeated?

TRADITIONAL SCIENTIFIC RESEARCH METHODS

There are research designs that all psychologists, including community psychologists, utilize. These include correlational and experimental methodologies. We will review these here first and then turn to some specific methods that are more likely to be utilized by community psychologists than most other types of psychologists (e.g., social psychologists).

Correlational Research

Traditional scientific research methods can be roughly classified into three broad types. Table 2.1 is a summary of their characteristics. **Correlational methods** include a class of designs (e.g., surveys) and measurement procedures, as well as techniques (e.g., self-report), that allow one to examine the associations or relationships between two or more variables in their natural environments. In other words, correlational methods do not contain active manipulations of the variables under study; rather, they are usually descriptive in nature. For example, using D'Ercole and associates' (1992) theory of drug abuse, one might want to investigate the relationship between the number of months pregnant and the severity of substance abuse; these variables are not manipulated. The fact that one has no control over them means that the distinction of independent from dependent variables may be arbitrary, albeit dictated by a theory.

Also, causation cannot be determined, because intervening or other unstudied variables could easily have produced the effects noted. Associations are said to be **spurious** when intervening or confounding variables are thought to be responsible for the relationships. In experimental research, intervening variables are controlled for through randomly assigning participants to groups, holding conditions constant, and manipulating the independent variable. In correlational research, these criteria are seldom, if ever, met.

In its simple form, the associations between two or more variables are quantified using a statistic known as the **Pearson Correlation Coefficient**, which ranges from +1.00 to –1.00. The sign (+ or –) indicates the direction of the association. For example, if the sign is positive (+), both variables move in the same direction, or as one gets smaller so does the other. A positive correlation can also mean that as one variable increases, so does the other. A negative or inverse correlation means that the variables move in opposite directions. For example, as one variable increases, the other decreases. The number (e.g., .35) indicates the magnitude or intensity of the relationship, with 1.00 being the largest correlation and 0.00 indicating little or no relationship.

Using D'Ercole and associates' (1992) theory of drug abuse, a Pearson Correlation Coefficient of –.80 between the number of months pregnant and substance abuse means that women who are at more advanced stages of pregnancy are less

TABLE 2.1   Characteristics of Three Broad Types of Scientific Research Methods

	Correlational	Quasi-Experimental	Experimental
Type of question	Are the variables of interest related to each other?	Does an independent variable that the researcher does not completely control affect the dependent variable or the research result?	Is there a relationship between independent and dependent variables that addresses the cause?
When used	Researcher is unable to manipulate an independent variable. Sometimes used in explanatory research.	Researcher wants to assess the impact of a real-life intervention in the community or elsewhere	Researcher has control over the independent variable and can minimize the number of confounding variables in the research.
Advantages	Convenience of data collection. May avoid certain ethical and/or practical problems.	Provides some information about cause-effect relationships. Permits assessment of more real-world interventions.	Ability to demonstrate cause-effect relationships. Permits control over confounding variables and the ruling out of alternative explanations.
Disadvantages	Cannot establish a cause-effect relationship.	Lack of control over confounding variables. Strong causal inference cannot be made.	Some questions cannot be studied experimentally for either practical or ethical reasons. May lead to artificial procedures.

Source: Adapted from "Techniques and Pitfalls of Applied Behavioral Science Research: The Case of Community Mediation" by F. Y. Wong, C. H. Blakely, & S. L. Worsham, in *Community Mediation: A Handbook for Practitioners and Researchers* (pp. 35–41) by K. G. Duffy, J. W. Grosch, & P. V. Olzack (Eds.), 1991, New York: Guilford. Copyright 1991 by Guilford Press. Used by permission.

likely to abuse drugs (a strong negative association). However, one *cannot* conclude that advanced stages of pregnancy *cause* decreases in substance abuse. Also, this association may be spurious when there is reason to suspect that pregnant women's perceived support from their spouses later in pregnancy is largely responsible for decreases in substance abuse rather than due to the pregnancy itself.

Experimental Research

The **experimental method** includes a class of designs (e.g., between-groups designs where no two groups receive the same treatment) and measurement procedures, as well as techniques (e.g., umbilical cord blood specimens), that allow one to manipulate independent and dependent variables. A common design is the **pretest-posttest control group design**, which involves the assessment of an effect or effects both *prior to* and *following* an experimental manipulation in one group (the experimental group) but not another (no-manipulation group or control group). That is, one group of participants is exposed to an independent variable and another group is not. In addition, assignment to the experimental or control group is random; thus, participants have an equal chance of being assigned to either the experimental or control group.

If the experimental manipulation is functioning as predicted by a theory, the dependent variable should ideally be observable as a change from premanipulation to postmanipulation scores within the experimental *but not* the control group. In other words, the pretest-posttest observations of participants in the control group should remain relatively constant over time, unless some natural maturation occurs or the initial pretest sensitizes all participants to the nature of the assessment being conducted. For example, using D'Ercole and associates' (1992) theory of drug abuse, pregnant substance abusers who participate in primary and secondary prevention or treatment programs should report an increase in days of sobriety from pretreatment to posttreatment compared to those who do not. Community experimentation is a fairly new idea in the history of psychology. The father of community experimentation, George Fairweather, is profiled in Profile 2.2.

Quasi-Experimental Research

Many variables (e.g., school climate) studied in the field of community psychology cannot be experimentally manipulated for practical and ethical reasons. Similarly, subjects cannot always be randomly assigned to groups. For example, since Sharon is already pregnant, it is not possible to randomly assign her to the nonpregnant group. In studies of pregnancy, one would probably end up using intact groups. Thus, a compromise is the use of the **quasi-experimental method**. A common quasi-experimental design is the **nonequivalent pretest-posttest control design**, which involves the comparison of a group before and after some experimental manipulation with another group that has not been exposed to the manipulation or treatment. As mentioned earlier, this design differs from the pretest-posttest design previously discussed in that *participants are not randomly assigned* to experimental or control conditions.

Experimental manipulation is often restricted by practical or ethical reasons. Although this allows for a more natural or realistic research design, initial differences between experimental and comparison groups may not be balanced. For example, using D'Ercole and colleagues' (1992) theory of drug abuse, pregnant women who voluntarily participate in primary and secondary prevention or treatment programs may be more educated than those in the comparison group, which may include women who are high school dropouts. Thus, differences already exist between the two groups before the study begins. Care must be taken in drawing conclusions about causal differences between the two groups as the two groups already differ at the onset of the research.

◆ *PROFILE 2.2*
George Fairweather

Although you will come to know him best in this book from his Lodge Societies, George Fairweather might well be called the father of modern community experimentation. His seminal book with William Davidson, *An Introduction to Community Experimentation: Theory, Methods, and Practice*, succinctly laid down characteristics of beneficial community research and programs for community specialists interested in social change. The book was published in 1986 and remains one of the foundations of the libraries of most community psychologists.

In the beginning of their book, Fairweather and Davidson clearly laid out the reasons why social change is important to solving human problems as well as disclosed the parameters of beneficial change. Fairweather encouraged *innovation*, especially in the service of solving social problems. However, Fairweather and Davidson also suggested that most social experiments and social programs designed to produce change should start small; otherwise, they are too expensive and too difficult to evaluate at the onset.

Fairweather acknowledged in the book that creating an appropriate experimental design and measuring outcomes adequately are no easy task in the laboratory and are even more difficult in field or in community settings. The authors also reminded psychologists that statistical tests are, by themselves, not socially significant. Understanding of the accompanying social problem is also important to the understanding of or interpretation of the statistics gleaned from any community experiment. "Simply finding that two social models yield significantly different statistical results without a concomitant knowledge of the problem itself from workaday observations can lead to erroneous conclusions made from collected data" (Fairweather & Davidson, 1986, p. 184).

Another important aspect of Fairweather and Davidson's book, which was also alluded to in Chapter 1 of this present textbook, is that *dissemination of beneficial innovations* are crucial to the betterment of communities. Ideas and programs that work in one community do not always work elsewhere, but if the ideas are not shared with others, how would people ever know where else ideas and programs will be beneficial?

Finally, Fairweather and Davidson suggested that community experimentalists might be called Renaissance persons. That is, community experimentalists need to have a variety of interests and skills. The authors noted that one of the important rewards for the young community scientist is the positive feeling of being involved in something meaningful and important. It is to that sentiment that our present book is dedicated.

At this point, some clarification about the terms *correlation, experimental*, and *field research* is necessary. **Field research** refers to the investigation of a set of related phenomena pertaining to an issue (or issues) *in natural settings*. Either correlational or experimental methods or both may be used in the field. We will briefly review three types of research methods or approaches frequently employed in field research—research that is far more typical in community psychology than in many other areas of psychology.

OTHER RESEARCH METHODS USED IN COMMUNITY PSYCHOLOGY

Ethnography

Due to the urgency of the issues in the field of community psychology, diverse methods or approaches are often employed. Ethnography is one such method. **Ethnography** is a research method that refers to a broad class of designs (e.g., semi-structured interviews) and measurement procedures and techniques (e.g., behavioral ratings) that allow one to conduct social interactions with participants of the study. The primary purpose of ethnography is to allow one to gain an understanding of *how* people view their own experiences.

Ethnography should allow an individual to describe his or her *own* experiences without having to translate them into the words of the researchers. In other words, the informants or participants should use their own language to describe their own experiences. An ethnographic interviewer should probably also provide an explanation of *why* he or she is asking particular questions so as to be more fully understood by the informants. Similarly, in contrast to the more traditional scientific definitions of objectivity or neutrality, in ethnography the value systems of the researcher may influence the social interactions between the researcher and the informants and thus influence the course of the research. Hence, a researcher is better off taking a stance of ignorance about the experiences of the informants than making predetermined judgments (Heller, Price, Reinharz, Riger, & Wandersman, 1984). Of course, no scientific research method is truly objective, because how one conceptualizes an issue logically dictates the course of its action.

Compared to cultural anthropologists and sociologists who first developed this technique, community psychologists use ethnography at a lower rate. However, as research issues become more socially oriented, these methods (which are correlational in nature) are more likely to be employed than experimental methods (Speer et al., 1992). Ethnography is perhaps most informative when research questions asked do not have a strong theoretical framework. Thus, *qualitative* information that is likely to be gleaned from ethnographic studies can inform the researcher about future directions of study, some of which may include field experiments where variables are actively manipulated.

Participant observation is a popular and special type of ethnographic technique. Although the researcher often assumes the role of an observer (i.e., systematic observation with neutrality) in participant observation and ethnography, a prototypical study using participant observation often involves ongoing dialogues between the researcher and participants. For example, a researcher who is interested in the study of teenage gangs often needs to "hang out" with the gangs for a period of time. Also, the researcher needs to acquire the language used by the gangs to facilitate his or her investigation of the gangs' social network characteristics as well as to establish trust. Meanwhile, the constant social interactions between the researcher and gang members may affect their perceptions of and relationships with each other. A consequence can be role ambiguity, where it becomes unclear to gang members what role the researcher is adopting. Is the researcher a member of the gang, a researcher, or both? Case in Point 2.2 introduces a researcher whose participant observational studies have been very controversial.

Epidemiology

A second set of methods or approaches used more by community psychologists than other psychologists is **epidemiology**, which is "the study of the occurrence and distribution of diseases and other health-related conditions in populations" (Kelsey, Thompson, & Evans, 1986, p. 3). This includes a broad class of designs (e.g., prospective or, loosely, "futuristic" studies and retrospective or, loosely, "historical" studies) and measurement procedures and techniques (e.g., random telephone dialing).

These methods allow for the establishment of two phenomena: prevalence and incidence. The **prevalence** of a disease or health-related condition is the total number of people within a given population who have it. The **incidence** refers to the number of people within a given population who have acquired the condition *within a specific time period*, usually a year. Incidence rates can be established using a **prospective design** or investigation of new cases. Prevalence rates can be established using a **retrospective design** or investigation of known cases. In their purest forms, neither the examination of prevalence rates nor incidence rates should disturb or change the behavior of the community. There are differences between the two, however, beyond the difference in their definitions. Prevalence rate is a more inclusive measure than incidence rate and is easier to calculate. However, the disadvantage of prevalence rates is that they are difficult to interpret, as they indicate both the incidence and duration of a disorder.

Depending on the objectives of the epidemiological investigation, measurement procedures as well as techniques used in the design can range from household interviews to random telephone digit dialing. Others include the use of birth certificates, death certificates, census records, or all of these.

Having defined these concepts, an example is in order of how epidemiology is used. **Human immunodeficiency virus (HIV)** is thought to be responsible for **acquired immune deficiency syndrome (AIDS)**, one of the deadly, incurable diseases of this century. Epidemiological surveys (mostly retrospective studies) conducted by the Center for Disease Control (CDC) in the early 1980s called attention to the onset of this epidemic. Subsequent investigations (including prospective studies) documented that groups at high risk of contracting HIV included homosexual and bisexual individuals, as well as intravenous drug users. Epidemiologists, then, would say that these groups are *high risk* or at *risk*. Recent investigations illustrate that children (via birth) and women (via partners

Going All the Way

When the Belgian government proclaimed in 1988 that its AIDS-education efforts had proved successful, that most gay men practiced safe sex and knew how HIV is transmitted, Ralph Bolton was impressed—too impressed. Suspecting "a massive case of denial," Bolton, a medical anthropologist at Pomona College then working in Brussels, sought further evidence, though not in a conventional manner. Gay himself, Bolton conducted an informal study in which he met dozens of men in local bars, parks and bathhouses, had sex with them and later noted their predilections for either moderate or high-risk activity.

Bolton's study exposed serious flaws in the government's data. Not only were most gay men still engaging in unprotected oral and anal sex and other high-risk behaviors, they also were lying about it to public-health interviewers. Bolton's unorthodox methodology, meanwhile, has raised questions of its own. Is it ethical for an anthropologist studying sexual behavior to have sex with his subjects? Has Bolton blurred the participant-observer distinction to the point of abandoning it?

Bolton contends that the traditional methods of gathering information do not work when applied to the intimate realm of sex. Many Belgian respondents admitted that when they are asked about their sexual practices in interviews or on questionnaires, they give the answers they think are expected of them rather than confess to risky behavior. Firsthand observation is not a viable approach either. Who but the most uninhibited couple would submit to such scrutiny? And even if willing subjects were found, could an anthropologist be sure that they were not engaging in less hazardous sex than they might when not observed?

And so Bolton took the advice of the late sociologist Erving Goffman: "Go to where the action is." He quickly notes that he never actually engaged in high-risk sexual behavior. Rather, Bolton would proceed during an encounter to the point at which the next logical step was a high-risk activity—and then tactfully insist on prophylaxis. "People didn't object to using condoms," he says. "But almost invariably it was I who raised a precaution."

Not everyone embraces Bolton's participatory methodology. Renee C. Fox, a sociologist at the University of Pennsylvania, has expressed concern that none of Bolton's subjects provided explicit informed consent, a standard ethical safeguard among anthropologists. Bolton counters that doing so would have biased the study. "Obviously I didn't introduce myself saying, 'Hi, I'm Ralph Bolton. I am doing sex research, and I'm going to observe you during our encounter.' But I never disguised that I was an anthropologist studying sexual behavior." Bolton concedes, however, "that information pretty much went in one ear and out the other."

Even without participation, a professional interest in sexual behavior can tarnish one's reputation. But Bolton says that his own image does not concern him. "I'm just interested in doing what has to be done to stop this epidemic. Frankly, I'd just as soon be studying sports behavior in Scandinavia."

Source: From "Going All the Way" by A. Burdick, 1993, *The Sciences*, March/April. Copyright 1993 by the New York Academy of Sciences. This article is reprinted by permission of *The Sciences* and is from the March/April 1993 issue. Individual subscriptions are $18.00 per year. Write to The Sciences, 2 East 63rd Street, New York, NY 10021 or call 1-800-THE-NYAS.

who are bisexuals or intravenous drug users or both) are the fastest growing groups who are at risk of contracting HIV. It is estimated that more than 20 million people in the world will be HIV positive by the end of 1995 (Tarantola & Mann, 1993).

Once the prevalance and/or incidence rates for a disorder have been determined, epidemiologists can attempt to isolate variables that seem to have caused the disorder. For example, once the CDC had an understanding of who was at risk for HIV, the CDC could next search for the cause of the disease, which was discovered (the exchange of blood or other body fluids from an infected individual to another).

Needs Assessment and Program Evaluation

Community psychologists are beginning to realize the benefits of the use of epidemiological methods in the development and refinement of activities related to prevention, intervention, and treatment. However, for these activities to be effective and efficient, it is important to understand the significant issues and needs of the individuals involved. **Needs assessment** refers to a set of methods or approaches that elucidate the magnitude of an issue or examine a set of issues in relation to the available resources for addressing the issues. In other words, it is a way of determining if there is a need for a certain program or intervention because the need is not yet well addressed.

For example, given that the incubation period of AIDS is about 10 years— much longer than the nine-month gestation period for Sharon's baby—it is important to estimate the needs for health care and services of individuals who are at various stages of HIV. Individuals who are newly diagnosed may need social support, whereas individuals who are in the late stages of AIDS may need intensive medical and hospice care. Also, in the absence of a cure or vaccine for HIV, needs assessment should emphasize the development or refinement of prevention and intervention strategies, including the practice of safe sex by using condoms and implementing needle exchange programs.

Needs assessments can be conducted via ethnographic interviews, surveys, and other observational or descriptive techniques, each of which has its own advantages and disadvantages. For example, in ethnographic interviews, individuals might be reluctant to reveal face to face that they are unmarried and pregnant, such as Sharon, or are HIV positive. They might be more likely to disclose this information in an anonymous survey. On the other hand, during an interview, the interviewer (or the informant, for that matter) can change the direction of the interview and thus reveal information not discovered on written surveys, which are less easily modified on the spot.

Having developed or refined a program to address needs related to a particular issue, whether it be AIDS or teen pregnancy, the effectiveness or efficiency of the program should be evaluated; this process is called program evaluation. **Program evaluation** refers to a broad class of designs (e.g., survey) as well as measurement procedures and techniques (e.g., birth certificate) that allow one to examine "social programs..., and the policies that spawn and justify them, [and] aim to improve the welfare of individuals, organizations, and society" (Shadish, Cook, & Leviton, 1991, p. 19). Given the sluggish economy in this country as well as worldwide, there is an increasing trend to hold social programs "accountable" for their performance, so program evaluation is becoming more and more important.

It is beyond the scope of this chapter to conduct an extensive discussion of the processes involved in the evaluation of a typical social program. Suffice it to say that an adequate evaluation consists of at least four related components: (1) the goals, (2) the objectives, (3) the activities, and (4) the milestones. The **goal** refers to the aim of the evaluation. A good evaluation is likely to be driven by theory. That is, the concept of goal addresses the question, What does the evaluation hope to achieve? (or, *Why* should an evaluation be conducted?). The construct of an **objective** refers to the plan. That is, objectives address the question *How* does one go about achieving the goal? The concept of **activity** refers to the specific task. That is, activity addresses the question, *What* does the plan consists of?) **Milestone** refers to the outcome; that is, Does the evaluation *achieve* its intended goal?

Using D'Ercole and colleagues' (1992) theory of drug abuse, one might want to investigate the differential effectiveness of profit versus not-for-profit primary and secondary prevention and treatment programs for African American adults (the *goal*). Therefore, one reviews records and interviews clients and staff of the two types of programs (the *objective* or design). Given the voluminous records and possible number of informants or interviewees, only a randomized stratified sample will be used (the *activity*, including analysis). It might be reasonable to hypothesize that a higher enrollment rate will be observed in the not-for-profit than for-profit programs because of different client fees, with the not-for-profits being less expensive. However, the two types of programs may not differ in dropout rates, because, as you know by now, intervention outcomes are often contingent on a host of factors other than program type (the *milestones*).

This example no doubt is a very simplistic picture of program evaluation. Although program evaluation may seem more "objective" as a scientific research method than ethnography, role ambiguity is still possible. Role ambiguity is most likely to occur with internal evaluation. That is, an evaluator who is also on the staff of the agency assumes not only the role of evaluator but also is someone interested in using data derived from the evaluation for future program development or refinement. To guard against this problem, agencies usually establish an advisory panel so that program development or refinement is executed by the panel rather than a single, internal evaluator. Another solution is to employ an external evaluator such as a community consultant. The U.S. General Accounting Office, a research arm of the U.S. Congress, conducts a fair amount of evaluation of publicly funded social programs. Private firms such as Abt Associates, the Rand Corporation, and Stanford Research International also assume a large share of program evaluations in this country.

In addition to methodological concerns (e.g., competing theories about a social issue and different operational definitions for a feature of the theory), social dynamics are crucial in evaluating any social program. That is, people do not like to be judged, especially when potentially negative consequences exist. Given the fact that not-for-profit social programs are more sensitive to funding issues and public scrutiny, if these programs have been demonstrated to be less than effective, they are likely to be eliminated. Even when they are effective but less than efficient (i.e., expensive to maintain), they may still be eliminated.

THE URGENCY OF RESEARCH IN COMMUNITY PSYCHOLOGY AND RELATED PITFALLS

The Value of Multiple Measures

We mentioned at the beginning of this chapter that research in the field of community psychology is often conducted with a sense of urgency not often seen in other areas of psychology. We have demonstrated some aspects of this urgency by using the example of drug abuse among pregnant women. Other related issues deserve some brief comment.

As you may recall from Chapter 1, Speer and associates (1992) indicated that there has been a shift in the field of community psychology. This shift has been toward the use of correlational designs and away from experimentation because topics of investigation often relate to major social issues. Even in those cases where quasi-experimental or experimental designs can be used, one may have to face a multitude of methodological issues or dilemmas. One class of issues or dilemmas concerns the logistics of implementing a research program. For example, how do researchers locate pregnant women like Sharon to investigate drug use? Not only are they hard to access, especially if they do not seek medical attention, but they may also be homeless or change addresses often.

Also, how do researchers increase the probability that these pregnant teens will tell the truth when using self-report measures? Another way to further validate self-reported alochol use would be to count the number of empty alcohol beverage containers that pregnant women have discarded. A nonreactive measure such as this, where people are not contacted face to face, is called an **unobtrusive measure**. Unobtrusive measures are ethically questionable, as participant consent is often not obtained. Likewise, unobtrusive measures do not speak to *why* a certain behavior occurs, only that it does occur. If you found beer cans in Sharon's garbage, you wouldn't know why she drank when pregnant; neither would you know whether the cans were hers or Tony's.

When working with complex social issues such as teen pregnancy, one should always make an attempt to use **multiple methods**. For example, self-reports, nonreactive or unobtrusive measures, as well as umbilical blood samples could be obtained to determine whether, indeed, pregnant women such as Sharon are using drugs or alcohol. However, multiple methods take more time than single methods and may generate different conclusions for the same issue. Although it is hoped that a theory is solid enough to guide the interpretation of results, one would need to reexamine the theory and research if different methods produce different outcomes.

The Importance of Cultural Sensitivity

Another class of methodological issues or dilemmas concerns **cultural sensitivity**, or awareness and appreciation of intragroup and intergroup differences. We have chosen to define cultural sensitivity in a very *liberal* sense. People belong to many categories and have multiple expectations or identities. For example, one can be an African American (racial or ethnic identity) who is also a college graduate (educational background) and a white-collar worker (socioeconomic status). This individual may have more in common with white college graduates (of similar educational background) who are also white-collar workers (similar socioeconomic status) than other African Americans who are high school drop-outs (different educational background) or living on welfare (different socioeconomic status).

In other words, cultural sensitivity underscores the importance of the issue of person-environment fit. For example, White researchers and consultants might encounter resistance from African American research participants or program clients. Similarly, male researchers who study pregnant women who are in drug treatment may encounter resistance not only from the women but also from the program staff. Neither the women nor the staff share the same goal or vision as the male researcher (i.e., effective treatment based on scientific knowledge). Rather, both the women and staff perceive the researcher as intrusive. In other words, there is a poor person-environment fit between the researcher and the pregnant women as well as staff. Ecologically valid research hinges on cultural sensitivity. The methodology used needs to enhance or at least take into account the person-environment fit.

Even when one is able to circumvent the preceding two classes of methodological dilemmas, there may be ethical dilemmas with which to contend. For example, when drug abuse among pregnant women is investigated, not only does one need to maintain the integrity of the study (including confidentiality) but one must also have a clear sense of ethical and legal responsibility. In other words, should one report to a legal authority those pregnant women one thinks are endangering themselves, their unborn child, and perhaps their other children? There are no easy answers. Although research in community psychology is crucial to a better society, the research is not easy to conduct.

SUMMARY

A major principle of the field of community psychology is to create or engage in some form of social change so that individuals may benefit. In order to sort the beneficial from the useless changes, psychologists need a way to help assess change. Scientific research provides that mechanism. Positive social changes are more likely than not to be driven by theory and evaluated with scientific research.

When scientists conduct research, they utilize a set of related assumptions and activities. Most scientific disciplines (especially the mature ones) are guided by theory. Within a theory, there may be more than one model (or blueprint) and paradigm (or framework). Thus, scientific research can be conducted with more than one design as well as various levels of measurement and analysis. These components are the defining features of scientific research.

A special category of theory often found in the literature of community psychology is systems theory. Systems theories presume that systems underlie the processes, behaviors, or issues being discussed. A system can be thought of as a set of objects that relate to each other. More precisely, a system is an organized, unified whole that is made up of parts, components, or subsystems that are interdependent, such that the whole is recognizable as a whole. An example of a system is a school.

The first set of steps in scientific research involves the translation of some related conceptual features of a theory into more concrete or measurable aspects, using the process of *operationalization*. The outcome of operationalization is some form of independent variable (the manipulated variable or cause) and dependent variable (the result or effect). The next two sets of steps involve some form of sampling strategy (e.g., random samples, convenience samples, purposive samples, and random assignment), followed by hypothesis testing (the null hypothesis vs. the alternative hypothesis) and analysis.

The fidelity of scientific research is a function of such things as ethics (which are examined by an institute review board), reliability, internal validity, and confounding effects. Reliability is the extent to which concrete or measurable features of a theory can be replicated. Internal validity refers to the degree to which an independent variable is responsible for changes in the dependent variable. External validity is the generalizability of results from one study to another or to other settings. Confounding effects are those variables other than the independent variable that could also account for the research results.

Scientific research can be conducted using the correlational method (which produces a statistic known as the Pearson Correlation Coefficient), the experimental method (e.g., pretest-posttest control group design), or the quasi-experimental method (e.g., nonequivalent pretest-posttest control design), or all three. Ethnography (e.g., participant observation), epidemiology, and needs assessment as well as program evaluation (including the processes of goal, objective, activity, and milestone) are descriptive types of methods frequently employed in field research. Each type of method has its advantages and disadvantages. Each is perhaps more likely to be utilized by community psychologists than any other type of psychologist.

Research in the field of community psychology is often conducted with a sense of urgency. This urgency is best achieved when multiple methods are used and cultural sensitivity is taken into account.

3

THE IMPORTANCE OF SOCIAL CHANGE

If a free society cannot help the many who are poor, it cannot save the few who are rich.

◆ *JOHN F. KENNEDY*

What a beautiful day July 1, 1899, was! The sun was shining; there wasn't a cloud in the sky as the day stretched into night. The Hayden family, all eight of them, sat down for a hearty meal to celebrate the harvest. As soon as the first forkfuls were in their mouths, the family dog, outside in the yard, started barking frantically. Joe Hayden, the father and owner of the farm, yelled for the dog to stop. When the dog continued its intrusive barking, Joe went to the back door to find the barn in flames.

All family members, children included, ran to the well and set up a bucket brigade. Not only were their efforts futile as the freshly cut hay continued to burn but the fire quickly spread to their old wood-frame house. Next, the fire spread to the neighbors' homes on the Hayden side of the street. Late that night, the neighbors whose homes had not been destroyed consoled the Haydens and the other community members on their losses. Although they did not lose any livestock in the fire, the Haydens lost their home and its contents, as well as the barn and their crop. Many of their neighbors lost their homes and personal possessions, too.

Some of the neighbor women whose homes still stood took two or three of the children home with them; the men told Joe that they would help him rebuild his house and barn. Within two months, the Haydens had a new house and barn, which the neighbors helped them build on the same piece of property. Some community members also donated feed for the livestock, and the Haydens were soon reunited again.

In those days, if you were sick, disabled, or old, it was no business of the government (Sarason, 1976). Neighbors helped neighbors; social support seemed commonplace.

INTRODUCTION

The preceding vignette illustrates several important dimensions that have changed in U.S. society in the least 90 years. Compared to the society in which the Haydens lived, today the United States is no longer an agrarian, rural society. Rather, this nation is an urbanized, industrialized society. Americans do not appear to be the neighborly, helping society we once were. Instead, people tend today to be less self-reliant and less cooperative with one another and more dependent on community services and government assistance, the latter perhaps an invitation to disaster according to some community psychologists (Sarason, 1976). The turning point in U.S. history, turning from helping each other to dependence on external agencies, probably arrived with the Great Depression (Wilcox, 1983).

In 1971, psychologist Leigh Marlowe wrote that the rate of social change was accelerating. Change, some planned and some unplanned, continues today at a breakneck pace. In fact, change seems to be a pervasive condition of modern times (Christensen & Robinson, 1989). As you learned in Chapter 1, actively participating in and fashioning social change is a fundamental value of community psychology (Jason, 1991).

Questions regarding social change for community psychologists are complex and interrelated. Social scientists want to know what causes change; how to predict change; how best to cope with change, and, most of all, how to fashion or direct change that improves the living conditions of community members. All members of society need also to consider whether today's solutions will become tomorrow's problems (Keys & Frank, 1987).

We will first look at what creates social change, whether planned or not (as in the Haydens' fire), particularly in the 1990s. In this endeavor, we can draw from all areas within psychology, as well as anthropology, medicine, public health, political science, sociology, and other disciplines (Wandersman, Hallman, & Berman, 1989). In fact, a multidisciplinary approach for examining and intervening in social change is often desirable (Seidman, 1983), especially if the diversity and challenges of the vast population are to be appreciated (Freedman, 1989; Salazar, 1988).

What are some of the phenomena that induce change in society? Factors such as diverse populations, declining resources, demands for accountability, expanding knowledge and/or changing technologies (Hess, Markson, & Stein, 1991; Kettner, Daley, & Nichols, 1985), economic changes, community conflict (Christensen & Robinson, 1989), dissatisfaction with traditional approaches to social problems, the desire for choices and the need for diversity of solutions to social problems (Heller, Price, Reinharz, Riger, & Wandersman, 1984), and other issues lead the list of reasons for social change. Although the list is not exhaustive, some of these forces need to be looked at in more detail to help you comprehend their roles in shaping social change.

REASONS FOR SOCIAL CHANGE

Diverse Populations

In Europe during the Middle Ages, the bubonic plague claimed 60 million lives. Other societies were later faced with typhus, smallpox, and cholera epidemics. Today, just when people thought cancer was the deadliest of contemporary diseases, society is faced with the fatal acquired immune deficiency syndrome (AIDS) epidemic. Cancer and AIDS patients have special needs, but other populations in today's society also create special demands. The increasing elderly population, pregnant teens, victims of violence, the bereaved, the unemployed, and other groups all have special situations that create the need for new programs and social changes. The Haydens would have experienced some of these problems in the early 1900s, such as the death of a family member, but they were less likely to experience violence, teen pregnancy, and drug problems than are families today.

A concrete example of how the needs of diverse groups are often not met but can be met in the community would be worthwhile. For a variety of reasons, few low-income people vote. The Haydens could vote even though they lost their home. However, today's homeless are often denied the right to vote because they do not have fixed street addresses. Because many minorities have low incomes, minority voter registration is also problematic due to transportation costs and so on. This situation creates the added problem that those individuals who most need to voice their political opinions on nutrition, health care, housing, and other programs do not go to the polls. Fawcett, Seekins, and Silber (1988) believed that making voter registration more accessible to the poor and to minorities would encourage more registrations and perhaps more voting. The researchers instituted voter registration at sites where cheese, butter, cornmeal, and other commodities were distributed to families with annual incomes less than the federally defined poverty level. This small change in accessibility to voter registration resulted in an amazing 100% increase in the number of people registered to vote and a 51% increase in subsequent voting in presidential elections. Taking the service to the people who most needed it empowered them to participate in social change.

Special populations (Fairweather & Davidson, 1986) cause changes in society and, in turn, create more social change by virtue of either their swelling ranks or special situations. In fact, never underestimate the importance of population trends in social change (Light & Keller, 1985). If formal, established institutions are insensitive to the special issues of diverse populations, these groups, themselves, can and will create change (Kettner et al., 1985). An early and remarkable example of self-created change came from the Gray Panthers, a group of aging activists inspired by Maggie Kuhn, who understood the importance of services for the growing numbers of elderly. We will discuss self-help or grass-roots efforts to create or deal with social change in the next chapter.

Another example, related to the opening vignette, is that as farmers mechanized their production in the early 1900s, many could not afford the expensive equipment. Knowing that the equipment would require less labor, cooperatives of farmers formed in which owners of one piece of equipment, such as a tractor, traded equipment and labor with owners of other pieces of equipment, such as a hay baler and a hay wagon.

Declining Resources

Since few community service programs are self-supporting, most are highly dependent on external funding (Kettner et al., 1985). External funding for community services generally comes in the form of legislated or government-sponsored funds as well as grants from public or private endowments or foundations. Both types of funds are likely to be awarded for experimental programs or services, which after some specified period must seek other sources of funding. New programs therefore compete with older programs for limited pools of money (Sarason, 1972; Levine & Perkins, 1987). Likewise, these "demonstration" programs are deemed insufficient because the time lag for them to be documented and disseminated to other communities is too long (Chavis, Florin, & Felix, 1992). Also, both the federal government and local governments have provided less and less funding for human services than in the past, thereby creating a sort of "Robin Hood in reverse" effect (Delgado, 1986).

Because government funding for community services is decreasing, there is more pressure on other granting institutions such as private foundations. Examples of such granting foundations for community services include the Ford Foundation, the Charles Stewart Mott Foundation, the Henry J. Kaiser Foundation, the Robert Wood Johnson Foundation, the McArthur Foundation, the Carnegie Foundation, and others (Chavis et al., 1992). More programs and human services agencies are applying for these limited funds; hence, the competition for both government and foundation monies is often fierce.

Although some agencies charge fees to clients for services, many are reluctant to become dependent on client fees, as such fees also fluctuate depending on caseload and other factors. Even those agencies that charge clients on a **sliding scale**, where fees are tied to income and/or number of dependents, are reluctant to increase charges to their most financially needy clients. A feeling exists that there has already been a trend for allocating resources away from the poor (Delgado, 1986). When funding issues become severe, and even when they are not so severe, clients and service administrators demand reform or social change. However, these groups are often answered just as vociferously by taxpayers angered that taxes will be raised again. All of these groups demand and/or create social change in response to already occurring social change.

One other source of funding for community service agencies is voluntary or charitable contributions from the public. Such contributions also vary as a function of the economy and other uncontrollable factors. Community service directors are therefore reluctant to become too dependent on charitable contributions. Funding issues for community services have been and will continue to be delicate and troublesome for years to come.

A newer source of funding is from socially conscious corporations such as Ben and Jerry's Ice Cream, Inc. Such companies often act in unison with community coalitions and advocacy groups to raise funds for community causes. The Ben and Jerry's story is detailed in Case in Point 3.1.

Accountability

Accountability and its sister term *cost effectiveness* seem to be the buzzwords for the 1990s. **Accountability** can be defined as the obligation to account for or be responsible for various transactions, monetary or otherwise. **Cost effectiveness**

❖ CASE IN POINT 3.1

Ben and Jerry's Ice Cream: The Corporation with a Social Conscience

How does Rain Forest Crunch preserve our environment? What does Cherry Garcia have to do with social change? Both are flavors of Ben and Jerry's ice cream, an upstart ice cream company in Vermont—a company that promotes "caring capitalism."

Bennet Cohen, the chief executive officer of Ben and Jerry's, is a baby boomer with a social conscience. He and Jerry Greenfield, his partner, firmly believe that "somehow, business has set itself up to be valueless, completely unspiritual, [but] it's very possible for business to make a profit and integrate a concern for the community into its day-to-day activity. If most businesses operated that way, we wouldn't have all these social and environmental problems we have" (Walker, 1992, p. B1).

Ben and Jerry—the entrepreneurs, not the ice cream—supposedly armed themselves with $5 diplomas from a correspondence course on making ice cream and decided to go into the ice cream business because they had been boyhood chums. In 1977, they experimented with Vermont cream and various goodies in an effort to create premium, "chunk-intensive" ice cream. Today, Ben and Jerry's ice cream nets almost $100 million a year and donates 7.5% of its pretax income to charity through the Ben and Jerry's Foundation.

For example, Ben and Jerry's ice cream boasts a circus bus that tours the country in conjunction with local charities. The bus attracts crowds wherever it goes. Besides offering a bit of summer fun and a free sample of ice cream, the bus and its occupants (clowns, jugglers, and so on) remind the audience about the purpose of the local charity and assist with fund raising. Interestingly, the bus is also environmentally conscious. It has 32 marine batteries and 180 feet of solar panels. In keeping with the flavor Rain Forest Crunch, the profits from the circus bus are used for the preservation of the Amazon Rain Forest.

Ben and Jerry's ice cream also treats its employees well. Employees receive up to three pints of ice cream a day, free day care, a health club, and a share in the company's profits. No one in the company can earn seven times more than anyone else.

There are other fledgling projects that offer hope that increased funding will be available through America's corporate giants. Recently, former President Jimmy Carter convinced corporations in the Atlanta area to sponsor the Atlanta Project, in which 20 different community clusters, each with a corporate sponsor such as Delta Air Lines and Coca Cola, decide what programs will be launched in the vicinity to better the community. Projects include home repairs for the elderly, transportation to jobs for city dwellers, immunizations for children, and a host of other services. Carter's philosophy is "Give people the resources to solve their own problems, neighborhood by neighborhood" (*USA Today*, 1993, p. 10A). Does this sound a bit like community psychology to you?

The next time you enjoy Chocolate Chip Cookie Dough ice cream or lick a Peace Pop, you might pause to wonder why all companies are not as socially conscious. Imagine how much significant and prosocial change could be supported if all companies were this caring.

means that money should be spent wisely; that is, there should be some return or profit on money expended. Cost effectiveness often refers to money; accountability can also refer to matters such as time expended, quality of decisions made, and so forth.

In the 1800s, citizens such as the Haydens were not bombarded by the media about the government and spending, legal or not. Spending has always been an important issue, but it is more likely to be historically in the forefront of the minds of today's citizens than it was in the past.

Who requests accountability? Almost anyone today: clients, staff, administrators, taxpayers, elected officials, licensing bureaus, and others. Any of these constituencies is likely to want to know the answers to such questions as: Where was my money spent? Did the targeted population benefit? Were goals accomplished, and if not, why not?

When answers to these questions are not forthcoming, are not the expected ones, or are not the best or most productive, the parties leveling the query are likely to demand change. Some individuals may want new administrators; others might want new spending guidelines. The list of demanded changes can be so exhaustive that the end result is the demise of any organization not readily accountable to its constituents. Again, the final outcome is likely to be some kind of ongoing change.

Knowledge-Based and Technological Change

In their day, the Haydens may have used some very innovative farm machinery that today would be called antiques. The Haydens probably felt timid and perhaps threatened the first time they used these machines. To give you some perspective, do you recall the first time you sat at a computer? You probably experienced trepidation and later felt the embarrassment caused by thinking a machine could get the better of you. **Technological changes** in the form of computer services and speedier communication systems have, in turn, created new demands on workforces in business as well as in human services. Some organizations and individuals adapt well to technological advances. Others—for a multitude of reasons such as reluctance to utilize new technologies or lack of funds—do not adapt well or quickly. For instance, many individuals can choose between electronic mail or fax machines for speedy communication. After toying with both methods, most communicators choose the fax machine because it is "high touch" as well as "high tech" (Naisbett & Aburdene, 1990).

People today may think that they are undergoing rapid and extreme technological changes more than ever before. Imagine, though, what adjustments the Hayden family would have undergone if they had changed from horse-driven equipment to gasoline-powered agricultural equipment in the early 1900s. What would they do with their teams of horses? Where would they get gasoline for their new tractors? Technological changes, whenever they occur, obligate further changes (Frank, 1983). Consider, for example, how your first experience with a computer changed you. If the experience was a positive one, perhaps today you complete your term papers, balance your checkbook, keep track of appointments, and pass your idle time playing video games with your computer. The computer has therefore changed your methods of conducting business, completing your work, and socializing. Imagine how computers have changed the rest of society!

If these "galloping technological changes" (Frank, 1983) are not enough, mainstream U.S. society is also experiencing a knowledge explosion. New methods for practicing anything from psychotherapy to landscape architecture, new guidelines for human resources management, additional legislation controlling all parts of people's lives, as well as other innovations and applications all requiring new understanding and new skills can overwhelm society's members, create additional change, and perhaps at the same time stimulate much anxiety.

Pilisuk and Acredolo (1988) surveyed nearly 500 residents of California and found a high level of expressed fear of technology. The fear of technology has been called **technophobia** in the psychological literature. The surveyed subjects reported fears that technology would contaminate drinking water, cause cancer and nuclear accidents, pollute the air, and make food and transportation dangerous. The researchers were also interested in who held the most fear. They found that women, minority group members, and less-educated persons were the most fearful. In other words, those with the least commerce with technology were probably most afraid of it. Perhaps as technological changes advance, the more these same individuals will continue to fear it. Few traditional community systems (such as the Department of Health) provide help in coping with technical disasters (Webb, 1989)—a situation that does not help to allay fears. One possible way to address these concerns is via education and information dissemination. These strategies are discussed in the next chapter on creating social change.

Community Conflict

The family in our opening vignette was fortunate to have neighbors who were so cooperative and caring. This is not always the case in communities, though. Some communities experience the strife of conflict. Conflict, however, does not always produce negative outcomes (Worchel & Lundgren, 1991). Sometimes a positive outcome of community conflict is social change. **Community conflict** involves two or more parties with incompatible goals that usually have specific values (positive and negative) attached to them. Because of the strongly held values, power struggles, and varying interest levels of the parties, conflict in the community can be difficult to resolve or manage (Christensen & Robinson, 1989). However, such conflict, whether resolved or unresolved, often results in social change, because goodwill alone does not always resolve or dissipate conflict (Fairweather & Tornatzky, 1977).

When diverse groups come together in any situation, there may be conflict. An example of change resulting from conflict within a diverse group occurred recently in the professional psychological community (Fowler, 1990). Within the large national organization for psychologists (the American Psychological Association, or APA), research psychologists grew increasingly dissatisfied with the perceived trend for the APA to cater more to the needs of practitioners than researchers. Such rifts between researchers and practitioners are seen as counter-productive (Duffy, Grosch, & Olczak, 1991). However, from the APA criticism grew a new psychological society—the American Psychological Society. The APS has a different mission than the APA, and its membership is heavily comprised of scientists. For another example of change resulting from community conflict, see Case in Point 3.2.

Dissatisfaction with Traditional Services

Probably no other cause has fostered social change more than consumer dissatisfaction with existing community services. In fact, you will recall from Chapter 1 that such dissatisfaction with traditional mental health services spawned the birth and growth of community psychology itself when psychologists at the Swampscott Conference expressed dismay with traditional forms of mental health treatment.

One example of dissatisfaction creating community change relates to this chapter's opening vignette. The Haydens lost their house because the bucket brigade they set up just was not fast enough to keep up with the damage from the fire. The Haydens might have asked for a town meeting to discuss with other citizens the formation of a fire district and fire department so that equipment such as a water wagon could be bought for everyone to use.

It is important to look at another, more modern example, though, of how dissatisfaction with services leads to change. As you may already know from your training in psychology and related disciplines, one of the earliest forms of psychotherapy (or "the talking cure") was psychoanalysis as designed by Sigmund Freud. Freud's own protégés such as Carl Jung and Alfred Adler became disenchanted with this brand of therapy and modified psychoanalysis as they knew it (Phares, 1991). Contemporary therapists, disgruntled with such concepts as pansexuality and the unconscious from Freudian theory have also developed a vast array of therapies exemplified by behavior modification, cognitive behavioral therapy, and humanistic counseling, to name a few. Today, the mental health client has a long menu of therapies from which to choose. You will read more about the history of the treatment of mental illness in future chapters.

Desire for Diversity of Solutions

Walk into any store in the United States and the display of goods available is overwhelming. Americans are used to choices between brands X, Y, and Z. Americans don't just want diversity among goods, however; they expect diversity and choice among services also. Individuals seeking psychotherapy want to know that they have options in the training of the therapist, the type of therapy, the payment plan, and the length of treatment. Similarly, Americans want to be able to choose between private and public educational institutions for their children and between law firms and lawyers when they want to recover damages or

❖ *CASE IN POINT 3.2*

Community Conflict: Adversity Turns to Opportunity

In the 1960s, an unfortunate but interesting instance of community conflict occurred in Rochester, New York. Surprisingly, from this adversity grew opportunity. An African American neighborhood decided to hold a neighborhood party. The party occurred on a hot summer night with many young adults showing up for the festivities. Halfway through the night, a group of White youths came to the party and were seen as intruders. One brusque remark led to another, which eventually erupted in violence. Rochester, New York, like many cities, quickly exploded in racial conflict.

Several community groups, concerned that such violence not repeat itself, came together in an attempt to find a solution to the city's problems. As a result, the American Arbitration Association was asked to consult on the design of a community program for handling many types of conflict. The **community mediation** program was born. This program (showcased in Chapter 11) manages community disputes between individuals or groups in a peaceful fashion by assigning a neutral third party—a **mediator**—to facilitate discussion and problem solving between the disputants (Duffy et al., 1991). The program also monitors community agency elections as well as urban renewal housing lotteries, "lemon law" (automobile owner/ manufacturer) arbitration, and other community projects where a neutral is needed. The initial community conflict, racial tension, was probably a part of the larger national civil rights movement—a movement that created sweeping social changes, which are not yet complete.

From the Rochester conflict, however, came more social change in the form of the Community Dispute Resolutions Centers Act (Christian, 1986). This legislation established in every county in New York a mediation center modeled after the one in Rochester. With New York as the pioneer state, other states followed. Today, there are hundreds of functioning mediation or neighborhood justice centers in this country. Some are adjuncts to the courts; others are run by religious and other charities (McGillis, 1980). All hope to inspire the peaceful resolution of conflict. Community conflict, then, creates snowballing social reform and social change, of which the Rochester experience is only one example.

close a real estate deal. Americans have come a long way since the 1800s when families like the Haydens had one doctor, one school, and one pharmacy in their towns. When individuals find agencies are insensitive or that there are few options from which to choose, and sometimes this is coupled with dissatisfaction with those existing options, the individuals often demand and create change.

Here is an example from the justice system of how the desire for more options creates change. Anyone who has watched Judge Wapner on television's "The People's Court" hand down a verdict knows that the courts often leave complainants and defendants alike disgruntled. Sometimes even the "winner" does not feel as if he or she has won. One answer to handling this dissatisfaction and to providing more diversity for users of the court system is to develop a **multidoor approach**, as is found in Washington, DC (Ostermeyer, 1991). This is a coordinated system of assisting citizens involved in the justice system to find the most appropriate option for them: various courts (small claims, city, state, and federal); mediation and arbitration programs; legal aid offices; public, private, and volunteer attorneys; and other agencies such as those assisting with mental health. The multidoor approach helps citizens and agencies avoid the frustration of multiple and overlapping referrals and lessens the perception that the justice system is a confusing maze of bureaucracies (Ostermeyer, 1991). The multidoor courthouse is discussed further in Chapter 9.

The preceding catalog of reasons for social change, which is not exhaustive, is summarized in Table 3.1. It will familiarize you with some of the causes for social changes. We next need to examine some of the ways in which change occurs, whether planned or unplanned.

TYPES OF SOCIAL CHANGE

Forecasting social trends is a tricky business. Children of the 1960s will tell you that they didn't think anyone could overthrow Elvis. Along came the British rock groups who toppled "The King." Educators riding the tide of the baby boom built

TABLE 3.1   Reasons for and Examples of Social Change

Reason for Change	Example of Social Change
Special population	AIDS patients desire emotional support from a group of other AIDS patients, and their families get together and form a support group.
Declining resources	The national economy is depressed; less grant money is available from private foundations.
Accountability	A taxpayer group attends a public hearing and demands to know how a tax increase will improve community services.
Technological advances	A corporation buys new personal computers for midlevel managers who now require training.
Community conflict	An agency seeks a halfway house in a residential neighborhood not zoned for multiple-family dwellings; two residents groups, one in support and one against, conflict at a public meeting.
Dissatisfaction with traditional services	An area's private practice psychologists charge high fees not covered by insurance, so citizens inquire about funding possibilities for a mental health clinic that will charge on a sliding scale.
Desire for diversity of solutions	A multidoor courthouse program offers a variety of options for solutions to neighbors fighting in the neighborhood.

schools and school annexes in the suburbs until the number of schools had soared. Today, schools are closing; few school boards and public officials realistically anticipated the decline in the number of school-age children during this decade. College enrollments are down, too. Community activists have much that they can learn from demographers and other forecasters about where change will occur next, particularly spontaneous or unplanned **change**.

Spontaneous or Unplanned Social Change

Naturally occurring change is called **unplanned** or **spontaneous change**. Most disasters are not planned. For instance, no one planned the fire at the Hayden farm, and, more recently, few predicted the disaster of the explosion of *The Challenger* space shuttle or the magnitude of the devastating earthquakes in California.

Natural disasters result in much distress as well as social change. Droughts, earthquakes, floods, fires, and other natural events displace community members from their homes and their jobs. Although these disasters are not necessarily always distressing (Bravo, Rubio-Stipec, Canino, Woodbury, & Ribera, 1990), they typically result in some large-scale change.

Unplanned, major shifts in the population also cause social change and, in fact, much social dissatisfaction and divisiveness (Katz, 1983). For example, as the swell of baby boomers moves through time, their needs change. Some baby boomers are now middle-aged and are caring for elderly parents (Naisbitt & Aburdene, 1990). They often find a dearth of community services that provide elder care, and this creates much stress in the boomers' lives. Some baby boomers also have young children who require day care, which can be in short supply. The stress of caring for both the younger and older generations in their lives has resulted in such adults being labeled the **sandwich generation**.

Similarly, other demographic shifts create other social changes. Today, for instance, there is an increase in the number of single working parents and two-career families (Hess et al., 1991), both of which need to find day care for their young children (Naisbitt & Aburdene, 1990). Likewise, the high divorce rate and the subsequent remarriages of parents create **blended families** of stepparents and stepchildren who sometimes do not adapt well to their changing family situations. These groups can also be assisted by services established in and designed for the community.

Behavioral changes in the population over time are often unplanned. A realistic example of these changes would be recent increases in crime, especially violent crimes (Baron & Byrne, 1994). Although high crimes rates do not always result in fear (Taylor & Shumaker, 1990), individuals who live in areas where they do fear the high crime rate may desire special community programs such as neighborhood watches or escort services for the elderly. One interesting study did establish that those who have been crime victims are not always the most afraid of crime. Rather, this research demonstrated that those most fearful of crime live in neighborhoods with abandoned buildings, vandalism, idle teens, and other signs of deterioration that indicate concomitant declines in social control within the community (Baba & Austin, 1989).

What makes unplanned or unintentional change stressful is that, although it is rare, it is often serious and uncontrollable, much as the Hayden's fire was. Research (Rodin, Timko, & Harris, 1986) has shown that uncontrollable events are quite stressful. In other words, when individuals feel they control their fates, they experience less stress; when they feel they have lost control, they experience distress (Boggiano & Katz, 1991; Taylor, Helgeson, Reed, & Skokan, 1991). Also, unplanned change is often confined to particular ecological situations in which individuals may unwittingly be placed. For example, crime and natural disasters are generally confined to particular environments (Taylor & Shumaker, 1990), so when individuals find themselves in those environments, they may experience stress.

Besides assisting in the design and development of community services, community psychologists can also assist with coping for unplanned change by playing a role in forecasting it. Remember that one of the tenets of community psychology is prevention. We do not mean to suggest that community psychologists can prevent these changes—certainly psychologists can't prevent floods—but learning how to predict unplanned changes can enable the community to prepare for the changes as they occur or even before they occur. Such preparation can prevent the change from being as severe and distressing as it otherwise might be.

The science of prediction is complex, but there are scientists who specialize in prediction and forecasting. In *Megatrends 2000*, content analyses of the print media were utilized to forecast coming trends (Naisbitt & Aburdene, 1990). Census data can also help forecast population changes. For instance, as the baby boomers age, they will represent the largest group of elderly this country has ever had, so if elder care is in short supply now, it may be in even shorter supply in two decades if no one prepares for it. **Social indicators** are measures of some aspect of society based on combined, corrected, and refined social statistics (Johnston, 1980) and can be used in social forecasting. By utilizing techniques such as extrapolative forecasting, network analysis, environmental prediction, and others, social trends can be forecasted and preventive measures can be prepared (Harrison, 1976). Indeed, the use of "future studies" can do much for prevention in communities (Sundberg, 1985), but not without some limitations. Lorion (1991), for example, raised the issue of the **base rate problem**. This issue pertains to the fact that although many individuals seem to have the antecedents of diagnosable disorders, for example, few may really actually develop the disorder.

Planned Change

Suppose people do not want to wait for change to happen, as in unplanned or unintended change (McGrath, 1983); instead, they want intentionally to create change, called **planned change** or **induced change** (Glidewell, 1976). How could people go about this seemingly monumental task? There are some venerated strategies suggested in the community psychology literature: self-help, including grass-roots activism; networking of services and social support; the use of external change agents or consultants; educational and informational programs; and involvement in public policy processes. All of these issues are detailed in the next chapter. None of these approaches is easy, and each has its advantages and disadvantages. With planned change, however, the desired effects are more likely to be obtained than with unplanned or spontaneous change.

Exactly what is planned change? Kettner and associates (1985) wrote a good working definition. *Planned change* is an intentional or deliberate intervention to change a situation—or for the present discussion, a part of or a whole community. Planned change is distinguished from unplanned change by four characteristics. First, planned change is *limited in scope*; that is, in planned change, what is to be changed is targeted or earmarked in advance. Second, planned change is directed toward *enhancing the quality of life* of the community members. This is the primary purpose of planned change in communities. Planned change should enhance, not inhibit, community life. Third, planned change usually *provides a role* for those affected by change. Community psychologists should not impose change on community members. Rather, their role is to inform citizens of the viable options, assist them in the selection of appropriate options, and then participate with them in the design and implementation of change. Finally, planned change is often but not always *guided by a person who acts as a change agent*. **Change agents** (Lippett, Watson, & Westley, 1958; Oskamp, 1984) are often trained professionals but can also be advocates for or from client groups, political activists, educational experts, or others interested in inducing change. Psychologists often act as consultants or change agents. The role of consultants is detailed in the next chapter.

Issues Related to Planned Change

A major issue regarding planned change is *who* decides change will occur and *when*, *how*, and *what* changes will take place. Suppose the Haydens had called a town meeting to discuss how the community should manage fire disasters. Who should decide what the town should do? All voters? Only taxpayers? Only those who owned farms where hay could combust? Did they need to discuss temporary housing issues for fire victims? Should they ask an outside agency such as the Red Cross?

Some change experts argue that administrators and managers are responsible for initiating change; others argue that the bottom of the organization such as staff, clients, or other laypersons should create change (Kettner et al., 1985). Many in the field of community development agree that almost anyone and everyone involved in the changes is the appropriate person (Christensen & Robinson, 1989; Heller et al., 1984; Kettner et al., 1985; Levine & Perkins, 1987).

In community psychology, the concept of *collaboration* is embraced (Bond, 1990; Fawcett, 1990; Oskamp, 1984; Rappaport, 1990; Rappaport et al., 1985; Serrano-Garcia, 1990). The idea of collaboration—of social scientists and clients coming together to examine and create solutions for social problems—is a major tradition in community psychology (Rappaport, 1990). Collaboration is also called **participatory decision making** or **collaborative problem solving** (Chavis et al., 1992) and has already been discussed in Chapter 1 as a process important to community psychology (Kelly, 1986a). As Christensen and Robinson (1989) suggested, self-determination has practical problem-solving utility in that those who live with the problem can best solve it. Acceptance is therefore higher than in imposed changes. Moreover, collaborative decision making helps build a stronger sense of community and avoids client-consultant conflict and duplication of effort because collaboration is a mutual influence process. The key to collaboration is empowerment, which enhances the possibility of self-determination.

Anyone embarking on planned social change needs to prepare carefully for the changes. Ongoing, carefully planned change requires hard work and a substantial investment of time, talent, money, and other resources that might otherwise be useful elsewhere (Kettner et al., 1985). The change agents should also prepare participants for change to take a long time (Fairweather & Davidson, 1986; Seidman, 1990), as it is likely to be resisted. Likewise, the more important the problem, the more difficult it will probably be to solve (Shadish, 1990).

Planners also need to consider whether change is really possible (e.g., Will all involved parties cooperate? Are funds available? etc.) and whether, in the end, the desired results can be realistically achieved. For example, although thousands of community programs and organizations exist across the country, many fail (Florin, 1989). Prestby and Wandersman (1985) found that 50% of voluntary neighborhood associations, many of which are designed to create and support social change, become inactive after only one year. Such organizations therefore seem particularly vulnerable to demise or failure (Chavis, et al., 1992).

Fairweather and Davidson (1986) have explained that a single attack on a social problem will not create substantial change. A multipronged and continual approach is generally more successful. A once-and-for-all solution probably will not be effective either (Levine & Perkins, 1987). Fairweather and Davidson have also cautioned that some old practices might work well, any useless approaches should be discarded. It is worthwhile to remember, too, that *complete* change might not always be necessary. Profile 3.1 provides an example of planned change efforts by discussing Marybeth Shinn, an outstanding community psychologist who works on some fascinating projects in New York City.

Besides the preceding dimensions, planners also need to consider the other parameters of beneficial change (Fairweather & Davidson, 1986). Change must be humane—that is, it must be socially responsible and represent humanitarian values that emphasize enhancing human potential. Change techniques should also be problem oriented—that is, they should be aimed at solutions of problems rather than merely be idealistic. Similarly, change strategies should focus on multiple social levels rather than on specific individuals. The techniques may need to be creative and innovative. Old, stale methods may not work; creativity is the constant companion of community activists. The change plans also need to be feasible in terms of dissemination to other groups or situations. Not all techniques

◆ PROFILE 3.1
Marybeth Shinn

As one of the prominent leaders in community psychology, Marybeth Shinn keeps the field invigorated. You will meet her in several places in this book, as her work relates to many ecological settings, such as life on the streets for America's homeless and in community organizations.

Educated at Radcliffe College and the University of Michigan in community and social psychology, Shinn landed her first teaching position at New York University and remains there today. Her plaudits are many. She has received a number of prestigious fellowships from private and public organizations and is a fellow of both the American Psychological Association and the American Psychological Society.

Shinn's work in community psychology has centered on several important topics; we will focus here on some of her more recent work. In various places in this book, you will read about her work on homelessness. Her work has clearly demonstrated why homeless is *not* just the homeless individual's problem but rather a *societal* problem that needs to be addressed on a broad spectrum. Shinn is also one of the leading researchers and authors in the area of social support—a topic about which you will read in Chapters 4 and 5. Her research has demonstrated that the support of others can, indeed, reduce stress in groups as diverse as working parents, child-care workers, and individuals with scoliosis.

Shinn has also been instrumental in prodding community psychologists to take a critical look at their field. Her publications on examining organizations through a community psychology lens and mixing and matching levels of conceptualization, measurement, and analysis in community psychology have been seminal in the field. In her own words,

> *Community psychology needs to pay more than lip service to issues of level in developing theory, defining variables, and testing relationships....There are promising statistical techniques for extracting information about extraindividual units and relationships from data collected about or from individuals....With better conceptualization, we can also develop more measures that match the level of theory. (Shinn, 1990, p. 126)*

fit all groups, but there are some communities that can adopt tried methods from other communities.

Change agents should plan globally or holistically (Newbrough, 1973), so as to see the whole picture rather than disjointed pieces of problems. Pluralistic (Freedman, 1989) or multilevel planning is likely to ensure success because the context or environment within which the change will occur will be more likely to have been considered.

As mentioned earlier, context or environment is a concept important to the ecological tradition of community psychology. In working with the Hayden family, a community psychologist would take into account the family's agrarian lifestyle as well as the social climate in the town they frequented. A contemporary example would be more useful, though. Suppose that a large corporation decides to open a health club as part of its wellness program. If the corporation was downsizing its workforce, the health club and perhaps the whole wellness concept could be resented and underutilized by employees because they perceive that the health club funding might have been used to save coworkers' jobs. Without taking into acount the context of the organization and the trends occurring in the organization, the change strategy of the health club would fail.

Change agents also need to value social experimentation and action research. In this regard, planners cannot be timid about innovation—neither can they be afraid to evaluate their innovations. Social experimentation and evaluation go hand in hand (Fairweather & Davidson, 1986). Any interventions and programs developed to create community change need to be honestly evaluated, modifed based on the evaluation, evaluated again, and so on. Then and only then do change agents and communities know that they have the best possible ideas in place.

Finally, planners or change agents need to be realists, particularly with regard to the prevailing political climate (Light & Keller, 1985). Change always makes something different that otherwise would not be changed (Benviente, 1989). Some individuals will like the change; others will not. Hence, the power struggles related to change are likely to commence as soon as change is suggested.

WHY CHANGE PLANS FAIL

Why do programs that are designed to create social change or provide alternative services fail? Why do the most well-intended efforts sometimes go awry? What if the Hayden family had called a town meeting to discuss what should or could happen when a family loses a home to a fire and no one came to the meeting? Or what if the citizens were divided as to what they should do? A multitude of reasons exist but we will mention only a few. One of the most important reasons for failure of planned change is resistance (Glidewell, 1976; Levine & Perkins, 1987), which can come from a variety of sources, including administrators, practitioners, clients, or any other community member.

Why does resistance occur? Societies tend to have built-in resistance to change (Bagby, 1981); members of groups seem trained to follow their own ways—the old ways—which they regard as safe or superior (Glidewell, 1976). Groups feel their existence is threatened by new groups or new ideas. Psychologists have long documented the effects of in-groups and out-groups in which people favor their own groups (the **in-group**) and stereotype or denigrate outsiders (the **out-group**) (Worchel, 1986). In the community, for instance, for-profit businesses, especially big private-sector corporations, often resist social change instituted by small nonprofit businesses or by new government policies because the for-profit enterprises think their revenues will be affected.

Change is often seen as unwelcome, not just by groups but by individuals as well (Kettner et al., 1985). Social psychologists know that individuals are also resistant to change, one of the causes of which is mere cognitive laziness or the desire not to have to think too hard. Most humans are **cognitive misers** who take the path of least effort in terms of decision making and thinking (Baron & Byrne, 1994). Other individuals are also closed-minded or **dogmatic** (Rockeach, 1960); they conserve their old ways and shun new ideas because of rigidity in their thinking. Individuals resist change for the same reasons as groups—because they feel that change threatens their reputation, job security, and well-being.

Other factors also create the failure of planned change. When a social movement is seen as promoting only a single cause or a cause alien to a large number of people, change is often slow or does not occur at all. For example, if the Haydens had proposed a temporary shelter for farm families only to the exclusion of townspeople, the Haydens might have failed. More contemporarily, had the March of Dimes, for example, stuck with the single issue of the defeat of polio, the organization would have assured its own demise. Refocusing on the elimination of *all* birth defects has ensured the health of that organization for a long time.

When those attempting to create change disregard others in the community or disregard other community problems, failure can also take place. A solution to avoiding isolated change is **networking**. A network is an interconnected and interactive social relationship among various individuals or organizations in which reciprocity of information, resources, and other support between individuals or organizations is maintained (Chavis et al., 1992). The next chapter contains more information on networking.

Often, agents of change and their programs fail because their tactics are unwelcome or negative. Alinsky (1971), Kettner and associates (1985), and Wolff (1987) see risk taking, including the risk that change will be unwelcome, as part and parcel of all change. However, the reality is that if those people planning change receive only negative exposure (by the media, for example) or fail to suggest their own solutions to the problems they are protesting, their protests are perceived as hollow or disruptive rather than productive. Agitation, protest, and confrontation do not always work, and published research supports this contention (Oskamp, 1984). If a community activist chooses a radical or confrontative route to change, Saul Alinsky's work will be of interest. Table 3.2 summarizes some of his approaches.

We have already suggested that collective planning for change is construed as good, but this is only true within limits. If the organization or individuals planning change are too loosely structured, if solid leadership does not exist, or if the decision makers show no discipline in their plans, then they, too, can fail. Often, as the planners begin to fail, conflict breaks out in the ranks (Levine &

TABLE 3.2   Ten Rules for Radicals

These are general guidelines. According to Saul Alinsky, they should be adapted to the uniquenesses of each situation.

1. Use whatever you've got to get attention.
2. Don't go outside the experience of your people.
3. But whenever possible, go outside the experience of the enemy.
4. Make the enemy live up to its own rules.
5. Ridicule is a potent weapon and it makes the opposition react to your advantage.
6. A good tactic is one that your people enjoy—if they don't enjoy it, there is something wrong.
7. A tactic that drags on too long becomes a drag.
8. The threat is usually more terrifying than the thing itself.
9. Power is what you have and what the enemy thinks you have.
10. Keep the pressure on.

Source: Adapted from *Rules for Radicals: A Practical Primer for Realistic Radicals* by S. Alinsky, 1971, New York: Random House.

Perkins, 1987). Delgado (1986) reviewed several organizations that had good intent but that evaporated because of the inadequacy of their own organizational infrastructures. Due to the concern over the survival of community organizations, recent work on infrastructures and phenotypes of organizations is under way (Luke, Rappaport, & Seidman, 1991; Maton, 1988; Schubert & Borkman, 1991; Zimmerman et al., 1991). Maton, for example, using three different support groups within the community, found that the groups with higher role differentiation, greater order and organization, and capable leaders reported more positive well-being and more positive group appraisal. We will take a closer look at community psychology and community organizations in Chapter 11.

One of the best solutions to prevent failure—and prevention is a critical part of all of community psychology—is to lay a good foundation for change by conducting research. Community psychologists regard research and practice as interdependent on one another (Kelly, 1986b). **Action research**, as you have already read, is scientific work grounded in theory but directed toward resolving problems (Lewin, 1948; Deutsch & Hornstein, 1975; Oskamp, 1984). Action research in the community is not without its problems (Price, 1990; Tolan, Keys, Chertak, & Jason, 1990). Problems include the lack of trust in the researcher by community members, breakdowns in negotiating with program and community administrators, the inability to randomly assign subjects to conditions, the selection of appropriate and adequate measures, and so on (Fairweather & Davidson, 1986). Research should not just be done at the front end of community change. Once an intervention has been implemented, it needs ongoing assessment. For example, one method for assessing interventions is program evaluation, as already reviewed in Chapter 2.

SUMMARY

Social change is a pervasive condition of today's world. There are many reasons change occurs. Diverse populations, such as the growing number of elderly and AIDS victims, have needs that must be addressed but for which society may not be prepared. Another reason for change is declining resources, which include money, space, and commodities such as food. On the other hand, galloping technological advances also necessitate change on the part of individuals as well as society. One technology that has caused all sorts of modification in our daily lives and in methods of conducting business is the addition of computers. On the other hand, many people fear the advance of technology (technophobia), and traditional community services do little to help individuals cope with the fear.

Demands for accountability also create change. People expect that funds will be expended wisely and grow concerned when spending is not accounted for. Related to accountability is cost effectiveness, which refers to how wisely money is spent (i.e., Is there a profit?).

Community conflict is yet another reason for change. Groups in communities experience ethnic strife, conflict over resources such as land use, and so on to create change. A growing sentiment against traditional methods for dealing with today's problems—for instance, the treatment of the mentally ill—as well as a desire for choices or diversity among solutions to problems also prompt change.

There are two types of change: planned (or induced) change and unplanned (or spontaneous) change. Planned change occurs when changes are intentional or deliberate. Planned change is limited by its scope, usually enhances the quality of life for community members, provides for a role for affected groups, and is often guided by a professional change agent or consultant. In unplanned or spontaneous change, change is unexpected, sometimes disastrous (as in a natural disaster such as a flood), and often of a large magnitude (such as when a segment of the population experiences growth as in the baby boom generation).

4

CREATING
AND SUSTAINING
SOCIAL CHANGE

Introduction

Creating Planned Change

Citizen Participation
 Issues Related to Citizen Participation
 Advantages and Disadvantages of Citizen Participation

Networking
❖ *CASE IN POINT 4.1 Grass-Roots Activism on a College Campus*
 Issues Related to Networks
 Advantages and Disadvantages of Networks

Professional Change Agents: Consultants
 Issues Related to Consultants
◆ *PROFILE 4.1 Thomas Wolff*
 Advantages and Disadvantages of Consultants

The Use of Education and Information Dissemination to Produce Social Change
 Issues Related to Information Dissemination
 Advantages and Disadvantages of Educational Change

Public Policy as a Means of Social Change
 Issues Related to the Use of Public Policy to Create Change
 Advantages and Disadvantages of Public Policy Changes

Summary

You can't say that civilization don't advance, for in every war they kill you a new way.

◆ *WILL ROGERS*

It was December 31, and the Marvin family—Melba, Harold, and their three young children—had just settled down to their New Year's Eve dinner. They were happy to be sharing a meal with each other. Their busy schedules often prohibited them from dining together. Harold's head suddenly snapped up as he asked what the popping sound was. Melba and the children giggled; they accused Harold of hearing noisemakers before midnight. They continued to eat, and this time they all heard the popping noise. Harold ran into the hall to find dense smoke pouring out of an upstairs bedroom.

Harold and Melba collected the children and ran into the street. Melba took the youngest child and ran in one direction while Harold ran in the opposite direction with the other two to find a neighbor at home who could call 911. By the time they found someone home down the street, the neighbor's house on the left of theirs was on fire. The police responded first to the call. After what seemed like an eternity but which was only about 20 minutes, the fire department arrived. By this time, several other of the old wooden homes had also caught fire. Gawking families from the rest of neighborhood ran out into the street when they heard the sirens. Everyone, including the dismayed Marvin family, stared in wonder as the burning houses shot flames like fireworks high into the New Year's sky.

Four of the houses were decimated by the fire; a few others had water and smoke damage. The Red Cross, having arrived when the police called them, gave the Marvins and the other displaced families temporary shelter and also found used clothing for the families.

Harold and Melba were surprised when they started negotiating with their insurance company. Neither the house nor the contents were fully covered; their insurance policy had failed to keep pace with inflation. The Marvins felt a deep sense of depression but vowed to find a new, albeit smaller, home in the same school district if possible. Both Harold and Melba worried about the prospect of finding another home, given that they both worked full time. They knew the other families would probably be looking in the same neighborhood, too, so competition might be fierce. At least, the Marvins reasoned, they were all safe and together, even if their New Year's celebration had been ruined.

INTRODUCTION

This opening vignette exemplifies the busy, daily life led by many working-class families in the United States. Both parents often work; young children are farmed out to caregivers, and the family rarely enjoys quality time together. Major tragedies upset the existence of the whole family, and in contrast to the opening story in the previous chapter, this situation is worsened by the fact that there is often little social and material support available to these families to help them cope.

Consider also how much more difficult daily life is for families who do not have the comforts of a two-parent income, a home in a secure neighborhood, good jobs, and healthy children. Finding food and clothing, seeking a safe shelter for the night, and caring for other basic needs are monumental, all-consuming daily chores.

CREATING PLANNED CHANGE

Society has never needed changing more than it does today. Creating and sustaining social change is not an easy task, but community psychologists are at the forefront of researching the best ways to create and maintain positive societal change. Participating in social change is a fundamental value in community psychology (Jason, 1991) as well as a basic property of social reality (Keys & Frank, 1987). This chapter will examine established methods for fashioning both small- and large-scale social change. For each technique, its use, its advantages and disadvantages, and related research will be discussed. When change is intentional and planned in advance, it is termed **planned change**.

CITIZEN PARTICIPATION

Melba and Harold Marvin, the contemporary homeowners in the opening vignette, could have banded together with other homeowners who found that their insurance did not cover their losses. The homeowners' group could have approached the insurance companies and demanded an accounting of why coverage of losses is not keeping pace with replacement costs. The homeowners could also have presented their solutions to the problem and asked that a committee be formed of community citizens and insurance carriers to address which proposed solution is best. Or a citizens' group could have asked the fire department why they did not respond faster to the blaze or the group could have formed a neighborhood watch so that when fires start in homes where no one is home, the fire still gets noticed and reported. Had the families taken any of these actions, they would have been citizens actively participating in social change.

Perhaps no other method of creating social change has received as much attention as participant-induced change, and interest in this type of change is mounting (Linney, 1990). Various authors have given different labels to this type of change, including citizen participation (Levi & Litwin, 1986), empowerment (Rappaport, Swift, & Hess, 1984), grass-roots activism (Alinsky, 1971), and self-help (Christensen & Robinson, 1989), among other terms. **Citizen participation** can be broadly defined as involvement in any organized activity in which the individual participates without pay in order to achieve a common goal (Zimmerman & Rappaport, 1988). At the root of this mechanism of change is "the premise that people can, will, and should collaborate to solve common problems" (Christensen & Robinson, 1989, p. 48). In fact, some hold self-help as the most promising mechanism for changing society (Florin & Wandersman, 1990). An example of citizen participation is **grass-roots activism,** which occurs when individuals define their own issues and press for social change to address these issues and work in a bottom-up rather than top-down fashion. For example, when citizens who are tired of lives being senselessly taken on our highways urge policy makers to pass laws with stiffer penalties against drunk driving, the citizens are practicing grass-roots activism.

Another example of this type of change but at a more personal level is **self-help groups**, such as Alcoholics Anonymous, where individuals with common issues come together to assist and emotionally support one another. Because self-help groups are often overseen by professionals, some psychologists prefer the term **mutual assistance** groups for groups comprised solely of laypeople (Levine, 1988). Often, individuals in these groups learn coping strategies from each other. At a personal level, community members—such as friends, family, and neighbors—can assist in supporting each other through difficult times by providing **social support**. Social support is an exchange of resources (such as emotional comfort or material goods) between two individuals where the provider intends the resources to enhance the well-being of the recipient (Shumaker & Brownell, 1984, 1985). Social support can be another means by which social change occurs, but all are discussed elsewhere in the book in some detail.

The usual settings for citizen participation are work settings, health care programs, architectural environments, neighborhood associations, public policy arenas, education programs, and situations applying science (especially social science) and technology. This type of participation can occur by electoral participation (voting or working for a particular candidate or issue), grass-roots efforts (when citizens start a group and define its goals and methods), or government-mandated citizen participation in which citizens are appointed to watchdog committees or attend public hearings. Table 4.1 provides more examples of mechanisms for citizen participation but which vary in terms of effort expended and commitment.

Issues Related to Citizen Participation

Not everyone wants to participate in social change nor believes that he or she can be effective in fashioning social change. Research by O'Neill, Duffy, Enman, Blackmer, and Goodwin (1988) examined what types of individuals are active in

---

TABLE 4.1   Examples of Citizen Participation

Voting

Signing a petition

Donating money or time to a cause

Reading media articles on community needs or change

Boycotting environmentally unsound products

Being interviewed for a community survey

Joining a self-help group

Participating in a question-answer session after a debate

Serving on an ad hoc committee or task force

Participating in sit-ins and marches

Leading a grass-roots activist group in the community

Doing volunteer work in the community

Conducting fund-raising for a community service

Offering consultation services

Serving in public office

---

trying to produce social change. The researchers administered a modified I-E Scale and an Injustice Scale to introductory psychology students and single mothers (both of whom were considered nonactivist groups), board members of a day-care center (a moderately activist group), and board members of a transition house for victims of domestic violence (the high activist group). The *I-E Scale* (Rotter, 1966) measures **internal** versus **external locus of control**. Individuals with an internal locus of control believe that they control their own reinforcers; individuals with an external locus of control believe that other people or perhaps fate (something external to the individual) controls reinforcers. The researchers modified Rotter's scale to measure personal power or the sense that a person is in control of his or her fate. The *Injustice Scale* measures individuals' perceptions about whether the world is just (for example, do the courts let the guilty go free and convict innocent people). O'Neill and associates found that neither construct alone, personal power nor a sense of injustice, is sufficient to predict who will be a social activist. Both a sense of personal power *and* a belief in the injustices of society combine to produce social activism. Figure 4.1 reproduces these results in graphic form.

Measuring the impact of citizen participation is difficult but it is necessary if one is to understand the process and to determine whether it works (Kelly, 1986b). The citizens—the stakeholders so to speak—might want hard evidence that their efforts were worthwhile, but such direct evidence is often difficult to obtain. Involved individuals might also disagree about what is solid evidence:

FIGURE 4.1   **Results of Research on Social Activism**

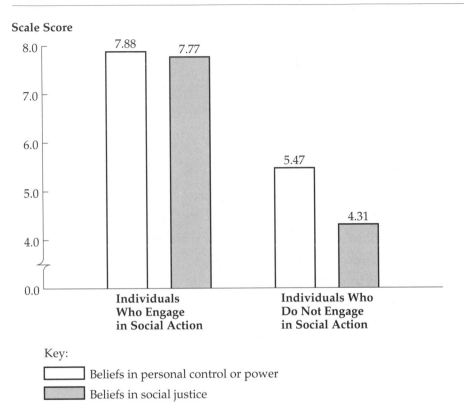

Scale Score

Citizens who believe in personal control (or power) and social injustice are likely to be social activists.

Source: From "Cognition and Citizen Participation in Social Action" by P. O'Neill, C. Duffy, M. Enman, E. Blackman, and J. Goodwin, 1988, *Journal of Applied Sociology, 18*, pp. 1067–1083.

cost savings, increased profits, higher client satisfaction, less stress, improved community relations, and so forth.

Some citizens may want to participate but lack the appropriate skills; few laypeople for example, know how to lobby for policy change or how to conduct meaningful and scientific research. Chavis, Florin, and Felix (1992) and Levin and Litwin (1986) noted that citizen groups might also need their group dynamics skills sharpened. Their leaders might need leadership development in the form of training in negotiations or incentive management (Prestby, Wandersman, Floren, Rich, & Chavis, 1990) or in strategic planning. The whole activist group might benefit from techniques borrowed from organizational development (see Chapter 11) such as **team building**. Team building is designed to assist a group to develop into a well-functioning team by helping it to define goals, to analyze tasks and the way tasks are performed, as well as to examine the relationship among people doing the work (Moorehead & Griffin, 1992).

Obtaining funding for citizen-initiated programs can be problematic. When is funding not problematic? Citizens often don't know where or how to access funds. For example, how many of you know how to write or have written successful grants large enough to support a community program?

Advantages and Disadvantages of Citizen Participation

Active participation in change efforts is highly motivational (Chavis et al., 1992; Christensen & Robinson, 1989). That is, people are more likely to accept change that they, themselves, have generated (Duffy, 1991). Involved individuals are also likely to know the problems that need addressing because they have lived with the problems. For that same reason, this type of community participation often helps build a sense of community (Levi & Litwin, 1986) or social consensus and cohesiveness (Heller, Price, Reinharz, Riger, & Wandersman, 1984). Conversely, feeling a sense of community also increases participation in grass-roots efforts (Chavis & Wandersman, 1990).

As desirable as this type of participation is, it is not without its pitfalls (Oskamp, 1984). Christensen and Robinson (1989) reported that not every citizen wants to participate. Although it is easy to level a charge of apathy against nonparticipants, the rights of those who prefer not to be involved need to be respected.

With this type of social change, results can be long in coming. The delay may cause some early and inspired individuals to run out of steam before their efforts show results. Studies in human services settings suggest that burnout is high (Maslach & Jackson, 1981; Ross, Altmeier, & Russell, 1989) and that those with the highest dedication often burn out first (Schultz & Schultz, 1990).

Finally, because they often are not comprised of all members of a community but rather comprised of a select few, citizen groups can fail. If these individuals are not representative of the affected groups or the population at large, the solutions might not be viable or acceptable for everyone. Furthermore, if this small group of activists is not representative of the larger constituency, then the large group might distrust or reject the smaller group (Worchel, Cooper, & Goethals, 1991), which also causes failure. Participants in community intervention need to recognize the politics of the conflicting goals and interests of the various involved parties (Riger, 1989). Similarly, if activity in the efforts costs more than any benefits that accrue, individuals are likely to become inactive (Prestby et al., 1990).

Zinobar and Dinkel (1981) have developed a manual and workshop for citizens interested in creating change. Although the thrust of this manual is toward citizens involved in community mental health programs, it provides suggestions helpful to most community groups, such as:

1. Make sure the suggestions are specific.
2. Give reasons the change is needed
3. Obtain media coverage by inviting reporters to meetings.

Likewise, citizens hoping to be involved in or expand self-help organizations would be well served by an article by Zimmerman and colleagues (1991) in which they describe the successful expansion of a typical organization. Such an organization needs to mobilize resources from a variety of sources, display flexibility in securing resources, be creative in defining organizational roles, and encourage individual involvement.

For more radical rules for participation you might want to see Alinksy's (1971) *Rules for Radicals* (mentioned in the previous chapter); however, be aware that Alinsky has been rebuked by others for his abrasiveness and lack of ideology (Delgado, 1986). Case in Point 4.1 discusses a case about the success of activism on a college campus.

NETWORKING

If Harold and Melba Marvin had formed their angry homeowners' group, they might have encountered trouble keeping the group organized and motivated. By joining a statewide coalition of homeowners for adequate insurance and insurance reform or an umbrella organization dedicated to oversight of local fire departments, the success of the Marvins' group might be greater. The formation of such coalitions is the focus of this section.

One means for fostering community development or community change is to develop enabling systems (Chavis, Florin, & Felix, 1992). **Enabling systems** are vehicles whereby multiple community initiatives can be simultaneously mobilized, supported, and sustained in an efficient and effective manner by developing specified links among the social actors (Chavis, Florin, & Felix, 1992). Chavis (1993) has offered a good example of enabling. He has empowered many community groups and organizations to conduct their own program evaluations by teaching them to design, conduct, and analyze research. He has therefore made them independent of the need for reliance on professionals in the future for their research needs.

Networks (Chavis, Florin, & Felix, 1992; Fischer, Jackson, Stueve, Gerson, & McAllister-Jones, 1977; Sarason, Carroll, Maton, Cohen, & Lorentz, 1977) are confederations or alliances of related community organizations or individuals. Members of networks regularly share funding sources, information, and ideas with one another. Thus, their futures are more secure by networking their information and sometimes their clients. Another advantage is that clients are less likely to fall through the cracks in the service system. **Umbrella organizations** are usually overarching organizations that oversee the health of member organizations. Again, they act as clearinghouses for information that members can share. A concrete example might prove useful. United Way of America is perhaps one of

❖ CASE IN POINT 4.1

Grass-Roots Activism on a College Campus

It seems inconceivable in this day and age that a college campus would be without gynecological and reproductive services for its students. Just a few short years ago, a medium-sized public college in the Northeast had no such services for male or female students. The student government president, an avant-garde young man undaunted by controversy, approached the college president to ask for a clinic. "No" was the answer he received repeatedly.

He next approached psychologists on his campus who recommended contacting sister schools with a survey to determine whether they housed gynecological services. Out of 21 campuses contacted, only 2 did not have such services. The results of the survey did not impress the college administrators, who exclaimed that the other college presidents must be violating policy.

The student government president next contacted the local family planning center, which reported being overwhelmed with student appointments. They needed to make room for other community members. Yes, the center would support him if only by way of moral support.

Without administrative support or funding, the student president knew he would have to look elsewhere. He examined the student government budget, which the elected student leaders controlled. He would have to spend student money, which was in short supply. With the help of a psychologist, he surveyed the student body and found that students indeed were desperate for the service. The money would be well spent, so the student leaders made allowance in their budget for gynecological and reproductive services through creative financial planning. Even then, college administrators would not let him establish the clinic on campus.

A subcommittee formed by the student president contacted local doctors to see whether they would provide the services to students for reasonable fees. One physician agreed. The student government used its van to transport students to the extra evening appointments the doctor had set aside just for them.

It occurred to the psychologists, however, that merely providing preventive and diagnostic services seemed inadequate. The student leaders concurred that educational programs were also needed. The subcommittee and the doctor agreed that his nurse practitioner (for slightly higher fees) would give sex education lectures in the dormitories. After all, they were all aware that sex education does not foster an increase in promiscuous behavior but rather causes a shift to more tolerant attitudes (Kilmann, 1984).

After the off-campus clinic had been in existence for several years, the college administration was replaced and a new college president came on board. The attitude of the campus administration changed, too. An on-campus gynecological and reproductive service was now more acceptable. However, there was no funding in the then current budget. The student government agreed to continue funding the clinic, to find the doctors and nurses, and to provide peer training to student counselors. In exchange, the campus administration agreed to house the clinic, still held in the evening, in the regular college health center where important student health

Continued

records would be more accessible. In the end, both groups (students and administrators) won, but change was a long time in coming.

This case also illustrates that a variety of appeals for change can be successfully used—in this case, a survey of other campuses, opinion polls, and support from another community agency. It also documents that sometimes compromise between two conflicting community groups is the most "winning" solution.

the best-known umbrella organizations in the United States. United Way, through charitable contributions, is known for its financial support of community agencies that might otherwise flounder. United Way also provides community service agencies with office supplies, furniture, and other desperately needed tangible provisions. However, United Way also offers expert consultation on fund-raising, staff training, development of publications, and other issues crucial for community agency survival.

Community development corporations (Vidal, Howitt, & Foster, 1986) and **neighborhood associations** (Speigel, 1987) are citizens' groups of communities and neighborhoods that have come together to conquer a community social problem or to ensure that the community develops in a healthy, planned fashion.

Issues Related to Networks

Networks and umbrella associations offer ongoing support to participants, use reciprocity in the sharing of ideas and resources, use role modeling for each other, and provide accessible resources to participants (Sarason et al., 1977). For instance, these systems allow small community agencies to share information about grants, staff-training opportunities, and resource libraries; to exchange successful publicity ideas; to refer clients to each other's services; to build lobbying coalitions; and so forth. Thus, the health and success of each smaller service is assisted or enabled. Research has documented the effectiveness of these networking systems for acquired immune deficiency syndrome (AIDS) services (Madera, 1986) and unemployed and deinstitutionalized populations (Wolff, 1987), among others.

A somewhat similar notion is that of a **clearinghouse**. Clearinghouses are typically umbrella organizations that individuals seeking self-help groups can contact for assistance in finding self-help. Of course, the clearinghouse concept means that the self-help groups, themselves, are loosely networked. These clearinghouses are reported to result in high consumer satisfaction and good community receptivity (Maton, Levanthal, Madara, & Julien, 1989; Wollert, 1987).

Enabling systems and networks represent a form of social change because they build on existing resources and develop more productive and creative relationships between already existing services. In other words, such systems reweave the social fabric of what might otherwise be a more tattered and frayed community and its services and thus ensure survival and continued growth of the services.

Advantages and Disadvantages of Networks

Besides enhancing the viability of many services, networks are advantageous because they assure that important systems come to know each other better, find effective ways to work together, and learn to plan or advocate for change in a collaborative rather than competitive manner (Wolff, 1987). Likewise, enabling systems better ensure that resources are equitably distributed (Biegel, 1984), help reduce community conflict (Christensen & Robinson, 1989), and focus collective pressure on public policy makers and other decision makers (Delgado, 1986; Seekins & Fawcett, 1987). Networks also enable related services to detect cracks in the service system. **Cracks** are defined as structural gaps in the service systems and are exemplified by missing or inaccessible services and missing information (Tausig, 1987).

Few authors have addressed the disadvantages of umbrella organizations, even though several disadvantages exist. For one, private sector businesses might feel threatened by and perhaps launch a successful attack against the collective power of activist community organizations (Delgado, 1986). Similarly, when umbrella organizations grow large, they develop their own set of problems in terms of sheer bureaucracy, conflict, and expense.

Another disadvantage is that when the umbrella organization, rather than being a loosely knit resource and support network, becomes a controlling, parental organization, member agencies can become dissatisfied. We know, for instance, of one rural domestic violence program that broke from a strong countywide coalition of churches over staffing and funding issues despite the domestic violence program's already precarious existence. The bad feelings between the smaller domestic violence program and the larger parent organization resulted in the establishment of a second, redundant domestic violence program in the same geographic region.

Another possible disadvantage of community coalitions is that different community services may be in different stages of development. The new ones need staff training; the older ones may be seeking to expand their client bases. Coordinating the different developmental needs of member organizations can be difficult for the parent organization. Finally, if the tentacles of the association grow beyond one particular community's boundaries because member organizations have satellites in other geographic areas, existing associations in neighboring communities may feel threatened and subvert each other's purpose.

PROFESSIONAL CHANGE AGENTS: CONSULTANTS

Harold, Melba, and the other homeowners from this chapter's vignette might find that, despite their numbers, they collectively know little about confronting insurance or fire companies. Melba might therefore suggest finding a consultant who would collaborate with them in an effort to successfully guide the group through the process of obtaining fairer insurance coverage or in researching fire departments in other communities or neighboorhood watch systems.

Professional change agents or expert consultants seek to create social change through modification, renewal, and improvement. A **consultant** or **professional change agent** is someone who engages in collaborative problem solving with one or more persons (the **consultees**) who are often responsible for providing some form of assistance to another third individual (the **client**) (Mowbray, 1979). As you read in Chapter 2, consultants are often professionals well versed in scientific research. They are typically called on to conduct program evaluations and needs assessments for community organizations.

Community psychologists seem uniquely qualified to be community consultants because they possess skills in community needs assessment, community organizing, group problem solving, and action research. The community psychologist is also likely to focus on the social systems and institutions within a community rather than on individuals (Weed, 1990). Weed suggested that community psychologists offer a community a cohesive perspective, which is, of course, one of the values cherished by community development specialists.

Issues Related to Consultants

An important issue related to the expense of consultants is whether they really do help the client. One general study of the use of consultants was conducted by Medway and Updyke (1985), who reviewed the literature on outcome of consultations. In the better-designed studies, the researchers found that, compared to control groups, both consultees and clients in the intervention groups (where consultants were utilized) made gains in solving their problems or promoting change as measured by such things as attitude scales, observed behaviors, and standardized scores. In the control groups (in which no consultants were used), there were fewer of these improvements. This literature review therefore offers clear statistical evidence for the value of consultants.

Weed (1990) identified several steps for community psychologists acting as consultants to primary prevention programs that are adaptable for almost all change agents—expert or not. The steps include, first, defining the goals to be accomplished. The second step is to raise the awareness of the individuals in the setting under consultation and then to introduce the new program or research. At this point, other related organizations or communities can be networked for collaboration, support, and learning about new techniques and funding sources. Consultants also need to collaborate on effective methods for evaluating changes. Favorable evaluation justifies the money, time, and effort expended. Evaluation also leads to modification and fine-tuning should that be necessary. Unfortunately, evaluation is a step sometimes forgotten in many change situations. Without evaluation, how would people know if the change worked and whether it ought to be repeated? Profile 4.1 showcases the work of community activist Thomas Wolff, whose work includes coalition building.

◆ PROFILE 4.1
Thomas Wolff

Thomas Wolff attributes his community activism and desire for change, in part, to his parents' flight from Nazi Germany. Years later, during his undergraduate education at Clark University, he was trained to question assumptions, something that he says, "I find critical to my daily work." His graduate degree is from the University of Rochester.

Familiarization with the works of Saul Alinsky, George Albee, and Seymour Sarason and contact and work with Carolyn Swift and Julian Rappaport also shaped his thinking and regard for the values of community psychology, in particular for the virtues of empowerment and reform. Thom Wolff's national reputation for reform landed him the position of Chair of the Prevention Division of the National Council of Community Mental Health Centers, where his lobbying for prevention was unrelenting and his challenges to the National Institute of Mental Health were passionate. Wolff has worked with a variety of community populations, including college students, the elderly, the unemployed, and the deinstitutionalized. We will highlight here his work on deinstitutionalization, which garnered him the prestigious Outstanding Contribution to Prevention in Mental Health award.

Deinstitutionalization is the moving of previously institutionalized populations, such as the mentally ill or the mentally disabled or retarded, into the community from the institution. This strategy is often motivated as much by a lack of funding for the institutions as by humanistic or scientific reasons. Wolff recognized that community services for the deinstitutionalized population were fragmented; various helping services did not work together. Thus, some services duplicated each other's efforts, and some clients "fell through the cracks." Likewise, the prevailing clinical mindset of treating the individual failed to take into account a sense of community so vital to the individual's well-being.

Working with the Mayor's Task Force on Deinstitutionalization, Wolff helped a particular community resolve its conflicts about deinstitutionalization and develop techniques to handle the community's concerns. The task force brought together a diverse group, including mental health advocates, city officials, criminal justice professionals, and others interested in this issue.

Wolff received the Award for Outstanding Contribution to Prevention in Mental Health from the National Council of Mental Health Centers in 1984. In 1985, Division 27 of the American Psychological Association awarded Thomas Wolff its Distinguished Practice Award in Community Psychology. In introducing Thom for the award, Carolyn Swift reminded the audience that the years on "the community mental health roller coaster" had not lessened Thom's commitment to prevention. Thom continues his commitment and work today. His most recent work involves planned community coalitions. Coalitions among and between community, regional or national groups give them more power and strength and therefore a more secure future. You will read about coalitons in Chapter 12.

Source: Adapted from the *American Journal of Community Psychology, 15* (1987), pages 149–166.

Advantages and Disadvantages of Consultants

There are several advantages to expert consultation. The first is obvious; the professional is expert at what he or she does. The professional change agent has been specially trained and has the knowledge base upon which to make wise decisions. Another not so apparent advantage is that the consultant is a neutral person. Because the consultant is not embroiled in the presenting problems and should have no vested interest in the community or organization, the consultant can make unencumbered, unbiased judgments and recommendations.

Consultants also generally take a long-term approach to problem solving. Individuals in the community or organization often focus on short-term issues because they are living with them day to day. However, for the continued health of the community or organization, a long-term approach might be best. As stated earlier, too many community groups fail quickly and easily; quick fixes may be one of the reasons.

Finally, if a consultant is experienced, she or he comes with a vast array of ideas, past successes, and relevant ideas because of experiences with past but similar situations. Consultants should not betray nor create a conflict of interest with past clients, but previous experiences can help them find common ground that might be useful to other similar communities or organizations.

Despite these somewhat apparent advantages, professional change agents are not without disadvantages; one is high cost. Cost can be a major factor and can thwart the best-laid plans of any community or organization needing expert assistance. We hope that community psychologists acting as change agents would consider *pro bono* or voluntary consultations. The national psychological association, the American Psychological Association, is encouraging *pro bono* work by psychologists.

Developing cooperation from all involved in the consultation can also be problematic. Outside consultants sometimes inspire fear (of job loss or criticism), defensiveness, and resistance to change. Consultants might want to consider utilizing less direct or nondirective techniques to avoid these problems (Heller et al., 1984).

Consultants' contacts with their clients are often time limited. They need to quickly assess the issues, assist in the development of solutions and their implementation, and foster maintenance strategies in a short period of time. Often, the issues on which they are asked to consult are complex compared to the amount of available resources, including time. For example, many communities and their organizations grew haphazardly rather than in a planned fashion. Redesign can be difficult, if not impossible. Some problems defy solutions; they are essentially insoluble (Sarason, 1978). Many of these issues can be short-circuited if consultants carefully match their skills and expertise to client situations.

Finally, clients sometimes hold high and unrealistic expectations of what a consultant can do. Other clients may "use" the consultant for their own misleading purposes, especially when there are conflicting views about what ought to be done. In these situations, the ethical consultant will probably leave clients feeling disappointed. Again, careful intake by a consultant to ensure that his or her expertise fits the clients' issues can help.

THE USE OF EDUCATION AND INFORMATION DISSEMINATION TO PRODUCE SOCIAL CHANGE

Harold and Melba Marvin, in dismay at the fact that they could no longer afford a home as comfortable as their former one, could take their story to the newspapers. The papers, by disseminating the Marvin's story to researchers, insurance companies, other homeowners, and elected officials, would be assisting in agenda setting and education of the community regarding the plight of underinsured homeowners. This shared information could be the beginning of an insurance reform movement.

The dissemination of information and the education of community members has perhaps received less attention in the community psychology literature than any other aspect of change (Blakely et al., 1987), yet information dissemination remains a vital part of social change efforts. In fact, some community psychologists have challenged their colleagues to renew efforts to disseminate useful information and innovative programs as a method of addressing social problems (Linney, 1990).

Just what do we mean by **information dissemination** or **education** in community psychology? As you now know, community psychologists seek to prevent, intercede in, and treat, if necessary, community problems with what are typically innovative programs. If innovative or experimental programs are researched and found to be successful but the results are never shared with other communities or adopted by others, the results are of limited use (Fairweather, 1986). Dissemination of information can save change agents working with similar populations or in similar settings much time, money, and effort. Thus dissemination of innovation is crucial.

Little research exists on the educational function of community psychology (Fairweather & Davidson, 1986). However, there has been much debate in the literature about how programs can be efficaciously transferred to other settings. Adopters of innovations from community psychology need to be careful in their translation efforts. Adopters should be faithful to the original change model, especially to the mechanism that caused change, but adopters may also need to do some reinventing to a limited extent given that not all settings will be the same (Blakely et al., 1987; Bowman, Stein, & Ireys, 1991).

Whenever information from community psychology is shared with community members, its main purpose should be to improve the community, to promote prevention in favor of treatment, and to empower community members to shape their own destiny (Fairweather & Davidson, 1986). Information for educational purposes can also be used to shape ideology and to direct action in a community as well as to inform those in a position of power (the **gatekeepers**) to understand others in the community better (Levine & Perkins, 1987).

Issues Related to Information Dissemination

There are several important issues that need to be carefully considered by community psychologists hoping to educate community members about research results or innovative programs. First, it is important to remember that not all individuals will be receptive nor receptive at the same time to the information and ideas. Despite great enthusiasm, some individuals will be slow but will eventually adopt what you wish to share, while some will never adopt what you have to offer (Rogers, 1982). Why will adoption be slow and somewhat diffuse? Fairweather and Davidson (1986) suggested that at least two phenomena will interfere: personal characteristics of adopters and the social context in which adopters find themselves. For instance, some individuals are closed minded or **dogmatic** (Rokeach, 1960). They will not accept new ideas readily; in fact, they might not accept the ideas at all. Other individuals may find themselves in a social situation or social context where the suggested change is unacceptable, so they conform with the group's wishes and do not adopt an idea, no matter how good it is.

Second, measuring whether the information dissemination is useful will be problematic. A variety of measures could be utilized, including number of adoptions, replication of previous results in the imitative program, and so on. Selecting several measures will result in better understanding of whether the shared information was successfully adopted. For example, Seitz, Apfel, and Rosenbaum (1991) used several measures—such as dropping out of school, failing grades, enrolling in vocational or alternate school programs, and grade-point average—to measure efficacy of an intervention program for pregnant teens. They found that on several different measures, the adolescents experiencing the special intervention were more likely to succeed in school. Had the researchers used only one measure, their results might have indicated otherwise.

Disseminators of information, especially those sharing information on new programs, should also be mindful that only some pieces of the program might be useful to adopters and that disseminators are collaborators rather than dictators about how the shared information should be utilized. Fairweather and Davidson (1986) suggested that anyone trying to diffuse innovation in a community needs to learn to be a graceful loser at times!

A final issue related to the use of education as a social change mechanism is that it must be culturally sensitive. What works for one ethnic group might not work in another. Snowden (1993) also commented that ethnic minority groups are often high users of public-sector community services. Even though innovations taking place are well intentioned and promising, equal benfits for minorities and equal avoidance of harm cannot be taken for granted. Researchers, policy makers, and advocates must give special attention to the impact of their interventions on the well-being of ethnic minority citizens.

An example might prove useful. Marin, Marin, Perez-Stable, Sabogal, and Otero-Sabogal (1990) tested a seven-month, media-based community intervention designed to increase levels of information on the damaging effects of cigarette smoking and on the availability of culturally appropriate cessation services. Knowing from their previous work (Marin et al., 1990) what messages best discriminated between Hispanics who quit versus those who continued to smoke assisted them in designing their campaign. The campaign was successful, especially given that change in knowledge occurred most in the less acculturated Hispanics. **Acculturation** generally means that the people in a minority group adopt as their own the norms, values, and behavior patterns of the dominant society but still are not admitted to more intimate social groups in that society (Hess, Markson, & Stein, 1991). In other words, in the Marin and colleagues (1990) study, those Hispanics least familiar with Anglo smoking cessation campaigns were most changed by the information dissemination *designed especially for them.*

Advantages and Disadvantages of Educational Change

Advantages of this method of social change are several. First, a wide audience can often be reached with these change efforts because a multiplex approach to disseminate ideas, especially by mass media such as television and newspapers, can be used. Second, education as a whole is generally revered in the United States, so the average community citizen as well as those in power are likely to accept this approach to change rather than more radical approaches. Finally, this may be one of the least expensive forms of social change for community activists to pursue if they use certain vehicles such as public media for dissemination. A picture may indeed be worth a thousand words. Similarly, a research report written in lay terminology can easily be distributed to many individuals at once.

There are disadvantages, however. Closed minds are not easily opened, no matter how much information is presented. Also, the vehicle for dissemination may have to be custom designed for the audience. For instance, consciousness-raising groups worked well to disseminate information about feminism in the women's movement (Levine & Perkins, 1987). However, for physicians' groups, professional journals may be the best vehicle.

One final disadvantage is that even the best-laid educational plans can go afoul. In one interesting study, Prince-Embury (1992) provided community members living near Three Mile Island (the site of a nuclear accident) with educational and health information that contained relevant and credible material on issues of concern to the community. Although psychological symptoms such as stress declined slightly after the educational information was distributed, many people reported less perceived control. In other words, knowing more about the disaster and the health implications decreased the sense of control of the community's members. Perceived control, as you will read elsewhere in the book, is considered to be a keystone in mental and physical health. Education and information dissemination, then, do not always have their desired effects.

PUBLIC POLICY AS A MEANS OF SOCIAL CHANGE

Suppose the newspapers followed the plight of the underinsured families discussed in this chapter's vignette, and the coverage attracted the attention of their state legislator. After interviewing the Marvins and similar families, this legislator could introduce a bill governing regulation of replacement cost insurance. Had this happened, the Marvin's situation would have affected public policy—the topic of this unit. Let's look briefly at the interrelated roles of public policy and community psychology.

Did you vote in the last election? It is often surprising at how many citizens, college students in particular, do not vote. Voting, drafting legislation, lobbying for particular interests, and so on comprise actions that change, and often change dramatically, our national and local social agendas. For citizens and community psychologists alike, participating in public policy endeavors opens a "window of opportunity" (Nikelly, 1990) for what can often be sweeping social changes.

Just what is **public policy**? The aim of public policy is to improve the quality of life for community members. Although the term is often used for government-mandated legislation, it can refer to policy at a specific agency or at the local community and state governmental levels. Public policy can also influence to what issues various resources are allocated (Levine & Perkins, 1987).

A concept relevant to public policy is **policy science**, which is the science of making findings from science (and in the case of community psychology, findings from social science) relevant to governmental and organizational policy (Oskamp, 1984). A well-known example of this is the use of actual scientific studies on desegregation of schools to shape policies on integration (Oskamp, 1984; Perkins, 1988).

Issues Related to the Use of Public Policy to Create Change

Politics and community psychology are deeply intertwined (Vogelman, 1990). There is general agreement among community psychologists that their science and politics are inseparable. However, community psychologists do not agree on how much science should impinge on policy and how much public policy should pervade science. Some argue that good policies are those based solely on scientific evidence. In other words, one should not attempt to influence any public policy until one has solid scientific evidence. Others argue that pressing social problems such as AIDS and homelessness do not afford one the luxury of time for conducting research. Society is not likely to have solutions to this complex situation for some time to come.

Most community psychologists do agree that the development of public policy should be a collaborative effort between researchers, affected populations, and the decision or policy makers. The idea of collaboration leads psychologists to avoid "colonial" relationships with the affected community members (Chavis et al., 1983). In fact, collaboration with appropriate community members, particularly those affected by policy research and/or policy decisions, is not only strategically sound, it is good ethics (Robinson, 1990).

Americans like to think that the public policy that guides social change is predicated on science, humanism, and logical thinking, but often what happens in Washington and elsewhere occurs whether or not rational thought enters the process (Johnson, 1991). The political climate, lobbying groups with cross-purposes, and other vicissitudes can often influence the end product in public policy as much or more than science and other logical factors. Phenomena such as a more sophisticated electorate than yesteryear's (Oskamp, 1984) and shifting public concern (e.g., from national defense issues to social problems) (Johnson, 1991) can sway the direction of public policy. Likewise, funding created for various policy changes will remain a heated issue in the foreseeable future, and behavioral and social scientists unfortunately are often the underdogs for social change funding (American Psychological Society, 1991). The media also sets an important emotional tone that shapes public policy in this country (Schmolling, Youkeles, & Burger, 1989) and influences what people think about. This is called **agenda setting** (Oskamp, 1984).

Policy science serves several functions: instrumental, conceptual, and persuasive (Shadish, 1990). We personally feel that research can and should also serve a predictive purpose. When research shapes the direction of change or of public policy, then it serves an **instrumental purpose**. Research can also be aimed at changing the way people think or conceptualize social problems and solutions. Research with this function serves a **conceptual purpose**. Third, research can persuade policy makers to support a particular position or solution to a social problem; it then functions in the **persuasive** mode. Finally, when research is designed to forecast what change will occur in the future or to predict whether change will be accepted, the function is **predictive**.

Is there any evidence that social science research influences legislators as they develop public policy? Yes, one can see the impact of researchers, in part, by what type of research is funded by the federal government. Except for economists, psychologists perhaps receive the largest amount of funding of all social scientists (Oskamp, 1984). Furthermore, public officials have reported utilizing social science in the drafting of policies with psychological research cited as the most influential of all these sciences (Caplan, Morrison, & Stambaugh, 1975). More recently, Trudy Vincent (1990), while on the staff of the United States Senate, reported that the activities in which members of Congress engage are very similar to those of ecologically minded community psychologists. That is, legislators also need to pay careful attention to the people, settings, events, and history of their districts before establishing policy. Directly and indirectly, then, psychology can influence public policy.

No matter what the role of research in policy development or in the community, it should always be "returned" to the community for application (Chavis, Stuckey, & Wandersman, 1983) and not kept solely in the scientific journals for consumption by scientists. Remember, though, that when research is given away to the community, it can also be used for political ammunition, manipulation, and self-serving purposes (Oskamp, 1984).

Research in the service of public policy is not the only way to address social change. Community psychologists and community members can also **lobby** to change policy. To lobby means to direct pressure at public officials to promote the passage of a particular piece of legislation or policy. Individuals wishing to influence policy can also disseminate appropriate pieces of information, such as public opinion polls and results of field research, to policy makers in an attempt to educate them (Perkins, 1988). Education and information dissemination as a means of social change have already been discussed.

The average citizen hoping to influence legislation may find the process bewildering, whether it is at the local, state, or federal level. Fortunately, there are materials available to the average citizen that will take the mystery out of the legislative process (Alderson & Sentman, 1979; Ebert-Flattau, 1980; Zigler & Goodman, 1982). The American Psychological Association (APA) has created a Public Interest Directorate, the mission of which is to advance the scientific and professional aspects of psychology as applied to human welfare. The directorate disseminates reports and other written materials to state and federal governments and legislators. Similarly, APA also developed a guide to advocacy in the public interest that includes sections on the legislative process and on effective means of communications with congressional staff.

A community psychologist or community member could also seek an elected office, work on the campaign of a particular candidate, or vote for a particular candidate supporting a favored social change program. While holding an important elected office may seem alien to some, it is often the ideal role for a scientist. Why? The community scientist's training places him or her in the position to be able to demand evidence for proposed programs. Scientists also best know the importance of evaluating change mechanisms such as new or experimental programs (Fairweather & Davidson, 1986).

Another role for politically active scientists is to act as expert witnesses and *amicus curiae* (friend of the court). A recent case of the *amicus curiae* role for psychologists in the courts was the use of sex stereotyping research by Susan Fiske in the *Price Waterhouse* v. *Hopkins* case heard and cited in the local, appellate, and Supreme Courts. The American Psychological Association also filed an *amicus curiae* brief in the case. The testimony about the psychology of stereotyping played a crucial role at each court level as well as in the eventual vindication of the wronged female employee (Fiske, Bersoff, Borgida, Deaux, & Heilman, 1991). Community psychologists in these endeavors play a role in shaping case law and setting precedents on which other cases may be based (Jacobs, 1980; Perkins, 1988).

Advantages and Disadvantages of Public Policy Changes

The advantages of using public policy efforts—including research, lobbying for or sponsoring a particular policy, and elections—are that sweeping social changes can often be induced, especially if the efforts of broad alliances are all aimed in the same direction. Another advantage is that the average American citizen is known to have considerable respect for the law (Kohlburg, 1984; Lempert & Sanders, 1986), and some people may accept the change because it is the law.

Often, the real issues underlying social problems are economic and political rather than psychological, so the policy solution might be the most appropriate anyway (Nikelly, 1990). Finally, policy makers often, but not always, have a broad perspective on the community that elected or appointed them so are likely to understand the interrelationships between seemingly segregated groups and isolated social problems. Therefore, solutions in the form of policy can take a broadbrush and long-term approach rather than a narrow or short-term focus, which is more likely to fail.

No method of social change is without problems, however, and policy science and public policy are not without theirs. For instance, much social science research is completed by academics operating in a "publish or perish" mode (Phares, 1991) to impress colleagues; the research is often not returned to the community for social change. Similarly, community researchers are often perceived as agents of a traditional system that has historically been oppressive and are consequently not perceived as guests or collaborators in the community (Robinson, 1990). Therefore, research participation, results, and dissemination efforts are shunned, rendering the research useless.

Another serious problem with using public policy avenues to create social change is the electorate. Bond issues, school budgets, referenda, and other elections are participated in by a select few. Most voters are disproportionately well educated and older than the average American. Hence, the voices of the poor, the young, and the minorities are not heard via voting. This means that those who may most benefit from prosocial change are not participating in the direction of these changes (Hess et al., 1991).

Perhaps the greatest disadvantage to using public policy efforts to create social change is that policy shaping can be a slow, cumbersome, politicized process. For instance, we estimate that the average time span from initial writing to passage of a bill in Congress is about a year. However, less controversial policies pass more quickly. More complex or controversial issues take much longer. In the meantime, the needs of the affected groups may have changed; indeed, the group, itself, may have evaporated, or their needs may have become more severe so that the original policy solution is insufficient.

SUMMARY

Many methods for creating and sustaining social change exist. Each has its own advantages and disadvantages. Activists hoping to fashion social change need to consider what strategies will work best for the issues they hope to address. Some combination of strategies will probably work better than a single strategy, and what worked once might not work again or in a different community or for a different issue.

Planned change, such as grass-roots activism and information dissemination, intentionally addresses and prepares the community for changes. The primary purpose of planned change should always be to improve the community. Each method of planned change has its disadvantages and advantages. Methods available for induced change include citizen participation, networking with other community resources, the use of professional consultants, education or knowledge dissemination, and participation in public policy efforts by citizens and scientists.

In citizen participation, citizens produce the changes they desire by mechanisms such as grass-roots activism, which is a type of bottom-up rather than top-down change. Such change results in empowerment, in which individuals feel they have power or control over their own lives.

When community agencies come together to aid one another, they are networking. Networking has been shown to directly assist in the longevity of community organizations. Sometimes umbrella organizations, such as United Way, also provide services to community agencies or enhance their functioning, thus again ensuring their success.

Professional change agents or consultants can also help communities evolve. Community consultants need to be careful not to overtake the community but rather empower the community to create its own changes.

Education and information dissemination are yet other means of producing social change. Although these methods of change sometimes produce vast changes, care must be taken to utilize the most appropriate information with sensitivity to the cultural diversity of the community.

Passing new legislation and policies or revamping existing laws and policies are other means of creating social change and are known collectively as public policy. Public policy changes can create sweeping social change but often such policy is fraught with the politics of competing groups and can take much time to fashion and implement.

5

STRESS, COPING, AND SOCIAL SUPPORT: TOWARD COMMUNITY MENTAL HEALTH

The renown which riches or beauty confer is fleeting and frail;
mental excellence is a splendid lasting possession.
    ◆ *GAIUS SALLUSTIUS CRISPUS, 86–34 B.C.*

Arthur, or Art to his friends, is filled with anxiety. He is a first-semester freshman and his midsemester grades are poor; in fact, Art is afraid that he will flunk
out between semesters. He feels that the main reason for his poor grades is that
his roommates have interfered with his studying. Most freshmen are in double
rooms; Art had the misfortune of ending up in a triple room. He hopes to have a
different rooming situation next semester, but for now he has to cope with the
living habits of not one but two other people—difficult people in Art's opinion.
One roommate is moody and unpredictable. The other is out until all hours of
the night and comes home and wakes up the whole floor of residents.

Adjusting to the rigors of academic life at college has been hard for Art, too.
He breezed through high school, where little studying and homework were
required. At college, Art sometimes has to read 30 pages a night per subject, and
the crush of examinations and papers all due at the same time are overwhelming
him.

To make matters worse, Art spent this past weekend at home. He was so
happy to get off campus and get away for a few days. However, when Art arrived home, his parents sat him in the living room and broke the distressing
news to him that they were divorcing after 25 years of marriage.

The depressed and dejected Art sat in his residence hall on the Sunday night
after his visit home and wondered how he would manage all the stress. Maybe
he should just drop out of school? Would working for a year ease the tension
between his mother and father by contributing needed income? Perhaps his
being home would make his parents understand how important a family is.

INTRODUCTION

In everyday life there are many factors to which people must adjust. Personal
relationships, changes in work schedules and living habits, and major happen-
ings such as a war, a poor economy, or a natural disaster are some of the events
that require good coping skills from almost everyone, no matter how healthy or
disabled. This chapter will examine what mental health is and what individuals
and communities can do to optimize (primary and secondary prevention) an
individual's mental health. First, three classic theories (and therapies) for promoting mental health and treating mental disorders will be discussed. You can

contrast them with more contemporary interventions from the field of community psychology, which are delineated in the last half of the chapter. The three major forces or theories in psychology are psychoanalysis, behaviorism, and humanism.

HISTORICAL NOTES ON MENTAL HEALTH AND MENTAL DISORDER

The Medical Model: Psychoanalysis

For those of you who are psychology majors or have taken a course in abnormal, child, or personality psychology (or are fans of Woody Allen movies), Sigmund Freud (1856–1939) will be no stranger. Freud is the father of psychoanalysis. Although many people today disagree with his theories, it cannot be denied that Freud's influence is felt in psychology as well as in psychiatry. Although Freud believed that biology played an important role in the development of psyches, he argued that most psychological disorders are treatable or curable with the use of free association or verbal therapy. Psychoanalytic treatment takes the form of individual verbal therapy up to five times a week over several years.

Somewhat later, the psychoanalytic approach began to split into two paths: traditional psychoanalytic individual verbal therapy versus biological psychiatry, or the **medical model**. A German contemporary of Freud's, Adolf Meyer (1866–1950), argued for the importance of the interplay between biology, psychology, and environment, but many others preferred only biology as an explanation for mental disorders, after a strict medical model. The traditional psychoanalytic individual verbal therapy model has consistently shown to be ineffective with the severely mentally ill (Wilson, O'Leary, & Nathan, 1992). Therefore, given the strength of the biological, or medical, model, the two authoritative references about mental illness (the *Diagnostic Statistical Manual [DSM]* and the *International Code of Diagnosis [ICD]*) were developed. The medical model left at least two important legacies in traditional psychology. One is the reliance on diagnostic labels, as found in the *DSM*. The other legacy is the assumption of authority and power by the professional over the patient. Both of these legacies, though, are eschewed by community psychologists.

The Behavioral Model: The Social-Learning Approach

As you may recall from your introductory psychology course, by using dogs as subjects, the Russian physiologist Ivan Pavlov (1849–1936) was able to demonstrate that behavior could be formed as a result of **classical conditioning.** This is the process by which a response comes to be elicited by a stimulus, an object, or a situation other than that which is the natural or normal stimulus. That is, Pavlov repeatedly exposed his dogs to a **conditioned stimulus** in the form of a bell whenever the **unconditioned stimulus** in the form of meat powder was present. Although the **unconditioned response** or natural response for meat powder was salivation, eventually these dogs learned to display a **conditioned response** or learned response in the form of salivation *in the absence of* meat powder. A more human example is necessary here. Returning to the vignette in this chapter, you might predict that if Art isolated himself in his room each time he felt depressed (the unconditioned stimulus or unlearned stimulus), he would soon perceive his room (conditioned stimulus or learned stimulus) as depressing. In fact, you might predict that the room itself would eventually trigger depression in Art (the conditioned response or learned response)

Dissatisfied with the psychoanalytic approach and rejecting the method of **introspection** or self-examination (a method advocated by Wilhelm Wundt, the father of experimental psychology), two American psychologists, John B. Watson (1878–1985) and B. F. Skinner (1904–1990), further developed Pavlov's theory by using humans as subjects. Instead of pairing a conditioned stimulus with an unconditioned stimulus, Skinner developed and preferred the use of **operant conditioning,** in which behavior is more likely to be engaged in when it is **reinforced** or rewarded. Often, the reinforcers and the conditioned and unconditioned stimuli are provided by something external to the organism. Thus, in part, behavioral tradition provides one with a sense that ecology is important. For example, Art would more likely be nice to his roommates if they returned in-kind behavior.

Extending the principles of learning theory, or the **behavioral model,** Martin Seligmen (1975) argued that depression can be explained as a form of **learned helplessness,** or a lack of perceived control due to uncontrollable events in the environment. In the case of Art, the social-learning approach would argue that the reason he felt depressed was due to the fact that he had experienced many life events over which he had little control. For example, he had little control over his parents' divorce. In other words, lack of control reinforced Art's feelings of depression or helplessness. Other advocates of the social-learning approach, such as British psychiatrist Han Eysenck, Sr., and American psychologist Joseph Wolpe, have developed techniques such as **desensitization** or step-by-step relaxation training to change phobic or fearful behavior.

Generally speaking, the social-learning model is an effective treatment with many forms of mental distress. However, it is labor intensive, because each behavioral treatment must be tailored to match the individual's needs. Moreover, to many critics, the social-learning approach appears to deal with the symptoms rather than the cause of mental distress. Finally, most community psychologists would note that this model treats one individual at a time—not a very efficient way to manage change.

The Humanistic Model

The 1960s witnessed the growth and emphasis of the movement of human rights, such as the introduction of the Civil Rights Act in 1969. This had a profound impact on how mental health and mental disorders were perceived or defined. That is, to some mental health care experts and professionals, such as American psychologists Abraham Maslow (1908–1970) and Thomas Szasz as well as British psychiatrist R. D. Laing, maladjustment had more to do with **labeling,** or an individual being told he or she is not healthy or is "sick," than with innate determinants. In other words, people sometimes behave in accord with what they are told. Thus, treatments should be designed to assist these people to understand and reflect on their unique feelings. In conjunction with this notion, American psychologist Carl Rogers (1902–1987) developed **client-centered therapy,** in which the role of the therapist is to facilitate the client's reflection on his or her experiences. Note the word **client** in the previous sentence. To humanistic psychologists, clients are not "sick" and thus are not labeled **patients.** If Art were to visit a counselor and the counselor diagnosed him as depressed, Art might indeed come to think of himself as a very depressed individual according to this labeling hypothesis.

Similar to the psychoanalytic model, the **humanistic model** emphasizes the use of verbal therapy. Unlike the psychoanalytic model, both individual and group verbal therapy are common to the humanistic model. However, the humanistic model suffers from some of the same criticisms as does the psychoanalysis theory. Faith, Wong, and Carpenter (1994) found that the effectiveness of a sensitivity training group (a form of humanistic group therapy) is not so much due to the fact that people gain a sense of self-worth but due to improved mental health as a function of social skills learned during therapy. Table 5.1 briefly summarizes the characteristics of the three major theories just discussed.

There are, however, at least two more major ideas derived from humanistic psychology that have been transplanted to the field of community psychology. One is that all people are worthy individuals and have the right to fulfill and discover this worth. The second is that the individual best knows himself or herself and thus needs to provide input on solutions to problematic issues. To that end, we turn next to how people handle a pervasive problem of today: stress.

TABLE 5.1   Characteristics of the Medical, Behavioral, and Humanistic Models for Studying Mental Illness/Health

	Medical	Behavioral	Humanistic
Philosophy	Unconscious sexual energy shapes human behaviors	Human behaviors can be molded or conditioned	Humans are innately striving for actualization or positive self-regard
Method of Investigation	Case study	Experimental	Case study and correlational experimental
Treatment	Psychoanalysis (may include medication)	Various behavioral techniques (e.g., biofeedback)	Individual and group psychotherapy

STRESS

A Definition

Stress is a complex concept but it can be briefly defined as "a call for action when one's capabilities are perceived as falling short of the needed personal resources" (Sarason, 1980, p. 74). Stress responses vary from physiological reactions, such as ulcers or high blood pressure, to psychological reactions, such as avoidance of a stressful event in the future, to the serious psychological condition called *learned helplessness* (described earlier).

Physical Responses to Stress

The typical reactions to stress have been described in the classic work of Hans Selye (1956, 1974) on the **general adaptation syndrome (GAS).** This syndrome includes a set of physical responses to stress in three different stages. The first stage is **alarm,** in which the sympathetic nervous system is activated so heart rate, respiration, and other physiological responses increase. The second stage of the GAS is **resistance,** where the body tries to resist the stress if it persists. Although the individual might appear fine, the bodily defenses are actually eroding, according to Selye. Finally, if the stress continues long term, the final stage of **exhaustion** will be reached. Exhaustion can lead to death.

Does stress lead to actual physical illness or ruin the immune system? The popular press likes to relate stories that this is indeed true. However, a review of the scientific literature shows two things. First, many of the studies are poorly designed. For instance, many are retrospective studies—that is, people are asked to remember backward in time, a technique that is susceptible to memory problems and other errors. Second, the literature as a whole shows a weak but positive correlation between stress and illness. The correlations usually range from .20 to .30, with the highest correlation possible being 1.0 (Lippa, 1990).

A sample study about stress, health, and college examinations ties in with the opening vignette about Art. Jemmet and Magloire (1988) followed students' physical well-being over the course of a semester. The researchers found more immunoglobin in the saliva of healthy college students during nonexamination periods than during periods of examination, such as finals week. Immunoglobin protects people from illness. Thus, students are more prone to colds and other ailments during examination periods (Dorian, Keystone, Garfinkel, & Brown, 1982) and thus may need additional support from the college (academic and medical) during exams.

Psychological Responses to Stress

Psychological reactions to stress are quite varied. Individuals can respond to stress by personal growth, by a decrease in psychological well-being (even psychopathology), or without any noticeable psychological change (Dohrenwend,

1978). What determines, in part, how an individual responds are **moderating factors** such as one's personal characteristics and one's social resources. A moderating factor is considered to be operative when, if in its presence, the relationship of stress to illness (mental or physical) is weaker than in its absence (Bloom, 1988). For example, if a person is hardy, then the effects of stress are less deleterious than for an individual who is less hardy but who experiences the same amount of stress. Moreover, hardy individuals perceive minor events such as everyday hassles as less stressful than individuals who are not hardy (Banks & Gannon, 1988). **Hardiness** is typified by a sense of personal control, a sense of commitment to work and self, and a tendency to perceive change as a challenge rather than as a threat (Kobasa, 1979).

Other personal characteristics may also moderate the effects of stress. Chan (1977) and Baum, Singer, and Baum (1981) postulated that locus of control (internal or external, as discussed elsewhere in this book), a sense of helplessness (described earlier in this chapter), chronic anxiety, and low self-esteem are central personality determinants of stress reactions. Other research (Nelson & Cohen, 1983), however, has sometimes failed to support that certain of these constructs actually do moderate the effects of stress.

Social resources can also moderate the effects of stress and include, when under stress, one's sense of social support in the community. In fact, the concept of social support has received enormous attention in the literature of community psychology.

FACTORS THAT INFLUENCE ADJUSTMENT AND COPING

Life Events as Sources of Stress

Holmes and Rahe (1967) asked individuals to assign 0 to 100 points to life events according to the degree of readjustment these people required, with 100 points indicating much readjustment. Topping off the eventual list of stressful events was the death of a spouse (100 points), followed by divorce (73 points) and marital separation (65 points). Other events high on the list of stressors were a jail term (63 points), personal injury or illness (53 points), and being fired from a job (47 points). Interestingly, some positive life events were also construed as stressful or requiring adjustment. For example, marriage (50 points), pregnancy (40 points), retirement (45 points), and holidays such as Christmas (12 points) were considered to be stressful as well. In other words, both positive and negative life changes probably produce stress because they require people to make adjustments. In fact, recent research (Kofkin & Repucci, 1991) has found that a single event can also be construed as both positive and negative at the same time. Those changes that are uncontrollable or unpredictable seem to be most stressful (Baron & Byrne, 1994; Vinokur & Caplan, 1986).

Horowitz, Schaefer, Hiroto, Wilner, and Levin (1977) have developed the **Life Events Questionnaire** in line with Holmes and Rahe's work. The questionnaire, however, takes into account the kind of life event *and* the time since the event occurred. Other research (Kale & Stenmark, 1983) has indicated that this particular questionnaire is a significantly good predictor of psychological adjustment compared to other available scales.

The research on stressful life events did not end there, however. Holmes and Masuda (1974) found that the more stress points (points accumulated by summing together the "score" for each stressor) an individual accumulated over the course of a year, the more likely that individual was to experience a major physical illness. In fact, individuals with over 300 points showed a high incidence of illness over the next nine months. We might predict that with Art's problematic adjustment to college life, the rigors of his studies, his roommate problems, and his parents' divorce, he might soon become seriously ill.

Hassles of Daily Life as Stressors

Major life events such as those already mentioned are relatively rare. What is more common are everyday hassles such as being caught in traffic or in long lines, losing money, forgetting phone numbers, having too much to do, and fearing confrontations with friends. Art, the freshman in the opening vignette, seems to be experiencing some of these hassles, too. Lazarus and Folkman (1984) developed a **Hassles Scale** for individuals; the researchers found that the more hassled an individual feels, the greater the reported stress. Scores on this scale are also related to an individual's psychological symptoms. That is, the more the minor irritants in a person's life, the poorer the individual's psychological well-being. Other research using the Hassles Scale and other measures of daily irritants has demonstrated that the presence numerous or accumulated daily annoyances rather than exposure to a single life trauma may result in poorer health (Lazarus, 1984). For example, studies in industry show that daily hassles on the job or mismatches between one's personal characteristics and one's job demands are especially good predictors of major illnesses (Chemers Hays, Rhodewalt, & Wysocki, 1985).

Chronic versus Acute Stress

Life events and daily hassles create **acute stress,** but what about long-term or chronic stress? McGonagle and Kessler (1990) suggested that emphasis would be better placed on chronic or continuous stress from continual financial or marital problems, prolonged illnesses, and other stressors that have no endpoint. Their research with nearly 2,000 men and women indeed demonstrates that chronic stresses are more strongly related to depressive symptoms than acute stress. Interestingly, by not aggregating the effects of chronic and acute stress in their sample, the researchers also discovered that depression created by acute stress is less pronounced among people who have preexisting chronic difficulties than those without such difficulties. One might logically expect something different— for example, that chronic stress is exacerbated by acute episodes of stress. It is not clear why this curious finding exists. McGonagle and Kessler suggested that chronic adversity facilitates the development of coping resources associated with resiliency to subsequent stress. A second possibility is that enmeshment in an ongoing stressful situation marshals more rapid mobilization of coping resources for subsequent stress. Perhaps acute stress might lead to resolution of chronic stress, as when a poor marriage (chronic stress) ends in divorce (acute stress).

The Environment

The Physical Environment

Sometimes environmental phenomena are distressing or demand adjustment. For example, noise, pollution, and other environmental stressors can cause adjustment problems. Prisons and schools are prime examples of how the effects of a physical environment can create stress. Art's rooming situation certainly was creating stress in his life. Likewise, inmates in overcrowded prisons have been shown to have higher blood pressure than inmates in less crowded prisons (Paulus, McCain, & Cox, 1978) as well as more complaints of illness (Wener & Keys, 1988).

Similarly, noise can be distressing. Cohen and colleagues (Cohen, Evans, Stokols, & Krantz, 1986) examined the health and performance of schoolchildren who lived in the flight paths of the Los Angeles airport. The researchers found that these children had higher blood pressure, lower mathematics scores, and were less persistent at problem solving than children from similar backgrounds who did not live near a major airport. Other research (Bronzaft, 1981) has confirmed that students on the noisy side of school buildings perform less well than children on the quiet side of the same school building, but performance improves when the children are moved to the quiet side of the building.

On the other hand, there are factors that one might intuitively predict would play a role in emotional well-being, but research indicates otherwise. For example, Adams (1992) examined urban versus suburban neighborhoods and their impact on psychological health. Classic urban theory would suggest that living in highly urbanized areas of a city results in social isolation, disorganization, and psychological problems. However, Adams's research found that people living in the suburbs were no more likely to express satisfaction with their neighborhood or with the quality of their lives than those living in cities.

The Psychosocial Environment

No other factor related to sources of distress has received more attention in the field of community psychology than the psychosocial environment. Specifically, community psychologists are concerned about the fit of the person to the psychosocial environment. If the fit is not good, then the consequence may be distress. Likewise, community psychologists acknowledge that the person and environment interact such that both the person and environment make demands on each other (Tracey, Sherry, & Keitel, 1986).

One psychological element of one's social settings is social integration. **Social integration** is defined as people's involvement with community institutions as well as their participation in the community's informal social life (Gottlieb, 1987). Holahan and colleagues (1983) examined the relationship of social integration and mental health in a biracial community. They were attempting to move the literature away from relying on intrapsychic dynamics, as seen in psychoanalytic and other traditional theories of mental disorder. The research resulted in complex but interesting findings. African Americans reported significantly more psychological symptoms than Whites. Perhaps prejudice against African Americans in mainstream society created this difference. However, some African Americans were less socially integrated into their communities than were Whites, thus providing another explanation for the first finding. In fact, African Americans low in social integration showed more symptoms than either Whites or other African Americans with high levels of social integration. In other words, social integration seems to contribute to one's sense of well-being. Quite possibly, the converse is true, too; one's lack of well-being keeps a person from being better integrated socially.

Culture or subculture is also another factor relevant to adjustment. Poverty surely is a factor that results in distress. However, cultural values that differ from mainstream or traditional U.S. values can also create distress. For example, Aldwin and Greenberger (1987) found that Korean youths overall were more depressed than Caucasians. However, different models accounted for or predicted depression in the two groups. For Koreans, perceived parental traditionalism was a strong predictor of depression, whereas for Caucasians, academic stress was a significant predictor of depression. These findings argue for greater attention to the importance of cultural values in studying adaptation to stress.

COPING STRATEGIES

Rather than utilize highly individualized methods such as client-centered therapy, psychoanalysis, or behavioral techniques (see Case in Point 5.1), community psychologists take several different approaches to promoting mental health (i.e., primary prevention) and managing stress (i.e., secondary prevention). This section will look at only a few of these approaches, including social support, information and education, and sports and recreation.

Social Support

Anyone who has experienced divorce of their parents, as Art is experiencing, knows the stress and sadness that divorce creates. Had a friend referred Art to a support group of others who had experienced parental divorce, Art might have benefitted. The friend would be providing social support by caring enough to make a referral for help with coping. The support group recommended by the friend would provide added support by providing Art with peers who have common emotional ground and therefore useful coping techniques to deal with their distress. Art might have learned some of these techniques from them.

❖ CASE IN POINT 5.1

Mental Health Care Professionals

Various professional services are available to help people cope with stress. Many of the mental health care services are delivered by individuals from four major professional disciplines. **Psychiatrists** are medical doctors (M.D.s). who specialize in psychiatry. They can be employed in either the public (governmental) or private sector (such as private practice). In addition to their training, psychiatrists must pass a licensing examination before they can practice the discipline. Within the field, there are subspecialties such as biological psychiatry and community psychiatry. Nonetheless, the role of psychiatry is usually medication maintenance, although mental health patients who are financially capable can often receive some form of therapy such as psychoanalytic therapy up to five times a week.

Many individuals who hold advanced degrees in any subfields of psychology consider themselves psychologists. **Clinical psychologists** are mental health care professionals who have advanced training (usually a doctoral degree) in clinical psychology and hold licenses from the states in which they practice. Similar to psychiatrists, clinical psychologists can be employed in either the public or private sector. Unlike psychiatrists, clinical psychologists cannot prescribe medication.

The long-standing professional conflict between the fields of psychiatry and clinical psychology has created many interesting twists as to who is qualified to be called a "psychologist." One outcome is that in many instances, the government (state and federal) recognizes as psychologists only those individuals with advanced training in clinical psychology or related areas such as counseling or industrial psychology and who have passed some licensing examination.

Furthermore, these scenarios are complicated by several other factors. Sometimes, the term **therapist** is used interchangeably with the terms *clinician* and *psychologist*, although not all "clinicians" and "therapists" (such as those in social work and psychiatric nursing) have training in clinical psychology. Also, many "doctoral-level psychologists" receive their training in nonclinical areas such as community psychology.

There are also disagreements within the subfield of clinical psychology. Traditionally, clinical psychologists were trained using the **scientist-practitioner model** or trained to be both scientists and practitioners. These psychologists hold a Doctor of Philosophy (Ph.D.), the highest degree in any scientific discipline. Now, there is a growing trend in the subfield of clinical psychology to train people as clinicians or "practitioners." A degree known as Doctor in Psychology (Psy.D.) has been created.

A third group of mental health care professionals who deliver services and treatments are **social workers,** who generally hold a degree called a Master of Social Work (M.S.W.). Unlike psychiatrists, they cannot prescribe medication. Similar to psychiatrists and clinical psychologists, social workers can be employed in either the public or private sector. The primary role of a social worker is as a "practitioner." Similar to clinical psychologists, social workers also sometime pose a professional threat to psychiatrists. Again, some of this controversy has to do with licensing.

What psychiatrists, clinical psychologists, and social workers have in common, though, is that they treat *individuals* who are experiencing stress. That is, they do little

Continued

to promote the mental health of large groups of people or the whole community. Another common feature is that all of these caregivers are usually construed as authority figures in the lives of the individuals they treat. Rarely do the individuals feel empowered to do something about their own situation.

A final and important issue related to these mental health care providers is the one of health insurance or third-party payments. Health insurance companies act as third parties who pay the mental health care provider, whether that professional is a psychiatrist or social worker, for the treatment of the client or person covered by the insurance. Many individuals in the United States have no insurance coverage. For those who do, there appears to be a somewhat disconcerting trend for insurance companies to reduce their payment costs such that those providers who charge less (for example, the psychiatric nurses and social workers) are the ones impaneled or covered by insurance. Community activists need to stay on top of this issue—for example by conducting research to ascertain whether there is a relationships between the success of treatment and the cost of the treatment. The issue of health insurance is addressed in more detail in Chapter 10.

Interestingly, community psychologists, who sit outside most of these territorial disputes, believe that an ounce of prevention is by far the most cost-effective intervention of all. Mental health education could go a long way toward preventing the need for treatment and health insurance coverage all together.

In groups such as Alcoholics Anonymous and Overeaters Anonymous, individuals with common issues come together to assist and support one another. The groups are usually comprised of individuals who are searching for useful coping strategies, such as better ways to provide parenting or to maintain sobriety, or who have special problems such as overeating, gambling, or reentering the community after a stay in a psychiatric institution. These **self-help groups** are sometimes led by a professional but more often they are simply comprised of laypeople whose experiences and common situations act as motivators and guides for others in the group. Hence, another name for these groups is **mutual help groups** (Levine, 1988).

Individuals need not belong to formal or organized groups to come to the assistance of each other. Friends, families, and coworkers often come to one another's aid in times of crisis or stress. Whether the support comes from an established mutual help group or from a caring friend, social support has become an important construct in the field of community psychology. **Social support** can be defined as an exchange of resources between two individuals perceived by the provider or the recipient to be intended to enhance the well-being of the recipient (Shumaker & Brownell, 1984).

The concept of social support was first identified by physician John Cassel (1974) and later elaborated upon by Gerald Caplan (1974). Interest in the definition, measurement, and effects of social support quickly grew. Within the two years that *Psychological Abstracts* first contained the term *social support* in its index, over 450 studies appeared (Brownell & Shumaker, 1984). We cannot do this vast literature justice here, but we will attempt to highlight its main thrust.

Most studies of social support examine support between adults, but a few have also studied support among children (Barrera, 1986). Interest in the effects of social support has also expanded worldwide (Gidron, Chesler, & Chesney, 1991), but no one is exactly sure how social support functions. In fact, there is no one accepted definition in the literature but the one given above generally captures the typically accepted elements of social support.

A matter related to the confusion over the definition is that social support has been criticized as too broad a concept (Barrera, 1986; Brownell & Shumaker, 1984). More concise and definitive terminology might be useful. Three other terms have been offered as composing the more generic concept of social support. Social embeddedness seems to be one aspect of the broader concept of social support. **Social embeddedness** is the number or quantity of connections an individual has to significant others who might offer assistance. In that regard, it is the opposite of social isolation. A socially embedded individual has many friends, family members, and associates upon whom he or she can draw when seeking social support. **Enacted support,** or the availability of actual support, refers to the very real actions others perform when they render assistance. In other words, an individual may have a large network of friends or be socially embedded, but the friends might not actually give support. The number of available supportive friends, then, is less than the number who actually support the needy individual. Finally, **perceived social support,** the most frequently examined construct in the literature, refers to the cognitive appraisal of being reliably connected to others. In other words, it is the perception of *how available* and *how adequate* social support is. For example, an individual might have many friends who offer support, but the support is useless or not consistently given. Both Barrera (1986) and Brownell and Shumaker (1984) suggested the field would be better served if researchers made these three distinctions before they commence their work.

Issues Related to Social Support

Perhaps the most important issue related to social support is its effect. The bulk of the research (cf. Brownell & Shumaker, 1984) shows that social support has beneficial effects. Early research (Brownell & Shumaker, 1984) has demonstrated beneficial effects of support groups for cancer patients, first-time parents, the bereaved, and rape victims. More recent research has shown positive effects for social support among early adolescents (Cauce, 1986), those suffering from chronic stress (Cummins, 1988), those who attempt suicide (Veiel, Brill, Hafner, & Welz, 1988), the elderly (Chapman & Pancoast, 1985; Heller & Mansbach, 1984), parents of children with cancer (Chesler & Barbarin, 1984), adolescent mothers (Unger & Wandersman, 1985b), scoliosis patients (Hinrichsen, Revenson, & Shinn, 1985), divorcing mothers (Tetzloff & Barrera, 1987), children with disabilities (Wallander & Varni, 1989), mothers charged with child abuse (Richey, Lovell, & Reid, 1991), caregivers to the elderly (Greene & Monahan, 1989), gamblers (Turner & Saunders,

1990), and the homeless (Rivlin & Imbimbo, 1989), among other groups. However, social support is *not always beneficial* (Barrera, 1986; Shinn, Lehmann, & Wong, 1984). We will discuss *why* shortly, under the topic of disadvantages of social support.

Related to the issue of whether social support is effective is the issue of *how* it is effective. The literature is replete with explanations, but three seem to stand out: the direct, indirect, and interactive effects of social support (Brownell & Shumaker, 1984). The **direct effects** of social support mean that interpersonal contact and assistance directly facilitate healthier behaviors. For instance, when friends encourage an ill individual to stick to his medical regime and eat a healthy diet, they are directly supporting and aiding the unhealthy individual.

The **indirect effects** of social support mean that social support influences an individual's well-being by decreasing the perceived severity of stressful events. For example, when parents convince a child that a difficult math class is a challenge rather than a stressful event, the parents are providing indirect support to that child. Another way to provide indirect support is to redefine the scale of a larger problem into a smaller, more controllable one or to help resolve a small problem before it becomes a bigger one (Brownell & Shumaker, 1984).

The largest portion of the research on social support, though, focuses on its **interactive effects** or its **buffering effects.** In this case, social support is interpreted to mitigate or ameliorate the adverse effects of stressful events by influencing the recognition, quality, and quantity of coping resources. An example of this would be that a friend points out that the distressed individual is coping as well as or better than others in the situation or that the distressed individual has many caring friends. More recently, another possible indirect effect has been identified, a **boostering effect** (Okun, Sandler, & Bauman, 1988) in which social support actually enhances the beneficial effects of positive life events. In this case, the social supporter points out the life-enhancing effects of some positive experience.

Research on exactly how social support works has not yet established a firm understanding of its functions in our literature. For example, Cohen, Teresi, and Holmes (1986) found a direct effect but no buffering effect for social support on psychological symptoms in an inner-city elderly population. On the other hand, Bowers and Gesten (1986) did find buffering effects in an experiment using college students who waited alone, with a friend, or with a stranger for an interview in which the students thought they would have to answer highly personal questions while being videotaped. Of course, the group of students waiting with friends reported the lowest anxiety of the three groups. Research continues to tease out the main mechanism by which social support functions.

One explanation for these differing research results could be the different methodologies and statistical techniques utilized. The first study primarily used correlational techniques (with surveys and network analysis, for example), whereas the second utilized an experimental paradigm with active manipulations. Depner, Wetherington, and Ingersoll-Dayton (1984) and Tebes and Kraemer (1991) more fully address these and other complex methodological and research issues in studies of social support.

Related to the issue of how social support functions is the **transactional nature of social support** (Shinn, Lehmann, & Wong, 1984). This transactional feature of social support has also been called the *exchange process* (Shumaker & Brownell, 1984). By *transactional* is meant that support is a two-way phenomenon. Social support affects how individuals function, and how individuals function influences the amount and kind of social support they receive. In times of distress, for example, individuals often seek social support to assist in their coping. Divorcing women sometimes turn to their friends for help in managing the emotional burden of divorce. On the other hand, in times of distress, social support can be disrupted by the individual's behavior. The woman who turns to her friends may find that her married friends shun her for fear she will disrupt their own marriages. Hence, social support is both a cause and an effect.

Another issue in the social support literature is its measurement—not a surprising circumstance given the disagreement over the construct's definition. A variety of measures have been developed, but the psychometric properties and soundness of these measures are still being examined (Fiore, Coppel, Becker, & Cox, 1986; Shinn, Lehmann, & Wong, 1984). Three such measures are the Inventory of Socially Supportive Behaviors (Barrera, Sandler, & Ramsey, 1981), the Social Support Behaviors Scale (Vaux, Riedel, & Stewart, 1987), and the Social Support Questionnaire (Sarason, 1983). Discussion of each of these scales is beyond the scope of this chapter, however.

Who the supporter is comprises another important issue in social support. For example, Dunkel-Schetter (1984) found that cancer patients reported that advice from health care professionals was helpful but that the same type of advice from friends and families was not beneficial. Research has also demonstrated that not all helpers or social supporters are equally adept. Toro (1986) coded and analyzed audiotapes of natural and professional helpers. He found that although there were many similarities between professionals and layhelpers, the type of advice offered, the amount of information given, and other similar dimensions varied as a function of the type of interpersonal interaction and who the helper was. For instance, of the professional helpers, lawyers did the most talking and showed the greatest proportion of information giving and closed questions—circumstances not beneficial in all crises.

Classic research on the **bystander effect** has curiously but clearly demonstrated that the larger the number of available helpers, the less likely it is that any of them will step forward to offer help (Latane & Darley, 1970). Psychologists assume that one of the main reasons for this phenomenon is **responsibility diffusion** (Baron & Byrne, 1994), in which one feels less responsible for another's fate when others present could also accept responsibility. When people are alone, they feel 100% responsible for another in need of help.

You might be curious to know what the profile of the typical natural helper is. Gottlieb and Peters (1991) completed a recent large-scale survey of Canadian mutual help group participants and found that the typical participant is a middle-class woman between the ages of 25 and 44. This does not mean that men or lower-income individuals do not participate; they simply did not dominate the sample of helpers. The ratio of men to women who reported participating in social support programs, for example, was four to six.

We should also caution you that Canadian data probably do not hold for other cultures. For example, Gidron, Chesler, and Chesney (1991) examined support groups in Israel and found that Israeli groups differed from those in North America. For instance, in Israel, groups are often facilitated by government professionals, which means that the groups do not always function as autonomously in Israel as they do in the United States.

Of course, who the recipient is also matters. When an individual in need of help is perceived as responsible for his or her problem, then that person is less likely to receive aid than one whose situation is attributed to uncontrollable or external causes (Schmidt & Weiner, 1988). In other words, if people blame the victim for his or her dilemma, they are far less likely to offer support. People are also more likely to aid others whom they perceive as similar to themselves (Dovidio, 1984) or whom they like (Schoenrade, Batson, Brandt, & Toud, 1986).

Much of the discussion on who the helper and recipient are reveals that the social support literature has focused on the individual level of analysis. Although that offers a beginning, experts in the field of community psychology are calling for psychologists to move beyond the individual to extra-individual levels. Psychologists need to expand notions of social support to examine the role of groups and networks and to explore the functional and structural characteristics of these social networks (Felton & Shinn, 1992).

Advantages and Disadvantages of
Support Groups and Social Support

Shumaker and Brownell (1984) provided an excellent review of the beneficial effects of social support from which we will borrow for this section. Of course, the main advantage of social support as a coping strategy is that it often has beneficial effects—that is, it enhances the well-being of the individual who receives the support. This general function can be reduced to several more specific functions.

Social support seems to gratify basic affiliative needs. In other words, through social support, individuals make contact with others and find companionship. When people perceive that others care for them, these people feel a sense of belonging.

Social support also seems to enhance self-identity and therefore self-esteem, which is part of one's identity. For instance, Thoits (1983) argued that it is through interactions with others that one's personality develops. Stated another way, through social exchanges, people acquire an awareness of who they are and where they fit in the social hierarchy. Here's a simple example. Suppose a professor returns an essay examination to you and at the top is a grade of 45. "Yikes," you think. "That's not a very good grade." You turn to a friend and see that she has a 35, while another classmate received a 28 and yet another a 17. "A-hah!" you say. "Now my 45 doesn't look so bad; I must be one of the smarter people in this class." By comparing yourself to appropriate others, you come to know yourself better.

Social support, as Shumaker and Brownell (1984) argued, also serves a stress-reducing function, so in that respect, support is beneficial. How does social support do this? First, social support at the prestress stage probably broadens an individual's cognitive appraisal of the stressful event. Hence, a clearer understanding of the stress is obtained. Second, social support from others can often assist individuals in finding a number of techniques for responding to the stress. For example, a trusted friend's of Art might have known to which professional agencies he could turn for counseling or might model appropriate emotions for Art because the friend had also been through a recent parental divorce. Social support might come in the form of direct aid, too. For instance, Art might have friends who take him out to dinner to get his mind off his problems. As mentioned earlier, a final advantage of social support is that it seems to work not just for individuals who have experienced losses but for all types of individuals experiencing life changes. Its possible applications seem endless.

Although the advantages of social support and self-help groups seem fairly obvious, the disadvantages are less so. First, as already mentioned, not everyone wants to be an involved citizen or participant. Some individuals are not natural caregivers nor feel comfortable with or motivated to help others. And some individuals who are continuous caregivers experience burnout (Brownell & Shumaker, 1984).

Second, research (Brownell & Shumaker, 1984) has uncovered that social support in some instances can be harmful. For example, Shinn, Lehmann, and Wong (1984) reported that aid sometimes threatens the recipient's self-esteem, especially if aid implies superiority-inferiority positions of the giver and recipient, respectively. Likewise, if the giver-recipient relationship requires the recipient to admit impairment, social support can be detrimental. Similarly, recipients often want to reciprocate the aid. In fact, in U.S. society there exists a **norm of reciprocity** (Baron & Byrne, 1994) in which people expect to reciprocate with those who do something for them. Often, there is no opportunity to repay a lay caregiver, thus embarrassing or humiliating the recipient. In this case, the professional caregiver, such as a client-centered therapist, where no expectation for reciprocity exists, is perhaps advantageous (Shinn, Lehmann, & Wong, 1984). These and other situations mean that social support does not always benefit and can, in fact, harm the receiver. A recently developed scale has been designed to test these negative social exchanges. It is the Test of Negative Social Exchange by Ruehlman and Karoly (1991).

A related notion is that the timing of social support is also important. Support given at the wrong time can perhaps be detrimental. For instance, Shinn, Lehmann, and Wong (1984) reviewed research on bereavement and reported that in early stages of grieving, empathy and emotional support are valuable. In the later stages, support that aids reintegration into normal social life is more valuable.

These and other factors related to social support indicate that support is not always beneficial, especially when it is not timely nor well introduced. As with any method of coping, social support is not without its drawbacks. Shinn, Lehmann, and Wong (1984) cautioned that in each support situation, the person-environment fit must be carefully examined. That is, one must consider the caregiver's intent and the recipient's perception of the assistance as well as the timing, amount, source, and function of the social support. Profile 5.1 introduces you to two individuals who recognized the relationships among distress, life circumstances, and social support before most other researchers discovered these same relationships.

◆ *PROFILE 5.1*
Bruce P. and Barbara Snell Dohrenwend

Many of the concepts as well as models or theories in the field of community psychology can be traced to the work of the Dohrenwends—pioneers of community psychiatry or psychiatric epidemiology. Although Barbara Snell Dohrenwend passed away a number of years ago, her husband continues to conduct research as well as train graduate students in psychiatric epidemiology. Both have received many national and international accolades for their scientific contributions. Barbara Snell Dohrenwend was a former president of Division 27 (Community Psychology) of the American Psychological Association as well as a corecipient with Bruce P. Dohrenwend of the Division of Community Psychology Distinguished Contribution Award in 1981. In her honor, the Barbara Snell Dohrenwend Memorial Lecture has been established by Division 27 for distinguished contribution to the field of community psychology.

More than 40 years ago, in a time when the medical model was the dominant paradigm used in the study of mental health and disorders and the field of community psychology had yet to be born, Bruce P. and Barbara Snell Dohrenwend began their scientific investigation of how environmental or stressful life events could contribute to the development of or further exacerbate psychiatric disorders. Their research serves as an impetus in the field of community psychology for studying how social support can serve as a buffering effect for stress, including the utility of case management or assertive community treatment (see Chapter 6).

Furthermore, the Dohrenwends argued that these events or experiences can be quantified using standardized procedures. This has led to the development of the *Psychiatric Epidemiology Research Interview,* a reliable and valid instrument for assessing different dimensions of psychopathology. Concepts such as *incidence* and *prevalence* have not only become standard nomenclatures in the study of mental disorders but also are part of the paradigms used today that emphasize ecological validity. Other contributions include the President's Commission on Mental Health, which is, in part, responsible for the enactment of the Community Mental Health Act and the development of the Epidemiological Catchment Area Study—a systematic assessment of mental illness.

Information and Education about Mental Health

Besides social support, there are other avenues for promoting emotional and physical well-being. In an earlier chapter of this book, we discussed education and information dissemination as a means of social change. Education can also pave the way toward better mental health. When education assists people in acquiring knowledge, skills, and attitudes that directly contribute to their mental health and to their effect on the mental health of others, it is known as **mental health education.** Moreover, Cowen (1980) argued that the goal of prevention (including mental health education) should emphasize teaching people *how* to think instead of *what* to think, thus enabling them to make reasonable choices and decisions as well as to have a sense of responsibility. In other words, the "ability to think straight paves the way for emotional relief, prevents dysfunction, and promotes health" (Shure & Spivack, 1988, p. 69).

Morrison (1980) asserted that mental health education is particularly valuable in "demythologizing" the public's perception of mental illness. Education can change public opinion away from the concept of mental illness as a disease to one of mental illness as having a psychosocial nature. Morrison reasoned that if community members view a mentally disordered person as less dangerous and more in need of skills to cope with problems in living, then the public is more likely to accept this person as a neighbor. The concept of educating the public about mental disorder and mental health is important to the present discussion as well as to the next chapter on deinstitutionalization of the seriously mentally disordered.

Ketterer (1981) suggested that mental health education is of two types: (1) improving the coping skills and competencies of normal and at-risk populations and (2) public information strategies that inform the public about mental health problems and preventive or treatment services. To accomplish these goals, mental health educators generally use three main techniques: the mass media, lectures and/or demonstrations, and small-group discussions.

Muñoz, Glish, Soo-Hoo, and Robertson (1982) provided an example of the first type of mental health education. They attempted to improve the knowledge of and competency of a community population by broadcasting a series of televised segments about depression, self-control, and social learning on a local televised news program. Citizens in the San Francisco area were selected at random from the telephone directory. They participated in pre- and postprogram interviews. The interviews contained behavioral questions as well as a measure of depression. The postprogram interview also contained questions about which segments the viewers had seen. Between the two interviews, the educators showed nine four-minute segments on a local news program three times daily. Each segment modeled a mentally healthy approach to daily life, such as telling oneself to stop thinking upsetting thoughts.

The results showed that two specific behaviors increased significantly as a consequence of the televised segments: stopping thinking about upsetting events and taking time to relax. A more general result was that individuals who had high initial levels of depression and who had viewed the segments showed a significant reduction in depressed mood in comparison to individuals who were depressed and who did not view the televised segments.

An example of the second type of mental health education again involves using the media but this time to inform the public about general mental health resources in the community. Sundel and Schanie (1978) investigated 21 television and radio announcements for use in the Louisville, Kentucky, area over a 60-week period. In the messages, the phone number of the local crisis intervention and information center was also provided. The results demonstrated that both well-educated and uneducated audiences benefitted from these messages, with uneducated audiences benefitting the most. Calls to the crisis and information center also increased as a result of the broadcast announcements. There was also a significant increase in knowledge about local community mental health resources, as indicated by pre- and postbroadcast interviews conducted every few weeks during the broadcasts with community members selected by random sampling.

A third example of use of the media in mental health education exists, too. Taylor, Lam, Roppel, and Barter (1984) developed a multimedia campaign entitled "Friends Can Be Good Medicine." This mental health campaign was conducted statewide in California. The program goals were to (1) encourage the development of supportive ties to others and (2) educate people about the relationship between social support and lower rates of psychopathology and health. Those who participated in the program reported greater gains in knowledge, attitudes, and intentions to socialize with others than those in the control group. These differences were maintained at one-year follow-up. Once again, the use of the mass media is an effective means for heightening community awareness and perhaps changing behaviors.

A follow-up study after one-year indicated that the gains in knowledge, attitudes, and intentions to seek social support were maintained (Hersey, Klibanoff, Lam, & Taylor, 1984). The authors noted that the campaign was most effective when it used *multiple channels of communication.* This is a most important point about education and information dissemination. Multiple approaches ordinarily result in stronger gains than narrowly focused efforts. For example, when a compaign uses both print *and* broadcast media, it is more likely to be successful than a print-only campaign.

Sports, Recreation, and Exercise

In his presidential address to the Division of Community Psychology of the American Psychological Association, Steve Danish (1983) encouraged community psychologists to involve themselves in the study of sports as related to the development of personal competence. He contended that sports have become cultural phenomena that permeate all of society; sports are a social institution comparable to other social institutions such as religion, law, government, neighborhoods, medicine, and human services systems. Danish also concluded that sports, when not ultra-competitive, help build character and heighten concern for others, as well as develop a sense of community, especially team sports.

There is also evidence that exercise and physical fitness help buffer the effects of stress (Brown, 1991). Brown measured the physical fitness of college under-graduates by observing them on a piece of exercise equipment. He also obtained self-reports of illnesses as well as measures of students' health from university health records. In addition, Brown obtained measures of the students' self-re-ported stressful life events. For students who were physically fit, high stress did not produce deterioration in their health, whereas high stress did lead to more illnesses and thus more visits to the infirmary for unfit students. In other studies, avid exercisers report improved quality of life, increased sense of accomplish-ment and well-being, and more feelings of relaxation (Sime, 1984).

Providing sufficient space for fitness and exercise is also related to a community's crime rate. In neighborhoods that provide adequate parks and recreational facilities, there is a lower crime rate than in neighborhoods that do not contain sufficient facilities for its residents, especially its youthful residents. Unfortunately, it is likely to be the affluent neighborhoods that house more recreational facilities per capita. In Chicago, for example, near the more affluent lake-front neighborhoods, there are 41 acres of park land per 1,000 residents. On the less advantaged west side of Chicago, there is only 0.5 acre per 1,000 residents (Grace, I-Chin Tu, Rochman, & Woodbury, 1994).

There are several problems with sports and physical fitness as answers to promotion of better mental and physical health, however. Danish (1983) reported that one problem is that when athletic participation takes on a physical fitness rationale, it feels like an obligation and loses some of its intrinsically motivating properties. This may be why adherence to physical fitness programs is so low despite the fact that physical fitness is so beneficial. As many as half of the people who start a physical fitness or exercise program drop out within the first few months; a year later the number drops dramatically again (Bloom, 1988).

To improve adherence to sport or physical fitness programs, some authorities recommend that exercise occur in group settings such as at school, at work, or with the whole family (Bloom, 1988). Group or communal participation seems to sustain adherence, thus reinforcing the idea that ecology is important. In fact, worksite physical fitness programs are increasing in popularity (Falkenberg, 1987). These worksite programs have been shown to reduce absenteeism, enhance productivity, and contribute to commitment toward the work organization (Shephard, Cox, & Corey, 1981). On the other hand, schools, where physical fitness can be introduced at early ages, *do not* seem to actively promote it as a means for developing a sense of mastery or for promoting better physical and mental health. Only about a third of the young people between the ages of 10 and 17 participate in daily physical education programs in schools (Iverson, Fielding, Crow, & Christenson, 1985). Nonetheless, the benefit of physical activities for mental health deserves closer examination. Physical activity benefits children. For example, in their meta-analytic review, Allison, Faith, and Franklin (1994) found that children with a diagnosis of disruptive behavior or related problems who engaged in some form of a physical activity regiment were significantly less likely to display disruptive behaviors than those who did not.

SUMMARY

The traditional models of mental health and mental disorder are derived from clinical psychology; therefore, they emphasize individualized forms of treatment such as psychotherapy. Freud's psychoanalytic theory, based on a medical model, is one of the older theories. The behavioral model offers individualized treatment also. In behaviorism, maladjustment is caused by faulty learning. Behavioral treatments involve the modification of learned responses or relearning of more appropriate responses. The humanistic model is another approach to individualized treatment based on the premise that people can be assisted to better understand their own unique feelings. Individuals might not be "sick" *per se* but rather are behaving in accord with labels that others have applied to them. One other theme of humanistic theory is that all individuals have worth and that worthiness should be promoted and enhanced perhaps through psychotherapy.

Today, people recognize that life events and daily hassles create stress in individuals and that many individuals need to adjust and cope with these problems. Both positive and negative changes as well as minor and major life events can trigger stress reactions. Adjusting to physical stressors in the environment or not being socially integrated into the community or social environment can also create the need to adjust.

Community psychologists have moved away from individual psychotherapy to interventions that promote mental health on a wider scale. Community psychologists also empower individuals to help themselves. Encouraging social support or developing self-help or mutual help groups is one such intervention. Another involves mental health education by which communities are educated about means for coping and about general mental health issues often via the mass media. One other suggested intervention involves noncompetitive group sports and physical fitness programs.

6

THE SERIOUSLY MENTALLY DISORDERED: BACK TO THE COMMUNITY

In individuals insanity is rare, but in groups, parties, Nations and epochs it is the rule.
   ◆ *FRIEDRICH WILHELM NIETZSCHE,* BEYOND GOOD
                AND EVIL, *1955 TRANSLATION*

Min was of Chinese descent and lived in the United States. Not only was she convinced that her psychiatrists did not understand her illness but she was also convinced that they did not understand her Chinese values.

Min had drifted in and out of a large state hospital because of what her doctors called her schizophrenia. Each time Min entered the hospital, she was given medication that eased her symptoms, particularly her hallucinations and imaginary voices talking to her. When medicated, Min would develop better contact with those around her, take better care of her daily needs, and then be released from the hospital to her family's care. However, her two parents worked hard to support themselves, her brother, her sister, and Min. Her siblings were in school. Therefore, Min was alone much of the time. Because her family was not available to supervise her medications, Min often forgot to take them. Eventually, she would become "out of control," which would prompt the family to call their psychiatrist, who, after some pleading from the family for intervention, would tell them to return Min to the hospital.

Such was Min's state. She would leave the hospital only to return. She would take her medication and momentarily be liberated from her symptoms only to forget the medication later. Min is one of the country's chronically mentally ill who seems to be in desperate need of long-term, coordinated intervention but who might not be receiving it.

INTRODUCTION

This chapter will examine the plight of Min and others like her. We will begin with some historical highlights and move next to the issue of deinstitutionalizing the mentally ill. While examining deinstitutionalization, we will discuss how to measure the success of moving individuals out of institutions as well as discuss the common alternatives to institutionalization. Interestingly, many contemporary alternatives are tantamount to reinstitutionalization.

IIISTORICAL NOTES ABOUT MENTAL DISORDERS

Although the ancient world has always been portrayed as less than civilized, some older cultures gave more emphasis to the study of mental health than others. For example, to most Chinese (ancient and modern), physical and psychological well-being is thought to depend on a balance of two natural forces: **Yin**, the female force, and **Yan**, the male force. Furthermore, these two forces are thought to regulate the five elements—gold, wood, water, fire, and earth—that are responsible for people's daily health. Among other things, the concentration of each element is thought to vary with the type of food group. Thus, a proper diet and regular exercise are important to maintain a balance between these elements.

According to Chinese folklore, a wise king named Sun Lone Tse, whose name meant "to cultivate," in ancient times (circa 600–700 B.C.) was thought to be responsible for the first classification system of herbs used in medicine. Also, Chinese historical texts mention a doctor named Wah Torr as the father of Chinese medicine. On one occasion, he performed minor surgery on a general's arm, using **acupuncture** as anesthetic. That is, needles were used to stick into the **meridians** (pressure points) to facilitate the release of **endorphins** (natural pain relievers) in the brain. Also, Wah Torr wrote many medical texts. These concepts relating mind and body are important to the fields of clinical psychology and behavioral medicine, sister disciplines to the field of community psychology. If Min were in ancient China or even modern-day China, the treatments for her disorder might indeed be different than they are in the United States.

As one moves through history, the ancient Greeks are also important. Hippocrates (circa 460–377 B.C.), who was known as the father of Western medicine, spoke about four natural **humors**, or fluids, that were thought to regulate people's mental health. Specifically, great fluctuations in mood were thought to be caused by an excess of blood. Fatigue was considered to be caused by an excess of phlegm or thick mucous. Anxiety was thought to be caused by an excess of yellow bile or liver fluid, and depression by an excess of black bile.

Whatever medical and psychological advancements achieved by the ancient Chinese and Greeks, the majority of their contemporaries relied on the supernatural to explain mental illness. After the collapse of the Roman Empire in Europe (circa 500 A.D.), supernatural or religious beliefs became the norms for explaining mental illness in Western society. For example, according to the church and those in power in many Western societies, the mentally ill and other disenfranchised people were "sinners." Religious zealotry reached its peak in 1484 when Pope Innocent VIII officially sanctioned the persecution of witches, some of whom were actually suffering from mental illness; many others were just dissenters of the "mainstream" cultures. This period of almost 900 years in Western societies has come to be associated with the infamous name, the Dark Ages.

In many Western societies during the Renaissance (revival) period (circa 1400–1700), the idea of **humanism** finally developed. Thus, the mentally ill gained indirect benefits from the notion that all people had certain inalienable rights and should be treated with dignity. Furthermore, some doctors began to challenge the concept that mental illness was a defection of moral character. By the middle of the 1600s, institutions known as **asylums** or madhouses were established to contain the mentally ill. Perhaps the most famous was London's Bethlehem Hospital, nicknamed "Bedlam," which is now a word meaning chaos and confusion. The first asylum in the United States was established in the late 1700s. Nonetheless, asylums were places where the socially undesirable or misfits were kept. More often than not, residents of the asylums were chained.

The further development of humanism during the American (1776) and French (1789) Revolutions provided more incentives to the mental health care reform movement throughout the European continent and in the United States. For example, two pioneers were instrumental in the movement in this country. Benjamin Rush (1745–1813), known as the father of American psychiatry, wrote the first treatise on psychiatry and established its first academic course. The second person was Dorothea Dix (1802–1887), whose experience with mental health care was derived from her teaching of women inmates. During her days, it was not unusual for the mentally ill to be kept in prisons. Dix traveled extensively in the country to raise money to build mental hospitals.

The mental health care reform movement further benefitted from the pioneer work of several doctors who devoted their lives to the development of scientific **nomenclatures**, or classifications, of mental illness. These classifications eventually led to the study of **etiology**, or the cause of mental illness. It was probably a French doctor named Phillipe Pinel (1745–1826) who first used the term **dementia** to describe a form of psychosis that was characterized by deterioration of judgment, memory loss, and personality change. A German doctor, Emil Kraepelin (1956–1926), further studied this condition and described it using the term **dementia praecox** (premature dementia). Subsequently, Swiss doctor Eugen Bleuler (1857–1930) gave the same disorder the name **schizophrenia**, which has become a household name in today's psychiatric practice. Also, Bleuler extended previous work by describing several subtypes of this illness.

Meanwhile, the **germ theory**, as advocated by Frenchman Louis Pasteur, had gained unprecedented recognition in the medical and scientific community. That is, many illnesses were thought to be caused by germ infections. Thus, the development of psychiatry as a field was destined to take on a medical, or biological, tone. In other words, under the influence of germ theory, mental illness was conceptualized as a *disease* rather than a *disorder* or psychological dysfunction.

At about the same time, the American Psychiatric Association and the American Psychological Association were formed in 1844 and 1892, respectively. Although the original mission of the American Psychological Association was not specifically concerned with issues relating to mental health and mental illness, as the subdiscipline of clinical psychology became more dominant, these issues became a priority. This emphasis no doubt does not sit well with the American Psychiatric Association, which sees itself as the sole guide in the field of mental health and mental illness since its inception. Over the years, these professional conflicts have been further complicated by a number of other factors, including the emergence of social work as a professional field.

After the work of Benjamin Rush and Dorothea Dix, the mental health care reform in this country can be roughly divided into three more eras: 1875–1940, 1940–1970 (Grob, 1991), and 1970–present (Shadish, Lurigio, & Lewis, 1989a). During the period from 1875 to 1940, the government assumed the major responsibility in caring for the mentally ill. Two-thirds of all the patients were living in state-run psychiatric hospitals. In many ways, this system was an extension of Dorothea Dix's thesis of moral management. More often than not, these patients received little treatment.

Meanwhile, there were a small number of privately owned psychiatric hospitals, such as the Menninger Foundation and the Institute of Living, providing services or treatments to those who could afford the costs. Although these services or treatments may be crude by today's standards, they contributed to the development of **community psychiatry**, a subdiscipline of psychiatry that argues that mental patients should be treated using the least restrictive method and in the least restrictive environment. Many of these private mental patients lived in small comfortable units, and they were encouraged to take lessons in cooking, sewing, and other self-improvement courses.

However, the initial optimism associated with moral management began diminishing in society. In almost all instances, psychiatric hospitals were no more than human warehouses. If treatments were provided, they tended to be **electroconvulsive therapy** or electric shock to the brain and **lobotomy** or brain surgery. Furthermore, the cost associated with these hospitals had become a major strain on society, especially during the Great Depression and the Second World War.

Beginning in the 1960s, the **zeitgeist**, or atmosphere, of the society began to change. For example, the introduction of **psychotropic drugs** (or mood-altering drugs) such as Thorazine rekindled the idea that the mentally ill could be treated with so-called dignity. Coupled with the ideology of community psychiatry, the use of medication allowed for the discharge of many mentally ill back into the community.

In this chapter's opening story, medications successfully allowed Min to return to her family. When she went off medication, her problems resurfaced. A consequence was the development of **outpatient treatment**, or nonhospitalized treatment (e.g., community mental health centers), as opposed to **inpatient treatment**, or hospitalized treatment. Also, to accommodate these newly released inpatients, alternative housing such as **community residences** or group homes were established but not without controversy.

Meanwhile, the fields of psychiatry and psychology began to recognize that not all the mentally ill could be treated the same way, such as those who had committed a crime due to their mental illness. **Forensic psychology**, or the study of crime and mental illness, started to emerge as a specialty (also see Chapter 9). The definition of treatment expanded to include issues such as vocational training. The rights of the clients have increasingly become a central issue. That is, clients who demonstrate competence have the right to decide on their treatment. Thus, organizations such as the National Alliance for the Mentally Ill were established to address or monitor client rights.

As the fields of psychiatry and psychology continue to expand, many have quickly learned that without systematic planning, many people who have mental disorders are likely to end up using the "revolving door" of an institution. That is, individuals who receive treatment are released, readmitted, and treated again in an unending cycle, as with Min, the woman in the opening vignette. Although former First Lady Rosalyn Carter was instrumental in reforming the mental health care system, during the Reagan and Bush Administrations many of her efforts were repealed. Meanwhile, as the national budget deficit continues to increase, less and less money is available for treatments and rehabilitation services. In the last decade, many urban cities such as Los Angles and New York witnessed a growing population of homeless mentally ill (Levine & Huebner, 1991; Susser, Moore, & Link, 1993).

DEINSTITUTIONALIZATION

Deinstitutionalization is usually defined as sending mental patients back into the community. Recall that Min was institutionalized and sent back to her community—in fact, she was repeatedly institutionalized and returned to the community. We must admit that this definition is too simplistic. A casual review of the field of mental disorders indicates that there is a great deal of controversy about what exactly *deinstitutionalization* is (Grob, 1991; Shadish et al., 1989a). Let's examine some of these definitions and related issues.

John Talbott (1975), a renowned psychiatrist, argued that the term *deinstitutionalization* is a misnomer. Instead, a better term is **transinstitutionalization** to describe "the chronically mentally ill patient who has his or her locus of living and care transferred from a single lousy institution to multiple wretched ones" (p. 530). The individual in the opening vignette, Min, presents a picture of this phenomenon. Min was in and out of institutions with residency with her family between institutionalizations. On a related note, Mathew Dumont (1982), another psychiatrist, argued that "deinstitutionalization is nothing more or less than a polite term for the cutting of mental health budgets" (p. 368).

The popular literature, such as the *New York Times*, defined *deinstitutionalization* as "moving mental patients from enormous, remote hospitals into small community residences" ("Willowbrook Plan," 1982). Another *New York Times* editorial stated that *deinstitutionalization* is "dumping mental patients out of state hospitals onto local communities, with promises of community treatment that never came true." Also, the *New York Times* claimed that *deinstitutionalization* is synonymous with *homelessness* ("Redeinstitutionalization," 1986, p. A24).

Indeed, these definitions illustrate the many different aspects of deinstitutionalization. Reconciling these differences, some mental health care experts (Bachrach, 1989; Rein & Schon, 1977; Shadish et al., 1989a) proposed that the term *deinstitutionalization* should be understood as a semantic mechanism to frame the complex, often conflicting, and seemingly unrelated sets of issues associated with ongoing mental health care reform. In other words, *deinstitutionalization*, like any term, has its concrete or explicit and implied or implicit meaning. More often than not, the concrete aspects of deinstitutionalization, such as budget constraints, are the impetus for the driving forces behind mental health care reform. Policy is likely to be the product of practical concern or "ideology" (Grob, 1991; Kiesler, 1992; Warner, 1989). However, a growing number of mental health care professionals are arguing that society must look beyond the immediate practical concern, to develop plans that can anticipate *long-term* consequences. For example, one concern is the growing number of the homeless mentally ill who also have the human immunodeficiency virus (HIV) or have acquired immune deficiency syndrome (AIDS). According to a survey conducted in a New York City shelter that housed homeless men, Susser, Valencia, and Conover (1993) found that 12 out of 62, or 19.4%, of the homeless mentally ill men tested positive for HIV. These men need all three issues (mental disorder, homelessness, and AIDS) addressed over the long run.

How and what can a society do to anticipate some of these long-term mental health care consequences? To that end, Bachrach (1989) provided a more heuristic or meaningful definition of *deinstitutionalization* as

> the shunning or avoidance of traditional institutional settings, particularly state mental hospitals, for chronic mentally ill individuals, and the concurrent development of community-based alternatives for the care of this population. *This definition assumes three primary processes:* depopulation—*the shrinking of state hospital censuses through release, transfer, or death;* diversion—*the deflection of potential institutional admissions to community-based service settings; and* decentralization—*the broadening of responsibility for patient care from a single physically discrete service entity to multiple and diverse entities, with an attendant fragmentation of authority. (p. 165)*

According to Bachrach (1989), this definition of *deinstitutionalization* underscores three related elements: facts, process, and philosophy. That is, sound mental health care policy must be based on credible research or evidence (the facts). In order to plan for long-term goals, one must know the characteristics of the mentally ill and the resources or systems where they receive their services (process). Also, sound policy is often the result of a thorough study of historical and philosophical precedents. That is, historical events and philosophical ideology often determine the direction of mental health care movement (philosophy).

The Many Aspects of Deinstitutionalization

What were some of the issues U.S. society (especially mental health care professionals and policy makers) did and did not anticipate about the "watershed effect" of deinstitutionalization beginning in the late 1960s? Although it is beyond the scope of this chapter to give a full account, these complex issues can be understood from several related perspectives: philosophical, biomedical, economic, sociological, and psychological.

If Sir Thomas Moore were alive in the 1960s, he probably would have felt the optimism in the United States that Americans were on their way to Utopia. Indeed, President John F. Kennedy was asking middle-class Americans to give to the less fortunate. Programs such as Project Head Start (e.g., including free meals for schoolchildren who come from low-income families) and the Peace Corps (e.g., teaching people in Third-World countries about family planning, including the practice of prenatal care as well as abortion as an option of family planning) were established. The notion or philosophy of humanism appeared to reach its peak. The field of mental health benefitted from these effects. Meanwhile, the advancement in medical technology also allowed people with mental disorders who were once unmanageable now to be "controllable" by using psychotropic drugs such as Elavil and Thorazine. Thus, professionals had one more reason to treat the mentally ill using the least restrictive method.

However, some mental health care experts (Kiernan, Toro, Rappaport, & Seidman, 1989; Warner, 1989) have argued that however admirable and persuasive the notion or philosophy of humanism is, a more heuristic explanation to account for the occurrence of deinstitutionalization is economics. Investigating deinstitutionalization in different Western countries in the past 30 years, Warner (1989) found that

> *the process was stimulated by the opportunity for cost savings created by the introduction of disability pensions and, in some countries, by postwar demand for labor. Where labor was in short supply, genuinely rehabilitative programs were developed. Where cost saving was the principal motivation, community treatment efforts were weak. (p. 17)*

Also, Kiernan and colleagues (1989) found that manufacturing employment was negatively related to both first admissions in state hospitals and case openings in community outpatient facilities. That is, when the economy was good, fewer people were admitted into state psychiatric hospitals.

Since World War II, the world economy had been relatively good until the 1970s. The argument that deinstitutionalization is associated with economic stability appears to be consistent with the number of psychiatric hospital beds per 10,000 individuals in the Western industrialized countries. That is, as long as there was a demand for a labor force, more people were deinstitutionalized.

On the other hand, use of mental health facilities is related to personal poverty. Banziger and Foos (1983) found that unemployment and welfare factors were strong predictors of utilization of mental health centers. More recently, Bruce, Takeuchi, and Leaf (1991) demonstrated a causal link between mental disorder and poverty. They examined the patterns of new disorders that developed over a six-month period in an epidemiologic study. Their sample included African Americans, Hispanics, and Whites. The researchers found that a significant proportion of new episodes of mental disorder could be attributed to poverty. In addition, Bruce and associates found that the risk for developing disorders was equal for men and women and for African Americans and Whites—in other words, poverty does not discriminate on the basis of race or gender.

❖ *CASE IN POINT 6.1*

Rosenhan's Experiment about Stigmatization

Researcher D. L. Rosenhan was especially interested in whether mental health professionals (particularly psychiatrists) could detect genuine mental disorders or problems from fake ones. He decided to conduct an experiment. First, Rosenhan (1973) trained his graduate students and others in how to fake symptoms of psychiatric disorders. For example, he instructed the pseudopatients (fake patients) to tell hospital staff that they heard a thudding sound or a voice saying "thud." Rosenhan then sent his pseudopatients to a psychiatric emergency facility.

To Rosenhan's amazement, the students were admitted. Soon after their admission to the psychiatric ward, the pseudopatients were each given diagnoses. All of them but one were labeled *schizophrenic*. The pseudopatients were kept in the hospital from 7 to 52 days, with the average stay being 19 days.

Not long after their admission, the pseudopatients began to act "normal." Curiously, many of the other patients realized that the pseudopatients were normal. The staff did not recognize this normal behavior when they saw it, which, according to Rosenhan, was not often, as the staff did not spend much time with the patients.

The pseudopatients began to request to be released from the psychiatric ward. However, the staff consistently told the students that they were not well enough to be released. Eventually, Rosenhan had to intervene so that some of the pseudopatients could be released. When the pseudopatients were released, many were labeled *schizophrenia in remission*.

Without minimizing the agony associated with mental disorders, Rosenhan demonstrated that many perceived disorders are due to the process of labeling. Although some mental health professionals might argue otherwise, Rosenhan demonstrated that, at times, diagnosing a patient is more of an art than a science, and that once labeled, it is difficult to overcome the label.

Although these findings appear to explain the reasoning behind deinstitutionalization, they do not adequately account for its falling short of its goal to enhance the quality of life of the mentally disordered.

Community psychologists and mental health care experts (Cheung, 1988; Earls & Nelson, 1988; Lovell, 1990; Mowbray, 1990; Mowbray, Herman, & Hazel, 1992; Struening & Padgett, 1990) have argued that sociological factors (such as adequate housing) and psychological factors (such as stigmatization) often hinder the progress of deinstitutionalization. Case in Point 6.1 discusses interesting research on stigmatization—research in which institutionalized patients faked their disorders.

In a case study, Cheung (1988) argued that the successful reintegration of the mentally disordered into the community to a large extent is dependent on public relations. That is, community members who are not familiar with mental illness are likely to be concerned with or resistant to having a halfway house built in their neighborhood. Earls and Nelson (1988) found that housing concern was positively correlated with negative affect. That is, former patients who had to worry about basic shelter were likely to have poor mental health. These two findings indicate the difficulty of balancing the seemingly incompatible forces of "public good" and "private want."

Also, many people with mental disorders are discharged from hospitals into the community without adequate planning or support systems. For example, Mowbray (1990) argued that many of them do not have adequate living or social skills (e.g., cooking and paying bills) to survive in an unstructured environment. In order for deinstitutionalization to be effective, adequate and appropriate treatments must be in place. Struening and Padgett (1990) found that homeless adults in New York City had high rates of alcohol and other drug abuse as well as mental illness. It is not unlikely that a large portion of these people were mental patients who were discharged from hospitals without adequate planning. Thus, they became homeless and had alcohol and other drug-abuse problems (Levine & Huebner, 1991; Susser, Moore, and Link, 1993). Meanwhile, a majority of the mentally disordered are continuously being discharged from hospitals into nursing homes or in board-and-care homes that are ill prepared to provide the services these patients need. Another consequence is a high burnout rate among staff at these agencies (Shadish et al., 1989b).

Deinstitutionalization of people with mental disorders is also viewed as one of the major reasons (Pogrebin & Poole, 1987; Pogrebin & Regoli, 1985) for the increasing number of former mental health patients in prisons (Jemelka, Trupin, & Chiles, 1989). Some view prisons as the new dumping grounds for the mentally disordered. Because prisons are secure places, judges perhaps believe that prisons will keep disturbed offenders from disrupting society (Toch & Adams, 1987). Prisons, however, offer little by way of treatment for these individuals.

In an interesting study of what happens to the chronically mentally disordered, Diamond and Schnee (1990) tracked 21 men who were perceived to be most at risk for potential violence and were also high users of jails. The men were tracked for two and a half years through various service systems. The men used up to 11 different systems, including the mental health, criminal justice, health care, and social services systems. Criminal justice services were the most frequently used ones, and mental health services were usually only short-term, crisis care services, although some of the men had been hospitalized for long-term psychiatric care. Diamond and Schnee believe that their figure is an *underestimate* but calculated that the cost of care of the 21 men in all service systems totaled $694,291. That figure does not include costs to victims nor property damaged in the men's violent episodes. The researchers called for a more coordinated effort of the various systems to better assist the men and to reduce costs.

Belcher (1988) suggested that when people with mental disorders are released from hospitals or institutions, they are often unable or unwilling to follow through on their own aftercare. This situation increases the likelihood of these individuals being involved in the criminal justice system. In addition, because the legal system and the mental health systems view mental disorders differently (Freeman & Roesch, 1989), the mentally disordered are not afforded the same level of therapeutic services for their disorder when they are incarcerated. The legal system narrowly deals with mental illness only as incompetence to testify in one's own behalf or as insanity, which is a defense against guilt. Hochstedler's (1986) research demonstrates that individuals with a history of mental disorder elicit more lenient penal sanctions and that the court uses its authority in these cases to impose mental health treatment. However, such coercive treatment of the mentally ill can violate both ethical standards of the professionals and patients' rights (Geller, 1986).

Treatment for the mentally disordered while in jail is rare because jail and prison personnel are not trained in mental health issues. Corrections staff are more concerned with custodial matters (Pogrebin & Regoli, 1985). The solution may be that mental health, criminal justice, and other professionals *need to collaborate in innovative and integrative ways to prevent* the mentally ill from being incarcerated in a correctional facility and to treat their disorders when they are incarcerated (Diamond & Schnee, 1990; Pogrebin & Regoli, 1985).

Common Alternatives to Institutionalization

The ideal setting for the institutionalized individual would be one that enhances his or her well-being because of the optimal fit between the individual's competencies and the support provided in the environment. However, this may be but a pipe dream. In reality, many community placements are based as much on what is available and on economics as on the individual's competencies.

If not in institutions, where are the people who have mental disorders? Ironically, today most chronic mental patients are still cared for either in institutions such as nursing homes or in other community settings often characterized by poverty, stigma, social isolation, and poor care that depict large psychiatric hospitals (Shadish et al., 1989a). About 1.15 million mentally disordered individuals reside in nursing homes; in fact, the nursing home industry is the largest system of long-term care for the severely and persistently mentally disordered (Bootzin, Shadish, & McSweeney, 1989). Research suggests that nursing homes do not return patients to mental hospitals as often as other forms of mental health care that is provided to deinstitutionalized persons (Bootzin et al., 1989). The reason, however, is not that the patients improve. Research demonstrates that symptomatology does not change; in fact, it might become slightly worse. The reason that nursing homes do not return patients to mental hospitals might be related to economics. More mental health dollars go to nursing home care than to any other mental health program (Kiesler, 1980). It behooves nursing homes to keep their clients!

Another type of community placement is **board-and-care homes**. These are typically community-based shelter-care facilities that include group homes and family care homes. The Public Health Service (1980) estimates that 400,000 people with chronic mental disorders may reside in these settings. This particular industry, compared to nursing homes, is relatively unregulated and more decentralized. The individuals in these settings tend to be younger and need less intensive care than those in nursing homes. Their care is typically paid for by Supplemental Security Income (disability checks), which they turn over to the shelter owners (Shadish et al., 1989a).

Segal, Silverman, and Baumohl (1989) examined these care facilities in the state of California and concluded that there are several types. The *family care home* is small, has a family-oriented atmosphere, and often is owner occupied. These homes typically shelter a couple of older, more emotionally stable residents. The homes are not medically oriented in that the residents are not treated like patients, but neither are any programs provided that are designed to make the residents more independent or to move them out of the shelter. The *small group home* has a typical bed capacity of 30 residents. These homes also serve an older population and do not emphasize control over the residents like the family homes. That is, there are no curfews or many rules or schedules for the residents to follow. However, the smaller group homes, unlike the family homes, use extramural staff for medical, social, and psychological services. The *larger group homes* offer some programs designed to enhance social skills and rehabilitation for their residents. Also, in the larger group homes there is more control over the residents' lives compared to the other two types of facilities.

The remainder of the deinstitutionalized individuals are scattered across many settings. About 250,000 remain in mental hospitals. Another 150,000 to 170,000 live with their families, and the rest are either homeless or live elsewhere such as in jails (Shadish et al., 1989a).

This fragmentation of care and the supposed economization of services implies that society has essentially moved from a mental health system to a welfare system (Kennedy, 1989). It is time to look at the success (or failure) of these changes in care for the mentally disordered.

Measuring "Success" of Deinstitutionalized Persons

Many in the mental health field would quickly jump to the conclusion that deinstitutionalization has not been successful. We have reviewed here some of the myriad problems that deinstitutionalization has created, including but not limited to transinstitutionalization, homelessness, and jail terms. How is successful integration into the community measured? The answer depends on whom you ask and what issues you discuss.

Society needs to take a closer look at the measurement of success of deinstitutionalization. Table 6.1 shows the names of famous individuals who at one time or another experienced mental impairment but who were also able to inegrate successfully into society.

The typical measures of success are social integration and recidivism. **Social integration** was defined in the last chapter as people's involvement with community institutions as well as their participation in the community's informal social

TABLE 6.1   Some Famous Individuals with Some Form of Mental Disorder

Person	Field	Mental Disorder
Dick Cavett	Contemporary American entertainment celebrity	Depression
Connie Francis	American 1950s singer	Manic-depressive disorder
Ernest Hemingway	American Nobel Prize writer	Depression
Abraham Lincoln	Sixteenth American president	Depression
Vincent Van Gogh	Late nineteenth-century Dutch painter	Psychosis
Virginia Woolf	Early twentieth-century American writer	Depression

life (Gottlieb, 1981). **Recidivism** means relapse or return to the institution or to care—in this case, return to the psychiatric hospital. However, both of these terms imply limited criteria. Recent efforts in the literature of the field of community psychology indicate that measurement of success is a more complex issue.

For example, Shadish, Thomas, and Bootzin (1982) found that different groups use different criteria for success. Residents, staff, and family members of community care facilities often express that the quality of life (e.g., a clean place to live and something to do) ought to serve as a measure of success. On the other hand, federal officials and academics cite psychosocial functioning (e.g., social integration and reduction of symptomatology) as good measures of success of community placement.

Clinicians (psychologists and psychiatrists) also use different criteria for different groups. Stack, Lannon, and Miley (1983) queried clinicians about their prognostic judgments for 269 patients in a state community mental health center. Specifically, the clinicians were asked to judge their expectations that the patients would be readmitted within the next two years. Clinicians' judgments were biased in regard to the patients' ethnicity; that is, they judged African American patients as more likely to be rehospitalized than White patients. The same clinicians were unduly influenced by their perceptions of the severity of the patients' disorder instead of other favorable factors such as lack of prior hospitalization, youthfulness, lack of severe impairment, and living in a residentially stable neighborhood.

Despite suspected clinician bias, do client characteristics help clinicians make accurate judgments about whether particular clients will be more successful once released from an institution? Mitchell's (1982) work seems to suggest this is so. Mitchell recruited 35 clients from outpatient psychiatric clinics, as well as their family members. The ability of the client to solve problems and to be independent positively related to the number of intimates or friends and the degree of support received from peers that the clients reported.

However, environmental factors also moderate the amount of success each deinstitutionalized individual will experience. Kruzich (1985) found that cities of

10,000 to 100,000 do have sufficient community resources for clients, but cities over 100,000 are so large that problems of distance and safety preclude high levels of involvement in community life or in accessing resources. Small towns and rural areas ranked in the middle of these other two sizes. Kruzich also found that depersonalizing care practices of the community facilities also predict the clients' level of integration into the community. **Depersonalization of services** means that the clients' individual needs are not attended to; that is, they do not have their own personal possessions, birthdays are not celebrated, and so on. When depersonalization is high, integration is low.

Another environmental factor related to whether former patients from psychiatric institutions will successfully integrate into the community is the attitude of the community citizens (Link & Cullen, 1983). There is a wealth of research indicating that Americans have negative and rejecting attitudes toward people with mental disabilities (Scott, Balch, & Flynn, 1983). Although the literature is somewhat inconsistent, various demographic variables have been suggested as related to attitudes toward the mentally disabled. Education is thought to increase tolerance of these individuals (Halpert, 1985) and low socioeconomic class is thought to decrease tolerance (Scott et al., 1983).

A few in the field of community integration of the chronically mentally disordered feel that the criteria for judging community competence of people with mental disabilities are amorphous and ambiguous. These professionals feel that a psychometric scale should be used to optimize the fit between the client and the community placement. Searight, Oliver, and Grisso (1986) suggested using the Community Competence Scale, which is a multiscale instrument of an individual's problem-solving skills, appropriateness of social judgment, and other factors related to social competence. In their research, Searight and associates found that the scale discriminated effectively between client groups requiring differing levels of guidance in the community.

BEYOND DEINSTITUTIONALIZATION

Certainly, the preceding scenarios do not reflect the optimism when deinstitutionalization began in the late 1960s. It was thought then that the introduction of the **Community Mental Health Act** could "reduce the census of state hospitals and to provide treatment to maintain psychiatric patients in the community" (Levine, Toro, & Perkins, 1993, p. 526). Now, with 20/20 hindsight, it seems obvious that one reason for the existing "patchwork" system is the lack of systematic planning, or poor coordination. However, some mental health care experts (Rein & Schon, 1977) argued that "the villain...is not poor coordination but the poor quality of services" (p. 244). Responding to this challenge, the National Institute of Mental Health (NIMH) and some state agencies have begun to collect data about the characteristics of the mentally disabled, including people who are not part of the "mainstream" population. That is, quality of services are dependent on professionals' knowledge about people who have mental disorders.

A First Step: Epidemiologic Catchment Area Study

In the early 1980s, the NIMH surveyed the psychiatric status of more than 20,000 people in five cities. Some of the findings from the **Epidemiologic Catchment Area Study (ECA)** are presented in (Tables 6.2 and 6.3). Findings from the ECA are consistent with the **Midtown Manhattan Study**, a longitudinal study investigating the prevalence of psychopathology from 1952 to 1960. That is, contrary to popular belief, some form of mental disorder is probably present in 1 of 10 American adults.

However, some mental health care experts argue that ethnic minorities are likely to be underrepresented in the ECA and Midtown Manhattan study due to certain cultural norms (cf. Wilson, O'Leary, & Nathan, 1992). For example, Sue, Fujino, Hu, Takechui, and Zane (1991) and Bui and Takeuchi (1992) found that Asian and Hispanic Americans tended to underutilize mental health care services, whereas African Americans tended to overutilize such services. Indeed, to many Chinese people, such as Min in the opening vignette, seeking mental health care services is not only a "loss of face" but a disgrace to the extended family. Many Chinese also believe the body and the mind are one and the same thing: the "body-mind duality" of Western society is alien to most Chinese (Cheung, 1986).

According to Sue and colleagues (1991), even when ethnic minorities do seek mental health care services, they tend to have a higher attrition or dropout rate than Whites. However, ethnic minorities are less likely to terminate treatments when the mental health care providers are of similar ethnic background. In addition to good planning and coordination, this finding illustrates the important thesis that for mental health care services to be efficient and effective, treatment models must be culturally sensitive.

TABLE 6.2   Lifetime Prevalence Rates of *DIS/DSM-III* Disorders (in Percentages)

Disorders	New Haven	Baltimore	St. Louis
Any Disorder	28.8	38.8	31.0
• Substance use	15.0	17.0	18.1
• Schizophrenia	2.0	1.9	1.1
• Affective	9.5	6.1	8.0
• Anxiety	10.4	25.1	11.1
• Eating disorder	0.0	0.1	0.1
• Antisocial	2.1	2.6	3.3
• Cognitive	1.3	1.3	1.0

Source: "Lifetime Prevalence Rates of DIS/DSM-III Disorders" by L. N. Robins et al., 1984, *Archives of General Psychiatry, 41*, page 952. Copyright 1984, American Medical Association.

TABLE 6.3   Six-Month Prevalence of Psychiatric Disorders in
Three Communities (in Percentages)*

	New Haven	Baltimore	St. Louis
Men			
18–24 years	23.8	25.1	18.9
25–44	18.9	23.5	19.8
45–65	11.9	18.7	9.4
65+	12.3	15.3	8.8
Total Men	16.7	21.1	15.4
Women			
18–24 years	24.6	26.1	17.8
25–44	21.2	27.1	17.2
45–64	10.3	21.5	10.9
65+	13.2	17.8	8.8
Total Women	17.1	23.6	14.3
Men and Women	16.9	22.5	14.8

*The psychiatric disorders included in this table are affective disorder, substance abuse/dependence, somatization disorder, antisocial personality disorder, schizophrenia, schizophreniform disorder, and cognitive impairment. All produce significant impairment in functioning.

Source: "Six Month Prevalence of Psychiatric Disorders in Three Communities" by J. K. Myers et al., 1984, *Archives of General Psychiatry, 41*, page 959. Copyright 1984, American Medical Association.

Model Programs for Individuals with Mental Disorders

It is sad to note that community psychologists and mental health care experts know more about what does *not* work rather than what *does* work with people who are mentally disordered. However, coupled with the knowledge gained from pioneer programs such as the **Lodge Society** (Fairweather, Sanders, Maynard, & Cressler, 1969) and epidemiological investigations, some innovative psychosocial rehabilitation models (Bond, Miller, & Krumweid, 1988; Bond, Witheridge, Dincin, & Wasmer, 1991; Bond, Witheridge, Dincin, Wasmer, Webb, & DeGraaf-Kaser, 1990; Olfson, 1990) have been developed for treating people with mental disorders. Fairweather's concept of Lodge Societies encompassed structured halfway houses or group homes for the mentally disabled that emphasized skill building and shared responsibility as well decision making.

Common to the newer models is the use of **case management** or intensive case support, including instruction in daily living skills (e.g., cooking and paying bills). Service delivery linking both the monitoring and brokering of delivery of a variety of services performed by the case manager is also advocated (Snowden, 1992). In other words, a case manager (usually a social worker) works *closely* with former mental patients, possibly including being on call 24 hours a day for any emergency that might arise. Also, case management can easily be integrated into **residential** *or* outpatient treatments.

It is thought that intensive social support in the form of case management should mitigate recidivism or relapse. This approach is consistent with the philosophy of the field of community psychology: **empowerment**. Compared to traditional treatments (e.g., outpatient), case management is labor intensive. However, research indicates that case management "repeatedly has been shown to reduce both hospital use and costs across a number of different studies performed in different communities..., although other desirable effects (e.g., symptom reduction, improved social relationships,...) have been less than robust (Levine et al., 1993, p. 529). These findings are understandable given the complex nature of mental disorder. As you may recall, even when housing is not a problem, improved social relationships are contingent on many different people—the patient being just one of the many.

One model case management program will be examined here. **Assertive community treatment (ACT)**, known variously as *mobile treatment teams* and *assertive case management*, is designed "to improve the community functioning of clients with serious and persistent mental illness, thereby diminishing their dependence on inpatient care while improving the quality of life" (Bond et al., 1990, p. 866). Assertive community treatment focuses on teaching practical living skills such as how to shop for groceries and maintain finances. More than that, in a single or team case manager (professional staff), ACT ensures attention to medications, service planning and coordination, as well as assessment and evaluations. Assertive community treatment usually also means a fairly low staff-client ratio—for example, 10:1. Moreover, clients do not visit staff offices but rather staff visit clients *in vivo*—that is, in their own environments.

Stein and Test (1985) developed one of the first such programs in this country in Madison, Wisconsin. Wanting more research on ACTs, Bond and colleagues (1990) compared ACT clients to clients at a drop-in center. Drop-in centers usually provide an informal meeting place for clients who typically are formerly institutionalized mental patients. These centers offer a range of social and recreational programs in a self-help atmosphere. In sharp contrast to ACT, drop-in centers have a central meeting place, a higher client-staff ratio, and no requirement for frequent staff contact.

Bond and associates found overall that after one year, 76% of the ACT clients were still involved in ACT, whereas only 7% of the drop-in clients were involved in their program. The ACT staff team averaged only two home and community visits per week per client but their clients averaged significantly fewer state hospital admissions and fewer days per hospital stay. The researchers estimated that ACT saved over $1,500 per client per year. The ACT clients themselves reported greater satisfaction with their program, fewer contacts with the police, and more stable community housing than clients from the drop-in center.

Assertive community treatment takes an ecological (in vivo) approach to clients. The staff is assertive in offering assistance to clients and in capitalizing on client strengths, the latter of which meets the tenets of community psychology.

Assertive community treatment prevents further client deterioration and provides a strong community alternative to hospitalization. Finally, ACT utilizes a holistic approach with each client as well as integration of services (Mowbray, 1990), all within the philosophies of the field of community psychology introduced at the beginning of this book.

This study, however, is not without criticism, although other reviewers (Mowbray, 1990) have questioned why community psychologists have not been *more* involved in research on ACT and the seriously mentally disordered. Toro (1990), for example, suggested that the study had differential and therefore biasing drop-in ratios in the two groups. Toro also argued that such research on ACT indicates that even though ACT prevents re-hospitalization, more research is needed on its impact in other domains such as employment and social relationships. Salem (1990) concluded that a more thorough investigation of consumer- or client-run programs is needed, as well as more diversity among interventions for people with mental disabilities.

Profile 6.1 introduces you to an individual who "practices" community psychology with the mentally disordered although she is not trained in community psychology.

The Battle Continues: Where Do We Go from Here?

Although having a mental disorder is still a stigma in society, the general public has become more familiar with mental health and mental illness. This awareness is responsible, in part, for the formation of the National Alliance for the Mentally Ill (NAMI). The NAMI functions as more than a self-help group; it also functions as a political lobbying body. It is estimated that the NAMI has about 1,050 affiliates in the country with a membership of about 130,000. The NAMI is a key player in the ongoing mental health care reform as proposed by President William Clinton and chaired by Tipper Gore, wife of Vice President Albert Gore. At the local level, individual chapter members provide support to each other as well as educate the public via educational activities, including education about medication and rehabilitative services.

Some psychosocial models based on the concept of case management and political efforts such as those engaged by the NAMI appear to be hopeful for the mentally disabled. However, mental health care reform is at a critical juncture. That is, although community psychologists and mental health care professionals can empower the mentally ill using appropriate and culturally sensitive treatment models, mental health care reform must *not* be carried out in isolation from other health agendas. Mental health care needs to be framed within a *unified* health care agenda. Research (D'Ercole, Skodol, Struening, Curtis, & Millman, 1991; Levine & Huebner, 1991; Susser et al., 1993) indicates that physical health and mental health are interdependent, such as is the case of drug abuse among many homeless mentally disordered. D'Ercole and colleagues found that physical illnesses among psychiatric patients tended to be underdiagnosed when using

❖ PROFILE 6.1
Edie H. Madden

Armed with two bachelor's degrees, one in art history and the other in oriental philosophy from an Ivy League college, Edie Madden first worked as a fashion buyer for a large department store. Feeling unfulfilled with her work and wanting to work with "real people," she decided to switch professions. Her journey through life soon became a mission.

Madden quit her job as a fashion buyer, but in the meantime, in order to have an income, she started a cleaning service. Unknown to her at the time, landing the contract with a group home agency subsequently turned out to be a life-long dream: working with and helping people. Given that her work environment was the group homes, Madden soon had many opportunities to interact with the residents. Being forever an optimist, she saw the residents as possessing strengths they had yet to realize themselves. She also gained their trust. Her persuasiveness not only led to her eventual employment at the agency but also convinced the administration to allow her to implement pilot rehabilitation programs for the residents. Madden's philosophy is to empower the residents and to emphasize the strengths they possess—a premise consistent with the field of community psychology (although she is not trained in community psychology).

Among the many programs Madden has implemented during her time at the agency is one that clearly resonates the philosophy of assertive community treatment as well as of community psychology: the "international dinner." Using the premise of cultural diversity, Madden persuaded the residents in the group homes to plan special dinners around cultural themes. Throughout the preparation of the dinner, she worked with the residents on shopping skills, cooking abilities, and table manners. In addition, using the premise of cultural diversity, she worked with the residents on how to deal with their mental problems. She helped them understand that they are not inadequate, but rather perhaps just different.

Today, Edie Madden is a senior rehabilitation counselor at Strong Ties, a facility of the Strong Memorial Hospital located in Rochester, New York. Using her experience from the group homes and ongoing classwork toward a doctoral degree in psychiatric rehabilitation psychology, she continues to work on her goal to empower people who have severe mental disorders. One of Madden's ongoing programs is to teach her clients *how* and *when* to utilize social support, including social service resources (see Cowen, 1980). This program consists of multifaceted, sequenced modules, building from basic activities such as daily living skills to advanced activities such as preparation for the examination for a General Education Diploma.

Madden's work is highly praised by the New York State Office of Mental Health, which emphasizes that people with mental disorders should be treated in the least restrictive environment or manner. Madden argues that "in order to feel empowered, these people must feel they are part of the community, capable of making decisions for themselves" (personal communication, 1993).

the traditional psychiatric diagnostic tools of the *DSM-III-R*. This was especially true for older and female patients. These findings suggest that poor physical health is likely to exacerbate existing poor mental health, which can become a vicious cycle.

Knowledge that community psychologists have gained in the past 30 years about health issues (mental health and mental illness in particular) strongly argues for the fact that we, as a nation, must not fall prey to the same false optimism of the 1960s. Also, no one should be denied mental health care services simply because she or he cannot afford to pay for such services; quality of services must *not* be contingent on amount of payment.

SUMMARY

A casual review of the field of mental health and illness indicates that there is a great deal of controversy about exactly what deinstitutionalization is. Some have argued that a better term is *transinstitutionalization* to describe the "dumping" of patients from one setting to another. Also, the characteristics of the mentally disabled have changed in the past 30 years. Now, ethnic minorities constitute a sizable sample of the mentally disordered, and they are likely to be undetected by the existing systems.

The most common placement for a deinstitutionalized individual is, interestingly, another institution, usually a nursing home. The functioning of a person who is mentally disordered in the community usually includes social integration and recidivism, or rate of return to the psychiatric hospital. Most analyses of success focus on problems of the individual; however, the environment, such as depersonalization of services, can also account for problems deinstitutionalized individuals face.

The ideal that led to the enactment of the Community Mental Health Act in the 1960s has not been fully realized. Now, it seems obvious that one reason for the existing "patchwork" system is the lack of systematic planning, or poor coordination. On the other hand, some mental health care experts argue that the villain is poor quality of services. Responding to this challenge, the National Institute of Mental Health and some state agencies have begun to collect data about the characteristics of the mentally disabled, including people who are not part of the "mainstream" population. That is, quality of services are dependent on knowledge about people who have mental disorders.

Coupled with the knowledge gained from epidemiological investigations such as the Epidemiologic Catchment Area Study and the Midtown Manhattan Study, some innovative psychosocial rehabilitation models have been developed for treating the mentally disordered. Common to these models is the use of case management or intensive social support (e.g., assertive community treatment), including some form of daily living skill training. Also, case management can be easily integrated into residential or outpatient treatments. It is thought that intensive social support in the form of case management should mitigate recidivism or relapse. However, research evidence is equivocal.

Mental health care reform is at a critical juncture. Although community psychologists and mental health care professionals can empower the mentally ill by using appropriate and culturally sensitive intervention models, mental health care reform must *not* be carried out in isolation from other health agendas. That is, mental health care needs to be framed within a *unified* health care agenda.

7

SOCIAL AND HUMAN SERVICES IN THE COMMUNITY

*This nation, this people, this generation, has man's first chance
to create a Great Society; a society of success without squalor,
beauty without barrenness, works of genius without the
wretchedness of poverty.*

♦ *LYNDON B. JOHNSON*

Rock was a high school junior. His girlfriend, Monique, was a sophomore in the same school. Both teenagers lived in middle-class suburban homes. Rock was bored with his humdrum life in the suburbs and liked to "live on the edge." It was his unpredictability and careless living that attracted Monique to Rock, although neither set of parents was thrilled with their child's choice of dating partner.

Rock and Monique were caught smoking marijuana in school. (Both also had a history of cutting classes and running away from home.) Because both were minors, the judge ordered Rock and Monique to enroll in a drug-treatment program.

The drug-treatment program was one of a dozen funded by a federal agency in collaboration with two state agencies. The goal was to *prevent* (not intervene or treat) youths from using alcohol and other drugs. Past research has shown that youths who have risk factors (e.g., cutting class and stealing) are more likely to use or abuse drugs than those who do not. Thus, youths who have risk factors are supposedly identified by the child and family welfare division and are referred to the drug-treatment programs at the other state agencies.

In the case of Rock, he was ordered by the court (rather than identified by the child and family welfare agency) to enroll in a drug-treatment program. After intake, Rock was immediately placed into one of the programs. He was to participate in both individual and group counseling. Family counseling with Rock's parents was provided on a limited basis, because the program was mainly designed for drug treatment.

Monique's placement was still pending. Incidentally, during intake, it was discovered that she was pregnant. The state agency responsible for the drug-treatment programs did not allow their clients to be pregnant. Meanwhile, staff at both state agencies did not know what to do with Monique. Also, both agencies were experiencing some difficulty in complying with the requirements of the federal agency that funded the drug-treatment programs.

This incident reflected one more symptom of the already strained relationship between the two state agencies. The road that led to the "collaboration" between the two agencies was shaky, at best. The original proposal to seek federal funds to establish drug-treatment programs for youths was largely engineered by the state agency that was responsible for drug-treatment services. Although its executive director had agreed in principle with the proposal, the state agency responsible for child and family welfare was more an observer than a player in the process.

Since the inception of the drug-treatment programs, several major political changes at the state level had led to a leadership vacuum at the two state agencies. For example, the two executive directors of the respective state agencies resigned after the governor announced that he would not seek reelection. A consequence was the lack of coordination of the patient referral process.

Meanwhile, direct-care staff felt strongly that alcohol and other drug abuse in youths was likely to be symptomatic of other issues, including parent-child and school problems. Moreover, most of these youths were already using or abusing some form of drug; therefore, to talk about "prevention" was a misnomer. However, since the federal funding agency focused on prevention, the staff were obligated to comply by educating about preventing the use of drugs.

INTRODUCTION

The preceding true story illustrates that, more often than not, social problems do not have a single cause or do not develop in isolation. In the case of Rock and Monique, direct-care staff appeared to be correct in stating that drug treatment for both was merely treating the symptom (drug habit) but not the cause(s) (e.g., school climate). Moreover, Monique needed a treatment program that specialized in drug rehabilitation for pregnant women. However, staff at the drug-treatment program were limited by their resources and expertise. Here is a good example of the inappropriate depletion of limited and sometimes scarce social and human resources. Effective social and human services delivery is contingent on good organizational infrastructure and management.

This chapter will begin with a review of how social welfare emerged in Western society and will be followed by a discussion of social welfare in this country. In particular, selected social and human services will be discussed, as well as affected groups.

HISTORICAL NOTES ABOUT SOCIAL WELFARE IN WESTERN SOCIETY

According to Handel (1982), **social welfare** is "a set of ideas and a set of activities and organizations for carrying those ideas, all of which have taken shape over many centuries, to provide people with income and other social benefits in ways that safeguard their dignity" (p. 31). Without sounding simplistic, this seemingly innocuous statement describes the complex nature of social welfare. Social welfare serves both ideological (e.g., political and religious) and practical (e.g., unable to provide for oneself) concerns. Some of the issues associated with these two broad categories of concern will be discussed.

Until modern times, the three major forms of social welfare were charity/philanthropy, public welfare, and mutual aid. **Charity/philanthropy** refers to social welfare in which a **donor** (giver) assists a **recipient** (taker). **Public welfare** is basically an extension of charity/philanthropy, in which the government assumes the responsibility for the poor.

Both charity/philanthropy and public welfare involve some form of religious ideologue (e.g., Christian love). They can be further understood from the perspectives of both the donor and the recipient. Specifically, to those who are in the position to assist the less fortunate, honor or salvation may be the driving force behind their generosity. On the other hand, the recipients must demonstrate their need (practical concern) for assistance (e.g., income or maintenance in the form of food). An indicator of need is the **standard of living** or economic means of subsistence of an individual. For example, people who are not able to adequately provide for themselves or their families or both are often considered in need of assistance. However, the notion of "needs" may be more elusive than people think. For instance, how does one classify people who live in poverty not because they cannot work but because they do not want to work? Also, notions of standards of living may vary. For example, everyone could live without televisions, but most don't want to. However, even many of the poorest people (likely to be recipients of some form of social welfare) in this country have televisions. In other words, does possessing a television mean that these people should not be entitled to social welfare?

Meanwhile, the processes inherent in charity/philanthropy and public welfare are likely to create social stigma. Handel (1982) argued that recipients of social welfare

> *are widely believed to be lazy and immoral....Although recipients must prove their need, their claims are often thought to be fraudulent....These people receive less social honor than other members of society. Such methods of providing income are therefore regarded as demeaning, as impairing the dignity of the people who depend upon them. (pp. 8–9)*

These statements are substantiated by laboratory (Worchel, Wong, & Scheltema, 1989) and field (Gergen, Morse, & Kristeller, 1973) research investigating the relationship between the donor and the recipient. For one, Gergen and associates (1973) found that although many developing countries welcome financial assistance from the United States, they complain that often the United States demands or mandates how the money should be spent. In other words, these countries perceived that the United States was infringing on their sovereignty.

Nadler and Fisher (1984) argued that "helping" creates differential status between the donor (e.g., feeling powerful) and the recipient (e.g., feeling a lack of control), which in turn threatens self-esteem. Furthermore, they concurred with Sherif, Harvey, White, Hood, and Sherif (1961) that cooperation or mutual aid is probably the more effective and equitable way to address social issues or prob-lems. In other words, to use the language of the field of community psychology, **empowerment** as part of the process of **mutual aid** is the preferred or perhaps the more effective tool for social ills such as poverty. Mutual aid is probably the precursor to today's **self-help groups,** or people who have similar problems and who help each other.

As noted earlier, the nature of social welfare is largely a function of the idealogy of the period. For example, research indicates that during religious seasons (e.g., Christmas and Easter), people are more likely to be charitable than nonreligious seasons. Furthermore, people who have been described as "poor" are considered to be more worthy of assistance than those who have been de-scribed as "welfare recipients" (Baron & Byrne, 1994). Although people might want to think of themselves as honorable and noble people, evidence suggests otherwise. In fact, these beliefs and perceptions (including the political climate) often shape how individuals think social and human services should be con-ducted and delivered.

Moving beyond these so-called traditional forms of social welfare, we turn next to two modern forms of social welfare: social insurance and social service. **Social insurance,** or public assistance, has its origin in the nineteenth century, around the time of the Industrial Revolution. Similar to public welfare, the basic premise of social insurance is that the government assumes responsibility for the poor. The funds for this derive from taxes. In other words, the *difference* between public welfare and social insurance (a consequence of the Industrial Revolution) is that "the recipients of social insurance are receiving benefits that have been earned by work, either their own, or work by someone else on their behalf" (Handel, 1982, p. 15), and recipients of public welfare do not contribute to this process. Some well-known programs of social insurance in this country include Assistance to Families with Dependent Children (AFDC), Food Stamps, Medicaid (for the poor), Medicare (for the elderly), Social Security (unemployment benefits or old-age pensions), and Veterans Benefits. Eligibility guidelines (e.g., poverty index as a function of household income) are established by the government, although they are often very cumbersome and lengthy.

Social services, or public charity (nonmaterialistic benefits that often overlap with social insurance), is an offshoot of charity/philanthropy. Derived from the nineteenth century or the Industrial Revolution, the government uses taxes to provide services. A major goal of social services is to ensure and maintain a productive workforce via prevention or intervention of social ills (Handel, 1982). Rock and Monique, the two teenagers in the opening vignette, were the recipients of social services from the child and family welfare agency and the substance-abuse agency in the state where they resided. It is hoped that these services can prevent (or intervene with) both youths from becoming more dependent on marijuana or other drugs without becoming a major burden to society in the years to come.

SOCIAL AND HUMAN SERVICES IN THE 1990s

Medicaid as an Intervention

It is beyond the scope of this book to cover the entire spectrum of social and human services (see Brown, 1988; Cottingham & Ellwood, 1989). Many U.S. presidents have difficulty passing their national budgets, including budgets for social programs. For example, in his first year of office, President Clinton had difficulty passing his budget of $496 billion. Vice President Al Gore had to cast the tie-breaking vote on a compromise budget despite the fact that Congress was dominated by fellow Democrats. Compromise budgets that result from political fighting often include spending cuts in some social and human services. Given that Medicaid is one of the most extensive and controversial public social welfare programs, it will be discussed here.

Before reviewing the advantages and disadvantages of Medicaid, we want briefly to review the concept of **poverty.** What is poverty? Does poverty merely mean the lack of (sufficient) money to acquire essential things in order to survive? Or does poverty mean being born and living in a ghetto or slum, which might lead to attending a school that is ill equipped (e.g., lack of funds to attract good teachers) and which might further lead to a vicious cycle for future generations? Probably, the latter notion is what President Lyndon B. Johnson had in mind when he made his 1964 State of Union address about the War on Poverty. Poverty can be a cause or an effect; it is multidimensional. Poverty is not just about lacking money; it is also about hopelessness, prejudice, and discrimination. For example, without a good education, one is likely to be discriminated against and unable to find a decent-paying job. Also, poorly educated people are less likely to be well-informed citizens compared to those who are educated, especially about their basic rights or entitlement. (This topic will be discussed later.) With these premises in mind, we are now ready to examine the effectiveness of Medicaid, one objective of which is to lift people from their misery so that they can move on to a better life.

Profile 7.1 introduces a pioneer in the study of poverty, Molly Orshansky, who first defined the poverty line. For a contemporary discussion of poverty levels see Shinn and Gillespie (1993).

Medicaid is one of the most extensive federal social welfare programs available to the poor. The benefits can include food stamps and medical care, among other things. It is estimated that one-quarter of all African Americans are enrolled in Medicaid (Darity & Myers, 1988). There is no single or simple answer to explain this figure. Suffice it to say that African Americans have long been suffering from political and social injustice. All things being equal, does Medicaid benefit those African Americans who are recipients? The answer depends on how one defines *benefit* and *success.*

◆ PROFILE 7.1
Mollie Orshansky

The **poverty line** (emphasis added) is a stock figure of American statistical and political culture. Most of us are at least dimly aware that it is an official level of income used to separate the poor from the non-poor, that the government somehow sets it, that it changes from time to time, and that it is the topic of periodic political fights. Even those who know its arcane details, however, usually forget that our official measure of poverty was once crafted by a real person with a passion and a pencil.

The person was Mollie Orshansky. In 1963, she published an article about poverty that set the U.S. government on a new path. "Children of the Poor" ran in the *Social Security Bulletin,* an otherwise rather dry publication of the Social Security Administration's Division of Research and Statistics. By the time the decade was over, Lyndon Johnson had included [Orshansky's] poverty estimates in his 1964 Economic Report of the President, the Office of Economic Opportunity had adopted her methods for determining eligibility to its programs, and the Bureau of the Budget had mandated the entire federal statistical establishment to use her definitions and methods in reporting poverty.

The story of Mollie Orshansky and poverty measurement is a case study in what makes political arithmetic persuasive. "I wanted to show what it was like not to have *enough* money....It's not just that the poor had less money—they didn't have enough. I knew you couldn't spend for one necessity without taking away from another."

Orshansky knew whereof she spoke. The child of Russian Jewish immigrants, she grew up in Brooklyn in the 1920s. Sometimes her father couldn't support his family of six daughters, even when he had work. Sometimes Molly went with her mother to apply for relief. ("If they gave you pork, you took it . . . you didn't want to seem ungrateful.") She learned easily to forgive the other women in line from her neighborhood who lowered their eyes and pretended not to see her and her mother.

The core of Orshansky's idea was to use the cost of a nutritionally adequate diet as the basis for a cost-of-living estimate and to calculate a cost of living for families of different sizes and composition. Because she had come to Social Security from the Bureau of Home Economics and Human Nutrition in the Department of Agriculture, Orshansky was eminently familiar with the Department's food plans. These plans set forth quantities of various food groups—meat, bread, potatoes, fats, fruits and vegetables, and so forth—necessary to sustain adults and children, and using current prices, found the cost of food necessary to feed families on these rations. The department calculated several levels of food plans, which were more or less generous but whose names were as opaque as canned-olive sizes: instead of jumbo, colossal, and extra-large, the Department of Agriculture called its food plans liberal, moderate, low-cost, and economy (in descending order), the latter renamed thrifty in 1975.

Orshansky developed 62 family types based on the number and ages of children, and for each she created a farm and non-farm version, making 124 categories. For each of these, she calculated a food budget based on the low-cost plan and one based on the economy plan, giving 248 categories in all. Here's where the pencil came in.

Food is not the only thing a family needs to live, but Orshansky chose it as the basis for her measure because there were relatively good studies of diets and their cost. She still needed a way to relate the cost of food to the cost of a family's total needs. A 1955 Department of Agriculture survey had shown that the average family spent one-third of its income on food. Orshansky assumed that families who must spend more than a third of their income on food were probably giving up other necessities—or food. She therefore made the elegant simplification of multiplying the cost of a family's necessary food basket by three, to arrive at an imputed total income that would put that family on the threshold of poverty.

For a non-farm family of two adults and two children, the low-cost food plan (multiplied by three) yielded an annual income of $3,995, enough to keep the family above poverty, and the economy plan yielded a figure of $3,165. Though Orshansky was dogged in creating 124 family types and income requirements, the media latched on to the archetypal family of four (minus cat or dog) as the magic number that would be called "the poverty line." In fact, the poverty line is the entire set of threshold incomes for different types of families.

Now that Orshansky had a way to measure poverty—to decide *whether* to count each household as poor—she needed a way to find out *how many* households were poor. For that, she needed to apply her definition to the whole population. With a $2,500 budget from the Social Security Administration, she went to the Census Bureau to get data on family and household income. The bureau had regularly calculated income for families of different sizes, but had never looked at income in relation to family composition: the number of children and adults and the ages of children, and the sex of the head of household. Orshansky used her $2,500 to buy these calculations, and when all was said and done, she concluded that somewhere between 17 million and 23 million children were poor.

"Children of the Poor" did for Washington bureaucracy what Michael Harrington's *The Other America* did for the broad reading public. Harrington had a journalist's flair for revealing the poverty Americans had ignored and for evoking empathy and outrage. Orshansky had the economist's capacity to give quasi-scientific backing to political will.

Preprints of "Children of the Poor" were circulated widely before publication and reached Sargent Shriver and others in the Office of Economic Opportunity (OEO). Legal advocates for the poor found inspiration in her measures as well. In 1964, the Justice Department called on her to help fight the poll tax; she fashioned the argument that even a $2 poll tax could deprive a poor family of a day's worth of food. In 1965, the OEO adopted her measures; in 1969, after a slight revision in the method of setting poverty thresholds, the Bureau of the Budget directed all federal agencies to use the Orshansky measures. In six years, her methods had become the indispensable tools of the poverty agencies and the standardized procedures of the statistical agencies.

Source: "Making the Poor Count" by D. A. Stone, 1994, *The American Prospect, 17,* pages 84–88. Reprinted with permission from *The American Prospect,* Spring 1994. © New Prospect Inc.

Financial Benefits

According to a study done by Darity and Myers (1987), poor people do have more money to spend (indicating a decrease in level of poverty) due to cash transfers as part of their Medicaid benefits. However, Whites (young and elderly) benefitted more than non-Whites. Darity and Myers found that Blacks received at least $4,000 to $5,000 less than Whites in assistance. These authors argued that this difference cannot be explained by the initially lower average levels of income for Whites.

You may recall from an earlier statement we made about how levels of education are correlated with being informed about one's basic rights and entitlement. You will soon learn in Chapter 8 that African Americans have a greater school dropout rate than Whites. If these African American school dropouts are illiterate or functionally illiterate, they are likely to have problems with filling out the Medicaid application form. In other words, when African Americans and other individuals cannot read, they are less likely to know what they are or are not entitled to. Winch, McCarthy, and Reese (1993) found that individuals who had more years of schooling were more likely to complete a welfare program than those who had not. Moreover, subsequent gainful employment was positively related to completion of the postsecondary training skills enrolled in the program. In other words, Medicaid or assistance is useful only if people know how to access it. Note that accessing public assistance is complicated by many factors of which only two are race and level of education.

SPECIFIC SOCIAL ISSUES AND SOCIAL SERVICES

Many groups access social and human services for a variety of reasons. To evaluate and judge the effectiveness or impact of these services, a consensus of standards is essential. According to Price, Cowen, Lorion, and Ramos-McKay (1988), model programs possess one or more of five characteristics:

1. These programs have a specific target audience.
2. The goal of these programs is to make a long-term and significant impact on the target groups, thus enhancing their well-being.
3. The programs provide the necessary skills for the recipients to achieve their objectives.
4. The programs strengthen the natural support from family, community, or school settings.
5. The programs have evaluative mechanisms to document their success.

Using these criteria as standards, we turn to four groups to examine the problems, the people, and approaches to addressing concerns within social and human services systems. We have selected these groups for several reasons. First, these groups are large or growing in number, such as the elderly and the homeless. Second, some of these groups are currently receiving much media attention, including maltreated children and pregnant teens. Third, all four groups have received significant attention in the field of community psychology.

Child Maltreatment

Causes of Maltreatment

It is estimated that over 2.2 million children a year are subject to maltreatment (American Association for Protecting Children, 1987). Abused children, as well as the abusers, are often the focus of intensive efforts from various social and human services specialists. Suspected cases of maltreatment are often investigated by the Department of Social Services. Abused children and their parents are often referred by judges and other professionals to mental health care providers for treatment. Children maltreatment can include physical and emotional abuse and neglect.

Besides the youthfulness of the parents, other predictors of abuse are prematurity of the infant, which is more probable in young mothers (Patteson & Barnard, 1990), past abuse of the parent when he or she was a child (Gil, 1979), and parental stress, including but not limited to low socioeconomic class (Rickel, 1989). Some studies have also linked certain parental personality traits to the tendency to maltreat. Egeland, Breitenbucher, and Rosenberg (1980), for example, found that parents who abused their children display higher levels of anxiety and defensiveness and that these parents had less understanding of the difficulties and demands of parenthood. In other words, these parents lack knowledge of appropriate child-rearing practices and skills (Rickel, 1989).

Research (Goleman, 1989) has demonstrated that some parents abuse because they, themselves, were abused as children, but they misconstrue and mislabel their own abuse as punishment. Besides sometimes becoming abusers later in their lives, maltreated children are considered to be at risk for serious residual problems, including emotional problems and social, intellectual, and motoric delays (Rickel, 1989).

Few studies, however, have shown that there is anything inherent in a child's behavior that triggers the abuse. Crittenden and Snell (1983) videotaped mother-infant dyads and found that maltreating interactions appeared to be set in motion by the mother and then maintained by the infant's behavior. However, the researchers also found that when the mother's behavior changed in a positive direction, the infant's behavior also improved.

Societal factors also contribute to child maltreatment. Poverty and economic hardship diminish the capacity for consistent and involved parenting (McLoyd, 1990). Paternal job loss in economic downturns, for example, can produce pessimism and irritability in the father. The father thus might become less nurturant and more punitive and arbitrary in his interactions with his children (McLoyd, 1989).

Community psychologists would be quick to point out that there are other ecological factors that contribute to child maltreatment. Garbarino (Garbarino & Kostelny, 1992) investigated community dimensions in child maltreatment. He examined two predominantly African American and two predominantly Hispanic areas of Chicago. Some 60,000 child maltreatment cases were plotted for location for the years 1980, 1983, and 1986. Garbarino found that there were significant location differences in maltreatment. As part of this same research, community leaders from social services agencies were also interviewed. The interviews revealed that high-risk locations were characterized by a lack of community identity, whereas low-risk areas were characterized by a sense of community or greater community cohesiveness. Garbarino concluded that abuse is not necessarily a sign of an individual or a family in trouble but rather a sign of a community in trouble.

Traditional efforts at intervention occur at the individual clinical level where maltreated children and their parents are given psychotherapy to help them overcome their personal problems and understand the abuse. Although these methods are laudable, they do little to prevent the abuse in the first place. This method of treatment is also difficult and expensive to implement on a wide scale. These methods focus only on the family and not on some systems that might also share responsibility.

Some people have argued that the best way to improve the caregiving system for abusers and their victims is through national policies aimed at creating jobs, reducing unemployment and other stressors, and income maintenance such as welfare or public assistance. Better and more realistic strategies, however, might be aimed at high-risk groups *before* the abuse commences (Olds, Henderson, Chamberlain, & Tatelbaum, 1986).

Several programs have been designed to do just that. For example, Minde, Shosenburg, and Marton (1982) developed a program to assist parents of premature infants in dealing with the stress of the premature birth. Mothers of low birth-weight infants attended peer-oriented self-help groups where parents had the opportunity to discuss their infants' prematurity. Following this intervention, positive results were tracked up to one year after the infants' hospital discharge. The mothers touched and talked to their infants more, felt more confident in caring for the infants, and allowed their infants greater freedom than the parents of premature infants not in this program.

Preventing Maltreatment

Perhaps one of the best known and highly acclaimed preventive programs is one designed by David Olds and his research team (Olds et al., 1986). Their project, known as the Prenatal/Early Infancy Project, provides nurse home visitation to prevent a wide range of maternal and child health problems associated with poverty, one of which is child abuse. One of the aspects of this program that makes it outstanding is that research was well designed; that is, randomly assigned experimental and control groups were used.

Primiparous mothers (women having their first child) who were less than 19 years old, of single-parent status, or who were from the lower socioeconomic class were welcomed into the study. The researchers wanted to avoid the appearance of being a program only for potential child abusers. By recruiting a heterogeneous group, the interventionists were better able to compare those who were not at risk for abuse with those who were at risk for abuse.

Nurses visited the homes during the prenatal (before birth) and the perinatal (after birth) periods every other week for 60 to 90 minutes. The mother's primary support person (perhaps her own mother, a friend, or the baby's father) was also invited to attend.

Social support from the nurses and significant others was a vital component of this program. Even when abuse has already occurred, social support is also important. Research (Goleman, 1989) has demonstrated that abused children who have someone they can turn to who is truly nurturing—a relative, teacher, minister, or friend—fare better than those children who have no or little social support.

The nurses carried out three major activities during their home visits: educating parents about fetal and infant development, promoting the involvement of family members and friends in support of the mother and care of the child, and developing linkages between family members and other formal health and human services in the community. In the education component, mothers and family members were encouraged to complete their own educations and to make decisions about employment and bearing additional children. Before birth, the nurses concentrated on educating the women to improve their diets and to eliminate the use of cigarettes, drugs, and alcohol; recognize pregnancy complications; and prepare the parents for labor, delivery, and care of the newborn. After the baby was born, the nurses concentrated on improving parents' understanding of the infants' temperaments and promoting the infants' socioemotional, cognitive, and physical development. The nurses also provided for the families to be linked to other formal services such as health providers, mental health counselors, nutritional supplement programs for mother and infants (Women, Infants, and Children [WIC] programs), as well as others.

One of the most important results of the program was on verified cases of child abuse and neglect. For women with all three risk characteristics (poor, unmarried, and adolescent) of abuse, there was a remarkable 75% reduction in the incident of verified cases of child abuse and neglect over the comparison group. The mothers in the nurse-visited group also reported that their infants were easier to care for. The interviewers of the mothers observed less punishment and restriction of the mothers toward their children and a greater number of growth-promoting playthings in the homes of the nurse-visited mothers. The medical records of the nurse-visited families showed there were fewer visits to emergency rooms for illnesses and childhood accidents. This was true even for the women who reported little sense of control over their lives when they first registered for the program. The results also hint at improved developmental life courses for the nurse-visited mothers as well. For example, once these mothers became older and more employable, they worked at their jobs more than their counterparts in the comparison group.

The causes of child maltreatment are many. Cases of abuse keep large numbers of social workers and mental health professionals busy with their aftermath. However, Old's work demonstrates that child abuse can be prevented. Expenditure of human and social services efforts at the outset may be more productive, less destructive, and more cost effective than efforts after the fact.

At present, psychologists also recognize that there are many children who are resistant to early childhood trauma. That is, they seem to be remarkably resilient children in that they adapt well to difficult life circumstances (Work, Cowen, Parker, & Wyman, 1990). Not all abused children suffer because of abuse and not all become abusers themselves (Goleman, 1986). The pathways by which these resilient children become hardy and the mechanisms by which they cope may teach society some valuable lessons in the future about dealing with abuse when it occurs.

Teen Pregnancy

Extent of the Problem

A possible consequence of teen pregnancy can be child abuse. In fact, one of the most pressing problems in society is how to enhance adolescent mothers' parenting skills so has to have a positive impact on the development of their children (Rickel, 1989). The United States has the highest teenage pregnancy rate (especially among African Americans) compared to other industrialized countries (Lawson & Rhode, 1993). Some critics argue that the social welfare system in this country may, in fact, be responsible for these pregnancies. That is, they believe that Assistance to Families with Dependent Children (another Medicaid benefit) as a source of income support actually promotes teen pregnancy and the growth of female-headed households. However, this assumption is not supported by research. Other industrialized countries, such as Sweden and the United Kingdom, that have more comprehensive welfare programs than the United States have lower teenage pregnancy rates (Kotch, Blakely, Brown, & Wong, 1992). Similarly, Darity and Myers (1988) stated,

> *Statistical inquiry does not indicate that the teens' decisions about childbearing are a response to the amounts [of money] made available. Their [teenagers'] decisions are not primarily pecuniary in character, anyway; the decisions are primarily affectional. The existence of welfare may facilitate black teen motherhood and increased female-headship, but it is not the fundamental cause. In fact, the decade of the 1970s was one in which the real value of AFDC and food stamps fell while black female-headship grew at an accelerating pace. (p. 285)*

Therefore, Medicaid does not cause young women to become or want to become pregnant.

In terms of absolute numbers of pregnancies, the concern that teen pregnancy is a an African American problem may in fact be misplaced. African American teenage pregnancies do not represent the majority of teen pregnancies. Although it is true that in the United States the rate of African American adolescent childbirth is significantly greater than the rate of Whites, in absolute numbers the incidence of White adolescent childbirth is much greater than that of African American adolescents (Meyer, 1991). In her article on teen pregnancy, Meyer chided researchers and the media for misplacing public opinion about teen pregnancy. Not only did Meyer feel that teen pregnancy is not just an African American issue, neither is it solely a female issue. She said that males, especially White males, are invisible in the research and intervention strategies in the literature.

Besides focusing mainly on females, mainstream psychological literature on adolescent pregnancy focuses on the individual and individual deficients. Reasons often cited for teen pregnancy include lack of self-esteem (Foster, Greene, & Smith, 1990), low expectancies (Scales, 1990), and psychopathology (Reppucci, 1987). Thus, the typical solution offered for lowering the pregnancy rate is counseling (Hofferth, 1991). Another usual approach to preventing adolescent pregnancy is sex education (Fielding & Williams, 1991). However, no one really knows the true effects of sex education (Reppucci, 1987). Other efforts involve assertiveness training ("Just Say No"), but these efforts often seem futile and misguided (Scales, 1987).

The overly rationalistic perspective that prevention efforts simply need to expose adolescents to more information or provide them with contraceptives is too narrow (Reppucci, 1987) and often disappointing. For example, Zabin and colleagues (1986) offered inner-city adolescent girls sex education as well as an in-school clinic at which contraceptives were available. These researchers found that in senior high school, 72.3% of the girls and 91% of the boys were sexually active. Before the program, 26% of the girls and 37% of the boys did not use contraceptives. The program seemed somewhat to have reduced unprotected intercourse: 18.1% of the girls and 32.2% of the boys reported not using contraception. Although these data show decreases, you must remember that the data indicate that large numbers of adolescents continued to have sexual experiences that were likely to result in pregnancy or abortion.

Many similar prevention programs for adolescent pregnancy have been disappointing. As Reppucci (1987) reiterated, "The limited effects of these changes are evident in the concomitant high rates of pregnancy, clinic dropouts, and contraceptive nonuse" (p. 7).

Preventive Programs

What is perhaps needed is less focus on the individual level of analysis (Patterson, 1990) and more focus on an ecological or transactional approach to teen pregnancy (Allen-Meares & Shore, 1986). The ecological approach suggests that there are ways of enhancing already existing environmental resources (such as the teens' parents) that might be effective (Reppucci, 1987). The ecological approach takes into account the environment surrounding the adolescent who is sexually active or about to be sexually active. However, the ecological perspective is complicated. It is complex because the adolescent may be confronted by differing viewpoints on sexuality by peers, family members, and the community. For example, up to three generations of family members may influence a teen's sexual decisions (Johnson, Lay, & Wilbrandt, 1988). Furthermore, the media to which the adolescent is exposed flagrantly exploits sexuality yet prohibits contraceptives from being advertised (Reppucci, 1987).

Finally, the issue of the status of women in the United States needs to be addressed. Early motherhood may be an attractive alternative to low-paying, dead-end jobs available to adolescent women (Lawson & Rhode, 1993).

One successful prevention program for teen pregnancy and school dropout is reported by Allen, Philliber, and Hoggson (1990). They attempted to assess which groups of participants and under what conditions a school-based prevention program was most effective. The program was the Teen Outreach Program of the Association of Junior Leagues. It used a curriculum that provided information on human development, information on skills for making life-option decisions, and supportive group decisions. The program also emphasized volunteer service to the community. The 632 participants in the program varied in terms of age, race, parents' educational level, and other factors. In other words, the study was not focused just on inner-city, African American youths. Program participants were compared to 855 similar others who did not participate. Results indicated that the Teen Outreach participants had lower levels of suspension, school dropout, and pregnancy. Moreover, the program worked best overall for older students *and* when the volunteer experience was emphasized. For younger students, the program worked best when the classroom component was intense. This study showed that there was no one best way to prevent school dropout, teen pregnancy, and other problems.

Secondary Prevention: Working with Pregnant Teens

Because many prevention programs have failed, teenage pregnancy rates are still high. As mentioned earlier, the United States leads nearly all industrialized countries in teenage pregnancy, abortion, and childbearing. More than one million teens become pregnant each year, and half of them give birth. This means that approximately 1 in 10 teenagers will become a mother by her nineteenth birthday (Turner & Robinson, 1993). Data also indicate that there is a trend for teens to become pregnant at younger ages (Thomas, Rickel, Butler, & Montgomery, 1990). There is a consensus that these high rates are a major concern for society (Meyer, 1991).

For these teens, primary prevention is too late. Programs are needed that will encourage them to continue their education and give them parenting skills. Seitz, Apfel, and Rosenbaum (1991) reported a successful school-based intervention program with inner-city African American, low-income school-aged mothers. The young mothers-to-be were placed in the Polly T. McCabe Center, a separate school for pregnant teens, yet fully a part of the New Haven (Connecticut) School System. The program was comprised of health care, education, and social services. Specifically, the program consisted of small academic classes augmented with counseling and prenatal health care services, as well as special classes to prepare the girls for parenthood. The parents of the pregnant girls were also invited to be involved in school events.

The primary concern of the researchers was what effect the program had on academic achievement, especially for those girls who had been poor students before becoming pregnant. Overall, 51% of the girls at two years postpartum were academically successful. What was most striking was that students who had never received grades as high as Cs were now successful. In fact, the poorer students became indistinguishable from the better students in terms of academic success. The results confirm that adolescents who appear to have minimal academic promise prior to their pregnancies are nevertheless very responsive to school-based intervention.

The Elderly

The population of the United States is aging. As the swell of baby boomers moves through time, the ranks of the aged are increasing. Medical advances allow people to live longer, with most women outliving men. By the year 2030, 20% of the population is expected to be over age 65 (Eisdorfer, 1983). Society needs to think carefully about programs and interventions with the elderly so that plans of action will be in place when needed as the population continues to age.

The stereotype of the elderly in the United States is that of a wrinkled, incoherent person rocking in a chair in a nursing home. Obviously, this stereotype is incorrect; only 4 to 5% of the elderly are institutionalized (Palmore, 1976). Most, in fact, live in their own homes and die in their homes rather than in intensive care in hospitals (Booth, 1991) or in nursing homes.

This is not to say that the aging population is not without problems, however. For example, two frequent and particularly impactful transitions of aging are loss of health and loss of spouse (Finch, Okun, Barrera, Zautra, & Reich, 1989). Loss of spouse and significant others in an elderly person's life can cause depression and stress (Siegel & Kuykendall, 1990). In addition, declining health is exacerbated by perceived lack of control over health matters, by personal barriers such as memory deficients, and by societal barriers such as lack of transportation and high cost of health care (Chipperfield, 1993). Families of the elderly who provide caregiving can also find themselves under stress and in declining health (Worcester, 1990), especially employed family members (Montgomery, Gonyea, & Hooyman, 1985).

The ecological situation in which the elderly find themselves also has a bearing on them. For example, married elderly are more likely to report wanting an energetic lifestyle (Rapkin & Fischer, 1992). A second environmental factor involves the actual setting in which the elderly find themselves; some are relocated in terms of their living arrangements. Many elderly who have to relocate often use various strategies such as reminiscence to preserve their sense of self despite their new surroundings.

Social Support

A myriad of programs exist for the elderly that focus on enhancing the quality of their lives. Only a few are mentioned here. One well-examined approach to preserving the emotional well-being and sense of security of the elderly is to provide them with social support. Social support by means of informal networks of family (Tice, 1991), confidants (Lowenthal & Haven, 1968), or other social supports (Abrahams & Patterson, 1978–1979) has been reputed to increase morale and buffer the effects of loss of loved ones.

In a well-scrutinized study, Heller, Thompson, Trueba, Hogg, and Vlachos-Weber, (1991) set up telephone dyads first among professional staff people and an elderly phone companion and then between pairs of elderly. Interestingly, there were no significant differences in well-being between the phone dyads and a no-contact group. There are several explanations as to why this was so.

One postulated reason was that the lonely elderly in this study did not see their phone companions as *reliable* sources of social support. In other words, the phone companion was not deemed as necessarily being available in a time of need (Willis, 1991) nor as an enduring source of support (Schiaffino, 1991). Another reason could have been that this was too new a relationship for the phone companion to be a true confidant (Vaux, 1991). Heller and associates also used random assignment—a strange mechanism by which to find a "friend"; similarly, the phone is a peculiar context in which to make a *good* friend (Vaux, 1991). Given some of these criticisms, perhaps phone dyads with family members would have been more successful (Roak, 1991). Social support, therefore, does not offer a panacea for the loneliness and isolation that some elderly experience.

Enhancing the self-esteem of the elderly has been another approach in the literature. A favored approach is to encourage the elderly to feel productive. Various projects (Becker & Zarit, 1978; Blonsky, 1973; Priddy & Knisely, 1982; Ruffini & Todd, 1979) employing senior citizens as voluntary helpers, senior companions, or peer counselors report positive effects. However, most of these intervention studies used either uncontrolled demonstration projects or preselected participants who are likely to be more motivated or of higher economic and educational backgrounds than the typical senior citizen (Heller et al., 1991).

Sense of Personal Control

Every facet of aging, such as health and cognitive functioning, involves the issue of personal control (Baltes & Baltes, 1986). Increasing the **sense of personal control** of the elderly is also a technique that has proven to produce positive results (Thompson & Spacespan, 1991), such as better mental health (Reich & Zautra, 1991). An enhanced sense of control leads to feelings of empowerment, a coveted principle of community psychology.

Langer and Rodin (1976) matched two groups of elderly in a nursing home on age, health, and other important considerations. One group was shown in detail how much control they had over their lives. They decided how to arrange their rooms, when to greet visitors, and how to spend spare time. Each of these residents was also given a plant to care for. The second group was told that their lives were mainly under staff control. For example, these elderly were also given a plant but were told the staff would take of it. Pre- and postintervention questionnaires about feelings of personal control, happiness, and activity were administered to the elderly and also completed by the staff about the elderly participants.

Almost all before-after comparisons favored the intervention group—the one with higher perceived control. Eighteen months later, Rodin and Langer (1977) conducted a follow-up. Half as many experimental participants had died as had control participants. This study demonstrates that the quality of life for the elderly can indeed be enhanced when they perceive they have control over it. The control the elderly had over their environment is reminiscent of Fairweather's Lodge Societies discussed in the previous chapter.

Finally, health education has the potential to have sweeping preventive effects on future generations as they age.

> *If it were possible to help our citizens more thoughtfully direct the course of their lives, prepare in advance for retirement, maintain appropriate health habits, develop satisfying avocational interests, and maintain a healthy self-esteem, the despair of millions of Americans could be drastically reduced. (Lombana, 1976, p. 144)*

Homelessness

We introduced you to the topic of homelessness in Chapter 1 when discussing the concept of *blaming the victim*. Very often, when people see homeless individuals on the street, they believe that these individuals caused their own problems. For example, many stereotype the homeless as drunk or mentally disabled old men who deserve what they get—a life of misery on the streets. Marybeth Shinn's research, which was reviewed in Chapter 1, clearly demonstrates that many of today's homeless are victims of problems they, themselves, did *not* create, such as lack of affordable housing. We will examine the issue of homelessness further here because the homeless often interface with a variety of social and human services systems.

Extent of the Problem

The extent of the problem of homelessness is difficult to determine. The main reason for this difficulty is that the homeless are a heterogeneous group; they include a variety of types of people (Breakey & Fischer, 1990). Estimates for the number of homeless in the United States range from 200,000 (Bobo, 1984) from the Department of Housing and Urban Development to 3,000,000 from an advocacy group for the homeless, the National Coalition for the Homeless (1988). The reasons the estimates vary relate to the motives of the groups doing the estimating. Dowell and Farmer (1992) contended that because the image of homelessness in a community is not good for business, government officials often underestimate or minimize the problem. Varying estimates of the homeless population can cause policy gridlock, too. If some people view the problem as small, then they will also view the problem as not necessitating immediate nor extensive attention. However, others might urgently press for sweeping solutions.

Who are today's homeless? The answer to this question varies, depending on which study one examines. Morse, Calsyn, and Burger (1992) found four types of homeless individuals: an economically disadvantaged group, an alcoholic group, a mentally disordered group (perhaps the deinstitutionalized individuals described in the preceding chapter), and a somewhat advantaged group who none-theless remain homeless. Mowbray, Bybee, and Cohen (1993) also found four clusters of homeless whom they call the depressed group, the substance abusers, the hostile-psychotics (perhaps approximating the mentally disordered group above), and the best-functioning group (perhaps approximating the advantaged group above).

Rossi (1990) has devised yet another way of classifying the homeless. He suggested that there are old homeless and new homeless. The **old homeless** are the individuals who are generally stereotyped as homeless. These are older, alcoholic men who sleep in cheap flophouses or skid-row hotels. They are "old" because they are the type of homeless who were seen on city streets after World War II. The **new homeless** are indeed truly homeless. They do not sleep in cheap hotels but rather sleep on the streets or find public buildings to escape into during inclement weather.

The new homeless also include many more women and children. Rossi (1990) estimated that among the old homeless, women made up fewer than 5% of that population; today, women comprise 25% of the homeless population. Likewise, there are age differences between the new and old homeless, with the new homeless being much younger. Indeed, the National Coalition for the Homeless (1988) estimated that there are as many as 750,000 homeless children. In general, fewer elderly homeless are seen on the streets today. Rossi also suggested that today's homeless suffer a much more profound degree of economic destitution than the old homeless. Many of them survive on 40% *or less* of a poverty-level income. Rossi's (Rossi, Fisher, & Willis, 1986) own research demonstrated that the median annual income of the homeless in Chicago was $1,198, or less than $3 a day. One final difference between the old homeless and the new homeless is that the ethnic and racial composition has changed over the years. Today's homeless are more likely to be from minority groups rather than White, as was true of the old homeless.

Homeless children suffer a number of compounding problems, largely due to their homelessness. Studies have consistently shown that homeless children have elevated levels of acute and chronic health problems compared to housed children (Wright, 1987), as well as poorer nutrition (Molnar, Rath, & Klein, 1990). Homeless children are also more likely to experience developmental delays such as short attention spans, speech delays, inappropriate social interactions (Molnar, 1988), and psychological problems in the areas of anxiety, behavioral problems, and depression (Bassuk & Rosenberg, 1988). Also, achievement scores on stan-dardized tests for homeless children are well below those of housed children (Rafferty, 1990). These children often move from school to school when they are lucky enough to be enrolled in school.

Causes of Homelessness

Studies show that homelessness is episodic, or at least is not a chronic condition for most individuals (Sosin, Piliavin, & Westerfelt, 1990); thus, environmental situations may account for much homelessness. For instance, the rate of psychiatric hospitalization for today's homeless is as low as 4% when the whole family is homeless (Shinn & Weitzman, 1990; Weitzman, Knickman, & Shinn, 1990). As for the homeless mentally ill, a lack of housing is more critical to the likelihood of their rehospitalization than is the quality of their psychiatric care (Rosenfeld, 1991). Unemployment is probably not a major consideration either. Koegel, Burnam, and Farr (1990) found that 33% of the homeless had been employed within the last month, and 59% had been employed in the last six months. Person-centered approaches such as mental disorders and unemployment are not particularly useful for explaining homelessness regardless of how popular these explanations are in the mass media.

Shinn (1992) conducted research to expand the understanding of whether structural or person-centered variables explain homelessness. In her study, a sample of 700 randomly selected homeless families requesting shelter were compared to 524 families selected randomly from the public assistance caseload. The first group represented "the homeless" and the second "the housed poor." Only 4%—a small percentage—of the homeless in the sample had been previously hospitalized for mental illness. Only 8% of the homeless and 2% of the housed poor had been in a detoxification center for substance abuse. The researcher concluded that individual deficits were relatively unimportant in differentiating the homeless from the housed poor. Corroborating this finding, Morse and colleagues (1992) identified various subgroups of homeless, including an economically disadvantaged group, an alcoholic group, a mentally disabled group, and a somewhat advantaged group of homeless. They searched for differences between these four groups and found few. They concluded that many policies and services should cut across these subgroups because many of their needs are the same.

To return to Shinn's (1992) research, she found that only 37% of the homeless, compared to 86% of the poor housed families, had broken into the housing market (i.e., had been primary tenants in a place they stayed a long time). In addition, 45% of the homeless versus 26% of the housed poor reported having three or more persons per bedroom in the place they had stayed the longest. The researcher regards poor housing opportunities and crowding to be better explanations for homelessness than personal deficits.

No social problem in the United States seems to originate from a single cause. Beyond the scarcity of low-income housing and the deinstitutionalization of the mentally disabled, what else makes some families more vulnerable than others to this crisis? Weitzman and associates (1990) studied the same families as those included in Shinn (1992) and who were new entrants to homelessness during a six-month period. These researchers compared the newly homeless who were receiving public assistance with another group of individuals who had housing but were also receiving public assistance. These families were interviewed about their housing histories, social support networks, welfare and work experiences, and physical and mental health. The results indicated that homeless families do not comprise a homogeneous population; instead, there are three distinct pathways to the door of the homeless shelter.

One group of families had relatively stable housing situations but something had gone awry; for example, they had recently been evicted from housing. These families made a rapid descent into homelessness. Weitzman and colleagues suggested eviction-prevention programs and more realistic public assistance allowances to assist these families.

Other families had a slow, painful slide into homelessness. These families had typically resided with others, moved around, and experienced some of the same problems (e.g., evictions, landlord harassment, and crowding) as the families whose descent to homelessness was more rapid. However, some of these families were experiencing multiple problems such as substance abuse and domestic violence. Weitzman and colleagues recommended some counseling programs for these homeless as well as a more adequate housing supply.

A third large group of families had never had the benefit of a primary residence. For these young families, doubling up with others in an overcrowded housing situation had been an ongoing way of life. This group contained a large number of young mothers whose own parents had themselves received public assistance. These women had few resources beyond public assistance and their own families. However, the women and their small families had never really become stable, independent, or self-reliant units. These individuals lack the search skills to cope with the dramatic scarcity of low-income housing units. Giving them priority in receiving permanent housing was a suggestion of Weitzman and associates. The researchers further suggested providing these families with day care and job training.

Providing job skills and job-relevant knowledge (e.g., the importance of meeting deadlines and respecting lines of authority) to those who want them can and does result in employment opportunities (Winch, McCarthy, & Reese, 1993). Wenzel (1992), however, conducted research that demonstrates that job training and employment alone do not "cure" homelessness. She found that for persons with low levels of social support and prolonged homelessness, poor employment outcomes resulted. The combined results of all of these studies imply that multiple solutions are most appropriate; simply providing adequate and affordable housing is not the only answer to homelessness (Sosin, Piliavin, & Westerfelt, 1990).

Other Solutions to the Homelessness Problem

Some of the suggestions for addressing homelessness reviewed here included increasing the amount of affordable housing, job training, and counseling. Given that these approaches take much time and money, what else is available to address homelessness?

The ultimate solutions to homelessness do not lie in the provision of temporary shelter. However, perhaps in the short run, society can improve the shelters or at least understand which shelters offer the best quality of life. Shinn, Knickman, Ward, Petrovi, and Muth (1990) examined various types of shelters for the homeless in New York City. In New York, shelters consist of "welfare hotels" (private hotels where the city rents rooms), congregate shelters (large barrack-type rooms), and shelters run by nonprofit organizations (such as churches). How was shelter quality judged in this study? The researchers determined that, first, shelters should not be expensive (i.e., they should not divert needed money from the development or construction of permanent housing). Second, shelters should provide services to help the homeless manage the trauma of homelessness and prepare to resume a normal life. Third, shelters should promote normative behavior by creating culturally normative conditions such that the shelters look like and feel like homes. Shelters should help residents preserve their dignity. In other words, they should not be filthy, regimented, and promote invasion of privacy. Shinn and colleagues found that the nonprofit organizations were doing an admirable job of enhancing the life of the homeless and that the city should continue to phase out the congregate and welfare hotel shelters.

Another solution to homelessness has been the American Psychological Association's (APA) *pro bono* program for the homeless that is being piloted in the Washington, DC, area. There are two objectives to this program. The APA wanted to provide psychologists with the opportunity to volunteer their services and the APA wanted to provide psychologists and other professionals with a *pro bono* or volunteer service delivery model.

Shelter staff in the Washington, DC, area were contacted to determine whether they perceived a need for psychological services. Of course, they did. Volunteers were recruited to serve as consultants in the development of the project, to assist in screening processes with the homeless, and to provide peer consultation to other volunteers. The APA also developed an orientation program for the volunteer psychologists, who provide life skills training, assessment of the mental health problems of the homeless, and psychotherapy to those who need it.

The best solution to the homeless problem in the United States, though, may be a concerted and organized federal public policy program. Charities and local governments alone cannot meet the growing needs of the homeless (Gore, 1990). One piece of legislation aimed at grappling with the homeless problem on a national level is the McKinney Act. It established an Interagency Council on Homelessness to coordinate, monitor, and improve the federal response to the problems of homelessness—in other words, to reduce duplication of effort. The act also established an Emergency Food Shelter Program National Board as well as local boards across the country to determine how program funds could best be used. Grants and demonstration programs—for example, for drug and alcohol-abuse treatment—were authorized by the act, and the Temporary Emergency Food Assistance Program was reauthorized by the act (Barak, 1991). A coherent policy of federal legislation needs to continue to pursue increased low-income housing, treatments for the mentally disabled and substance-abusing homeless, and education and job training for homeless individuals (Gore, 1990).

Case in Point 7.1 introduces research and model programs aimed at reducing unemployment (and related stress) and therefore at reducing poverty.

❖ *CASE IN POINT 7.1*

Community Psychology and Unemployment

Hard economic times bring unemployment and various strains and stresses. Unemployment affects nearly 10 million people in the United States every year (U.S. Bureau of Labor Statistics, 1992). The negative effects of unemployment are well documented and include anxiety, depression, and physical illness; in fact, the experience of unemployment has been documented to be severe enough so as to warrant intervention by a professional (Kessler, Turner, & House, 1988). Much of the distress is traceable directly or indirectly to financial hardship (Aubrey, Tefft, & Kingsbury, 1990; Broman, Hamilton, & Hoffman, 1990). The negative impact is not just on the unemployed individual. The families (Broman et al., 1990), and in particular the development of the children in those families (Liem & Liem, 1988), are adversely affected.

Traditional interventions for the unemployed focus on treating the individual by teaching stress reduction (Kessler, Turner, & House, 1989) or by providing a job counselor armed with information about job openings and who assumes responsibility for the unemployed client's job placement (Gray & Braddy, 1988). Community psychologists would offer other alternatives. First, community psychologists would empower individuals to participate in client-centered job-seeking programs such as job clubs. **Job clubs** are self-help groups where job-search skills are shared and participants are encouraged to set job-seeking goals each week (Gray & Braddy, 1988).

Community psychologists would also focus on strengths and competencies of the unemployed rather than on their weaknesses. Following this line of thought, Turner, Kessler, and House (1991) wanted to identify the kinds of resources people use to cope with unemployment and the points in the stress process at which each resource exerts a positive influence. They wanted to assess both personal (e.g., self-esteem) and social (e.g., a supportive social network) resources. The participants they interviewed were selected from census tracts in Michigan where there were high unemployment rates due to a recession that created plummeting car sales.

Turner and colleagues found that both personal and social resources can modify the effects of employment. More specifically, the researchers reported that integrating into a social network or having a confidant—someone to confide in—buffers the impact of financial strain on both physical health and emotional well-being. The researchers found that self-esteem is important, too. Self-esteem, or a feeling of self-worth, increases resistance to other stressors that might occur during unemployment. Self-esteem also motivates a person to seek reemployment, which has been shown in previous research to enhance well-being to the same level (or higher) found during prior employment. The researchers also admonished others to bear in mind that because reemployment is difficult in a poor economy, the unemployed need to be realistic—that is, flexible in their job searches.

Turner, Kessler, and House's research suggests that the unemployed need not suffer from as much stress as research suggests they do. Their research also has ramifications for intervention, particular in making available a supportive network on which the unemployed can draw in times of stress.

Other scientists have developed alternative interventions for the unemployed. Caplan, Vinokur, Price, and van Ryn (1989) in a randomized field experiment followed over 900 unemployed individuals who either attended workshops on job seeking or who simply received a self-help pamphlet on job seeking. Not surprisingly, those who found employment were less anxious and depressed than those who remained unemployed. Those who attended the workshops found better jobs and higher job satisfaction than those who received only the pamphlets. Similarly, the workshop participants who did not find reemployment were more motivated to keep looking than those who received only the pamphlet.

More recently, van Ryne and Vinokur (1992) discovered an important mechanism that underlies job-search behavior as provided for in such workshops. In other words, the researchers examined *how* programs on job-search training prompt the unemployed to seek work. van Ryne and Vinokur found that self-efficacy seems initially to be responsible for job seeking in the unemployed who have been through job-search skills programs. **Self-efficacy** is the belief that one can successfully execute a behavior or course of action under possibly stressful or novel circumstances (Bandura, 1977, 1986). Self-efficacy generally affects the likelihood of initiating a behavior, persistence at the behavior, and quality of performance of the behavior. van Ryne and Vinokur found that immediately after the job-search skills programs, self-efficacy directly and indirectly affected the participants' intentions to search for a job, actual job-seeking behaviors, and attitudes toward seeking a job (such as how hard it would be to find employment). Studies such as these indicate that interventions with the unemployed can be successful in abating the pain and poverty of unemployment. Research in this area continues.

SUMMARY

Social welfare or ideas and activities to promote social good have a long history in Western society. Until modern times, the three major forms of social welfare were charity/philanthropy (private assistance), public welfare (public assistance), and mutual aid (self-help). During the nineteenth century (around the time of the Industrial Revolution), two other forms of social welfare were born: social insurance (public assistance derived from taxation) and social service (public nonmaterialistic human services derived from taxation). With the exception of mutual aid, in order to receive social welfare, people must demonstrate their need, usually in the form of a low standard of living or poor economic means.

It is generally believed (i.e., stereotyped) that recipients of social welfare are lazy, despite the fact that these people might genuinely need such assistance. On the other hand, donors are perceived to be honorable people, although research indicates that willingness to help often is a function of environmental factors (e.g., people are more generous during religious seasons). These scenarios suggest that the nature of social welfare is largely a function of the idealogy of the period. Social welfare in this country is no exception to the rule.

Four groups that interface regularly with human services in U.S. communities are maltreated children and their families, pregnant teens, the elderly, and the homeless.

Teen parents and others—such as people who themselves were abused children—are predicted to be at risk for committing child abuse. Providing social support, parenting and prenatal education, and links between the parents and services in the community can sometimes prevent child abuse.

The problem of pregnant adolescents is a major one; the United States leads other countries in this statistic. Many Americans, however, view this as an African American problem as well as a female problem. It is not. Programs to reach teenagers before they become sexually active include sex education. The prevailing culture does not provide good role models, however; thus, the problem persists. Community programs to provide teen parents with further education, job training, and day care can better ensure that they will not be stuck in the welfare quagmire.

The elderly sometimes interface with services in the community, too. Declining health, loss of mobility, death of loved ones, and loss of control are problems for the elderly. As is true with other groups, not all community interventions are effective. However, encouraging the elderly to volunteer as companions or peer counselors and increasing their sense of control and personal responsibility can maintain the self-esteem of the elderly and perhaps maintain their health for longer periods.

Homelessness is an increasing problem in the United States. Stereotypically, the homeless are drunk or mentally disabled old men. The new homeless, however, include many children and women, as well as previously employed and previously housed individuals. Providing more affordable housing, *pro bono* services from professionals, and better and coordinated public policies will go a long way toward solving this problem.

What has been learned from the examination of abused children, pregnant teens, the elderly, and the homeless? For one, not all interventions work equally well and no single intervention works for all groups. Not all interventions require professional help, however. Many social support and mutual help groups are organized and run by laypeople and often are free and effective. Finally, interventions need to be multifaceted; that is, they must address multiple issues and utilize multiple approaches. For example, when professionals are involved, their efforts should be combined with peer or family efforts as well as take into account ecological factors. Efforts also need to be well coordinated so as to avoid duplication or "cracks" in the system.

8

SCHOOLS, CHILDREN, AND COMMUNITIES

Mi nombre es Roberto. Nací en Mexico y me mude a los Estados Unidos cuando era un niño. En mi casa, solamente se hablaba español. Un día, cuando estaba en el séptimo grado, mi maestra me pidió que leyera en frente de la clase. Yo trate de leer, pero no pude reconocer algunas de las palabras en inglés. La maestra me interrumpió y me dijo que yo no sabía leer muy bien y que debía sentarome. Después, ella llamó a un niño americano, quien leía mejor que yo. Yo me senti bastante avergonzado.

How many of you could read this passage? Imagine how frustrating text-books, television programs, and public announcements are to individuals for whom English is a second or third language. We will restart, this time in English.

My name is Roberto. I was born in Mexico and I moved to the United States when I was a child. In my house, only Spanish was spoken. One day, when I was in the second grade, my teacher asked that I read in front of the class. I tried to read, but I was not able to recognize some of the English words. The teacher interrupted me and told me that I did not know how to read very well and to sit down. After, she called on an American child who read better than I. I was quite embarrassed.

I had to repeat the second grade but this time with a different teacher, Miss Martinez. She had experienced much the same embarrassment when she was a child, so she was sympathetic to my situation. Her extra help inspired me to do my best. In no time, I was speaking and reading English well, almost as well as my classmates. By high school, I was a very good student. My good grades and my ability to play soccer well had endeared to my fellow classmates enough so that they liked me. Unlike some of the other Hipsanic students, I was quite popular, which made my life easier than theirs.

Today, I am in college; I am studying to be a lawyer. Actually, I don't want to be a lawyer; I want to be a legislator. I view law as the avenue to a political career. One of my goals as a legislator is to reform American schools so that all children will feel welcome and comfortable in them.

INTRODUCTION

Consider for a moment how it feels to be a child whom others view as different, either because of a different skin color, a foreign-sounding name, an accent or language other than English, or the use of a wheelchair. This chapter will explore the world of schools as they relate to children and families. The schools, themselves, are small communities as well as integral parts of the communities they serve. We cannot possibly cover all issues here, but we will touch on some of the more salient ones: child care, diversity in the classroom, and stressful events such as parental divorce. It is in the domain of education that social scientists and policy makers have perhaps created the most changes and thus had the most impact in the last few decades (Sarason & Klaber, 1985).

THE EARLY CHILDHOOD ENVIRONMENT

In 1979, Urie Bronfenbrenner presented what he considered an unorthodox approach to child development. Bronfenbrenner formulated the ecological perspective of human development. **Development**, to Bronfenbrenner and other psychologists, usually means "a lasting change in the way in which the individual perceives and deals with the environment" (p. 3). The **ecological setting** refers to a set of nested structures, or settings, one inside the other. At the innermost level is the immediate setting in which the individual finds himself or herself, such as the home or a classroom. The next layer consists of the interrelationship between these settings, as in the links between the child's home and the school. The third level, interestingly, is the environment that the child or individual is not in but that has an effect anyway, such as the policies of the parents' place of employment that have an impact on the child (e.g., day care). All levels are interconnected rather than independent of one another. The way the individual transacts with these settings and how the individual perceives them is important in influencing the course of the individual's development. As you may already know, the ecological perspective and the transactional nature of the individual's encounters with various elements in the environment is of utmost importance in community psychology.

A concrete example might further your understanding. Suppose Johnnie is having trouble focusing his attention on his studies in the third grade. Using the individual level of analysis, his teacher might believe that Johnnie needs extra tutoring and additional assistance with his math and spelling or that Johnnie needs medication for his attention-deficit disorder. An ecological perspective would take into account other contexts, such as Johnnie's home and neighborhood or even the playground at the school. The reality might be that Johnnie's home life is distressing because his parents are divorcing. Furthermore, his father might be unemployed, which is contributing to his parents' discord and Johnnie's inattention. Perhaps what would most assist Johnnie is some social support from other children whose parents' have divorced, not extra tutoring from the teacher.

As Bronfenbrenner suggests, then, advances in understanding development require its investigation in the actual environments, both immediate and remote, in which human beings live. This chapter will examine settings in which children develop, especially educational ones such as day-care centers and schools. Although some of the topics presented will be discrete for the sake of parsimony, it is important to remember that children do not enter each situation in a vacuum; they bring connections and experiences from a myriad of other contexts as well, regardless of their stage of development. For example, immediately following this paragraph, the topic of day care will be discussed. Research has demonstrated that the tripod of family structure (one versus two parents), the day-care structure (in-home care or day-care center), and the day-care process (content of the activities) influence a child's language development in very complex ways (Goelman, 1988). Because we are using a chronological (i.e., human developmental) organization in this chapter, early childhood care will be discussed first.

Day Care

"Day care is not just for children, it's for working mothers. It's for fathers, so their wives can help support the family. It's for families, so their children can grow up in a healthy environment. And it's for people who don't have children, so the economy can run smoothly" (Zigler & Goodman, 1982). Few individuals would argue with those sentiments. However, day care in the United States is not without controversy. Some individuals believe that day care, which means separation in early life from the parents, can be harmful to young children. Others argue that it is not *whether* care is provided but *the type and quality of care* that is provided that make a difference in the children's lives. Yet others comment that availability of *good* care at a reasonable cost is this nation's biggest problem. These and other issues will be explored here in more detail.

Necessity for Day Care

Child day care can be defined as all the ways children are cared for when they are not being cared for by a nonemployed parent or during regular school classes (Morgan, 1983). In the opening vignette, Roberto did not reveal whether his parents worked and what his early life at home was like. However, if his parents worked and he was left with a neighbor, he would have been in child day care. Child-care or day-care providers can include licensed and unlicensed centers, family members or relatives other than the parents, neighbors, or in-home sitters.

Approximately two-thirds of all mothers work outside the home (National Commission on Working Women, 1989). For these working women, there is high dependency on day care. Half of all preschoolers of employed mothers in the United States are in some form of nonfamilial care such as a day-care center (Scarr & Eisenberg, 1993). Many other children are left with relatives. Some children are not in day care at all; they fend for themselves. They are called **latchkey children** because they often carry their housekeys on chains around their necks (Zigler & Stevenson, 1993).

Effects of Day Care

In the 1970s, a popular question asked by parents and researchers was: "How much damage is done to infants and young children by working mothers?" (Scarr & Eisenberg, 1993). What was really being asked was whether nonmaternal care was a threat to the child. For example, if Roberto was left with a neighbor, would that affect his development differently than if his mother cared for him at home? In a summary of research on maternal employment and children's adjustment, Gottfried and Gottfried (1988) concluded that working mothers and working fathers do not impair their children's adjustment.

A second important issue, however, is what effect nonmaternal care has on the rest of the child's development: social, cognitive, language, and other abilities. Scarr and Eisenberg (1993) have warned that there is no simple answer. For example, child care includes for-profit (such as the large national chains) and not-for-profit centers (such as church-sponsored centers, family-based care, and other permutations of child care). Not only are there different types of care but there are also differences in the *quality* of care within the same category of care. Grandmother probably cuddles, reads to, and plays with her grandchild more than would a neighbor who also has her own children to attend to.

Quality is often measured by such factors as health and safety of the children, responsiveness and warmth between the staff and children, a developmentally appropriate curriculum, limited group size, adequate indoor and outdoor space, caregiver training, and staff turnover, among other variables (Scarr & Eisenberg, 1993). Well-designed studies, however, can control these factors so that useful conclusions can be drawn about the effects of early child care on child development. It is also important to control for family and socioeconomic backgrounds of the children, as these variables alone can often explain developmental differences among children (Scarr & Eisenberg, 1993).

A complete review of this literature is beyond the scope of this book, but there are several sample studies that can be mentioned. A consistent finding about child care is that nonmaternal care generally has either no effect (Scarr, 1984) or even has positive effects on cognitive development (McCartney, Scarr, Phillips, & Grajek, 1985). As for social skills, a child-care study conducted in Sweden found that the factors of family background and socioeconomic class, more than type of child care, better predicted social competence and the ability to get along with peers. Of course, caution should be exercised in applying Swedish results to U.S. children; however, one might tentatively conclude that type of child care (e.g., center based or in home) probably does not produce drastic developmental differences (Lamb, Hwang, Bookstein, Broberg, Hult, & Frodi, 1988).

Importance of High-Quality Care

Despite this good news about child care, there is also bad news. *Quality* day care is the number-one need of American families and children (Zigler & Goodman, 1982). This is more than a rhetorical matter; research has demonstrated that *high-quality* care is related to improved language, cognitive, and social development (Wasik, Ramey, Bryant, & Starling, 1990), whereas *poor care* might actually be detrimental to the child. Gamble and Zigler (1986) stated that poor child care increases the chance for developmental damage because such damage increases as a function of the number and magnitude of negative environmental encounters. In other words, a child who comes from a highly stressed home environment is at further risk if placed in poor day care.

Just how many poor-quality child care facilities exist? The answer is unknown because the U.S. child-care system at this point has developed in such happenstantial fashion that it is a patchwork system at best (Klein, 1992). One can deduce, though, that the number is probably high. Kamerman and Kahn (1987) found that 60 to 90% of all family day-care homes are unregulated; they operate "underground"—these homes are the most common form of child care.

Regulations such as the Federal Interagency Day Care Requirements (FIDCR), adopted in 1968, were intended to prevent poor child care, but experts view these regulations as inadequate. For example, these regulations do not include provisions for noncenter care (such as private family day-care homes) or children under age 2 or children who have disabilities. Neither do the regulations clearly delineate the responsibilities of the centers (Zigler & Goodman, 1982).

Does regulation or licensing guarantee higher-quality care? Phillips, Howes, and Whitebook (1992) examined this issue. They assessed 227 different child-care centers in five metropolitan areas in several states. The states in which the centers were located varied in terms of how stringent their child-care regulations were; however, all were subject to the FIDCR regulations. In general, the results demonstrated that centers in more stringently regulated states tended to have better staff-child ratios, staff with more child-related training, and lower staff turnover rates. Centers that complied with the regulations had significantly more age-appropriate classroom activities, less harsh, more sensitive teachers, and teachers who possessed specialized training. Interestingly, the researchers also found that nonprofit centers, such as those affiliated with churches, offered better-quality care than for-profit centers, such as the national chains. In fact, some authors believe that churches are ideal day-care facilities because they are in prime locations in most communities and have space that is not normally utilized during the week (Klein, 1992).

Possible Remedies to the Day-Care Dilemma

"The question is not whether there is a child care problem but rather what can be done about it" (Winget, 1982, p. 351). The child-care literature has suggested solutions to the problem of *affordable, available, high-quality* child care for American parents. Most experts call for policy changes (Morgan, 1983; Phillips, Howes, & Whitebook, 1992; Scarr & Eisenberg, 1993; Winget, 1982). Based on their research, Phillips and associates (1992) favor more federal intervention because state policies vary from good regulations to nonexistent or unenforced ones. However, this might be easier said than done. Despite the lobbying efforts of women's groups and child advocates, there has been very little progress made in terms of policy (Zigler & Goodman, 1982).

What other ideas does the literature hold for improved child care? Some early childhood experts have suggested parental involvement in the child-care centers (Zigler & Turner, 1982). However, research has documented that parents actually spend a minuscule amount of time in centers, even when the centers promote parental involvement (Zigler & Turner, 1982). On the other hand, parent education about the key ingredients of quality care might help replace the weak policy and regulation system now in existence (Phillips et al., 1992). After all, parents are the so-called consumers of the child-care delivery system in the United States; perhaps the centers, especially the for-profit ones, might be responsive to consumer demands.

Zigler and Goodman (1982) also suggested training high school students and senior citizens in child development; they would be good regular or emergency child-care workers. Switzerland has a law that no institution for the elderly can be established unless it is adjacent to and shares facilities with a day-care center, school, or some other kind of institution serving children (Bronfenbrenner, 1986).

Private industry also holds great potential for child-care improvement. Zigler and Goodman (1982) have suggested that companies can offer on-premise day care or reimbursements to employees for child-care costs. Extended maternity leave as well as paternity leave are other corporate possibilities. Such benefits are regularly provided in the European community (Scarr & Eisenberg, 1992). Finally, corporations could donate some of their profits to charitable causes such as nonprofit day-care centers (Zigler & Goodman, 1982). Abella (1991) also detailed information about **satellite learning centers** that link businesses with schools. The pupils are the children of employees and are students in kindergarten through second grade. They are taught on the grounds of private companies that share the costs with the public school systems. In Chapter 11 we discuss other accommodations modern organizations can make for employees and their family members.

Compensatory Education and Early Intervention

Except for Roberto's story, economically disadvantaged children or children from various ethnic or racial groups have not yet been discussed. We would be remiss if we omitted them, because several major historical controversies in the psychological and educational literature have focused on these groups.

In 1961, J. McVicker Hunt published a book, *Intelligence and Experience*, in which he likened a child's mind to a field waiting to be cultivated; the key to an IQ (intelligence quotient) harvest was proper stimulation. Hunt believed that by governing the encounters that children had with their early environments—that is, by providing children with adequate stimulus enrichment—their intellectual development could be enhanced. This "naive environmentalism" (Zigler & Muenchow, 1992) promoted a belief in the importance of early childhood education. Programs designed to assist so-called disadvantaged children—those believed to be living in impoverished environments—came to be known as **compensatory education** programs.

The children most targeted for these programs were primarily from the lower socioeconomic class and included many African American, Hispanic, and other minority children. These startling statistics indicate that the children of families living in poverty confront more problems than the children from more economically advantaged backgrounds. Consider the following:

- Of the 33 million poor Americans, 13 million are children, 500,000 of whom are homeless (Kozol, 1990).
- Of all students placed in classes for the educable mentally retarded, 41% are African Americans (Moore, 1982).
- Sickness and debility levels among Native American children in New Mexico, Arizona, and Texas approach those in Bangladesh (Ford Foundation Report, 1983). Indeed, family income is more strongly related to health status than any other sociodemographic characteristic (Starfield, 1982).
- Poor children are 40% more likely to miss school because of illness and to have these problems interfere with their schoolwork than children from affluent families (Hart, 1985).
- Less than half of the homeless and impoverished children score at a level indicative of normal development on standardized tests (Molnar, Rath, Klein, Lowe, & Hartmann, 1991).
- Studies have consistently identified low-income inner-city African American children as running a disproportionately higher risk for negative psychosocial and educational outcomes than more affluent African American and White children (Myers, Taylor, Alvy, Arrington, & Richardson, 1992).

Are compensatory education programs really beneficial to these children? For example, if Roberto had attended a preschool designed especially for Hispanic children about to enter mainstream public schools, would his early elementary education have been easier and more productive? To address this question, we will explore the best-known compensatory education program: **Head Start.**

The Economic Opportunity Act of 1964 established a variety of ways that children might benefit from social programs, one of which was Project Head Start. The goal of Head Start is to reach children between the ages of 3 and 5 from low-income families through a comprehensive preschool program. It is a total program in that it attempts to meet the children's mental, emotional, health, and educational needs. Specifically, its major goals are to:

- Improve children's health and physical being.
- Assist in the emotional and social development of the children by encouraging self-confidence, curiosity, and self-discipline.
- Improve mental, verbal, and conceptual processes.
- Establish expectations for success in the children.
- Increase the children's capacity to relate positively to family members and the family members to the children.
- Develop in the children and their families a responsible and constructive attitude toward society.

- Increase the sense of self-worth of the children and their families (Grotberg, 1969).

By 1965, the summer program had 13,344 centers in 2,000 communities (Ross, 1966). Project Head Start quickly expanded to a long-term program. Despite the impressiveness of these figures, Head Start today reaches only one in five of the eligible children (Kozol, 1990). The federal government picks up much of the cost, although under various administrations the program has fared better or worse (Zigler & Muenchow, 1992). Although the federal government is facing major economic problems, Project Head Start has recently received some of its largest budget increases ever (Zigler & Muenchow, 1992).

Head Start is somewhat unique among compensatory education programs. Because of some of these unique features, it approximates community psychology philosophy as outlined in Chapter 1. First, it is a nationwide program; others are local demonstration projects or at least not as broadly based. Second, Head Start was one of the first programs to demonstrate that a single approach or a single intervention is insufficient. For example, Project Head Start is not just a preschool program. One of the revolutionary ideas of this program is to involve parents as decision makers and learners (Zigler & Muenchow, 1992). Many Head Start parents have become certified Head Start teachers (Levenson, 1977). In fact, parental involvement is now fairly standard in most intervention programs for young children (Honing, 1988).

Although not meant to substitute for regular health care, Head Start was also designed to ensure that the children received health screening and follow-up treatment. Many other programs simply develop educational programs in a vacuum or provide one or two services (Zigler & Muenchow, 1992). Researchers have discovered that full-service programs result in more gains for children than partial-service programs (King & Kirschenbaum, 1990). Moreover, Project Head Start was not designed simply to enrich children's environments so as to enhance IQ. Rather, the program was developed so that children would be motivated to make the most of their lives (Zigler & Muenchow, 1992).

Throughout these pages, you have seen Zigler's name as a source of reference. Profile 8.1 discusses Edward Zigler, the shaper of child-care policies and programs.

Head Start isn't the only early intervention program available, but it probably is the best known one. The High/Scope Perry Preschool program was also designed to alter the causal chain that leads from childhood poverty to school failure to subsequent adult poverty and related social problems. This program incorporates into its design developmentally appropriate learning materials based on psychological principles of development, small class sizes, staff trained in early childhood development, in-service training for staff, parental involvement, and sensitivity to the noneducational needs of the child and family. What is fairly unique about this program is that it views the child as an active, self-initiating learner. The child selects his or her own activities from among a variety of learning areas the teacher prepares (Schweinhart & Weikart, 1988).

◆ *PROFILE 8.1*
Edward Zigler

In 1990, Edward Zigler of the Bush Center for Child Development and Social Policy of Yale University received the Division of Community Psychology's award for Distinguished Contributions to Community Psychology and Community Mental Health. In large part, the honor was due to his significant 20-year effort to develop and implement solutions to America's child-care crisis.

In his acceptance remarks, Zigler noted that there is still not enough child care in this country for every child who needs it. Furthermore, there is even less *high-quality* child care available. He cited these startling statistics:

- Of all school-age children, 70% have working mothers.
- Of all preschoolers, 60% have working mothers.
- Of all babies less than 1 year old, 52% have working mothers.
- Of the women who provide family day care, 90% have annual incomes *below* the poverty level.

Zigler's interest in child care grew from his early graduate work when he was studying mental retardation. He became poignantly aware of the deleterious effects of institutionalization on the retarded. In fact, he was one of the first psychologists to demonstrate that social support and social interaction were important factors in human devlopment. Thus, institutionalization and the isolation it creates for various populations have a negative effect. Zigler later was instrumental in establishing Project Head Start, an early intervention program for at-risk preschool children. This program is widely known in the United States today and is detailed in this book.

Zigler also pursued what he called "terribly radical and outstandingly simple and attainable" ideas for revamping our child-care situation (Iscoe, 1990). His concept, called "Educare," involves local schools in providing developmentally appropriate day-care facilities for children of working parents. The schools also provide outreach and other services. For example, schools can train, monitor, and network other caregivers who provide alternate child-care services outside of the schools. To that end, Zigler also consults and provides support to legislators, assisting in revamping social policy related to child development in this country.

Edward Zigler is a prominent and active community psychologist who puts his social change ideas and research into action, both in the community and in influencing public policy.

Source: Adapted from "Shaping Child Care Policies and Programs in America" by E. Zigler, 1990, *American Journal of Community Psychology, 18*, pages 183–216.

Medical findings have suggested that Project Head Start has been successful. Of the first 2 million children participating in Head Start, screening tests determined that 180,000 failed the vision test, 60,000 had a skin disease, 180,000 had anemia, and 20,000 had joint or bone problems. Over two-thirds of these children received the medical attention they needed (U.S. Government Printing Office, 1970). But what about other gains, as measured by the goals mentioned earlier? The most controversial measure of success of early education programs is intelligence or the intelligence quotient (IQ). IQ in and of itself is a controversial concept within psychology; a complete discussion of the concept cannot be given here. In an early review of Head Start and compensatory education programs, Moore (1977) summarized the findings of many assessments of these programs:

- Gains seem to be short-lived.
- Head Start children are less likely to be placed in special classrooms or to be held back compared to similar non–Head Start children.
- Early intervention is a complex process; it must involve the home and family.
- The more structured models seem to produce the best results, at least temporarily.

Some of these results merit further elaboration. The fact that gains seem to be short-lived was a startling and disheartening finding—one that dampened the popularity of such programs (Zigler & Stevenson, 1993). Head Start children, for example, score higher than non–Head Start children in "readiness to enter school," but this advantage disappears after a few months (Zigler & Muenchow, 1992). In terms of IQ, some studies demonstrated an initial increase that "faded out" after several years of formal schooling. Other early intervention programs, such as the High/Scope Perry Preschool Program, have also resulted in early IQ gains that faded over time (Weikart, Bond, & McNeil, 1978). Some of the proponents of Project Head Start attribute this fade-out not to a subsequent decline in IQ but rather to changes in motivational factors (Zigler & Muenchow, 1992).

In response to this problem of fade-out, companion programs were developed, such as Follow Through, a program designed to help Head Start children adapt to and continue the gains from Head Start into early elementary school. Seitz, Apfel, and Efron (1977) reported research comparing Head Start/Follow Through children to a control group. There were academic gains (e.g., mathematics achievement) for the Head Start/Follow Through children compared to control children, and these gains lasted four to five years. Subsequent studies have found that parents and siblings are also affected positively by early intervention efforts (Lamb-Parker, Piotrkowski, & Peay, 1987). Unfortunately, Follow Through has never become more than an experimental program in about 40 schools throughout the country (Zigler & Muenchow, 1992).

Because many of these early intervention programs have been in operation for several decades, professionals can now study their long-term effects. Much of this research is conducted using **longitudinal research** in which participants are followed for a designated period of time, such as several years. This type of research is frought with many problems, especially participant attrition. Jordan, Grallo, Deutsch, and Deustch (1985), despite the problems of longitudinal studies, recovered over 70 experimental participants who were previously enrolled in an early education program and over 70 original comparison subjects. Their results revealed a number of personality and skill benefits in adults who, as children, were availed of early opportunities. For example, the experimental group had superior employment status, educational attainment, vocabulary skills, self-concepts, and sense of self-control. Such gains indicate that these individuals may be "moving away from poverty" (p. 412). Curiously, these results held only for men. The authors explained that the early education interventions prompted children to be curious and assertive and to demand hands-on participation—characteristics less acceptable to society in girls than boys. More research is needed to determine whether these results are specific to this cohort group of participants, especially females. Follow-up research on the Perry Preschool Program indicated that that program later led to better grades in secondary school, fewer arrests, and better and more jobs with higher job satisfaction for participants than nonparticipants (Schweinhart & Weikart, 1988).

Some early research on Head Start also demonstrated positive fallout for the community (Zigler & Valentine, 1979). In 42 different communities with Head Start programs, there were 1,496 instances of positive community change compared to communities with no Head Start programs. For example, in one community with Head Start, the parents banded together and pressured the public schools to make changes. In another community, the parents' council from Head Start formed a consumer cooperative at which they could buy fresh fruits and vegetables.

In terms of cost effectiveness, early intervention programs pay their way. Cost effectiveness is a measure of interest to taxpayers and legislators. Several studies indicate that society can save $4.00 to $7.00 in costs for remediation, welfare, and crime for every dollar spent on early intervention (Zigler & Muenchow, 1992). Despite all this good news, some early childhood experts believe that for very high-risk children, good preschool intervention is still not sufficient for success (Halpern, 1991).

What does the future hold for these early childhood education programs? No one knows for sure, given the vagaries of federal and local budgets and the changing political climate. However, in his personalized book on the "inside story" of Project Head Start, Edward Zigler revealed a wish list for the next generation. His recommendations build on those of the Silver Ribbon Panel of the National Head Start Association. This wish list is presented in Table 8.1.

THE PUBLIC SCHOOLS

Although education law varies state by state, at the age of 5, or 6, most children in the United States are attending public schools: elementary school first and then high school. These schools are remarkable social institutions shaped by political

TABLE 8.1   Head Start: Recommendations for "The Next Generation"

1. Provide "full-quality" Head Start. That is, provide funding to attract and retain leading teachers, enhance comprehensive services to multiproblem families, strengthen the health care component, reduce class size, and acquire space specially designed for children.
2. Recognize Head Start as a full partner in welfare reform by offering full-day, full-year services to assist working parents. Also, broaden job search and training opportunities for parents.
3. Allow Head Start to serve infants and toddlers, which will require expanded funding and program discretion.
4. Raise the income eligibility guidelines to at least the Medicaid level, which is 133% of the poverty level. Regional variations in income and poverty levels also need to be taken into account. Medicaid is medical insurance for certain impoverished individuals such as those on public assistance.
5. Revamp Chapter 1 to sustain Head Start benefits in elementary school. Chapter 1, to date, does not involve parents, is not a comprehensive program but rather only a reading program, and is administered differently at different schools, which include over 90% of the nation's schools.

Source: Adapted from *Head Start: The Inside Story of America's Most Successful Educational Experiment* by E. F. Zigler and S. Muenchow, 1992, New York: Basic Books.

and social events (Sarason & Klaber, 1985), some of which are exemplified by the Civil Rights movement, the introduction of computers into schools, and the changing demographic trends such as the current high divorce rates. A few events—either historical or contemporary   of importance will be reviewed in the following passages.

Desegregration, Ethnicity, and Prejudice in the Schools

Because Roberto, the young man in the opening vignette, is now about 20 years old, he has probably benefited from the Civil Rights movement of the 1950s and 1960s. Or has he? It is necessary to examine the complex effects of societal prejudice as well as public policy designed to confront prejudice, discrimination, and segregation of families—in particular, the children and the schools.

The Historical Context
Perhaps in the arena of desegregation, psychologists have possibly had their greatest public influence (Oskamp, 1984). Despite the fact that amendments to the Constitution had long ago given equal protection of the laws and the right to vote to all citizens, it wasn't until the 1950s that events took place that today have had a lasting and sweeping effect on our schools.

In 1954, the Supreme Court of the United States decided the case of *Brown* v. *Board of Education of Topeka, Kansas*. In fashioning their decision, the Supreme Court justices heard major testimony from social scientists about the detrimental effects of segregation on African American pupils (see, for example, Clark &

Clark, 1947). In the official rendering, the unanimous judges cited social science research as being influential in their deliberations (Levine & Perkins, 1987). The consequence of the decision was that there would no longer be a place for segregation in schools, not even for separate but equal educational facilities. Interestingly, the judges were not initially concerned with implementing their decision nor in the precise effects of desegregation on children once it was instituted.

Some school authorities scrambled to come into compliance with the ruling. The chosen method for desegregation was often "one-way busing" (Oskamp, 1984), where inner-city children were bused to the suburbs and to all-White districts. Some school systems dragged their heels and some openly defied the ruling; subsequent court-ordered desegregation plans were imposed on them. Public policy changed some discriminatory behaviors, voluntarily or involuntarily, but did it change all related behaviors? An equally important matter was whether the children were better off with this policy. Social scientists quickly became concerned with these and other issues of desegregation. Given that 1994 was the fortieth anniversary of the *Brown* v. *Board of Education*, how far has the United States come?

Prejudice and Its Companions

In the opening vignette, Roberto revealed to us that he thought the other children believed he was dumb. Is this a form of prejudice?

Prejudice is an attitude (usually negative) toward the members of some group, based solely on their group membership (Baron & Byrne, 1994). If Roberto's classmates thought he was dumb because he was Hispanic, then they indeed were prejudiced. A companion to prejudice is discrimination. **Discrimination** involves what are often prejudiced actions toward particular groups based almost solely on group membership (Baron & Byrne, 1994). If Roberto's classmates refused to play with him on the playground because of his ethnic background, they would have been discriminating against him. Interestingly, studies in social psychology have demonstrated that people can be prejudiced without discriminating or can discriminate without harboring prejudices (e.g., La Piere, 1934). **Stereotypes**, a highly related concept, are beliefs that all members of certain groups share the same or common traits or characteristics (Baron & Byrne, 1994). In keeping with the same example, if Roberto's classmates classified all Hispanics as dumb, then they would have held a stereotype.

Important historical research on stereotyping in classrooms was conducted by Rosenthal and Jacobson (1968). In their study, teachers were told that perfectly normal children were either "bloomers" or "normal." Teachers were *not* told to treat these two groups differently. By the end of the study, the so-called bloomers showed dramatic improvements in classroom performance and IQ scores, probably because they had been the beneficiaries of positive prejudice. It is important to remember that all children were *randomly* assigned to the conditions of "normal" or "bloomer." This study demonstrates that teachers' labels and stereotypes of children somehow fulfill the teachers' prophecies. This phenomenon where a labeled individual fulfills someone else's forecast is called the **self-fulfilling prophecy**. Studies have shown that teachers' expectations in a variety of classroom settings do influence student achievement and motivation (Weinstein, Soule, Collins, Cone, Mehlhorn, & Simontacchi, 1991).

Research on contemporary society indicates that people's prejudices and labels may be quite different from those of the cohort groups previous to the Civil Rights movement. Before 1950, there was more *overt* racism with open name calling, different laws for certain groups ("Negroes ride in the back of the bus"), and, in fact, mob actions against and lynchings of certain groups. In **modern prejudice** (Dovidio & Gaertner, 1986; Duffy, Olczak, & Grosch, 1993), people's attitudes are more *covert* and subtle. In other words, these subtle forms of prejudice and discrimination allow their users to conceal the hidden, negative views they really hold. Chidester (1986) offered a fascinating version of modern prejudice. White participants in this study were introduced to African American and White strangers and later asked how much they liked each. The White participants indicated they liked the *African American* stranger best. This "leaning over backwards" is construed as trying to cover up prejudice and is an example of modern prejudice.

Prejudice, then, has not disappeared because the courts have ruled that desegregation and equal opportunity must prevail. Prejudice has just taken on a different appearance—a more subtle hue. Given that prejudice probably still pervades society, the question becomes: When children from different backgrounds are intermingled in school classrooms, what can adults do to lessen the effects of any prejudices they bring from home? Psychologists have some innovative responses to this question.

Fostering Acceptance of Diversity in the Classroom

In a famous demonstration with children called "The Eye of the Storm," teacher Jane Elliot told the dark-eyed children that they were inferior to the light-eyed children. In fact, she said they were so inferior that the light-eyed children were not to play or have contact with the dark-eyed children. The light-eyed children soon segregated, taunted, and mistreated the dark-eyed children. Elliot then reversed the roles; the light-eyed children were now the inferior ones. When Elliot debriefed the children and they discussed their feelings, the children talked about how horrible it felt to be the victims of such intense prejudice. This demonstration reveals but one means by which children in schools can be familiarized with what prejudice feels like. What other techniques are in the psychological arsenal for fostering acceptance of diversity in classrooms?

In U.S. society, it appears to be a reality that different groups have little contact with each other (Braddock, 1985). In general, people prefer to be with their own kind. Most African Americans talk to and socialize with other African Americans more than with Whites. Whites primarily do business with other Whites more than with other groups. Perhaps on your campus you have noticed these trends, too. If there are Greek organizations, you may have noticed that the members of one fraternity eat and socialize with each other more than members of other fraternities or nonmembers. This type of *voluntary* segregation does nothing to diminish prejudice and stereotypes. In fact, it probably fuels them. Segregation may thus be said to perpetuate itself. People now know that simply placing African American and White children in the same classroom does not reduce prejudice (Levine & Perkins, 1987).

Scientists needed to develop more sophisticated techniques for *actively* involving children with one another. One such approach to reduce prejudice is **intergroup contact** in which two conflicting groups come together, and the contact enables them to better understand and appreciate one another. Research demonstrates that only certain intergroup contacts enhance people's understanding and acceptance of each other.

Stuart Cook has been a leading proponent of the **contact hypothesis** for reducing prejudice. The contact hypothesis states that personal contact between people from disliked groups works to decrease the negative attitudes *but only under certain conditions*. The five conditions are:

1. The groups or individuals must be of equal status.
2. The attributes of the disliked group that become apparent during the contact must be such as to disconfirm the prevailing stereotyped beliefs about the group.
3. The contact situation must encourage, or perhaps require, a mutually independent relationship or cooperation to achieve a joint goal.
4. The contact situation must promote association of the sort that will reveal enough details about members of the disliked group to encourage seeing them as individuals rather than as persons with stereotyped group characteristics.
5. The social norms of contact must favor the concept of group equality and egalitarian intergroup association (Allport, 1954; Cook, 1985).

Several quasi-experimental and laboratory experimental studies of the intergroup contact hypothesis have been conducted. The one most relevant to this present discussion took place in a newly desegregated junior and senior high school. Racially mixed learning teams were developed; they were comprised of one Hispanic, one African American, and three Anglo students (the experimental condition). Other students remained in a control condition in which the team approach was not used. Experimental teams were to turn in team-created work, and everyone on the team received the same rewards for good work. The interracial team work resulted in less interracial and ethnic conflict for the intervention groups than for the control groups. Many Anglo students also increased their favorability ratings of the minority students on their teams. Within the team condition, cross-racial or cross-ethnic friendships were more likely to develop than in the control condition (Weigel, Wiser, & Cook, 1975). Thus, the intergroup contact hypothesis for reducing prejudice and increasing cooperation among students in racially desegregated classrooms was supported.

Elliot Aronson and his colleagues pioneered a seemingly similar technique called the **jigsaw classroom**. In this classroom, students intially work on a project in mastery groups. In this first type of group, students all learn the same material, but each group learns different material. The mastery groups then break into jigsaw groups such that one student from each mastery group comprises the jigsaw group. For example, if students were learning about prejudice, one mastery group would learn the definitions and examples for *prejudice, discrimination,* and *stereotypes.* A second mastery group would learn about the detrimental effects of prejudice. A third might learn about ways to reduce prejudice, and so on. In the jigsaw groups, one student from the definition group, one student from the detrimental effects group, and one from the how-to-reduce-prejudice group would come together and teach the others the appropriate module. In this way, isolated students become more central to the group, and competitive students learn to cooperate. Without everyone's interdependence and cooperation in the jigsaw group, the group cannot achieve its learning goals. Students who trip over English words are prompted and assisted by the other children; otherwise, no one can learn (Aronson, Blaney, Stephan, Sikes, & Snapp, 1978).

In one of the first major experiments on the jigsaw technique, Blaney, Stephan, Rosenfield, Aronson, and Sikes (1977) found that liking for classmates and the school environment, self-esteem, learning from others, and school performance all improved over control students in standard classrooms. Of course, competitiveness also declined. More recent research has documented that peer teaching, as utilized in the jigsaw method, improves peer liking, learning, and perceptions of the classroom climate (Slavin, 1985; Wright & Cowen, 1985). Exciting news is that positive results from cooperative strategies such as peer teaching seem to generalize to other minority children not in the immediate school environment (Miller, Brewer, & Edwards, 1985).

Some states have experimented with **magnet schools** where students from a variety of school districts attend because the school specializes in a particular discipline such as music or foreign languages. Interested students are thus attracted to the schools like steel to a magnet. These schools create a natural experiment on intergroup contact because students of many backgrounds can attend. Rossell (1988) compared the effectiveness of *voluntary* plans at magnet schools to *mandatory* reassignment desegregation plans. She found that magnet schools produce greater long-term interracial exposure than mandatory reassignment, probably because of what she and others have called "White flight" from the reassigned districts.

One can conclude that once classrooms are desegregated, by court order or by voluntary design, there are researched means by which the children can become more accepting and helpful to one another. But what happens to the academic performance of these students? If the courts determined that separate education was not only unequal but inferior for many economically disadvantaged students, did desegregation accelerate the academic achievement of the targeted children?

Effects of Desegregation on Academic Achievement

Some early studies of the effects of desegregation on academic achievement of minority students showed that desegregation did not improve the academic achievement of any of the affected students. For instance, Gerard and Miller's (1975) large study of the Riverside, California, system showed that minority students' marks generally fell because teachers who were initially lenient made an effort to move to a more uniform standard of grading for all students. The data showed a trend for the minority children's being less adjusted than the White children. Furthermore, sociometric ratings showed that few minority students were selected as workmates or friends. Not surprisingly, the teachers' attitudes also influenced some of these measures. The students in the classrooms of the more biased teachers showed the greatest drops in verbal achievement scores. You will recognize this as the self-fulfilling prophecy.

Other studies produced mixed results with some gains and declines in achievement, whereas still others showed only positive effects or no effects at all of desegregation. What conclusions can be made from these mixed results? First, consider that most studies are not well done. That is, many studies are not longitudinal; they do not track the long-term effects of desegregation from before the desegregation to afterward. Second, many studies are correlational in nature, thus cause and effect cannot adequately be determined. Another important element is that few of the conditions for intergroup contact, as described earlier, are met in most desegregated school settings (Cook, 1984). Finally, and very importantly, all of the studies are *reactive*. That is, the researchers wait for desegregation to occur and then examine it to declare it a success or failure. Cook (1985) suggested that this approach is bound not to support desegregation. Researchers ought to be *proactive*, according to Cook. They should be looking for innovative means to carry out school desegregation *before* it occurs so as to enhance the academic achievement of all involved students (Cook, 1985).

Because desegregation has been part of mainstream America for four decades now, one is able to study its long-term effects, those beyond the classroom. In a review of research on desegregated versus segregated schools and their long-term effects on assimilation of African Americans into adult life, Braddock (1985) revealed that African Americans who attended desegregated schools were more likely than those attending segregated schools to attend desegregated colleges, have more White friends and work associates, earn higher incomes, and hold higher-status jobs. Desegregation alone might not explain these results. Other processes—such as access to social networks, reduced social inertia, avoidance of stereotypical behavior, being shunned by employers, and other factors—might also account for the apparent advantages of desegregation. Furthermore, some African Americans might argue that their assimilation into mainstream American culture is a disaster; it diminishes the preservation of their own, rich cultures. Regardless of the reasons, school desegregation may be the most significant example of a national-policy innovation (Braddock, 1985) with far-reaching, long-term effects.

In conclusion, school desegregation and diversity in the classroom are controversial issues, but they are not going away. By the year 2000, one-third of all schoolchildren will be minority (U.S. Bureau of the Census, 1987). Society must continue its efforts to understand the effects of diversity and foster its acceptance.

The Schools and Adolescents

Despite nationwide efforts to desegregate U.S. schools and despite the best-laid plans to provide early intervention programs for targeted children, it remains true that many children isolated in the inner city continue to be economically disadvantaged. These children are usually from a racial or ethnic minority, yet they have never benefited from these programs. Inner-city children mature to adolescence still trapped in poverty. Inner-city adolescents are the ones that psychologists consider most at risk for academic failure, dropping out of school, teen pregnancy, drug use, and myriad other problems that interfere with obtaining an education so that the cycle of poverty can be broken (Children's Defense Fund, 1991). As adults, they are more likely to experience life's stresses and strains (Golding, Potts, & Aneshensel, 1991). In the interest of space, we will examine one issue here—dropping out of school—in some detail.

Dropping Out of School

In the opening vignette, Roberto wisely chose to stay in his school despite his early feelings of alienation from the school and from the other children. Some students, however, do not choose to stay in school; they drop out. The nationwide school dropout rate is estimated to be about 20% overall (Baker & Sansone, 1990), but dropout rates for certain groups are higher. For example, the school dropout rate for African Americans is estimated to be about 23%, for Hispanics 36%, but for Whites only 12% (Weinstein et al., 1991). Others estimate higher dropout rates, such as 40 to 60% for young African American males (Reed, 1988). Interestingly, the overall rate of young people failing to complete school has declined dramatically; in 1940, the dropout rate was a whopping 60%. There is, however, more interest today in school dropouts than ever before (U.S. Bureau of the Census, 1985). Rumberger (1987) elucidated some reasons for this high interest. He stated that some schools are raising their academic requirements which may alienate students who are already uncommitted to school.

Rumberger (1987) also believes that the educational requirements of most jobs will increase in the future, which would render dropping out of school an extreme disadvantage to obtaining employment. Also, minority students who have always had higher dropout rates than Whites are more likely to enter school than in the past. In fact, in some districts in cities such as Newark, Atlanta, and San Antonio, minorities comprise 90% of the student body (Plisko & Stern, 1985).

Why do students drop out? Many factors have been identified besides alienation from school. School failure and behavior problems in school are two other school-related elements. Family factors such as low socioecnomic class, English as a second language, and the absence of learning materials in the home have been implicated. Students who have friends who drop out are likely to drop out, too. Some young people drop out because they would rather work and earn money. Finally, personality variables such as low self-esteem and loss of a sense of control have also been identified as related to dropping out (Rumberger, 1987; Reyes & Jason, 1991).

What can be done about the dropout problem in the United States? Many school programs are rightly aimed at preventing dropping out and are assisted by the fact that it can now be predicted who is at risk (Evans & DiBenedetto, 1990; O'Sullivan, 1990). Many of the efforts are focused on the individual student and include counseling (Baker, 1991; Downing & Harrison, 1990; Rose-Gold, 1992) or improvement of self-image or self-esteem (Muha & Cole, 1990). In discussing dropping out and other adolescent problems, Reppucci (1987) said that concerned mental health professionals cannot be content with the current techniques of individual and family therapy and counseling. In too many instances, this arsenal has proven ineffective.

Because there are *multiple causes* of dropping out (Svec, 1987), a more ecological approach is desirable (Dunham & Alpert, 1987; Rumberger, 1987). An ecological approach would take into account the environment (such as the characteristics of the school) as well as of the individual who is about to drop out. A more sophisticated approach is also desirable because there are so many differences among individuals in their reasons for dropping out of school. For example, Streeter and Franklin (1991) have identified differences for dropping out between middle socioeconomic-class students and lower socioeconomic-class students. Middle-class students tend to drop out because of family problems or behavioral problems; lower-class students are more likely to drop out for academic and economic reasons. Similarly, there are school environment and school structure factors that probably influence the decisions of some adolescents to drop out. Pittman's (1986) research determined that teachers' attitudes toward the student who might drop out are just as important as any characteristic possessed by the student. Likewise, Fine (1986) has identified school-related variables such as poor facilities and inadequate teaching staffs that also affect students' decisions to leave.

One of the more successful, better-known prevention programs for students at risk for dropping out is one designed by Felner, Ginter, and Primavera (1982). The program was designed to address multiple issues, but it will be discussed here as a model program to address school dropouts. Felner and associates redefined the role of the homeroom teacher to provide counseling and guidance to incoming freshmen making the transition from junior to senior high school. The homerooms were also comprised solely of program participants. The program's other component was aimed at reducing the complexity of the school; participants were in several classes together in only one wing of a large school. With these ecological changes, the program resulted in better attendance, higher grade-point averages, and more stable self-concepts compared to a nonparticipating control group. Reorganizing or restructing the environment will be examined again in Chapter 11.

Another program, HUGS (Help Us Guarantee Success), has more recently been reported by Fortune Bruce, Williams, and Jones (1991). Students who had dropped out were interviewed to assess their reasons for dropping out. Students reported dropping out because they (1) felt they were being ignored, helpless, or unwanted in school; (2) were new parents; or (3) were having academic difficulties. These three primary reasons for dropping out were addressed in the program that was designed after the interviews. The HUGS program therefore included a one-day weekly after-school teacher-student interaction period, a weekly tutor program, and a student options program with provisions for work release and child care. The program resulted in significant declines in dropout rates. In the year before HUGS was implemented, the dropout rate was 107 students out of 2,500; after implementation, only 64 of 2,500 dropped out. Notice that the HUGS program did not stop all dropping out because, as the researchers noted, there were more than the three cited reasons for dropping out.

One issue related to this intervention is important to community psychologists. It appears that students did *not* participate in the design of the HUGS program; perhaps if they had been empowered and consulted, dropout rates would have been further reduced. Note, however, that there is at least one study that demonstrates that empowerment in schools does not always enhance the situation. Gruber and Trickett (1987), working in an alternative school, helped develop a policy council comprised of the various constituents in the school. The council was not as productive as hoped because there was an inherent imbalance of power among members of the council. Gruber and Trickett concluded that there is a fundamental paradox with the idea of one set of people empowering others. The very institutional structure that puts one group in a position to empower also works to undermine the act of empowerment!

Although some programs were successful, others have been less successful for a variety of reasons, such as larger school size (Reyes & Jason, 1991). Other ideas are therefore needed. Organized youth sports offer untapped potential for diverting youths from all sorts of problems, including dropping out of school (Reppucci, 1987).

The School Climate

It is not just inner-city and minority children who have problems in school. There are a multitude of reasons middle-class students drop out, get pregnant, fail, or underachieve in school. Some of the reasons are the same as for the inner-city students. Remember also that not all minorities live in the inner city. Those in the suburbs need to be tapped for research as well (Milburn, Gary, Booth, & Brown, 1991). A student need not be failing nor be an underachiever to experience school problems. Gifted children often become bored with or disinterested in school, too (Feldhusen, 1989; Meade, 1991).

Earlier, we alluded to the construct of **alienation from school**. According to Bronfenbrenner (1986), *alienation* means lacking a sense of belonging, feeling cut off. *School alienation* means lacking a sense of belonging in school. This phenomenon has received much attention in the community psychology literature.

It would be easy to blame students for being alienated, for having some personality flaw that makes them young and restless. However, developmental and educational specialists have also focused on the circumstances in which the alienated child finds himself or herself. In 1983, Seymour Sarason authored *Schooling in America: Scapegoat and Salvation* in which he suggested that schools are relatively uninteresting places for both children and teachers. Sarason contended that children often exhibit more intellectual curiosity and learn faster outside of school (Sarason, 1983; Weinstein, 1990). Bronfenbrenner (1986) suggested that children under stress at home can easily feel distracted and alienated at school.

My own (Duffy) research with students in two community psychology classes reveals another interesting feature of schools. I asked two different classes of students six years apart (1985 and 1991) to record their most memorable experience from school. Out of 40 students, only 1 reported a positive academic experience, 4 reported positive nonacademic experiences, and 34 reported negative nonacademic experiences. The students most remembered sad or frightening incidents involving fights between students or students and teachers, fires, bombs, child abuse, and other unfortunate events. The 4 positive nonacademic experiences all pertained to championship sports teams. In other words, at least retrospectively, the salient features of schools seem to be negative and unrelated to learning. Some of the students' experiences are revealed in Case in Point 8.1.

There is little doubt that the school environment itself serves as a risk factor to children (Weinstein et al., 1991). Understanding the school and its environment are therefore important. Several scales are available to measure school climate; one well-known one is the Classroom Environment Scale by Moos (1979). The scale measures dimensions such as task orientation, order, organization, and relationships. There are discernible individual differences in student perception and behavior based on different climates (Harpin & Sandler, 1985). For example, in classes where relationships are emphasized, students report higher levels of satisfaction and friendship. In an atmosphere of order and organization, student achievement is higher (Moos, 1979).

Heller (1990) suggested that changing classroom or school climate is difficult. Schools as social institutions are relatively intractable places. For instance, the assumption that learning best takes place in the classroom rather than anywhere else is rarely challenged (Sarason & Klaber, 1985). To expect underappreciated teachers with their low salaries to institute change is also unreasonable (Leitenberg, 1987). Besides, student and teacher perceptions of the environment in a classroom are often different anyway (Toro, Cowen, Gesten, Weissberg, Rapkin, & Davidson, 1985), so a solution from one may represent a problem for the other.

Some educational experts argue that what today's educational reformers need is for American schools to imitate Japanese schools—to increase the amount of homework and to lengthen the schoolday and the schoolyear (Morton, 1990). Why? Many Asian children perform better in school than do middle-class White students. One study demonstrates that it is the home environment, not the longer Japanese schoolday, that contributes to the success of Asian schoolchildren (Stevenson & Lee, 1990). The Asian mothers in the study were supportive of their children's achievement. The mothers provided their children with quiet study

❖ CASE IN POINT 8.1

Students' Memories of Public School

As described in your reading, I (Duffy) asked students in my community psychology classes to record their most memorable experience in school. No other instructions were given. For example, I did not tell them to think of a positive or negative experience. Most incidents recalled by the students were negative and almost all pertained to nonacademic events such as fights, disagreements between teachers and students, bombs, and so on. Here are some randomly selected ones:

In tenth grade I had a chemistry teacher who enjoyed belittling students. One girl was the brunt of almost every joke. She was overweight and he called her a whale and would make comments like "Nuke the whales!" Not surprisingly, she dropped out of the class, but the joking didn't stop. One day, disgusted with my teacher, I raised my hand in the middle of one of his rampages. When he called on me, I proceeded to tell him that I thought he was the most immature, cruel, vindictive, and irresponsible teacher I'd ever met.... He told me that since I felt I had to come to [this overweight girl's] rescue that he'd just pick on me. From then on, his teasing of me became nastier than it had been before.

Four honor students planted a bomb in my high school one night, attempting to blow up the school. They were all caught, tried, and sentenced. One culprit would have probably been salutatorian. The administration hush-hushed the incident, so I don't know why they did it or how long their sentences were.

It was the last day of school and my teacher was in the process of distributing our report cards. After he had done about three-fourths of the class, he announced that anyone he hadn't given one to had to line up at his desk and get their birthday spanking from him before they got the report card (their birthdays were in the summer, so everyone else had gotten their [spanking] during the course of the school year).... Three years later my teacher was convicted of over 100 counts of child molestation involving his step-daughter. I guess these spankings meant a lot more to him than we could have ever known.

I had a [Black] friend who got into an argument with a White kid. The White kid called [him] a Nigger at one point (big mistake). [My friend] punched the kid once, square in the nose. The kid wobbled around for a second or two before he fell unconscious on the floor. His nose had a metal plate on it for about a month. [My friend] had to pay medical expenses.... A day without a physical fight was very rare.

Schools are indeed places of learning but not just of reading, writing, and arithmetic. The whole school environment is a learning experience that can sometimes place the students at risk.

space, time for homework, and tutoring when the child needed it. Without parental concern or involvement in the schools, it is difficult for educators to induce American parents to create this same atmophere in their homes.

American educational planners have turned to **alternative education** as the answer. Alternative education or alternate schools have components that differ from traditional schools. For example, in traditional schools, the curriculum and requirements are designed by teachers and administrators. In alternative settings, the students and perhaps their parents in consultation with teachers design the curriculum or select classes in which the student will enroll. In alternative education, the classes might be smaller, and learning sometimes occurs outside of a traditional classroom setting.

Several studies indicate that alternative education is successful in creating higher student and teacher satisfaction with the schools and often better student achievement (Catterall & Stern, 1986; Gray & Chanoff, 1986; Trickett, McConahay, Phillips, & Ginter, 1985). What are the mechanisms by which alternative education creates these effects? Studies have identified the elements of student participation, self-direction, and empowerment (Gray & Chanoff, 1986; Matthews, 1991); innovative and relaxed atmospheres (Fraser, Williamson, & Tobin, 1987; Matthews, 1991); and empathic teachers (Taylor, 1986–1987). All of these factors are *outside* the student; they are not personality attributes of the students in the alternate settings but rather factors related to the ecology of the alternate setting.

Other Factors Related to School Adjustment

The school climate is not the only school-related risk factor for children. Students who transfer from one school to another and those who are moving from elementary to junior high or junior high to high school (Compas, Wagner, Slavin, Vannatta, 1986; Reyes & Jason, 1991) are also considered at risk for problems. These and a host of other factors require attention from educators if children are to adjust to various processes within the schools. This is true today more than ever before. Weissberg and colleagues (1987) compared cohort groups from 1974 and 1987 and discovered that children from the more recent group were rated by their teachers as significantly more maladjusted than the earlier sample. Also important is the finding that poor marks in school, absence of positive coping behaviors, and the presence of negative coping behaviors in kindergarten are indicators of later mental health problems some 15 years later (Spivack & Marcus, 1987).

One of the most promising approaches to ensure healthy adjustment—not just in school but throughout life—is **cognitive problem solving** (Cowen, 1980). This type of problem solving involves generating alternative strategies to reach one's goal as well considering the consequences of each alternative. Cognitive problem solving also generally includes developing specific ideas for carrying out one's chosen solution (Elias, Gara, Ubriaco, Rothbaum, Clabby, & Schuyler, 1986).

Cognitive problem solving can be used for interpersonal problems such as conflicts, for school-related problems, and many other areas of concern. When used for interpersonal problems, it is called **interpersonal cognitive problem solving** (Shure & Spivack, 1988). Research has uncovered the fact that a significant difference between well-adjusted and maladjusted children is that the maladjusted children fail to generate and evaluate a variety of solutions for coping with a personal problem. Although this method is not without controversy (Gillespie, Durlak, & Sherman, 1982; Rickel & Burgio, 1982), training in cognitive problem solving has been used successfully as an intervention to assist children with coping with stressors. Both teachers and parents can be trained to teach children to use cognitive problem solving.

Using a pre-post design, Elias and colleagues (1986) taught elementary children interpersonal cognitive problem-solving skills and compared them to a no-treatment group upon entry into middle school. The intervention group's curriculum included training in interpersonal sensitivity, generating alternative methods to reach goals, discovering obstacles for solving problems, and creating in the children expectancies that their initiatives could result in positive resolution of their problems. The training was significantly related to reductions in the severity of a variety of middle-school stressors, such as finding one's way around a new school, establishing new peer relations, and resisting pressure to engage in certain behaviors (e.g., smoking). Work and Olsen's (1990) research also demonstrated that training in problem solving improves adjustment in children and is probably effective because of increases in empathy in the trained children. Elias and associates (1986) suggested that the reason some studies show equivocal results for cognitive problem-solving training is that they are conducted simultaneously in too many different and varied settings.

There have been well over 50 child and adolescent interventions conducted based on the premise that cognitive problem-solving skills mediate adjustment (Denham & Almeida, 1987; Weissberg, 1985). Although many of the studies support this strategy as competency enhancing, cognitive problem solving is not without its critics. Durlak (1983), for example, advocates task-specific rather than generic problem-solving training.

One other issue related to school adjustment is **readiness** of young children to enter kindergarten. Readiness as a concept is discussed in Case in Point 8.2.

THE HOME ENVIRONMENT AND ITS EFFECTS ON STUDENTS

By now, you should be convinced that a complex transaction between the student, the parents, and the school as well as with other unseen forces affect students' school performance (Garbarino & Abramowitz, 1992). Despite this complex interaction, for the sake of parsimony, we have generally examined one element at a time in this chapter. Our remaining topic is the students' home environment as it affects school performance. There are many aspects of family life we could cover—such as single-parent homes, step-siblings or blended families, dual-career families, unemployment of a parent, and so on. Again, we have chosen to focus on just one aspect—divorce—because it has received much attention in the adjustment literature and because it now affects so many U.S. children, as one in every two families is touched by divorce.

There is little disagreement in the literature that divorce is an upsetting event for parents and their children. Divorce seems to have a negative impact on

❖ *CASE IN POINT 8.2*

Readiness for School

The concept of *readiness* has recently captured the attention of educators, the media, and policy makers (Graue, 1992). Although each school district and various teachers define *readiness* differently (Graue, 1992), it generally means that a child's developmental level is mature enough for the experience the child is about to have in school. Readiness usually means that a child about to enter kindergarten is developmentally prepared to enter kindergarten, or it can sometimes mean that when children are going to learn to read, they are ready to read. Readiness is important and has been tied to American child-care issues by certain authors (Kagan, 1990).

Much of the effort to determine whether a child is developmentally ready and to assist children who do not appear to be ready has been targeted at the individual level of analysis. For example, there are many developmental tests available to detect readiness (Ellwein, Walsh, Eades, & Miller, 1991). Districts expend much money administering these tests to predict who is and is not ready for certain academic experiences (Tramontana, Hooper, & Selzer, 1988). Unfortunately, these tests have very poor predictive validity and probably should not be used to make decisions that change the whole life course of a child (Graue, 1992).

When a child does not appear to be ready, some experts suggest inducing readiness for kindergarten in the child by sending him or her to prekindergarten (Reynolds, 1991) or retaining the child in the same grade before promoting him or her to the next (Smith & Shepard, 1988). Teachers who view readiness as an individual difference, as a trait, are most likely to subscribe to retention as a solution for lack of preparedness (Smith & Shepard, 1988).

Different patterns of retention among schools suggest that each school has its own view of what readiness is (Shepard, Graue, & Catto, 1989). In ethnographic research, Graue (1992) discovered that each community seems to adopt its own definitions and standards for readiness. Graue was a participant observer in three different classrooms in three different schools within the same school district. She also interviewed teachers and parents as well as examined school records to determine how each constituency and each school construed readiness. Each school community had different notions of what readiness entailed. Thus, readiness is context specific rather than specific to the child. Complicating this is that national associations are attempting to define readiness and set national standards of readiness (National Association of State Boards of Education, 1988).

It seldom occurs to many educators to change the schools rather than the children and the standards for the children (Graue, 1992). Changing the schools might be just the solution to the readiness controversy because it may be the schools that are not ready for the diversity of children attending them.

Graue (1992) believes that schools can be altered to accommodate children. For example, rather than being keepers of arbitrary curriculum standards, teachers could plan curricula that span a variety of age levels. Schools also need to engender more cooperation and collaboration between teachers of various grade levels within a school, which would make sorting children by readiness level less likely. Finally, Graue proposed comprehensive community plans for the transition between home and school, which could tie together the concerns of the home, the preschool, and the elementary school. Schools need to collaborate more with parents. Graue's participant observer study showed that not all parents have an equal opportunity to be heard about the issue of readiness.

children and therefore on their schoolwork. The effects of divorce are not limited just to parental conflict and schoolwork. Surveys of children of divorce indicate that there are various life changes that accompany parental divorce, including but not limited to decreased family income, decreased time with the custodial and noncustodial parent, disruption in family household routine, and less effective, less positive parenting (Sandler, Wolchik, & Braver, 1988).

Other life events can also be distressing for children (Brown & Cowen, 1988; Chandler, Million, & Shermis, 1985) but because children are intensely and negatively impacted by divorce (Wolchik, Sandler, Braver, & Fogas, 1985) and because divorce is so prevalent, it has been a major thrust of intervention work with children and their families. Research on this topic has found that children's perceptions of the negativeness of parental divorce differs from that of their parents and other adults, including clinical psychologists (Wolchik et al., 1985). In much of the research, then, children, not their parents or teachers, are the primary participants.

Studies of divorce have indicated that in the child's natural environment, several factors can moderate the effects of stress from parental divorce, such as the distance between homes of the adolescent children, the availability of support from other family members (Farber, Felner, & Primavera, 1985), and, to a lesser extent, peer support (Lustig, Wolchik, & Braver, 1992). In fact, there is a consistent and fairly strong negative correlation between the child's adjustment to divorce and the availability of social support, especially from other adults (Wolchik, Ruehlman, Braver, & Sandler, 1989). However, in this same research, it was discovered that social support is a complex issue. The effectiveness of support depends on the level of stress *and* the source of support. For example, children under *high* levels of stress with support from both nonfamily and family adults report fewer adjustment problems than children with no support. However, children under *low* levels of stress with high support from nonfamily adults were significantly more poorly adjusted than were children with no or low support.

Some interventionists prefer not to take a passive role by waiting to see whether there are tools available in the child's natural environment that can help the child cope. These proactive interventionists are busy designing programs to assist children of divorce. Pedro-Carroll, Cowen, Hightower, and Guare (1986) examined the effects of the Children of Divorce Intervention Program, which emphasizes establishing social support, identifying feelings related to divorce, training in communication and anger control, and developing methods for en-hancing self-esteem. By comparing program participants to demographically matched peers using a pre-post design, the researchers were able to assess the effects of the program. Before the intervention, the children of divorce were less well adjusted than their peers. The children in the program showed marked improvement after participation—so much so that their adjustment approached that of the comparison or control group's.

Stolberg and Garrison (1985) designed a different program, one that also involved the mothers. Divorced mothers and their children participated in one of three groups: children-only support group, mothers-only support group, and mother and child support group. The researchers also included a no-treatment control group. Children who participated in their own support group showed improved self-concept and better adaptive social skills. Mothers also improved the most in their own support group.

Both of the preceding studies demonstrate the efficacy of postdivorce inter-ventions, especially in the form of social support. Other successful programs have been developed to assist newly separated individuals that are more truly preven-tive, as they intervene at an early stage in divorce (Bloom & Hodges, 1988).

Unfortunately, not all divorced families will avail themselves of these pro-grams (Bowen & Richman, 1991). Braver (1990) reported discouraging statistics related to divorce intervention. Court documents revealed 2,200 families eligible for his program; he was able to contact only 962. In the end, only 70 families, a mere 2.8%, finished the whole program. The lesson to be learned is that even if programs are in place, not everyone will or can participate, and, even then, some participants might not benefit from the programs. Family life and school life are indeed intricately intertwined. It is best that they meet each other half way (Garbarino & Benn, 1992).

SUMMARY

The world of schools, children, families, and communities is a fascinating and complex one. Some children enter school at risk for a variety of problems, but innovative programs are available to prevent or treat the children and their families. Traditional interventions have focused mostly on deficits of the child or the family, but the more effective programs usually take into account the setting, such as the school's climate, as well as the actors in it.

Psychologists recognize how important the early childhood environment is. Children who are advantaged economically or otherwise in early childhood often have fewer problems in later life than disadvantaged children. Intervention pro-grams for young children at risk include quality child day care and compensatory education programs such as Project Head Start. Research has demonstrated that children of working mothers are not disadvantaged. However, these mothers need day care if they are to stay employed. On the other hand, inner-city and some minority children are at risk for a variety of problems day care cannot adequately address. Programs designed to give them the early push they need to later succeed in school are often successful. Project Head Start is one such example. Although early research demonstrated that Head Start was not successful in increasing IQ, its proponents argue that Head Start was not designed for that purpose. Head Start programs are all-encompassing programs; for example, they include parental involvement. Studies demonstrate that children who have attended Head Start have an easier transition into elementary school, achieve at higher levels, and have had their health problems attended to compared to children who do not enroll in such programs.

Desegregation has had an interesting effect on U.S. schools. Desegregation touches children of all ages and races. When the courts ordered the schools to desegregate, the Supreme Court justices did not envision the effects of desegregation on children nor formulate methods for fostering acceptance of diversity in schools. Those jobs fell to psychologists, who have demonstrated that desegregation often has positive effects for minority as well as White children. Various active methods for decreasing prejudice include intergroup contact, the jigsaw classroom, and the "Eye of the Storm" technique. The more passive means seem to fail.

Young children are not the only ones facing problems in this country. Adolescents often use drugs, drop out of school, or become pregnant. Most of the programs that are successful in preventing school dropout do not just try to change the at-risk individual but make adjustments in the school environment to better accommodate the individual learner.

The home environment as it relates to the school environment is important. Children faced with problems at home experience difficulty concentrating and attending to learning. Children of divorce are often considered at risk for a variety of school-related as well as other problems. Once again, intervention programs for children of divorce have proven successful when they provide for changes in the home environment as well as in the child.

9

LAW, CRIME, AND THE COMMUNITY

Two men look out through the same bars; one sees the mud, and one the stars.

◆ *FREDERICK LANGBRIDGE*

Mike was only 4 months old when he was adopted by a middle-class, older couple, Edna and Walt Farnsworth, who had always wanted children but were unable to bear their own. Mike's childhood was uneventful, although Mike's father, Walt, felt that his wife "doted on the boy a bit too much."

During his childhood, Mike was an average student in school. By junior high school, he seemed more interested in sports and cars than in his studies. When Mike reached puberty, he grew quickly, and by the time he was 16, he soared to 6 feet 2 inches, 210 pounds. His imposing size and apparent boredom with school inspired consternation in his teachers who were unsure how to manage Mike.

It was at this point that trouble came to the Farnsworth home. Mike realized that his father, Walt, who was a slender man of slight frame, was intimidated by him. Mike would yell at his mother and disrespect his father. Mike called his father "old man" as often as he could to embarrass Walt. Mike reasoned that his parents were older than his friends' parents.

When Mike was old enough to drive, he wanted nothing but to take his parents' car after school and drive around his small town, showing off to his friends or assessing what "action was going down" on Main Street. The town had few organized activities for its youths. He and his father argued often about the car, Mike's coming home late, and Mike's school grades.

One night, Mike had been drinking beer despite knowing that he was under age. His father was particularly angry when he smelled his son's breath. When Walt yelled at Mike, "You could have killed somebody with *my* car!" Mike struck out at his father. Walt went crashing through the drywall of their small home. Mike fled into the night, which left his poor mother, Edna, with immense worry as to what Mike would do next and great sorrow that her husband had been injured in the fracas.

This scenario was repeated again and again between Mike and Walt, who raged at both his wife and his son that he "didn't want this kid around any more." Edna tried to referee these fights between Mike and Walt but to little avail. As the conflicts escalated, Mike asserted his size and independence more and more.

Taking matters into his own hands and without consulting Edna, Walt went to the local police department to have his son arrested for "anything you can arrest him for—just get him out of my house." The police were used to such domestic squabbles and didn't feel an arrest was in order. Instead, they referred Walt Farnsworth to the probation department so that he could have Mike declared PINS (Person in Need of Supervision). The Probation Department was not surprised to see Walt; they had interviewed many parents just like him, all making the same request.

INTRODUCTION

Was Mike really headed for a life of crime? Was the family at fault for the turmoil in their home? Were any community systems also to blame? For example, was the school environment so alienating that Mike's disenchantment with school was displaced onto his family? How would the justice system ordinarily manage this family dispute?

This chapter will examine the criminal justice system in the United States. We will again look at the traditional system and how it manages those individuals who interact with it. We will also address some alternative and innovative programs designed to humanize this same system. As community psychologists, we will also examine how the environment or context contributes to crime, fear of victimization, and other justice system processes.

THE TRADITIONAL JUSTICE SYSTEM

Criminal Justice Processes

Pick up any newspaper from a major city in the United States and you see splashed across its pages reports of crime—crime in the streets, conflict in homes, corruption in business and government, crime just about everywhere. Community psychologists share the average citizen's concern about "the grim reality" (Thompson & Norris, 1992) of interpersonal violence and crime in our communities. Citizens and psychologists want to know what can be done to prevent crime and treat so-called offenders so that they will not return to a life of crime. Community psychologists also share the concern that victims be assisted in their recovery from crime.

In a special edition of the *American Journal of Community Psychology*, Ronald Roesch (1988) called for increased involvement by community psychologists in criminal justice proceedings by going beyond the individual level of analysis to the examination of situational and environmental factors that contribute to criminal behavior. He called for community psychologists to help predict problematic behavior and adopt preventive measures for at-risk individuals. Before addressing what community psychologists know about crime and the community, we will look at the justice and enforcement systems in U.S. society. This will enable you to contrast what usually happens in these systems with the reforms that community psychologists and concerned citizens are trying to institute.

The justice and enforcement systems in society are multilayered. They involve the various courts (municipal, state and federal, civil and criminal, and higher and lower) as well as the judges, juries, lawyers, plaintiffs, and defendants; the prisons, jails, and corrections officers; the police, sheriffs, and other enforcement agencies; the departments of parole and probation; as well as the multitude of ancillary services such as legal aid societies and neighborhood justice centers. Reviewing what would have happened to Mike, the youth in the opening vignette, had he been an adult arrested for assault might benefit your understanding.

Had he been arrested as an adult, Mike would have been officially charged with the crime (**indicted**), asked to address the charge by pleading guilty or not guilty (**arraigned**), and perhaps asked to post bail. As an unemployed person, Mike probably would not have had bail money, so if his friends or family did not assist him, he would have had to remain in jail, especially if deemed dangerous. Many others like Mike, including members of the lower socioeconomic classes, have not been tried but are serving time. They have not been found guilty; they simply do not have bail money. Today, the time in jail awaiting trial usually counts toward any subsequent prison sentences, but this was not always true in the past.

Mike also probably could not afford a lawyer, so the court would appoint a public defender for him. The public defender might convince Mike to plea bargain his case *before* it went to trial. A **plea bargain** is a behind-the-scenes negotiation where the prosecution would agree to a reduced charge if Mike pleaded guilty (Maynard, 1984). Critics of plea bargaining believe that this strategy is used to the disadvantage of the poor and the uneducated. Supporters favor plea bargaining because it saves taxpayers the expense of a trial (Hess, Markson, & Stein, 1991). If Mike refused to bargain, he would have gone to trial, where, if found guilty, he would have been sentenced perhaps to a prison term, to community service, or to probation. The process might not end here if Mike appealed the verdict or the sentence. The trial and appeals process can be a long one, sometimes taking years due to overloaded court dockets. Some of these processes and participants will be examined in more detail.

Crime and Criminals

Did Mike commit a crime because he hit his father? Some would argue he did. Others would suggest that Mike was simply a confused or frustrated adolescent—a person in need of some counseling, but certainly not a criminal.

Just what is a crime? It is beyond the scope of this book to argue about definitions of the term *crime*. Just as laws are never perfect, definitions are never perfect. Laws that determine and therefore define *crime* change from society to society and from one historical era to the next (Hess et al., 1991), making the definition of the term difficult. Nonetheless, a rudimentary definition of crime might assist you in understanding its complexity. A **crime** is an intentional act that violates the prescriptions or proscriptions of the criminal law under conditions in which no legal excuse applies and where there is a state with power to codify such laws and to enforce penalties in response to their breach (Nettler, 1980). As a means of further clarification, consider the following:

- There is no crime without laws and without a state to punish the breach of the law, the implication being that laws are political.
- There is no crime where an act that would otherwise be offensive is justified by law (such as killing another person in self-defense).
- There is no crime without intention (prosecutors must establish the purpose of the crime).
- There is no crime where the offender is deemed incompetent (as in "insanity") (Nettler, 1980).

Thus, self-defense, mental illness, the absence of a law, and so on can "save" a person from breaking the law and being labeled a criminal or offender.

Given the daily headlines about crimes and violence, just how frequent is crime in the United States? And what are the causes of crime? These difficult questions require one to venture into the area of **forensic psychology**, the study of the impact of legal phenomena on individual behavior. Inciardi (1990) reviewed the history and issues related to crime statistics. *The Uniform Crime Reports*, the first national effort at crime data collection, have been collected by the Federal Bureau of Investigation (FBI) since 1930. These statistics are based on the compilations of reported crimes of local law enforcement agencies such as city police and county sheriffs departments throughout the nation. The data, however, include only crimes *known* to the police. There is often little correspondence between the crimes that are committed in a community and the crimes that are reported. Research suggests that often the committed crimes, especially violent ones, are about twice the reported crimes in number (U.S. Department of Justice, 1991). An example of an unreported crime would be a storekeeper who catches his neighbor's son shoplifting but who admonishes the boy not to shoplift rather than face the boy's father with the news that the son is a thief who will be prosecuted. A more extreme and unfortunate example is the case of rape; slightly more than half of the rapes that occur go unreported (Bureau of Justice Statistics, 1993). On the other hand, homicide is almost always reported to the police.

Larceny and theft are the most often committed crimes in the United States, with about 3,100 reported per 100,000 people. These crimes are followed in frequency by burglary, motor vehicle theft, assault, robbery, rape, and, finally, murder/manslaughter, which has a frequency of 8 per 100,000 in the general population in the United States (U.S. Bureau of the Census, 1989). However, 1992 and 1993 were record years for violent crimes (Bureau of Justice Statistics, 1993). Men in the United States are more likely to die in a homicide than men of many other countries (Inciardi, 1980). The question is *Why*?

Perhaps the number of guns available in the United States explains this country's homicide rate. Unlike similar countries, such as Canada, where the handgun homicide rate is much lower, Americans have a constitutional right to bear arms. However, cross-national comparisons are sticky business. One cannot simply examine gun ownership and gun homicide rates. Often, in a particular country, other types of homicide rates (e.g., with a knife) are high yet one would not readily say that high rates of knife ownership caused the killing (Kleck, 1991). One needs to know more about a nation's cultural and ethnic homogeneity, history of racial conflict, rigidity and obedience to authority, subjective sense of unjust deprivation, and so on before one can make claims that gun control within a nation causes fewer handgun deaths (Kleck, 1991).

Many cross-national studies of gun control are also correlational (e.g., Killias, 1993), meaning that conclusions cannot be drawn about causality. If a positive correlation is found between the number of guns held by citizens and the number of homicides, it might be that (1) gun ownership levels are a *response* to already existing high violence rates or (2) gun ownership levels may serve as indicators of the population's willingness to inflict lethal violence on others (Kleck, 1991).

In the United States, Jung and Jason (1988) did find that U.S. gun control legislation has some impact, if only temporary, on firearm assaults. On the other hand, Lester and Murrell (1986) discovered that states with stricter handgun control statutes have lower suicide rates but not lower homicide rates than states with no such statues. In a similar vein, studies of owners of registered handguns reveal that gun owners are White, middle-class males, yet they are not the ones likely to die in nor cause homicides (Hess et al., 1991). Young African American men have the highest death rates from homicides (45 out of every 100,000, or six times the rate of Whites) (U.S. Department of Justice, 1991), especially when their assailants are African American.

As concerned citizens, Americans need to understand the reasons for Black-on-Black violence. One postulated reason is the low income or poverty level of African Americans. Poverty, however, cannot be the only explanation because other minorities (e.g., Hispanic Americans) also have low incomes, yet their homicide rates are significantly lower than that for African Americans (Silberman, 1980).

Inciardi (1980) offered another explanation. He suggested that violence was not part of the cultural heritage African Americans carried from Africa; hence, violence was learned in the United States. Inciardi argued that African Americans are the only minority group that came to U.S. shores involuntarily as slaves. Additionally, they are the group that is most salient in terms of racial features. Because of this, perhaps Whites harbor more prejudice against them than any other group. Of all the minorities and powerless peoples, African Americans seem to be the most frustrated by historical circumstances and present conditions. Frustration and blocked opportunities perhaps cause Black-on-Black violence (Hess et al., 1991) as much as or more than handguns or poverty. Wheeler, Cartwright, Kagan, and Friedman (1987) have confirmed, in part, the role played by social power in the United States. By analyzing court case data from as early as the 1870s, they concluded that the "haves" (Whites) have been coming out ahead of the "have nots" (minorities) in this country's justice system for a long time.

Given those last few statements, it is not surprising that forensic psychologists have discovered that race is a major predictor of outcomes of jury verdicts (Stewart, 1980) and sentencing decisions (Nakell & Hardy, 1987). Minorities are more likely to receive guilty verdicts and more severe sentences than Whites. As for the death penalty, or **capital punishment**, there are many minorities on Death Row, their numbers being disproportionate to their numbers in the general population. Likewise, studies verify that murderers of Whites are more likely to be sentenced to death than are murderers of African Americans (Hess et al., 1991; Henderson & Taylor, 1985). Race also plays a key role in judges' prosecutorial decisions in homicide cases (Radelet & Pierce, 1985). Prejudice may indeed be the underlying cause of much criminal behavior, as well as the vehicle that drives outcome in the justice system.

The Prisons

The traditional means to address violent crime is to arrest, prosecute, convict, and imprison, or **incarcerate**, the guilty individual. When Walt Farnsworth approached his local police department in the opening vignette, he had this process in mind. He wanted his son arrested, taken out of the home, and removed from him and the rest of society. At the least, Walt wanted Mike declared as a **person in need of supervision (PINS)**. Do these procedures remedy the crime situation in the country? We have already presented the skewed results of these processes for African Americans; we need now to examine broader data to answer this question.

Of the total adult population in the United States, 1 in every 46 adults (or 4.1 million people) is under some type of justice system supervision. This may involve incarceration; a community alternative in which the individual is supervised, such as **probation**; or **parole**, which is early release of a prisoner before the sentence expires (U.S. Department of Justice, 1991). (Figure 9.1 depicts the increase in the number of adults under the care or custody of a corrections agency.)

The philosophy of incarceration and legal supervision is generally retribution, not rehabilitation. **Retribution** in the legal system is supposed to mean repayment for the crime, but it translates in reality to punishment for the crime. If anyone is repaid, it is usually not the victim. Indeed, the victim is the only person who has no official role in the process; the victim need not even appear at the trial (Forer, 1980). The "state" is the entity that administers the punishment and receives the remuneration, if any. For instance, if an individual is found guilty and is fined, the fine does not go to the victim but rather to the state. If the guilty party is sent to prison, the state decides the sentence and the type of prison. In the past, the victim rarely got to speak out about any of these issues.

Does this retributional approach work? That is, Is the convicted person reformed? Does he or she return to a better life or **recidivate** (return to) a life of crime? Data show that of all released felons, 43%—nearly half—are rearrested within three years of release (U.S. Department of Justice, 1991). Retribution does not seem to work according to these statistics.

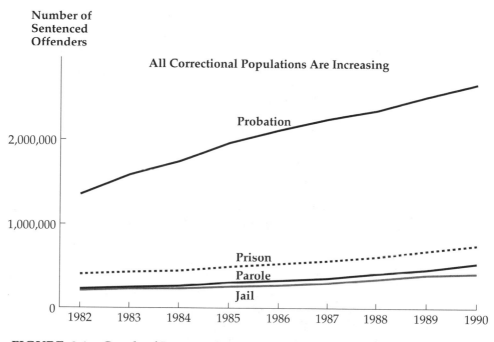

FIGURE 9.1   **Graph of Increase in Number of Adults Under the Care or Custody of a Corrections Agency**

Source: Bureau of Justice Statistics National Update, Vol. 1, No. 3, January 1992, p. 4.

A classic study in psychology highlights what occurs in prisons that makes reform unlikely. Philip Zimbardo and his colleagues (Haney, Banks, & Zimbardo, 1973) obtained volunteers to act either as prisoners or guards in a mock prison. Subjects were all mentally healthy before the study began and were randomly assigned to their roles. The researchers told the guards to do only what was necessary to keep order. The prisoners were all "arrested" unexpectedly at their homes and driven to the mock prison by real police officers. The prisoners were stripped, searched, dressed in hospital-style gowns, and given identification numbers by the guards. Within a few days of assuming their roles, the guards became abusive of the prisoners. They harassed the prisoners, forced them into crowded cells, awakened them in the night, forced them into frequent countdowns, and subjected them to hard labor and solitary confinement. Conditions in the mock prison became so brutal, the prisoners so depressed, and the guards so involved in their roles that Zimbardo and his colleagues prematurely ended the study. The prison experience, even for these "normal" men, proved overwhelming.

Prisons are **total institutions**; they handle an individual's diverse needs through bureaucracy (Goffman, 1961), which can be degrading, dehumanizing (Paulus, 1988), and humiliating for the inmates (Smith, 1992). Prisoners today often live in overcrowded conditions where they are exposed to acquired immune deficiency syndrome (AIDS), prisoner-to-prisoner violence, and a prison culture that is not conducive to their successful and productive return to mainstream society. In fact, one set of justice experts wrote that local jails serve only to brutalize and embitter men, further preventing them from returning to a useful role in society (Allen & Simonsen, 1992). Perhaps had Walter Farnsworth known the state of the corrections system, he would not have jumped so quickly at the notion of having his adopted son arrested.

Case in Point 9.1 highlights another interesting phenomenon found in today's prisons—women correctional officers who guard male inmates. This case illustrates another way in which prisons are peculiar psychological and social institutions.

Courts have ruled that the prison system must be restructured (*Ruiz* v. *Estelle*), but this restructuring has only escalated inmate-inmate and inmate-guard violence (Marquart & Crouch, 1985). Similarly, inmate lawsuits over the crowded conditions in prisons have led to many inmates' early release, which sometimes results in higher recidivism rates and return to the crowded prisons (Kelly & Ekland-Olson, 1991). Although legal decrees to change total institutions (loosely called *institutional laws*) do exist, there is concern that the decrees will not translate readily into *real* institutional change (Haney & Pettigrew, 1986). In the meantime, the growth in the number of prisoners continues to exceed the growth in prison space, which leads only to more overcrowding. Since 1980, the nation's prison population has ballooned by almost 134% (U.S. Department of Justice, 1991).

The threat of stiffer penalties and laws does little to deter potential law breakers (Paternoster, 1989; Singer & McDowall, 1988). In the meantime, the cost of imprisonment for an inmate is escalating; the cost to house the typical juvenile offender—such as Mike Farnsworth, for example—is estimated to be $25,000 annually (U.S. Bureau of the Census, 1989). Experts in corrections have adopted some imaginative but as yet unproven methods for addressing cost and crowding in prisons, such as house arrest (where an individual convicted of a crime must remain confined to his or her home) (Bingham & Piotrowski, 1989; Sandhu, Dodder, & Davis, 1990), short-term prison "boot camps" or **shock incarceration programs** (Sechrest, 1989), community service programs (McDonald, 1986), and electronic monitoring (Quinn & Holman, 1991) while serving time in the community at large. In fact, prisons are so crowded that about 75% of all convicted offenders are being supervised in the community, not in jails or prisons (U.S. Department of Justice, 1991).

Victims and Fear of Being Victimized

Harris (1985) reported that 32% of U.S. citizens are uneasy walking on their own streets. In 1990, 34.8 million people were victimized by crime in the United States (National Crime Survey, 1991). Community psychologists are interested both in fear of crime and in actual victimization (Thompson & Norris, 1992). Those who are the most fearful are sometimes the least likely to be victimized—a phenom-

❖ CASE IN POINT 9.1

Women Guarding Men

Sociologist Lynn Zimmer is interested in developing a comprehensive theory of women's occupational experiences. To build her theory, she conducted *ethnographic research* with two sets of women guards at two different prisons for men. In ethnographic research, the issue under study is first described. Interviews with individuals involved with the issue are typically conducted to piece together the description. Next, the issue is related to important features of relevant social contexts—in this case, the prison environment.

Women guarding men is an interesting and relatively new phenomenon and is also the title of Zimmer's book on the subject (Zimmer, 1986). Before 1972, there were no female guards in men's prisons (Freedman, 1974). Federal antidiscrimination laws changed all of this. However, less than 10% of the guards at men's prisons today are women. Therefore, women guarding men in prison is still a very nontraditional role for women.

Zimmer's contributions to the understanding of the stresses and strains on women guards are considered to be threefold (Crouch, 1988). In her books, she emphasized the extent and depth of resistance to the women officers, discovered the coping strategies the women utilized, and explained the pattern of adjustment of the women officers.

In terms of the women officers' acceptance into the culture of the prison, "they all share one common experience: working on a job in which they are unwanted and unappreciated by nearly everyone in their work environment" (p. 51). The male guards displayed resentment toward the women officers, and even the women's own labor union thought them unsuitable. The prison administrators seemed more acquiescent—resigned—than supportive to the women employees. Interestingly, the only ones who partly supported the hiring of women guards were the inmates, the very individuals the women were expected to guard.

How did the women officers cope with this resentment and resistance as well as the harassment from coworkers and occasional sexual misconduct of inmates? Zimmer's research suggested various coping strategies. The smallest number of women officers (11%) worked to the letter of their job descriptions. The remaining women fit one of two other modes. A large group of them (43%) avoided inmate contact as much as possible, and when they did have contact, they were backed up by male coworkers. Another large group (46%) adopted the "inventive" role—one in which they ally themselves with supportive inmates who control the trouble-makers among their peers.

Zimmer concluded that in the future, how the women perform this job will depend not just on the laws, but the policy decisions of reluctant prison officials and on the actions and interactions of those in the prison environment.

enon called the **fear-victimization paradox**. Not all research supports the inverse relationship between fear and actual victimization (Mawby, 1986; Taylor & Shumaker, 1990; Thompson & Norris, 1992), but the phenomenon is an interesting one. Discussed here are data that support the paradox.

Young men are the most likely to be victimized yet the least afraid of violent crime. Conversely, elderly women are most fearful yet least likely to be victimized (Mawby, 1986; U.S. Department of Justice, 1988). Young women also fear crime more than young men but are less likely to be victimized than young men (Roll & Habemeier, 1991). Actual victim or not, the cost of fear and suffering to potential or real victims is enormous. Cohen (1988), by means of sophisticated calculations, arrived at the amount of $92.6 billion annually as the real cost to victims identified by the FBI crime index in terms of actual losses *plus* pain, suffering, and fear. Thompson and Norris (1992) found that victims of violent crimes, especially those of low status, suffer pervasive consequences of the crime, including alienation, fear of crime, avoidance, and other behaviors.

Why do some individuals fear crime even if they are not likely to be victimized? For one, people often perceive urban environments as dangerous (Glaberson, 1990). City residents with the greatest fear are usually dissatisfied with their neighborhoods. When an area contains abandoned buildings, vandalism, graffiti, litter, idle teenagers, and other signs of "incivilities" (Taylor & Shumaker, 1990), its residents are more fearful because these signs suggest deterioration of the social controls on which their safety depends (Lewis & Salem, 1981). Other factors, such as population size of the city (Baron & Byrne, 1994) and desirability of the city as a place of residence (Levine, Miyake, & Lee, 1989), are not necessarily related to true crime rates.

As already mentioned, the fear of victimization and actual victimization is not always supported by empirical research. Taylor and Shumaker (1990) offered an interesting explanation for why there is only a marginal link between fear and likelihood of being victimized in a crime. They suggested that individuals in high-crime areas become desensitized to the probability of crime. This desensitization is adaptive in that losing the fear of crime perhaps lowers one's stress level. Actual victims of crime also respond adaptively to fear of further crime; they sometimes express less fear than nonvictims, much as if the original crime experience inoculates them from more fear. Taylor and Shumaker offered data from research on natural disaster victims that support their contentions that a disaster inoculates and desensitizes the victims in the future.

Taylor and Shumaker (1990) have suggested that their heuristic of crime as a natural disaster holds important policy ramifications. For one, in high-crime areas, individualized crime-prevention strategies may merely serve to continually resensitize and therefore distress the residents. A better approach, they have advised, might be to adopt a social problems orientation. That is, treat high-risk neighborhoods by finding global solutions to social problems such as unemployment and lack of recreational facilities for youth that might otherwise contribute to crime. On the other hand, in low-crime communities where individuals need to be somewhat sensitized to crime, an individualized orientation to crime prevention (adding security systems or learning self defense) might be more appropriate. In sum, Taylor and Shumaker recommended that not all crime-prevention programs are equally good for all neighborhoods. They and other community psychologists (Norris & Kaniasty, 1992) have recommended policies that create a "fit" between the neighborhoods, the residents, and the programs. This is especially true because citizen-initiated preventions on their own appear highly inadequate, according to Taylor and Shumaker.

Aside from fear of crime, there are concerns about how the justice system treats actual victims. We commented earlier on the small role, if any, the victim plays in courtroom dramas. Everyone in a courtroom has an officially sanctioned role except the victim. Criminal law is not structured to take into account the victim's needs or to give the victim what he or she might be due. The failure of the justice system to provide for the victims, in the opinion of some, is a major source of public dissatisfaction with legal processes (Forer, 1980; Finn & Lee, 1988). In 1974, only 35% of the victims were ever informed of the results of prosecutorial deliberations related to their victimization (U.S. Department of Justice, 1992). At least there has been an increase in the number of prosecutors who inform the victims of the outcome of their cases.

When victims *are* asked to play a role in the courts of law, how are they treated? Some studies show that in certain cases, victims are not treated well or are treated differently from others in the courtroom drama. For example, in sexual assaults, the victims are subjected to more negative questioning and are required to give more personal forms of testimony than are other victims, including assault victims. Surprisingly, sexual assault cases are convicted less often than other cases. This occurs even when laws are intentionally designed to make it easier to prosecute sexual assault (Sahjpaul & Renner, 1988).

Furthermore, research by O'Barr and Conley (1985) indicated that although litigants in small claims court are provided with significant opportunity to tell their stories, there is frequently a failure in small claims court to include components critical to establishing *legally adequate* claims. Research by Van Koppen and Malsch (1991) demonstrated that although plaintiffs (victims) are likely to win cases in civil court, they have much difficulty collecting their awards. The researchers further discovered that only those who repeatedly return to court are likely to collect anything at all. One might conclude, then, that certain actual victims do not fare well in court, even when their stories are heard.

Therefore, it should come as no surprise to learn that there are now over 4,000 victim assistance programs in the United States, many of them arising as grassroots efforts (Finn & Lee, 1988). Because of the lack of responsiveness of the courts to victim concerns in the past, some courts have revamped the way they deal with victims. For an example of a new approach, see Profile 9.1 on Melinda Ostermeyer and the Multi-Door Court House.

Enforcement Agencies

Some see the police as peace officers who assist in keeping communities harmonious and free of crime. Perhaps this attitude led Walt Farnsworth to the police when the conflict with Mike escalated. Others sometimes see the police as brutish and intrusive, as "pigs." Many of you may recall the videotape of the Los Angeles police beating Rodney King. The acquittal of the police in that incident triggered

◆ *PROFILE 9.1*
Melinda Ostermeyer

Melinda Ostermeyer is the director of the Multi-Door Dispute Resolution Division of the Superior Court of the District of Columbia. She was previously the director of the Dispute Resolution Center in Houston, Texas, where she also served as staff director of the Alternative Dispute Resolution Committees of the Houston Bar Association and the State Bar of Texas.

The Multi-Door Court House Program that Ostermeyer oversees is an innovative approach designed to enhance access to justice, decrease court backlog, and provide alternative methods of dispute resolution. The purpose of providing this program to the justice system is to reduce people's dissatisfaction with the legal system. Judge Frank E. A. Saunders (1976) of the Harvard Law School believed that the program benefits the entire legal system because it offers faster, less expensive, and more satisfying solutions to litigants.

The Multi-Door approach allows a case to pass through any of a number of "doors" for settlement. The case begins with a professional and well-reasoned initial case evaluation. The intake specialist examines case characteristics, the complexity of the issues, the intensity of the relationship between the disputing parties, their financial status, their emotional support systems, and the willingness of all parties to actively participate in the process (Ostermeyer, 1991).

Next, in collaboration with the involved parties, the case is directed toward an appropriate "door" (and occasionally multiple doors), including but not limited to mediation, arbitration, court, other community services such as mental health counseling or legal aid societies, and so on. Even if the "door" does not solve the problem, the citizens leave armed with information about where else they can turn (Ostermeyer, 1991).

Because the Multi-Door staff guide the citizens through what otherwise might be a bewildering maze of services, 90% of the users of the Multi-Door system report high satisfaction with it (Roehl, 1986). Moreover, research indicates that Multi-Door users report that they learned new tools for conflict management and communication because of their involvement in the program (Roehl, 1986). Finally, the Multi-Door approach to justice means that citizens avoid the frustrating and often unproductive sequence of multiple and overlapping referrals (Ostermeyer, 1991).

riots in Los Angeles in the spring of 1992. Regardless of one's views of the police, interesting research has demonstrated how difficult the job of policing communities can be. In fact, there is mounting interest in police burnout (Goodman, 1990) and in the frequency of murder of police (Lester, 1987).

Why is the career of an enforcement officer so difficult? One reason is that the police force and the community's citizens hold different views of the role of the officers. New police recruits often maintain a "serve and protect" orientation toward the community, but after training, their attitudes often shift toward one of remoteness from the community. In fact, police officers increasingly see themselves as hampered by community attitudes and constraints (Ellis, 1991) and as holding differing views from the community as to which policing style is effective (Alpert & Dunham, 1986). For example, police often have a machismo identity (Keys & Fuehrer, 1987) that is sometimes not welcomed by the community.

Defensiveness about the community's attitudes toward its police creates solidarity among police (Shernock, 1988). However, defensiveness coupled with the unique socialization of police into their enforcement role (Fielding, 1986) serve to increase the distance between the officers and the community. The history of policing also gives it a double and contradictory function (Robinson & Scaglion, 1987). At the same time and in the same society, the police may be both the agent of the people it polices and the dominant class controlling these same people.

The police force and citizens also hold different views as to which community incidents ought to involve the police. Police are often called by citizens for public nuisance offenses (e.g., loud noise or drunkenness), traffic accidents, illegally parked vehicles, and investigation of suspicious persons (Nishimura & Suzuki, 1986)—not very glamorous tasks and surely not the exciting roles portrayed in televised, fictional dramas about the police. The police are also likely to be called to intervene in family conflicts—a role for which they need more training—which can sometimes lead to assault on the officer if managed ineffectively (Buchanon & Chasnoff, 1986). Another frequent role of the police is to intervene in psychiatric crises; that is, the police are asked to intercede in a mental health crisis, make a quick evaluation, and decide whether to utilize placement in a hospital or jail if the person is a danger to self or others. Police officers do not relish this job and are often required to make quick mental health decisions without much training in mental health issues (Pogrebin, 1986–1987). To worsen matters, Reuss-Ianni (1983) has found that police "on the beat" (on the street) feel that their supervisors or those in police management positions have little understanding of what street work is like.

A primary question about policing is whether active enforcement and a police presence in a community affect the crime rate. Sampson and Cohen (1988) examined effects of proactive policing in 171 U.S. cities. The overall results suggest that there is an inverse effect of policing on robbery rates. In other words, the larger the police presence, the lower the robbery rates. In another study, Watson (1986) examined the effects of awareness of increased police enforcement as a general deterrent in noncompliance with seat belt laws. Using a field experiment and media campaign, Watson found that the increased threat of legal punishment reduced by one-half the number of noncompliers. The threat of police enforcement, then, is sometimes effective in reducing crime, but is it the only way or the best way?

Community psychologists are concerned about the division between the police and the communities they serve. Community psychologists are also concerned about burnout and stress in all careers, including that of enforcement officers. In addition, community psychologists, of course, believe that crime prevention is better than arrest and prosecution after the fact. We will turn now to programs designed by community psychologists and others interested in addressing the diverse needs of the citizens, victims, offenders, and professionals involved in the criminal justice system.

ADDRESSING DIVERSE JUSTICE SYSTEM NEEDS WITH COMMUNITY PSYCHOLOGY

Preventive Measures

Predicting At-Risk Behavior

Was there anything in Mike Farnsworth's background that would have helped someone predict that he would turn into an irascible and difficult adolescent? Perhaps his adoption, being placed with older parents, his large size, school alienation, and other factors contributed to his family difficulties. This section will examine predictors of criminal and violent behavior.

Professionals and laypeople such as jurors are often asked to make predictions about criminal and dangerous behavior. What does science tell us about jurors' accuracy? Marquart, Ekland-Olson and Sorensen (1989) have documented how jurors perform when they are asked to predict dangerousness in capital cases where a death sentence can be applied. Jurors, in essence, are asked to predict whether a defendant presents a continuing violent threat to society. In Marquart and colleagues' study, the patterns of behavior in prison and upon release of 92 individuals with commuted death sentences were examined. Because the juries predicted the prisoners would be violent, the criminals were sentenced to death rather than life in prison. Someone later commuted or reversed the death sentence.

The researchers reported that these prisoners were model inmates while incarcerated. Of the 92, only 1 committed a murder while in prison. Eventually, 12 of the inmates were released to the community, and 1 of the 12 committed a second slaying. Marquart and associates claimed that juries err in the direction of false positives; juries judge far more individuals to be dangerous than really are. Would it have been better to execute all 92 to prevent the 2 subsequent slayings? Or would it have been better to eventually free all 92 inmates and have only 2 commit further offenses? Since there is nothing that guarantees 100% certainty in the prediction of violence, the researchers suggested that jurors at least be told of the poor predictive record of their predecessors before they assign sentences.

Can psychologists and other professionals predict *better* than jurors which individuals are at risk for breaking the law or committing violence? If psychologists are good fortune tellers, then they ought to be able to prevent by way of intervention targeted at-risk individuals from fulfilling their prophecies (Coates, 1981; Roesch, 1988).

Is it possible to predict who those individuals at risk are? Roesch (1988) reviewed longitudinal research in England where 411 youthful male offenders were followed for several years. Crimes were more likely to be committed by youths when they were unemployed and when they had prior convictions for other crimes. Similarly, Tolan and Lorion (1988) reported research where they attempted to identify delinquency proneness in 337 adolescent males. Tolan and Lorion found that early onset of delinquent behavior is a good predictor of subsequent delinquent behavior.

These same researchers documented that family patterns are also important. Low-conflict, religious, highly cohesive families translated into lower delinquency rates for their young members. Such families may inculcate in their children the bond to conventional society that is so necessary to preventing delinquent behavior (Hawkins & Weis, 1985; Hoshino, 1989). On the other hand, many juvenile offenders report that other members of their families have been incarcerated (U.S. Department of Justice, 1991). The exact percents for various family members are given in Figure 9.2. The family has a decided impact on a felon's mental health when the felon is under community supervision (Quinn & Holman, 1991). Tolan and Lorion also noted that self-reported delinquency is a better measure than official records. Official records contain only crimes that were detected, not those that were actually committed.

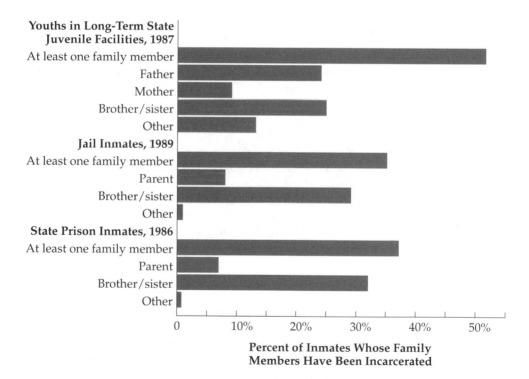

FIGURE 9.2   Percentage of Inmates Reporting Their Family Members Have Also Been Incarcerated

Source: Bureau of Justice Statistics National Update, April 1992, p. 7.

Coates (1981) also found that the broader social network—the one beyond the families of the youths—is important in predicting delinquency. If the youth reports being affiliated with peers who are crime-prone, then the youth is more likely to become delinquent or repeat an offense upon release from a youth detention center.

Although the emphasis on prediction of delinquency is on males, females can also be delinquent. Research shows that most female delinquents have experienced some type of childhood trauma, such as sexual abuse. Female delinquency might really be a sign of disclosure that victimization (e.g., sexual molestation) is occurring (Bowers, 1990). All of these studies bring one to the conclusion that people *can* forecast who is at risk for breaking the law. Community psychologists also need to try to be able to predict group behavior better, too. In the meantime, the next question logically becomes: Once these at-risk individuals have been discovered, what can one do to intercede in their lives to prevent misconduct?

Prevention with At-Risk Individuals

In an informative review comparing state detention centers with community-based treatments for delinquents, Coates (1981) suggested that much could be done by way of prevention. Before commencing this unit, though, we remind you that in Chapters 3 and 4 on social change, reasons for resisting social programs were reviewed. Despite the probable soundness of what you are about to read, such programs are not readily nor frequently adopted for a variety of reasons.

Coates (1981) remarked that working one to one with youths will not in itself prevent delinquency. Interventions must be focused on the youth's environment and social network. One could intervene with peers who are likely to negatively influence the at-risk youth. Or one could intervene with the youth's family or provide foster parents, a positive adult role model, or a more stimulating school environment if no parents are available. In other words, treating Mike Farnsworth without regard to his family, environment, or his friends probably would not have altered Mike's behavior.

Coates also noted that abrupt separation from helping services, even if they are correctional facilities, also causes declines in post release behaviors. Rather, youths need to be eased into the community by advocates and human services workers. Coates showcased the Pennsylvania Youth Advocate Program in which a parent receives intensive training in negotiations with the schools and other agencies on behalf of the youth and is provided back-up child care so the parent is free to keep youth-related appointments.

Coates also suggested that youths should not just be recipient's of services but instead should have some decision-making power in the design and use of the services they receive. There is some evidence to suggest that he is correct; also, this view is in keeping with community psychology's premise that affected individuals should participate in decision making. Martin and Osgood (1987) found that autonomy or participation in decision making resulted in prosocial outcomes for incarcerated youths. Data were collected from 434 residents and 156 staff members of residential institutions for adjudicated adolescents. The data demonstrated both direct and indirect influences of autonomy, which contributed to greater acceptance of treatment goals and more prosocial values in the youths allowed more autonomy.

Another noteworthy study with at-risk individuals and one that incorporates some of these ideas focused on youth gangs. Efforts by social scientists usually attempt to reduce the likelihood of being recruited into such gangs or of gang members returning to the gangs once they have been apprehended and incarcerated (Agopian, 1989). In the study under consideration here, recruitment into gangs was the important measure. Thompson and Jason (1988) worked with 117 eighth-graders at risk for joining gangs. The intent was one of primary prevention—to prevent eventual gang membership. Thompson and Jason used classroom sessions with structured after-school activities such as sports and job skills training. They later compared participants to a control or no-treatment group and asked gang informants to disclose which students had indeed joined gangs. Four members of the control group but only one from an experimental group were joiners. Intensive intervention seemed to reduce recruitment into gangs. However, one may also deduce from these results that prevention is not 100% effective either.

Designing the Environment to Prevent Crime

We reviewed here how the environment contributes to perceptions that an individual is likely to be the victim of crime. This issue needs to be examined further. **Environmental psychologists**—those who study the effect of the environment on behavior—have much to offer community psychologists in terms of recommendations for arranging the environment so that crime is less likely to occur.

Do characteristics of the environment influence crime? Research suggests the answer is yes. For example, several studies indicate that as the ambient temperature increases, so does aggression. Anderson and Anderson (1984) studied the number of aggressive crimes in two different U.S. cities as well as the temperatures on the days the crimes were committed. There was a positive correlation between the two. Similarly, **crowding**, the subjective experience of too many people for the amount of space, has also been linked to negative affect and behavior (Baron & Byrne, 1994). For example, in prisons, as the number of inmates increases, the number of discipline problems, deaths, and suicides increases (Cox, Paulus, & McCain, 1984). It can safely be said that features of the environments *do* influence crime rates.

Traditional approaches to crime deterrence in various environments would include installing burglar alarms, motion sensors, and other devices designed to catch someone in the act of breaking the law. However, recent research on environments proposes that built environments can incorporate safety features that deter or prevent crime. For example, D'Alessio and Stolzenberg (1990) found that the location in the neighborhood, the parking lot size, and the number of hours convenience stores were open determined whether the stores were robbed. The researchers suggested that changes along these dimensions might prevent robberies at stores built in the future. For example, stores with large parking lots were robbed more often. Smaller lots for future stores might deter robbers.

Levine, Wachs, and Shirazi (1986) studied high- and low-crime bus stops and found that the particularly dangerous stops shared common environmental features. For example, crime was higher at bus stops where those waiting mingled with passersby. Levine and associates recommended that locational and environmental information should be used when planning the development of future bus stops in order to reduce crime. For instance, plexiglass shelters that shield those waiting for the bus from passersby might reduce certain crimes.

With regard to residences, MacDonald and Gifford (1989) asked 43 individuals arrested for breaking and entering what cues various homes possessed that would prohibit them from being burgled. Houses that were easily surveillable were rated as least vulnerable, whereas houses with frequent *symbolic* barriers (e.g., door decorations) increased vulnerability because the barriers communicate both the value of and the availability of high-quality care for the house. Similarly, Riga and Morganti (1992) found that owner-occupied homes, compared to rental homes, had more *actual* barriers (e.g., fences) that help prevent crime as well as signify an effort to exert control over the environment (Altman, Wohlwill, & Werner, 1985).

Finally, there is a huge amount of literature on how the presence of violent cues triggers aggression. The largest piece of this literature pertains to televised violence, which can only be summarized here in the interest of space. Researchers have endeavored to show that televised aggression leads to increased aggression in children and adults. The average U.S. household has a television on for about seven hours a day. In those hours, 90% of all children's cartoons and 80% of all adult programs contain some violence. Laboratory studies on the two phenomena leave little doubt that televised violence and subsequent behavioral aggression are linked (Geen & Thomas, 1986; Liebert & Sprafkin, 1988; Wood, Wong, & Chachere, 1991). However, naturalistic research monitoring children's TV watching and their aggressive acts has yet to determine definitively whether aggressive children seek out televised aggression or whether televised violence causes aggression in children (Huesmann & Eron, 1986).

Evidence also exists that aggression as described in the mass media correlates with adult violence (Phillips, 1983). In addition, continued exposure can desensitize people to the pain of violence and thus diminish emotional reactions (Geen, 1981). Correlations, though, do not provide evidence for cause. Nonetheless, society might be well served by reducing the number of aggressive stories and dramas adults and children are exposed to by the mass media.

Interestingly, the media distort the reality of violence anyway. Mawby and Brown (1984) analyzed news coverage of crime of nine different newspapers. Young females and high-status victims were overrepresented in crime news. Such victims are atypical, so the authors suggested that the papers are reaching for entertaining stories when a focus on the real threats to social order might be more useful. Of course, the media could also be used to influence prosocial behaviors by exposing viewers and readers to prosocial models (Sprafkin, Liebert, & Poulous, 1975).

In summary, violence and crime tend to be magnified in certain environments. Individual characteristics alone do not always account for crime. Attending to environments and reducing problematic environmental characteristics could perhaps reduce crime and violence in society.

Reducing the Fear of Crime

We have already discussed that many individuals harbor fear about being victimized by crime, whether they are potential or actual victims. These fears create stress in the individuals. Community and other psychologists have developed methods by which these sometimes unrealistic fears can be addressed.

Taylor and Shumaker (1990) stated that responses to hazards, real or imagined, include protection of the self or property, avoidance of dangerous situations, and joining collective anticrime efforts. Although private security measures such as burglar alarms are increasing in number (Klein, Luxemburg, & King, 1989), these devices are not affordable by everyone and perhaps only serve to remind people of crime potential. Thus, community citizens must turn to other strategies. One imaginative idea is to develop a **neighborhood crime watch** (National Crime Prevention Council, 1989). In neighborhood crime watches, neighbors are on active alert for suspicious activity or actual break-ins to each other's homes (Bennett, 1989). Fear of crime is one of the factors that seems to differentiate neighbors who do or do not join watches. Certain environmental factors also predict who will and will not join neighborhood watches as well as other neighborhood associations (Perkins, Florin, Rich, Wandersman, & Chavis, 1990). Crime watches as collaborative activities among neighbors not only help build a sense of community (Levine, 1986) but sometimes they are also the only strategy that does not increase fear of crime (Norris & Kaniasty, 1992).

Some communities have resorted to formal crime prevention groups such as the Guardian Angels. The impact of such groups on crime is uneven. The Guardian Angels tend to reduce property crimes somewhat but have no impact on violent interpersonal crimes (Pennell, Curtis, Henderson, & Tayman, 1989). Although the Guardian Angels are to be admired in that they attempt to recruit minority youths and serve as positive role models, not all communities adopt their rather vigilante approach.

Other community scientists have also recommended actual fear-reduction programs. A police presence is often used to reduce fear of crime as well as actual crime in neighborhoods, but such actions have not been shown to actually reduce fear (Bennett, 1991). On the other hand, programs that empower citizens to take control of preventive and intervention measures do seem to reduce fear. In one program, Burke and Hayes (1986) taught "senior security" to elderly citizens. Participants learned practical self-protection methods and awareness strategies by means of films, lectures, and discussions. In a related program, Burke and Hayes taught seniors to counsel other senior citizens who had been victimized by crime. Participants in these programs reported better knowledge of community services as well as an increase in problem-solving abilities designed to reduce their fear of victimization.

Citizen Involvement in Police Matters

The discrepancies between police attitudes and community attitudes about how the police should serve their communities has already been reviewed. Programs that reduce these discrepancies might give citizens more confidence in their police, reduce citizens' fears, and allow the police to better serve their communities. We can only highlight sample programs here.

Walker and Walker (1990) describe a **Community Police Station Program** in which citizens play a major role in the determination, design, and delivery of crime-prevention programs. Citizens from the community see to the daily operation of the station and to the delivery of specific programs such as "Seniors Calling Seniors," a program designed to give shut-in or isolated seniors a sense of contact with others. The program also includes a citizens advisory board that helps identify the crime-prevention needs of each area of the city and sees that programs are developed to address those needs. In the Community Police Station Program, the police and citizens collaborate to make police services more acceptable and effective. In other communities, citizens and community members have been used to help recruit and select new police officers, again allowing collaboration and building a sense of community among citizens and enforcement personnel (Ellison, 1985).

Secondary Prevention: Early Intervention Efforts

This section will explore exemplary measures designed to intercede as early as possible after an individual has started down a path of crime. Prevention at this point is too late. The strategy thus becomes early detection and treatment. In the case of Mike Farnsworth in the chapter vignette, when Mike first argued with his father or stayed out beyond the agreed-upon curfew or missed school, someone should have or could have intervened before the situation deteriorated. This is *secondary prevention*. Efforts in secondary prevention have focused primarily on juvenile delinquents, so it is this emphasis we will address first. Efforts have been geared either toward intervening in delinquency by training parents to better deal with delinquent behaviors or by reducing recidivism rates after the first contact with the criminal justice system.

Parental Training

Families and or contexts in which youths live cannot be ignored in the development of delinquent and other at-risk behaviors (Allen, 1990; Fendrich, 1991). Perhaps Walt Farnsworth's own combativeness stirred Mike's anger and fueled Mike's reactions. Could Mike's parents have learned to deal with him more effectively? Research says yes. In one study (Bank et al., 1991), parents of delinquent youths were randomly assigned to one of three groups: parental training groups, groups provided with more traditional community services such as those offered by juvenile courts (e.g., PINS), or groups offered no services (the control condition). The parent training group learned how to handle their children more effectively and to communicate better. Dependent measures included offense rates, time spent in institutions, and subsequent police contacts, all of which were lowest for the parent training group. The trained families resorted less frequently to incarceration for their difficult youths and instead depended on their own newly acquired strengths and resources for coping with the delinquency. Some believe that parental training is among the most promising methods for dealing with problem youngsters (Tolan, Cromwell, & Brasswell, 1986; U.S. Department of Justice, Crime File Study Guide).

Reducing Recidivism in Juvenile Delinquents

Community psychologists and others involved with the criminal justice system are concerned about recidivism rates for youthful offenders, and not without good cause. A reliable but unfortunate predictor of conviction often is number of prior convictions (Coates, 1981; U.S. Department of Justice, 1991). Before addressing recidivism, though, we must describe how the process through which juveniles pass differs from that of adults (described earlier).

The **juvenile court system** was designed to prevent children and adolescents from undergoing the stress of adult court procedures. The juvenile system is therefore less formal than the adult one, although the U.S. Supreme Court has reduced informality to safeguard due process rights of youths (Hess et al., 1991). One result of the informality is that in juvenile court, professional decisions can be quite disparate. One youth guilty of larceny might be incarcerated; another youth facing the same charge might receive rehabilitative treatment; and a a third might receive probation. Mulvey and Reppucci (1988) found that service availability has as much as or more impact on treatment recommendations for juveniles than do characteristics of the individual juvenile. When alternative services are unavailable, the youth is likely to be incarcerated.

Furthermore, many youths in this system are minorities or from single-parent families. For these and other reasons, judges often adopt a protectionist attitude toward youthful offenders, and their treatment decisions are colored by their protectionism, especially for girls (Schutt & Dannefer, 1988). Certain youths, then, are likely to be diverted to foster care, treatment programs, or other alternatives such as halfway houses rather than be incarcerated. Hence, a variety of outcomes is possible for delinquent youths; guilty youths are not always incarcerated.

In Coates's (1981) review of services for delinquent youths, he differentiated between community-based services and traditional incarceration in youth detention centers, or what used to be euphemistically labeled *reform schools*. Coates was quick to point out that there is no agreement on exactly what *community-based services* means. A halfway house? Foster care? A group home? Coates noted that there are different types and degrees of community-based services. When a youth is remanded to his or her own community for "treatment," research provides mixed results at best on whether the community-based service is better than incarceration. A myriad of variables—such as the youth's dysfunction and geographic proximity of family, purpose and climate of the treatment program, and so on—need to be taken into account when interpreting research results.

Selection of dependent variables is important, too. Improvement in self-esteem is sometimes found in community-based programs but not in cases of incarceration. However, recidivism is higher for community-based programs than for incarceration because a youth returned to his or her community often joins the same social network that seduced that youth into a life of crime in the first place.

With that discussion in mind, we will examine a community-based program developed by Tolan, Perry, and Jones (1987). The program involved multiagency consultation developed through the family court by a representative from the local mental health center. All juveniles appearing before the court for the first time were required to attend program sessions with at least one parent, because, as noted earlier, family characteristics have been found to be important in determining delinquency (Tolan & Lorion, 1988). The program sessions were presented by appropriate community agencies (e.g., police, judges, probation, and the schools). Each youth was required to attend two four-hour sessions a month. Sessions consisted of information on the juvenile justice process, the consequences of repeat offenses, attitudes of others toward repeat offenders, strategies the youth could try to decrease involvement in illegal activities, and local agencies available to support prosocial behavior. Family relations, parenting skills, the relationship between drug or alcohol use and delinquency, and a tour of the local juvenile facility were also included.

Treatment and no-treatment groups were tracked for seven months and compared for recidivism rates, time between first and second offenses, if any, and other relevant dependent measures. The most significant finding was that the program participants had a recidivism rate that was only one-fourth that of their no-treatment cohorts. Results are attributable to the program's success in managing juvenile offenders. This program also provides **intermediate treatment** by allowing the youth to stay in his or her own home but bringing the youth into contact with environments other than just his or her home (Smith, 1986). Such in-home treatment programs are, of course, much less expensive and are more humanistic than instituionalization (Rosenthal & Glass, 1990).

Another interesting approach to early intervention with problem youths is New York's Mobile Mental Health Teams (Fagan, 1991). This program is jointly sponsored by the Office of Mental Health and the Division for Youth. The teams travel to youth correctional facilities to assess youths, assist staff in developing treatment plans, and provide follow-up and crisis intervention at the facilities. The Mobile Mental Health Teams also train correctional staff in youth mental health issues.

Early Assistance for Victims

So far, we have not mentioned victims and programs of secondary prevention for them. They, too, need their concerns addressed as early as possible after the crime. Some immediate steps can be taken for victims.

Victims may experience a wide variety of emotions, ranging from fright, rage, a sense of violation, and vengefulness to sorrow, depression, despair, and shock.

The justice system, though, does little for the victim, who, as we noted earlier, does not even have an official role to play in the trial, if there is one (Forer, 1980). The National Victims Resource Center, a national clearinghouse that provides victims with educational materials, funds victim-related studies, makes referrals to assistance programs, and provides information on compensation programs. Some state governments have also developed victim assistance programs (Woolpert, 1991) where victims are compensated for their injuries or awarded money from the offender's selling his or her story to the media or where victims can participate in parole decisions related to their offenders (Educational Conference on Psychiatry, Psychology and the Law, 1989). However, victim compensation programs are rare because an offender in prison does not earn much money toward restitution (Forer, 1980).

Financial compensation alone, though, cannot take away the psychological pain of being victimized nor assist the victim in reducing vengeful or angry thoughts about being victimized. Even with a trial, victims may have to wait months or years before their side of the story is aired in court. There are three types of programs available to victims that afford them early and substantially successful interventions for their victimization: crisis intervention, neighborhood justice centers, and problem-focused and emotion-focused coping.

Crisis Intervention.   The first type of program available to victims is very much psychological in nature. **Crisis intervention** is developed as a set of procedures to help individuals recover from the effects of temporary or time-limited but extreme stress. Early efforts at crisis intervention were focused on potential suicides and victims of extreme violence, unpredictable or dangerous situations, and natural disasters (Caplan, 1989).

Crisis intervention is usually a face-to-face or phone (hot line) intervention that utilizes immediate intercession in the form of social support and focused problem solving to assist a victim in a state of elevated crisis or trauma. The immediate purpose of crisis intervention is to avert catastrophe. Crisis intervention centers can be staffed by professionals or trained volunteers and are often open 24 hours a day.

Since its early days, crisis intervention has expanded to assisting victims of major school accidents (Blom, 1986; Weinberg, 1990), military disasters (McCaughey, 1987), sexual assaults (Kitchen, 1991), the chronically mentally ill (Dobmeyer et al., 1990; Holcomb & Ahr, 1986), students in a disciplinary crisis (Hagborg, 1988), and even victims of international terrorism (Lanza, 1986). Its potential uses seem limitless. There are now an estimated 500 known crisis intervention centers in the United States and Canada (Slaikeu & Leff-Simon, 1984).

A pertinent question about crisis intervention is whether it is an effective means of providing help at the onset of the crisis and thus of preventing future problems. Most studies on crisis intervention were conducted in the 1970s, when many of the crisis intervention hot lines were developed. We would like to review a more recent study here.

Echterling and Hartsough (1989) randomly selected evenings on which crisis telephone calls were sampled. Some 59 calls were monitored by the trained crisis intervention volunteers using a standardized monitoring form. In particular, the volunteer helpers' statements to the callers were recorded and coded to determine the sequence and usefulness of the steps in the process. The outcome of the call, whether it successfully averted the crisis, was also tracked. The researchers found that there are three important phases of short-term crisis intervention: assessment, emotional integration or responding to the caller's feelings, and problem solving or focusing on the specific actions to be taken after the call. These three phases, in this order, were most likely to result in a successful outcome for the caller.

How else has successful crisis intervention been used? Baumann, Schultz, Brown, Paredes, and Hepeworth (1987) recognized that the police are often called on to do crisis intervention work, but this is not a good use of police time. Police work is designed to collect information related to the commission of a crime rather than to attend to the emotional state of a victim. In an innovative program, the Baumann group trained lay community citizens on police safety procedures and crisis intervention techniques. After the training, two-person lay teams could be called by any police officer to assist in a crisis. The program resulted in less police time spent on each crisis call except in cases of domestic disputes. In some crises, the police were able to depart the scene even while the crisis was in progress, as long as the trained citizen participants were available to assist. As for family disturbances, the researchers explained that these calls seemed to have a higher degree of danger of physical violence than other calls. Hence, police presence was required throughout the disturbance. The study demonstrates that trained citizens can assist the police in performing some of their duties, which include crisis intervention. Both of these studies suggest that crisis intervention is an effective and immediate means for assisting victims.

Neighborhood Justice Centers.   **Neighborhood justice centers** or **community mediation centers** comprise the secondary category of early intervention programs. These centers are established in the local community and are designed to handle cases from criminal and civil courts or from other community agencies such as community mental health centers, probation departments, and family courts. The centers dispense with cases in a more timely fashion than is provided by court (Duffy, Grosch, & Olczak, 1991). One state reports a 15-day turn-around time from intake to resolution at its mediation centers (Crosson & Christian, 1990; Duffy, 1991).

At these neighborhood justice centers, a trained person hears the case as presented by both the victim (or claimant) and the respondent (the person responding to the charge). This trained neutral, the **mediator**, assists the two parties in understanding their conflict and in fashioning a resolution that is satisfactory to each. The resolutions in most programs are legally binding, do not require decisions about guilt or innocence (thus can "clear" an arrest record), and must be mutually agreeable (Duffy, 1991).

Most victims or claimants are highly satisfied with the process of mediation (Carnevale & Pruitt, 1992; Duffy, 1991) because they get to tell their version of the story soon after their victimization. They are also allowed to ventilate their emotions (something usually prohibited in court) and they are availed of the opportunity to address the person they believe caused their distress. Respondents or defendants appreciate the process because they typically do not come out of it with a guilty verdict or a criminal record. Likewise, they are afforded the opportunity to provide evidence that the victim sometimes plays a role in the "crime" (as in harassment, where both parties have actually harassed each other).

Mediators utilize a variety of strategies to facilitate discussion and guide the two parties toward solutions (Carnevale & Pruitt, 1992; Ostermeyer, 1991). Mediators use reality testing (a process in which one person is asked to "get in the other person's shoes"), a futuristic (rather than retrospective) orientation, turn taking, compromise, reciprocity in concession making, and active listening, among other skills. In some respects, mediation and psychotherapy are parallel processes, but mediation focuses more on problems and issues rather than emotions or relationships (Forlenza, 1991; Milne, 1985; Weaver, 1986). The end result in about 85 to 90% of the cases is an agreement or contract between the parties (Duffy, 1991). What is equally important is that 80 to 90% of victims and defendants emerge from the process satisfied (Duffy, 1991). The agreements can contain anything from restitution and apologies to guidelines as to how in the future the parties will interact. Just about anything that both parties agree to that is legal can be part of the mediated settlement. Mediation has been successfully utilized in landlord-tenant and consumer-merchant disputes; neighborhood conflicts; crimes such as assault, harassment, and larceny; family dysfunction; racial conflict; environmental disputes (Duffy et al., 1991), and a host of other areas where individuals disagree or infract on each other's rights.

In fact, the vignette of Mike Farnsworth is a true story; Mike and his parents were referred to a mediation center by the probation department. Although the hearing was a long one, Mike and his parents eventually agreed on rules for Mike (e.g., curfews) and a "reward" system for Mike (which had been missing before the mediation). A "punishment" system had long been in place. The reward system would be used when Mike's grades were good or when his behavior was positive. During the hearing, Mike and his father finally listened to one another (rather than bellowed) and began to better understand each other's perspective. Mike's mother, Edna, learned some valuable skills from the mediator, such as compromise and reciprocity of concessions, for use in refereeing future disagreements between Mike and his father should they arise. To our knowledge, the Farnsworths (whose name we changed to protect their anonymity) have lived much more harmoniously since their mediation.

Neighborhood justice centers have experienced phenomenal growth in the last two decades (Duffy, 1991; Emery & Wyer, 1987; Meehan, 1986) but are not without their critics (e.g., Greatbatch & Dingwall, 1989; Vidmar, 1992). The centers and the process of mediation embody many of the values of community psychology, too. The centers are generally available to the parties in or near their own communities. The centers provide an *alternative* to the sometimes oppressive, bureaucratic, and almost always adversarial court system (Duffy, 1991). Mediation *empowers* the parties to play a major and active role in determining their own solutions. Research on compliance with the contracts suggests that they usually *prevent* conflicts from recurring in the future (Duffy, 1991). Similarly, the centers are generally available to every community citizen regardless of income, race, or creed (Crosson & Christian, 1990; Duffy, 1991; Harrington, 1985), and the mediators are trained to *respect the unique perspective* and *diversity* of the parties (Duffy, 1991). Empirical research has demonstrated that mediation is a humanistic process because it enhances the functioning of both participants as measured by Maslow's hierarchy of needs (Duffy & Thompson, 1992). Research has also demonstrated that individuals who utilize mediation instead of court trials are respected and admired by others because they are seen as flexible and conciliatory (Duffy & Olczak, 1989).

Problem-Focused and Emotion-Focused Coping.   There are two immediate problems of victims. One is coping with the emotional watershed of being victimized; the other is developing problem-focused skills to deal with the reality of revictimization, which is perhaps unlikely in reality but prominent in the victim's mind. Winkel and Vrij (1993) developed a program designed to help victims cope in both ways soon after the crime. A police crisis intervention program was developed in which the police conducted a criminal investigation of the burglary victim's home, provided oral and written crime prevention information, and performed a security check. Later measures of coping found that this program instilled in the victims enhanced perceptions that the police were protecting them, reduced fear of future crime, and increased preventive awareness and responsibility on the part of the victim.

Tertiary Programs: After-the-Fact Interventions for Chronic Justice System Problems

You know now that Mike Farnsworth's story had a fairly happy ending. The outcomes for others involved in criminal justice processes, both victims and offenders, is not always so happy. This section will review the role of and treatment of chronicity. Specifically, programs designed primarily for individuals involved long term in the turmoil of criminality will be reviewed.

Innovative Programs for Chronic Offenders

Despite the development of primary and secondary prevention programs, the approach of the traditional justice system tends to be punishment and use of restrictive institutional settings, especially for juvenile delinquents (Gendrau & Ross, 1987; Lundman, 1986). Research has traditionally focused on two areas: efficacy of incarceration (imprisonment) compared to alternative programs and the effectiveness of prerelease programs during incarceration on recidivism rates.

Incarceration remains controversial in community psychology and is not a simple issue to examine (Coates, 1981; Martinson, 1980). Many research projects that attempt to compare forms of incarceration to alternative community programs have sampling problems. For instance, judges are reluctant to divert dangerous or chronic offenders to community programs. Researchers therefore find different populations in each setting, thus creating differences at the outset of the study. Furthermore, community programs differ as much from each other as do prisons; program idiosyncrasies therefore become an issue and prevent drawing generalizations from one program to the next. We will therefore examine only a few sample programs and research findings.

Incarceration and Its Alternatives.   The problems of incarceration have been well documented. They include reduced social status; isolation from family and community; feelings of guilt and self-rejection; lack of employment opportunities upon release (Chattoraj, 1985); racial divisions, cliques, and gangs within the prison walls (Irwin, 1980); drugs (Peters, May, Alaimo, Dolente, & Hecht, 1990); and the spread of AIDS among the prison population. Some of these problems are severe, too. May, Peters, and Kearns (1990) reported that there is high drug use during incarceration (i.e., at least 60% of all inmates) but that as few as 7% of the inmates are enrolled in in-house drug-treatment programs. Because of these and other problems caused by incarceration, the preference in community psychology seems to be to avoid incarceration and coercive punishment.

Mounting evidence suggests that alternative forms of punishment outside of the traditional prison system are not good alternatives either. Several studies have demonstrated that shock incarceration camps or **boot camps** that are run by corrections personnel but resemble intensive army training camps fall short of their goals (Palmer & Wedge, 1989; Sechrest, 1989). In Palmer and Wedge's study, 65% of the juveniles from the 53 different juvenile camps studied recidivated to crime. In other words, the inmates in the camps were not "shocked" out of their criminality.

Untangling the effects of incarceration versus alternative programs is sticky, too. Using parole violations and parole maladjustment measures, Fendrich (1991) found that the use of alternative programs was inversely associated with both measures. In other words, on both measures, the alternative programs came out better. However, in Fendrich's study, nonprogram variables such as family problems were *more* useful predictors of parole behavior. Thus, the alternative programs themselves are not always solely responsible for postrelease behavior.

If incarceration must be used for individuals who have committed crimes, can programs be developed to rehabilitate them in prison? Mathias and Sindberg (1986) reported on a group therapy program at a correctional facility. Ten therapy sessions were led by a psychologist and took place three to six months before release of each participant. At the end of therapy, interview and questionnaire data indicated that therapy reduced the participants' suspicion, distrust, and anxiety levels and increased their sense of self-acceptance and self-worth. One must be careful in rejoicing over these results, however. The participants were all from a minimum security facility, so they were not dangerous or repeat offenders. Also, there was no provision for a control group. Sometimes it is not therapy per se in correctional environments that produces positive results but rather the extra attention paid to the inmates (Hollin, Huff, Clarkson, & Edmondson, 1986).

Some studies compare incarceration to community alternatives and, as noted on several other occasions, the studies are replete with design problems. In one fairly well-designed study (Chamberlain, 1990), juveniles remanded to a correctional facility were matched on age, sex, and date of commitment with two other groups of youths. One group was diverted to alternative but specialized foster care in the community and another group received traditional community placements. All youths were considered to be seriously delinquent. The results indicated that the youths in the specialized foster care were more likely to succeed in their diversionary programs than those placed in traditional community settings such as group homes. At one and two years posttreatment, the group receiving specialized foster care was less likely to be reincarcerated or incarcerated for as long as the two other groups of youths. Again, one must be cautioned that not all research demonstrates that alternative community programs are this successful (Coates, 1981).

Prerelease Programs.   Imagine how Mike Farnsworth would feel upon release had he been imprisoned for, say, five years because of his repeated assaults on his father. Mike would have learned much in prison, most of it counterproductive. He may have learned how to make weapons out of ordinary household implements such as mirrors and cigarette lighters. He may have learned how to intimidate others merely by staring at them in a certain way, and he may have learned how to commit more heinous crimes than the assault on his father. But, even though prison may have hardened Mike, he might also have felt intimidated about his reentry into society and felt insecure about his newly acquired freedom. Where would he find a job? How would he feel about going to see his parole officer? Would his parents allow him to come home? What would his neighbors think? **Prerelease programs** that ease entry back into the community can perhaps prevent stress and future problems for inmates.

There is probably no other inmate for whom release is more problematic than forensic patients. These are the mentally disordered, incarcerated individuals discussed earlier in the book. These individuals suffer not only the social stigma of incarceration but of mental disability as well. They are probably less well received upon return to their communities than any other individual. Maier, Morrow, and Miller (1989) described a highly successful prerelease program for forensic patients that eases them back into the community rather than abruptly casts them out of the forensic unit. The participants had been hospitalized in a forensic unit for 2 to 10 years. The program contained modules that reoriented the participants to the community and to community living skills as well as contained provisions for release planning groups, buddy systems, debriefings upon visits to the community, and meetings with community leaders. In other words, the researchers encouraged the participants to take "small steps at a time" before release to the community. Over a 24-month period, only one crime was committed in the institution (but it was a fairly serious one of sexual assault) and none in the community in more than 11,000 excursions to it. Although this program did not guarantee that the community would be more accepting of the participants, it did assist the participants in successfully controlling behaviors in the community that otherwise would result in their return to the forensic unit.

Interventions for Victims

In other chapters of this book, long-term treatment for victims of a variety of abuses, such as child abuse, have been addressed. Here, we will showcase research by Kaniasty and Norris (1992) addressing the role of social support in long-term, crime victim assistance. Social support, as you already have learned from Chapter 4, often has beneficial buffering effects for distressed individuals.

Kaniasty and Norris have pointed out that criminal victimization results in depression, anxiety, fear, and hostility. Especially in the instance of violent crime, these feelings can persist for months. The more the perceived seriousness of the crime, the more vulnerable and wronged the victim feels (Beach, Greenberg, & Yee, 1992). Kaniasty and Norris wondered what role **social support**—support from significant others such as friends and family—played in the victims' coping with these diverse emotions.

Kaniasty and Norris took measures of several types of *perceived* support as well as several types of support *actually received* by victims of property and violent crimes. Analyses revealed that the positive or buffering effects of *perceived* support were more pervasive than those of *actual* or received support for victims of both types of crimes. On the other hand, received support in the form of information and material goods seemed to assist only victims of violent crimes and then more by way of reducing their fear of future victimization. Social support tends to be sought frequently from friends and family but often professional support is more helpful, especially in certain crimes such as sexual assault where rape crisis centers have been reported by victims as highly useful (Golding, Siegel, Sorenson, Burnam, & Stein, 1989). In other words, the victim, the crime, and the type of social support need to be carefully matched. Formal victim support programs tend to focus mainly on emotional support when what the victim may need is advice and material support. Kaniasty and Norris concluded that "providing support to crime victims is a very complex, involving, and delicate process. What is needed is a more proactive approach of educating the public about the role of social support, both perceived and received, in coping with criminal victimization" (p. 236).

A second approach to assisting victims after their victimization is to offer **victim-offender reconciliation programs (VORPs)**. These programs are very new and somewhat controversial. In fact, they are so new that not all communities provide them and not much research is available on them at present. These programs are showcased in Case in Point 9.2.

In conclusion, the criminal justice system is a complex one comprised of many different players with a variety of motives and functions. Community psychologists are collaborating with individuals involved in the justice system

❖ *CASE IN POINT 9.2*

Victim-Offender Reconciliation Programs

New programs that use mediation as their core and that focus on the needs of the victim are victim-offender reconciliation programs (VORPs). Victim-offender reconciliation programs are so new that they are not offered in all community mediation centers. In victim-offender reconciliation, the victim and the offender are brought together to explore their impact on and feelings about each other. Their meeting is facilitated by a mediator. As in mediation, the two parties are empowered to develop plans for restitution if appropriate (Woolpert, 1991). Restitution is not the only strategy that the victim and offender use; if they both agree, the offender can provide services to the community or victim or offer an apology. The victim can also request that the offender seek counseling; if the offender agrees, therapy becomes part of the agreement. Although VORP is not appropriate for all victims and all offenders, it has been applied in property offenses, robbery, assault, rape, and even manslaughter cases (Woolpert, 1991). The programs are thought to be more expedient than court in recompensing victims and are believed to be somewhat therapeutic for both the victim and the offender (Woolpert, 1991).

Research demonstrates that most victims will voluntarily participate in VORPs (Galaway, 1985; Reeves, 1989). In fact, some victims want to help rehabilitate their offenders (Coates & Gehm, 1989), and this may be their major motive for participation. Again, settlement rates, especially restitution, are fairly high (i.e., 90%) (Gehm & Umbreit, 1986), and victim satisfaction is also high (Coates & Gehm, 1989; Launay & Murray, 1989; Ruddick, 1989). VORP also seems to reduce victim anger and facilitate understanding of the offender's motives (Davis, Tichane, & Grayson, 1980). Research has also demonstrated that some offenders feel "rehabilitated" by meeting their victims; that is, their attitudes about crime change (Coates & Gehm, 1989). Schneider (1986) also demonstrated that programs such as VORPs, where offenders are empowered to some extent to determine their own case dispositions, result in lower recidivism rates. It is important to note, though, that VORP is so new that researchers have not yet given it the attention it needs (Woolpert, 1991) and some communities are not always open to accepting victim reparation programs (Walklate, 1986).

and together they are making headway on preventing crime and assisting those involved in the crime once it occurs.

SUMMARY

The traditional justice system includes enforcement agencies such as the police, the courts, the prisons, and related programs. Such programs allow a small role, if any, for the victim and tend to seek retribution or punishment for the offender.

Psychologists who have tried to parcel out the causes of crime know that guns, gun control, and related factors are not the only predictors of crime. Certain ecological settings and certain groups of individuals are likely to be involved in crime. Young African American men are most likely to be victimized by crime and most likely to be convicted of and incarcerated (imprisoned) for crime. Societal prejudice and the history of African Americans in the United States may, in part, be what underlie some of the statistics.

Prisons are bleak, total institutions, which are overcrowded and often fraught with problems such as violence, AIDS, and illegal substances. Prisons do not tend to rehabilitate nor treat offenders.

Victims and those who fear crime have been neglected populations in the traditional criminal justice system. An interesting phenomenon, the crime-victimization paradox, which has limited support in the literature, suggests that those who fear crime the most are often least likely to be victimized. An example would be an elderly woman who fears crime but is very unlikely to be victimized. Multi-Door Court House Programs have helped reduce the bewilderment faced by victims as they approach the vast array of legal services that might be available.

Police are asked to play a variety of roles in a community. Some are roles for which they are ill prepared, such as intervention in domestic disputes. Police officers often report that they feel alienated from the communities they serve and feel that their superiors offer little understanding for street life.

Community psychologists believe that criminal behavior can be predicted. Some studies have successfully predicted delinquent behavior in at-risk youths. Environments can also be altered to reduce the probability of crime. An example is removing violent cues from the media, which usually tend to bias its reports of crime any way.

Community programs such as a neighborhood crime watch are also successfully reducing the fear of crime. Other innovative programs involve citizens in collaborative efforts with officers at enforcement agencies.

In terms of secondary prevention, parental training for parents of at-risk or delinquent youths shows much promise for intervening in the cycle of delinquency. There also exist programs for early assistance to actual crime victims. Two such programs include crisis intervention and neighborhood justice centers or community mediation centers.

Programs comparing incarceration to alternative community services are difficult to assess with research due to research confounds, but many community programs offer hope that even chronic offenders can be assisted. An especially important type of program is a prerelease program that is designed to ease adjustment of an incarcerated person into the community.

Victims may also need follow-up services long after the crime. One new and interesting program is the victim-offender reconciliation program in which the victim and offender meet face to face and discuss their impact on one another as well as plans for restitution to the victim.

10

THE HEALTH CARE SYSTEM

It is probable that, before medicine becomes truly preventive, there must be a radical alternation in the basis of payment for medical service. It is extremely unlikely that the average individual will ever resort to his physician until he experiences compelling symptoms of disease if the incurring of an immediate financial obligation is specifically involved.

◆ *CHARLES-EDWARD AMORY WINSLOW, 1923*

Erika placed a single red rose on Tom's casket and then turned toward their children, Jessica and Scott. Grasping each other's hands, the three walked slowly away from Tom's grave.

Upon returning home, Erika weighed the events of the past 20 years. Erika met Tom at college in Michigan. She graduated with a teaching certificate in music; he earned his diploma in accounting. In August of their graduation year, they were married. Life seemed good during their early married life. Erika and Tom were both employed and making plans for their first child, Scott, who was born two years later. In another three years, Jessica was born.

While Erika taught music at the junior high, Tom's work for a large, successful accounting firm sent him all through the Midwest. Both of them were pleased that their lives were relatively carefree. Each had a good-paying job, the children never gave them trouble, and the family was able to afford a beautiful home in a respected neighborhood.

Everything changed suddenly in the twenty-fifth year of their marriage. Tom was not feeling well. He complained of a fever, night sweats, and swollen glands. Erika was stunned to learn that Tom had acquired immune deficiency syndrome (AIDS). On his business trips and at the urging of his accounting buddies who were traveling with him, Tom had engaged prostitutes for "a few hours of fun." That fun eventually turned into a fatal illness: AIDS.

Erika could hardly forgive Tom for his indiscretion, but she was relieved that she, herself, had tested negative for AIDS. Her busy life and his travels ironically saved her from the illness. Erika felt guilty for the anger she held for Tom while he was dying. The day of his funeral, the guilt gave way to anguish. During the last half year of Tom's illness, he was unable to work, which forced Erika to teach private music lessons. She worked night and day. Erika's saving graces were that Scott and Jessica were old enough to care for themselves and that Tom's sister and Jessica were able to look after Tom's needs as his frailness progressed.

What frustrated Erika the most, though, were the mounting medical bills. Tom owned an excellent health insurance policy while he was with the accounting firm. When he resigned due to his illness, the family was covered by her insurance through the school. However, this insurance plan did not cover some of the major expenses, experimental drugs, and frequent doctor visits.

Erika sat alone in her house after the funeral and pondered the unpaid expenses. Tom's funeral alone had cost over $6,000, but the medical bills were the monumental cost. Erika wondered how she would ever pay the hundreds of thousands of dollars she owed the doctors and the hospitals. All the private music lessons in the world would never help her tackle those bills.

INTRODUCTION

Despite the pioneer public health work of Charles-Edward Amory Winslow in the 1920s and those who followed him, Erika and Tom's story is tragic and, unfortunately, told all too often. Whether the catastrophic illness is AIDS, cancer, Alzheimer's disease, emphysema, or another disease, many Americans today are still faced with major health problems and have no way to cover all the expenses. The pain of the illness is magnified by the despair over the state of health care in this country. The health-related issues that face Erika and other Americans are the crucial ones explored in this chapter.

Americans pride themselves on living in one of the freest, richest, and most technologically advanced countries. Over 2,000 magnetic resonance imaging (MRI) scanners are available to perform diagnosis at a cost of $600 to $1,000 per session. MRI costs one to two million dollars apiece and allows doctors to peek into the body's internal workings. The state of California has more MRI than all of Canada combined (Public Agenda Foundation, 1992). Given this wealth of technology, Americans should be able to choose the types of health care services (e.g., outpatient mental health counseling or therapy) that best fit our needs. Unfortunately, people cannot agree on which health care model is best nor how health care should be funded. Perhaps part of the answer lies in empowering individuals and communities to adopt healthier lifestyles in the first place.

THE PUBLIC HEALTH MODEL

Some health care experts turn to the **public health model,** which emphasizes the importance of **preventive medicine.** That is, people who practice a healthy lifestyle are less likely to develop illnessess and thus lessen the burden (money) to the health care service delivery system. If Tom, the husband in the opening vignette, had been educated about safe sex, perhaps he would have avoided contracting the human immunodeficiency virus (HIV) which led to the development of his AIDS.

The public health model has been around for more than 120 years. The American Public Health Association was established in 1872 and included Margaret Sanger's pioneering work on the establishment of maternity clinics for low-income women in the often hostile, early nineteenth-century New York City.

However, not until the leadership of Julian Richmond, M.D., former U.S. Surgeon General, was public health given its long-overdue credit.

Specifically, based on scientific data as well as consultation with health care experts, Dr. Richmond outlined a set of goals and objectives (e.g., reduce the number of people who smoke) to improve the health of Americans within a 10-year period. Not all goals and objectives have been achieved, and some objectives and goals are less than optimal. For example, infant mortality rates had sharply decreased until the onset of the Reagan and Bush Administrations, whose many social agendas were not completely congruent with the philosophy of the public health model. Dr. Richmond's work established the "public health" and prevention foundations by challenging the American public: people need to rethink what they *must* do in order to be healthy. Today, another set of goals and objectives entitled *Healthy People 2000: National Health Promotion and Disease Prevention Objectives* have been established (U.S. Department of Health and Human Services, 1991). One goal is to reduce the amount of lead in drinking water, which has been shown to adversely affect health. Other goals and objectives include further reduction in infant mortality and morbidity rates.

The public health model is consistent with the philosophy of the field of community psychology. An important goal is to **empower** individuals by having them practice preventive medicine, although **intervention** and **treatment** must be available when needed. For instance, the model is noted for its relative success in preventing or reducing cigarette use, which has been linked to various forms of cardiovascular disease and cancer in later life (LeFebvre, Lasater, Carleton, & Peterson, 1987). Prevention or intervention programs against cigarette smoking generally use the mass media (e.g., Dr. Louis Sullivan, former Secretary of the Health and Human Services openly criticized the tobacco industry on national television) in conjunction with laws. For example, warning labels on cigarette packages and a ban on smoking on all domestic flights have both been legislated. Other successful smoking prevention programs are school based, which usually involve educating and teaching school-aged children assertiveness skills (Botvin & Wills, 1987).

Moreover, the public health model argues that health care service delivery should be sensitive to cultural and individual differences. For example, although research indicates that alcohol abuse tends to increase with acculturation among Mexican Americans, acculturated Mexican American females reported more alcohol abuse than their male counterparts (Gilbert & Cervantes, 1986). Therefore, these differences would need to be taken into account when designing an alcohol intervention program with Mexian Americans.

The use of certain traditional treatment modalities (e.g., psychotherapy) may be appropriate for some ethnic minorities and inappropriate for others. For example, "In traditional Chinese Medicine,...the state of mind and the state of health are considered simultaneously" (Cheung, 1986, p. 207). That is, the use of medicine cannot be separated from the use of psychological treatment in the Chinese culture.

These scenarios are further complicated by the fact that American medicine is derived from a male-biased model. For example, dependent behavior (relying on others) in males is less likely to be associated with histrionic or dependent personality disorders than in females (Kaplan, 1983). In other words, it is possible that when women seek relief from male physicians, the physicians interpret distress due to social problems or dependency as symptomatic of psychological disorders rather than of women's station in life (Muller, 1990).

The public health model is not without controversy. Some advocates argue that preventive care should *not* be equated with **health promotion,** which may consist of governmental interventions or **socialized medicine.** That is, in countries such as Canada and Singapore, governments not only educate their citizens about preventive care but also those who do not adhere to governmental health standards (e.g., no more than two children per family in Singapore) can be penalized. Americans who value their freedom to choose often find health promotion intrusive (Terris & Terris, 1990). As Erika and Tom, the couple in the opening vignette, might have believed, many Americans think that the government should not legislate morality. For example, although many Americans acknowledge that smoking is associated with a higher chance of developing cancer, they also perceive a smoking ban as an infringement on personal freedom. In brief, these arguments demonstrate the intertwining relationship between health care service delivery and practice, personal attitudes and culture, and governmental regulation. Profile 10.1 introduces you to a well-known physician who was bold but controversial about public health issues.

This chapter will look at three specific public health problems and some suggested solutions found in the literature of the field of community. We have chosen these three public health problems for two main reasons. First, they have each received enormous attention in the media. Second, each is highly preventable if certain activities are practiced. In addition, a large number of people are affected or have the potential to be affected if prevention does not occur.

TOBACCO-RELATED DISEASES: PREVENTABLE DEATHS

Extent of the Problem

One of every six deaths in the United States is attributable to **tobacco use,** or **smoking.** These terms are often used interchangeably; note, however, that tobacco use also includes smokeless tobacco (see Table 10.1), which is linked to various oral cancers. Regular tobacco use increases the risk for developing a number of serious diseases, including heart and blood problems, chronic bronchitis and emphysema, and cancer of the lung, just to name a few. Smoking alone is responsible for 21% of all coronary heart disease deaths (40% of those under age 65), 87% of lung cancer deaths, and 30% of all cancer deaths (Office on Smoking and Health, 1989).

Smoking during pregnancy is a major risk for giving birth to **low-weight infants** (less than 2,500 grams or 5.5 pounds), which accounts for 20 to 30% of

◆ PROFILE 10.1
C. Everett Koop

C. Everett Koop, M.D., a pediatrician, was U.S. Surgeon General during the Reagan administration. When he was nominated by President Reagan for the post, many democrats and civil libertarian leaders were concerned. For example, Dr. Koop was perceived by advocates of abortion as antichoice. For others, he was perceived as a conservative in line with Reagan's "ideology." In other words, if confirmed, Dr. Koop would be in the position to carry out many of Reagan's conservative agenda items, which tended to have negative impacts on less fortunate individuals. Nonetheless, Dr. Koop was confirmed by the U.S. Senate. During his tenure as U.S. Surgeon General, Dr. Koop surprised many people, including both critics and supporters alike.

One of Dr. Koop's crowning achievements as U.S. Surgeon General was his handling of the issue of abortion. As an antiabortion advocate, President Reagan asked Dr. Koop to convene a scientific panel to examine the impact of abortion. Meanwhile, both sides of the abortion issue were conducting aggressive lobbying to try to sway the scientific panel. Dr. Koop had made it clear that his personal ideology, which is antiabortion, would not influence his evaluation of the scientific data. In consultation with the scientific panel, Dr. Koop concluded that there is not sufficient evidence to suggest that abortion has a detrimental impact on a woman and her family. This conclusion was a stunning defeat for President Reagan.

Dr. Koop argued that family planning, planning child birth in advance of pregnancy and a form of prevention, should be practiced by people (both men and women) to minimize the use of abortion as an option of unwanted pregnancy. As U.S. Surgeon General, Dr. Koop was also well known for his opposition to tobacco use. He argued consistently that lung cancer is preventable when the major culprit is smoking.

By advocating for prevention, U.S. Surgeon General Everett Koop was practicing community psychology—and he might not even have known it!

TABLE 10.1   Some Ingredients in Smokeless Tobacco

Acetaldehyde (irritant)
Benzopyrene (cancer-causing agent)
Cadmium (used in car batteries)
Formaldehyde (embalming fluid)
Lead (nerve poison)
Nicotine (addictive drug)
N-Nitrosamines (cancer-causing agents)
Polonium 210 (nuclear waste)
Uranium 235 (used in nuclear weapons)

these infants (Kleinman & Madanas, 1985). Birth weight is directly correlated with chances of survival. Also, 14% of **preterm births** (usually less than 37 weeks of gestation) are attributable to smoking, as are 10% of all infant deaths (Office on Smoking and Health, 1989). Meanwhile, 25% of pregnant women continue to smoke throughout their pregnancies (National Center for Health Statistics, 1989).

Although some progress has been made in the reduction of tobacco use in the past 30 years (e.g., 40% of adults smoked in 1965 versus 29% of adults in 1987; U.S. Department of Health and Human Services, 1991), the fight for a smoke-free society is far from over. The fight was never more vivid and clear than when First Lady Hillary Rodham Clinton declared the White House a smoke-free environment. Mrs. Clinton's effort is substantiated with scientific evidence gathered by the Environmental Protection Agency in classifying **environmental tobacco smoke (ETS),** better known as **secondhand smoke,** as a Group A (known human) carcinogen. Exposure to ETS is responsible for approximately 3,000 lung cancer deaths per year in nonsmoking adults. Also, an estimated 150,000 to 300,000 cases of lower respiratory tract infections (e.g., bronchitis and pneumonia) every year in infants and children up to 18 months of age alone are attributed to ETS (Massachusetts Department of Public Health, 1991).

Antitobacco Efforts

Antitobacco efforts include smoking bans by the Pentagon in all military facilities as well as proposed laws to regulate tobacco products by the Federal and Food Administration (FDA) due the addictive nature of nicotine. Also, the **National Cancer Institute** (NCI, 1991) funds 17 longitudinal demonstration projects in 17 states. In brief, the NCI emphasizes a tripartite model that uses (1) media (i.e., mass media), (2) policy (e.g, regulations or laws and taxation), and (3) services and programs (e.g., cessation programs) to target specific vulnerable groups, such as ethnic minorities, youth, and women, via multiple channels (e.g., hospitals and schools).

Based on these standards and funds from an increase in the tobacco excise tax, the states of California and Massachusetts are engaging in the most comprehensive tobacco prevention and control programs in the United States. In 1994, the Massachusetts Tobacco Control Program funded more than 300 programs ($96 million), ranging from media campaigns to smoking cessation programs in primary care settings, as well as school-based interventions.

Despite these antitobacco efforts, every year the tobacco industry spends millions of dollars in advertising and promoting tobacco (e.g., free coupons, leather jackets with logos of the product, etc.). In addition, the industry is quick to use image-based propaganda, which has been demonstrated to be effective with youth as well as the less educated. For example, DiFranza and colleagues (1991) found that Joe Camel (a cartoon character smoking a Camel cigarette) was more readily recognized by children than Mickey Mouse. Meanwhile, the prevalence of smoking remains disproportionately high among African Americans, blue-collar workers, and the less educated (U.S. Department of Health and Human Services, 1991). Also, although the use of illicit drugs among youth has actually *decreased* in the past decade, smoking among adolescent females *appears to be on the rise* (Johnston, O'Malley, & Bachman, 1993).

In constant dollars, money spent by the tobacco industry on advertising and promotion has tripled since 1975. The total expenditure for cigarette advertising and promotion in 1988 was $3.3 billion, a 27% increase over 1987 expenditures (Centers for Disease Control, 1990). Also, there is evidence to indicate that the industry is focusing more attention on the use of indirect strategies, such as the use of "front groups" to conceal its own involvement in fighting local tobacco control ordinances (Traynor, Begay, & Glantz, 1993). In other words, those who engage in antitobacco efforts (including the NCI) are facing a Herculean task. Case in Point 10.1 introduces you further to the issue of tobacco advertising and its effect on children.

A Community Psychology Approach

Community psychologist Leonard Jason and Police Sargent Bruce Talbot wanted to stop merchants from selling cigarettes to minors, so they collaborated on a scheme designed to do just that. Talbot first had the police chief write a letter to merchants, reminding the merchants that it is illegal to sell cigarettes to minors. However, Jason's research showed that the letter and a fine had little effect on sales to minors. During Jason's research, he sent 13-year-olds, the age at which youngsters usually experiment with cigarettes, into stores and had one of his undergraduate students observe the transactions. Up to 79% of the merchants sold the youths cigarettes.

Talbot and Jason next convinced the village board, which had access to the data, to pass a law that used a system of progressive warnings, eventually culminating in loss of the merchant's license to sell cigarettes as well as in a fine for selling cigarettes to minors. At first, this new policy was not totally successful, but the more it was enforced, the more sales dropped. Eventually, sales dropped to zero and stayed at zero. Merchants who refused to sell cigarettes to youths also received a letter of thanks from the mayor.

Changing the public policy was not the only result of this problem, though. Jason also wanted to know if minors were indeed smoking less; that is, did the youths understand the intent of the policy to reduce the danger of cigarettes to minors? (In other words, if youthful smoking seemed reduced, was it because the youths understood the message or were youths simply finding older friends and siblings to buy them the forbidden substance?) By design, both before and after the policy was instituted, Jason surveyed 650 seventh- and eighth-graders to determine if they had experimented with or smoked cigarettes. Many had, but there was a dramatic decline in reports of both experimentation and use after enacting of the law (Youngstram, 1991).

Consistent with the model of the NCI, this research illustrates the use of information dissemination and public policy to change behavior for the good of the community. It also demonstrates how various community services such as the police, elected officials, and psychologists can collaborate on programs for the community.

❖ *CASE IN POINT 10.1*

Kid Stuff

The tobacco industry claims it does not want children to smoke. However, tobacco control experts point to tobacco advertisements and promotional items that they say have great appeal to children....From early years on, candy cigarettes and realistic toy cigarettes...let children play-smoke. These and other gimmicks make tobacco seem an acceptable, if not desirable, part of life. For adolescent fun on the beach, promotional Camel flip-flops (rubber sandals) stamp *"Camel"* into the sand with each step. The *Salem* toy challenges players to get all the plastic cigarettes through a hole on the top of the pack.

Many cigarette advertisements also contain sexual messages that link tobacco products with sexual desirability, gratification, performance, and conquest. The provocatively posed young women on the *Kool* billboard and the Marlboro cowboy— well endowed with a box of smokes—are promising more than nicotine pleasure to sexually awakening adolescents. While they may appeal to some adults, promotional items, such as the *Virginia Slims* water bottle, often have great appeal for teenagers and younger children. Last year, Connecticut's Department of Consumer Protection asked Phillip Morris to recall a *Marlboro* promotional lighter after children started a fire in their home with the lighter that the department says "is extremely attractive to children" (*JAMA*, 1993, *269:* 1353–1356). Phillip Morris complied. The department also asked RJR Nabisco to stop distributing promotional lighters decorated with the Joe Camel cartoon character. The department says the cartoons make the non-child-resistant lighter attractive to children. The company did NOT comply.

Endorsements of smokeless tobacco products by major league baseball players, bubblegum made to resemble chewing tobacco, and a plethora of product promotions and giveaways over the last decade—such as the U.S. Tobacco Company sponsored "Skoal Bandit Day" at New York Yankee Stadium—have contributed to the sharp rise in "spit" tobacco use in the United States, especially among children. By sponsoring auto races, tennis tournaments, and other sporting events, tobacco companies maintain a high profile among young impressionable fans. Such sponsorship helps to associate tobacco with success, glamour, social popularity, and lots of fun, rather than deadly drug addiction.

Source: "Kid Stuff" by A. A. Skolnick, 1994, *JAMA, 271,* pages 578–579. Copyright 1994, American Medical Association. Reprinted with permission.

SEAT BELT USE: ROAD WARRIORS

Table 10.2 presents a set of questions addressing another activity people frequently do not practice on a consistent basis: highway safety.

TABLE 10.2   War Against War on the Highways

Many Americans do not practice automobile safety although the behaviors are quite simple. How many safe practices do you follow?

1. Do you always wear your seat belt when you are a driver or passenger in a car?
2. Do you make sure that you do not exceed the speed limit when driving a car?
3. Do you carefully signal your intentions when you change lanes on a highway or intend to turn?
4. Do you come to a complete stop at stop signs?
5. Do you refrain from disposing of litter on the highways?
6. Do you play your car radio at a low enough volume so that you can hear oncoming sirens?
7. Do you only pass on the left?
8. Do you thoroughly clean snow and other debris that could disrupt your vision from your windshield before starting out in the morning?
9. Do you frequently inspect your windshield wipers, lights, and tires to make sure that they are in good working order?
10. Do you only drive when sober?

Extent of the Problem

The laws related to highway safety were designed to keep you and other citizens safe on the nation's highway. Yet, each day, thousands of motorists ignore these precautions, which is probably why there are 125 traffic deaths *each day* in the United States. Consider this staggering fact—more Americans die in vehicle crashes in 1½ years than soldiers were killed *in all 10 years* of the Vietnam War (Geller, 1990). Given these statistics, why do intelligent adults put their lives at risk when simple actions on the nation's roads could prevent such tragedy?

Interventions Designed to Increase Safety

Because the average citizen is so resistant to common safety needs, psychologists have begun to experiment with means to increase highway safety. Berry and Geller (1991) tinkered with reminder systems to "buckle up." The systems were visual (e.g., lights) or auditory (e.g., chimes) reminders to buckle seat belts. Some drivers were given two consecutive rather than one reminder. The results indicated that these prompts increased safety belt use for some but not all drivers.

In a second study, Ludwig and Geller (1991) used group meetings of pizza deliverers who made a personal commitment to utilize their seat belts. Again, there was an increase above baseline in seat belt (143% increase) and turn signal (25%) use among but not all of the drivers.

In yet a third study, Nimmer and Geller (1988) attempted to improve safety belt use of employees at a community hospital. Employees signed a pledge card, displayed a signed pledge in their vehicles, and had to wear their seat belts in order to receive an extra $5.00 in their paychecks at the week's end. Seat belt use increased overall, especially for the card signers, from 29.4% to 75.1% during the period in which they received extra pay for improved safety. Although there was some decrease in safety belt use when the reinforcer was removed, use was higher than the initial baseline measures for those individuals who had been reinforced with the extra pay.

Other research has demonstrated that these programs are effective with children as well. Roberts, Fanurik, and Wilson (1988) developed a safety belt program at 25 schools. Children who buckled up received a reward (stickers, bumper strips, and chances on pizza dinners). The rewards increased compliance from 18.1% to 62.4% in the children.

As you can see from all three of these studies, a variety of methods must be utilized to improve seat belt use (Geller, 1988). It is also apparent that not all methods are 100% effective. Some individuals are resistant, no matter how beneficial the behavior might be!

One last study demonstrates the importance of cultural context, too. Hayden (1989) examined the effects of laws in Illinois and then Yugoslavia. The laws mandated seat belt use in both geographic areas. Interestingly, in Illinois, there was marked public opposition to the laws, whereas in Yugoslavia, there was little open opposition to the laws (when the study was conducted, Yugoslavia was under Communist control). Curiously, compliance to the laws was greater in Illinois than in Yugoslavia. The results raise larger questions about the importance of cultural context, especially the cultural differences in receptivity and response to public policy changes.

AIDS: A PUBLIC HEALTH CRISIS

Extent of the Problem

At the time of this writing, more than 15 million people in the world have been infected with the **human immunodeficiency virus (HIV),** which is thought to be responsible for the **acquired immune deficiency syndrome (AIDS),** an incurable disease. It is estimated that more than 20 million in the world will be HIV positive by the year of 1995 (Tarantola & Mann, 1993). Aids is one of the nine leading causes of death in children (likely to be transmitted by mothers through birth); it is estimated that it will be in the top five by the year 2000. However, HIV is *not* the cause for AIDS. Rather, being HIV positive weakens one's immune system, thus opening the door for "opportunistic infections" that lead to AIDS (see Table 10.3). However, there is a small group of dissenting scientists who do not believe HIV is responsible for AIDS; they are generally ignored by the mainstream scientific community.

In the late 1970s and early 1980s, the medical community began to notice a strange disease, mostly infecting homosexual men and **intravenous drug users (IVDUs).** Very soon, terms such as *HIV, AIDS,* and *ARC* (AIDS-related complex) became household words. Although HIV and AIDS were first recognized in homosexual men in this country, the disease has now been shown to infect all

TABLE 10.3   Characteristics of People with HIV or AIDS

Brain lesions (advanced stage of AIDS)
Frequent diarrhea
Loss of appetite
Low-grade fever that will not go away
Low T-cell count (below 400; T-cells are involved in fighting infection)
Oral thrush (e.g., lesions inside the mouth)
Pneumonia
Skin lesions (e.g., Kacopsi Sarcoma)
Swollen glands
Weight loss

men, including heterosexual men such as Tom (the husband in the opening story) and women (17 to 22% more likely than men).

Scientists and laypeople alike speculate about the origin of HIV and AIDS; theories range from the "green monkey theory" (a specie of African monkeys that is thought to be the genesis of the incurable disease) to biological warfare conducted by the U.S. Central Intelligence Agency. Still others (Eigen, 1993) have argued that HIV has been present in human beings for more than 120 years, only to wait for the right circumstances to attack the human immune system.

Possible Solutions

Probably not since the bubonic plague in the Middle Ages has a single other epidemic presented a bigger challenge to the public health care system. The present challenge, however, includes more than preventing the further spread of AIDS. It also includes how health care services should be delivered to deal with this incurable disease. With no cure in sight, education is an important weapon (see Table 10.4).

AIDS education, however, raises many controversial questions. As part of education, should condoms be distributed in schools to prevent the spread of AIDS? If so, at what grade level of education? Such controversy has almost torn the New York City school system apart. Moreover, many people who are HIV positive or who have AIDS, such as Tom, are denied health care insurance or have to stop working, which results in their insurance coverage ending. People with AIDS are growing impatient with the Food and Drug Administration (FDA) in the regulation of experimental drugs and treatment criteria. In order to be treated with the two popular experimental drugs, AZT and ddI, people must have more than 20 symptoms as defined by the Centers of Disease of Control and Prevention (CDC), a federal agency that oversees most HIV and AIDS surveillance. However, it took a lot of political lobbying before the CDC added to its list symptoms specific to women with AIDS (e.g., cervical cancer). Meanwhile, many people with AIDS have died from taking illegal treatments (usually smuggled into this

TABLE 10.4   How Much Do You Know about AIDS?

1. Most people who have the AIDS virus look sick   (F)
2. Anal (rectal) intercourse is risky because it transmits the AIDS virus.   (T)
3. You can get the AIDS virus during oral sex.   (T)
4. A person can get the AIDS virus in one sexual contact.   (T)
5. Keeping in good physical shape is the best way to keep from getting AIDS.   (F)
6. Condoms make intercourse completely safe.   (F)
7. A shower after sex reduces the risk of getting AIDS.   (F)
8. When people don't have other partners, they don't need to practice safe sex.   (F)
9. Oral sex is safe if partners don't swallow.   (F)
10. People who have the AIDS virus quickly get sick.   (F)
11. By having just one sex partner at a time you can protect yourself from AIDS.   (F)
12. The AIDS virus doesn't go through unbroken skin.   (F)
13. Semen carries the AIDS virus.   (T)
14. A person must have a lot of different sex partners to be at risk for AIDS.   (F)
15. People who have AIDS feel quite sick.   (F)
16. If the man pulls out (withdraws) before orgasm, then intercourse is safe.   (F)
17. A good diet and plenty of sleep will keep a person from getting AIDS.   (F)
18. A negative result on the HIV test can happen even if somebody has the AIDS virus.   (T)
19. It's more important for people to protect themselves against AIDS in big cities than in small cities.   (F)
20. Only receptive anal sex transmits AIDS.   (F)
21. Most people who have the AIDS virus know they have it.   (F)
22. No case of AIDS was ever caused by social (dry) kissing.   (T)
23. Mutual masturbation or body rubbing are low in AIDS risk.   (T)
24. All sexually transmitted diseases can be cured.   (F)

Source: "African-American Adolescents' Knowledge, Health-Related Attitudes, Sexual Behavior, and Contraceptive Decisions: Implications for the Prevention of Adolescent HIV Infection" by J. St. Lawrence, 1993, *Journal of Consulting and Clinical Psychology, 61,* page 107. Copyright 1993 by the American Psychological Association. Reprinted by permission.

country). The American Foundation for AIDS Research (Honorable Chairperson Elizabeth Taylor) publishes a listing of all drugs for treating AIDS, including those that do not have FDA approval. The listing is available free of charge.

Morality and politics aside, community psychologists and public health advocates have learned to use the public health model to slow down the spread of AIDS. After a decade of fighting the epidemic, it has been widely recognized that behavioral changes are paramount in *preventing* the transmission of HIV (National Commission on AIDS, 1993). Moreover, attitudinal variables are often viewed as determinants of compliance with HIV prevention recommendations (Fisher & Fisher, 1992). According to the **Health Belief Model** (Becker, 1974; Rosenstock, 1966), readiness to perform health-related behaviors is seen as a function of perceived vulnerability, perceived severity of disease, perceived barriers to health-protective action, and feelings of self-efficacy concerning ability to protect oneself from disease. This meta-model has since been adapted or modified to meet the challenges and needs of the specific populations participating in HIV prevention programs. (The term *prevention* is used here in an inclusive sense to capture the overlap of primary, secondary, and tertiary modalities that occur in the AIDS literature and in the implementation of clinical programs.)

At the broadest level, HIV prevention programs may include multifaceted components such as mass media educational campaigns, distribution of condoms, needle exchange, and safer sex outreach workshops. Many programs have utilized these approaches, with notable success with gay men in large urban areas (Coates, 1990) and IVDUs (Des Jarles et al., 1987).

Crawford and Jason (1990) provided a good model of a media program for AIDS prevention. For six consecutive days, 5- to 10-minute segments addressing AIDS and the family were broadcast during the noon and 9 P.M. newscasts of a major local TV station in the Midwest. The researchers randomly assigned 151 children and 94 parents to one of two conditions. In the experimental condition, the children were prompted (encouraged) to watch the broadcasts, and their families were given educational manuals. The printed material provided viewers with more in-depth coverage of the issues presented on television. In the other (control) condition, the children were not prompted nor provided the supplemental material. The children who were encouraged to watch the program viewed significantly more of the broadcasts, talked more about sexual issues with their families, and were more knowledgeable about AIDS than the control children (Crawford, Jason, Riordan, & Kaufman, 1990).

Other HIV prevention programs have opted for more focused strategies. As you may recall from Case in Point 2.2 in Chapter 2, although the general public is relatively knowledgeable about HIV and AIDS (i.e., attitudes and knowledge), knowledge alone is not sufficient for people to practice preventive medicine such as using condoms when engaging in sex (i.e., behavior). One mechanism to increase the synchronicity between attitudes and behavior is the use of **perceived social norms.** Social norms are those unwritten rules that society expects people to follow. For example, because Tom's accounting buddies frequented prostitutes, Tom perceived that he, too, should visit prostitutes, even though he was married to Erika. Often, the majority of people in a community feel that they should be able to sanction those who fail to comply with the norms. Kelly and associates (1991) have demonstrated that peer influence or pressure is a significant predictor in the use of condoms by gay and bisexual men. The researchers first collected baseline data about attitudes and knowledge of HIV and AIDS in a gay community. Leaders were identified and recruited for a HIV communitywide prevention program. They were trained about communication skills and ways to prevent contracting HIV. Upon completion of the training, these leaders disseminated their knowledge in the community. People who were exposed to these leaders were significantly more likely to report an increase in knowledge about HIV and AIDS as well as to practice safe sex than those who were not.

Based on Kelly and colleagues' (1991) **diffusion model,** Miller and Klotz (1993) implemented a HIV prevention program for Latino hustlers in New York

City. Opinion leaders were identified by bartenders and were recruited and trained about communication skills and ways to prevent contracting HIV. Results indicated that "the intervention had direct effects on HIV risk knowledge, HIV risk norms, and risk behaviors; knowledge of unsafe sexual practices for HIV transmission increased with time, and many important HIV risk behaviors decreased following the intervention" (p. 43).

The diffusion model has also been demonstrated to be effective for HIV prevention targeting intraveneous drug users (IVDUs). For example, Watters, Downing, Case, Lorvick, Cheng, and Fergusson (1990) identified community leaders who distributed one-ounce plastic vials of ordinary household bleach per IVDU along with a set of behavioral instructions (including instructions regarding safe sex). Results indicated that a significant percentage of IVDUs reported using bleach to decontaminate syringes and not sharing needles in the past year. Increased condom use was also reported.

Other researchers have opted for even more focused strategies such as cognitive-behavioral skill training in HIV prevention programs for runaway and homeless youths (Rotheram-Borus, Koopman, & Haignere, 1991) and homeless, mentally disabled men (Colson et al., 1993). For example, one of the most basic tasks of HIV prevention is to empower individuals to use a latex condom in all sexual activities. Negative perceptions and myths about condom use may impede successful utilization during activity. These obstacles can be minimized by using cognitive-behavioral skill training.

In an ongoing randomized clinical intervention trial study (Colson et at., 1993), homeless, mentally disabled men participated in a program known as Sex, Play, and Games. First, the participants' attitudes about HIV and AIDS as well as conditions surrounding their sexual behaviors were assessed. They then participated in cognitive-behavioral skill training, including role-plays. Finally, they competed against each other in various games by reenacting what they had learned. The winner received a small prize. Upon graduation from the program, participants received a certificate. Preliminary data suggest that those who had participated in the intervention reported not only increased knowledge about HIV and AIDS but also were more likely to practice safe sex.

No doubt, the preceding three public health problems and suggested solutions generate hope for community psychologists. However, it is naive to think that effective and efficient health care service delivery can be achieved at a more massive level with little governmental involvement and funding. The question is: How much involvement? This question deserves a top priority in the continuous effort to provide effective and efficient health care to the American people (Terris & Terris, 1990).

SUMMARY

With no adequate solution in sight for the existing health care service delivery systems, some health care experts turn to the public health model, which emphasizes the importance of preventive medicine. That is, people who practice healthy lifestyles are less likely to develop illnesses, thus lessening the burden (e.g., financial) to the health care service delivery system. We conducted a review of three public problems and suggested solutions found in the literature of the field of community psychology: tobacco use, seat belt use, and AIDS.

One of every six deaths in the United States is still attributable to tobacco use. Consistent with the model of the National Cancer Institute, community psychologist Len Jason illustrated the use of information dissemination and public policy to change behavior (cigarette smoking of minors) for the good of the community. Jason's research also demonstrated how various community services such as the police, elected officials, merchants, and psychologists can collaborate on programs for the community.

Another major cause of premature death is the failure to use seat belts. Each day, thousands of motorists ignore this precaution, which is probably why there are 125 traffic deaths each day in this country. Research has demonstrated that information dissemination is a major factor in persuading people to use seat belts; behavioral intervention is also necessary.

In the absence of a cure or a vaccine, prevention and information dissemination, in the form of behavioral intervention (e.g., the diffusion model), appear to be the only hope to slow the spread of human immunodeficiency virus (HIV), which is thought to be responsible for the acquired immune deficiency syndrome (AIDS). By the year 2000, AIDS will be the fifth leading cause of death among children.

11

COMMUNITY ORGANIZATIONAL PSYCHOLOGY

A business that makes nothing but business is a poor kind of business.

◆ *HENRY FORD*

As Sarah Anderson walked out the door of Harmony House, she glanced back at the building that had been her home away from home for the last eight months. She felt a sense of relief and a paradoxical sense of sadness as she exited for the last time. "What went wrong?" she wondered. "How could my job have become such a sore point in my life when only a few short months ago I had accepted it so enthusiastically?"

Harmony House was run by a private nonprofit corporation that managed eight different group homes for at-risk adolescents in Sarah's city. The adolescents were sent to the homes, including Harmony House, by judges, probation officers, schools, and parents. The group homes boasted the ability to "turn kids around"—that is, get them off drugs, raise their school grades, and make them productive citizens again, in about six months.

A psychology major with a human services minor from a small liberal arts college, Sarah had been actively recruited by Harmony House after her summer volunteer work there. Her grades were very good, and the combination of training in college and her volunteer work plus her winning personality during interviews made her eagerly sought after by several community organizations. She had always wanted to be a case manager for one of them. Harmony House won her over because they offered the best salary, an excellent training program, and had a good reputation. Harmony House seemed to be on the leading edge of innovations in treatment, which Sarah thought would give her the upper hand when she sought to move on to bigger and better agencies.

The idealistic and perhaps naive Sarah approached her first few days at Harmony House with immense enthusiasm. Her supervisor, Jan Hayes, mentored and coached her for the first few months. Sarah felt she was getting plenty of attention and good training under Jan. Sarah was slowly developing a sense of confidence in handling each new difficult youth as he or she entered Harmony House.

Six months into her service, Sarah's career took a downturn that mirrored the many changes occurring at corporate headquarters. Jan Hayes was moved from Harmony House to headquarters to become their chief trainer, and Sarah received a new supervisor, one who cared much less about mentoring Sarah and more about keeping costs low at Harmony House. Sarah explained to her new supervisor that she was fairly new to the job so would like to be mentored, but her new supervisor told her to stop complaining and start performing.

As the weeks passed, Sarah realized that not only was she without the tute-lage and attention afforded her by Jan but that the budget cuts at the group home were taking their toll on the clients. The television broke, which left the youths with more free time than they needed. The furniture was in need of replacement, and the menu each day was much less appetizing. There were fewer field trips and fewer group therapy sessions, too. All these changes and others made the youths more discontented and harder to work with.

Sarah approached her supervisor and commented on these negative changes. His response was, "Sarah, these are tough times; I have to make these cuts and changes. I suggest that, if you think things are better elsewhere, you find another job." Sarah worked another two months before she resigned. She did not have any active job prospects, but she was so utterly dismayed with the changes at Harmony house, she felt she had to quit.

INTRODUCTION

Sarah's story is told to introduce this chapter on organizations, which, in a community psychology book, could be controversial. However, we and others (Keys & Frank, 1987; Klein & D'Aunno, 1986; Shinn & Perkins, 1990) feel that there is much that community psychologists can learn from organizational psychologists and just as much that organizational psychologists can learn from community psychologists. By now, both fields have built enough strength so that neither will be overwhelmed by the other (Hirsch & David, 1983). Hence, we include this chapter that weds community and organizational psychology.

WHAT DO ORGANIZATIONAL AND COMMUNITY PSYCHOLOGY SHARE?

As you now know, community psychology is the psychology that examines the effects of social and environmental factors on behavior as it occurs in various levels in communities, including the organizational level, in order to produce beneficial change. To understand the effects of environmental factors or settings on individuals, one must understand something about the setting—in this case, organizations, whether they be private sector businesses, mental health clinics, prisons, or any other community organization. In fact, it is futile to attempt to understand individuals apart from the settings to which they belong (Keys & Frank, 1987). This chapter will look at the effects of the organization on the individual and the effects of the individual on the organization with an eye toward the goals of community psychology. In specific, discussions will attend to ways in which organizations adversely affect their members, both staff and clients, and means by which organizations can be improved to better serve their members and the community.

Organizational behavior and organizational psychology, which are the study of how groups and individuals interface with the organizations they are in

(Moorehead & Griffin, 1992), has much to offer community psychology. **Organizational psychology** approaches the examination of organizations from the perspective of the individual, whereas **organizational behavior** approaches the study of organizations from a systems perspective or as if organizations are systems (Smither, in press).

It is obvious what organizational psychology and organizational behavior have in common, but what do they share with community psychology? First, organizational specialists have developed paradigms, or models, as well as constructs and measurement techniques that go beyond the individual level of analysis (Riger, 1990). This is a goal of community psychology. For instance, from the study of organizations comes **organizational development (OD)**. OD is a set of social science techniques designed to plan and implement long-term change in organizational settings for purposes of improving the effectiveness of organizational functioning and enhancing the individuals within the organizations (Baron & Greenberg, 1990; French & Bell, 1990). In other words, concern for the organization and the individual in the organization should be equal (Beer & Walton, 1990).

One OD technique is **survey guided feedback,** which has been found to reduce the rate that community service organizations become inactive by 50 % (Chavis & Florin, 1990). In this technique, periodic surveys are conducted throughout an organization to assess employee and/or client feelings and attitudes. The results are communicated to all levels of the organization so that all groups and individuals develop procedures for correcting the problems identified in the surveys (Schultz & Schultz, 1990). Indeed, as pointed out in an earlier chapter, human service organizations in communities often create their own demise by not paying attention to their infrastructures and internal problems. Understanding organizational psychology can often help fledgling and even mature community organizations cope with inadequate or faulty organizational structures, procedures, and problems.

Another aspect of organizational psychology important to community psychology is the understanding that individuals and organizations have a dynamic relationship—that is, an ever changing, transactional relationship over time (Keys & Frank, 1987). For instance, at one point, an individual might be highly motivated to stay in an organization, while at another time, he or she may be motivated to leave, as did Sarah. However, just when the disgruntled individual wants to leave the organization, the organization most needs that person. The cycle then continues. The study of such dynamic relationships is the domain of both community psychology and organizational psychology.

Organizational scientists have a long tradition of conducting research from a systems perspective. They know how to include all organizational participants (e.g., managers and employees) as well as coordinating mechanisms and processes in their research endeavors as they attempt to study and change the overall organization. It is this multilevel or holistic type of research that community psychologists hope to achieve rather than endeavors focused merely on the individual. However, some in community psychology feel attempts at researching individuals *and* supraindividual levels in organizations are antithetical (Keys & Frank, 1987). In fact, the community psychology literature in some respects reflects this. In 1980, McClure and others found that less than 10% of the articles in one of the leading journals of community psychology, *The American Journal of Community Psychology*, emphasized a systems or organizational focus.

Another aspect of similarity between organizational psychology and community psychology is that for most individuals, work is part of their self-concept. Therefore, work has consequences for well-being, the promotion of which is a goal of community psychology (Price, 1985). Furthermore, there is "spillover" between work organizations and communities. Work influences how people feel; hence, if people emotionally withdraw from work, they might also feel alienated from their families and our communities. Likewise, feelings about community also "spill" into the work world. Working mothers, for example, probably experience more work stress than any other employee because they experience the most stress at home (Price, 1985).

Interestingly, there is a serious point at which the study of organizations and community psychology part company (Riger, 1990). In the field of organizational behavior, most efforts are aimed at improving organizational efficiency and profits, sometimes at the expense of the individuals in the organizations. If the organizational effort benefits individuals, it is often only incidental to the main task of improving the organization (Riger, 1990). For instance, if Sarah's new supervisor had taken into consideration Sarah's concerns about the budget cuts, he probably would have done so only if it affected Harmony House and not because it would have made Sarah happier. More specifically, suppose Sarah knew of a dangerous circumstance that might have resulted in Harmony House being sued, such as an elevator that was in disrepair. Sarah's new supervisor might likely have listened to her but not to please Sarah. Rather, he would have been concerned about the financial well-being of the organization.

On the other hand, the primary aim in community psychology is usually to enhance the functioning of individuals *and* organizations. The intent is to empower individuals within organizations to create innovative solutions to the problems facing them, to ensure that the innovations and changes are humanistic, and to promote a sense of community within the organization. From these values, organizational specialists can also learn. For instance, community psychologists feel that creating a sense of community within an organization or a sense of belonging to the organization can enhance human functioning. Organizational psychologists focusing less on the organization and more on the sense of community or cohesiveness are beginning to understand that work group cohesiveness and productivity often go hand in hand (Tziner & Vardi, 1982).

Managers of organizations have now come to understand that empowering those under them to participate in decision making in **quality of work life (QWL) programs** or programs of participatory decision making that create long-term change in organizations is a good idea (French & Bell, 1990). One example of a QWL program is a quality circle. **Quality circles** are small groups of volunteer employees (or volunteer clients of any community service) who meet regularly to identify and solve problems related to organizational conditions. Quality circles are considered to humanize organizational environments as well as to increase participants' satisfaction with the organization (Baron & Greenberg, 1990). If Sarah and other employees of Harmony House had participated in a quality circle, they might have realized that they were all discontented with the changes and so developed innovative solutions to the organization's problems *before* staff turnover became high.

A second example of the use of quality circles in organizations might be useful. In a rural mental health center, volunteer clients and staff might meet as a quality circle to discuss what to do about the lack of a public transportation system for clients without cars. Together, they could develop some innovative and workable solutions so that clients could more predictably obtain services from week to week.

Those living with the issues best know how to address them, and quality circles and other participatory methods in organizations take advantage of this fact by empowering involved individuals to solve their own problems. In matters of empowerment, community psychologists lead the way for the organizational specialists.

EVERYDAY PROBLEMS IN COMMUNITY ORGANIZATIONS

Why this interest in organizations? People spend a great deal of their adult lives in organizations, particularly in their place of employment but also in volunteer, recreational, educational, and other organizations. One's organizational affiliations often bring economic well-being, emotional security, happiness, a sense of self-esteem and status, as well as the social rewards of belonging to a group and a sense of accomplishment (Schultz & Schultz, 1990). On the other hand, organizations can also frustrate and alienate people and cause much stress. In fact, Hendrix, Steel, and Schultz (1987) reported that the most common source of stress is a person's job. With that in mind, we will turn to a sampling of the problems of today's organizations.

Stress

Stress was defined earlier in this book as a call for action when one's capabilities are perceived as falling short of the needed personal resources (Sarason, 1980). For instance, changes in the environment, especially unpredictable or uncontrollable ones (Baron & Byrne, 1994; Vinokaur & Caplan, 1986), can be stressful when they exceed one's coping resources. That means that even positive changes can bring stress. Receiving a promotion can be as stressful as being fired. But remember, these situations are construed as stressful *only if* the individual perceives them as taxing or exceeding his or her resources and endangering well-being (Lazarus & Folkman, 1984). Major readjustments, such as a new job (Holmes & Rahe, 1967), as well as everyday hassles (Kanner, Coyne, Schaefer, & Lazarus, 1981), such as rising prices, too many things to do, and being late for work, can be stressful. Imagine with her relatively new job, dissatisfaction, and eventual unemployment how much stress Sarah must have experienced!

Stress can occur in any facet of people's lives, but we are concerned here with causes of stress in organizations. Organizational causes of stress are varied and sometimes complex. Organizational members can be too busy *or* too bored, both of which can cause stress. There may exist interpersonal conflicts between coworkers, or the individual may not feel competent or sufficiently trained to do the work. Likewise, the individual may have a dangerous job such as working on a ward with violent individuals or be in a demanding environment where noise, fumes, poor lighting, or other environmental conditions produce stress. The person might also have a supervisor with whom he or she does not get along. There may be too many or too few rules or too much or too little structure. Or the individual might have problems at home that he or she brings to work.

Burnout

A concept related to but slightly different from stress is burnout. **Burnout** is a feeling of overall exhaustion that is the result of too much pressure and not enough sources of satisfaction (Moss, 1981). Burnout has three components:

1. The feeling of being drained or exhausted
2. Depersonalization or insensitivity to others, including clients (which, in human services, certainly is counterproductive)
3. A sense of low personal accomplishment or the feeling that one's efforts are futile (Jackson, Schwab & Schuler, 1986) Symptoms of burnout include loss of interest in one's job, apathy, depression, irritability, and finding fault with others. The quality of the individual's work also deteriorates, and the individual often blindly and superficially follows rules and procedures (Schultz & Schultz, 1990), topics soon discussed in this chapter.

Burnout is most likely to affect those organizational members who are initially eager, motivated, and perhaps idealistic (Van Fleet, 1991). Because many community activists and human services professionals fit this description, burnout ought to be a major concern to community psychologists (Stevens & O'Neill, 1983). Research has demonstrated that many individuals in community service organizations—including police officers, social security agency employees, and social workers—indeed suffer from burnout (Jones & DuBois, 1987). Staff burnout is a critical problem for the human services professions (Shinn et al., 1984). Burnout in community services is especially high when expectations are pinned to clients' progress rather than on the service staff's own increasing level of competence or self-efficacy (Stevens & O'Neill, 1983). In other words, in combating burnout, feedback to the organizational employee is important as client feedback to the same staff person (Eisenstat & Felner, 1984). Sarah's feelings that the clients were poorly served and that she was not as appreciated by her second supervisor might eventually have contributed to her burnout had she not resigned.

Workaholism

In other psychology courses you may have heard of the **Type A/Type B person-alities** (Friedman & Rosenman, 1974). Type A individuals, as opposed to the relaxed Type Bs, have a chronic sense of time urgency, have a distaste for "down time" or idleness, are impatient, and are competitive. Type As also work near maximum capacity, even when no deadlines are set, and are motivated by an intense desire to master their environments and to maintain control (Phares, 1991). Therefore, the Type As of an organization tend to be the **workaholics.** Of interest also is that Type As are often found in industrialized and densely popu-lated cities, and the relaxed Type Bs in small, rural communities (Rosenman & Chesney, 1982).

The early literature on Type-A behavior linked the personality syndrome to heart disease and stroke. In fact, Type-A personality was previously called the *coronary-prone personality,* as it was thought that Type As were twice as likely to have coronary heart disease than others (Phares, 1991). However, recent research has found that not all Type-A traits induce heart disease. What most seems to link Type-A behavior to heart attacks is the hostility toward or cynicism about others held by many Type As (Moser & Dyck, 1989).

Organizational Culture

Why is it that as individuals come and go from organizations, much as Sarah did, organizations do not seem to change much, even though their members do? The answer is organizational culture (Baron & Greenberg, 1990). Earlier in the history of its study, and as a narrower concept, organizational culture was referred to as *organizational climate.* Just as Type-A is related to an individual's style, organiza-tional culture is related to the personality of the organization. **Organizational culture** consists of the beliefs, attitudes, values, and expectations shared by most members of the organization (Schein, 1985, 1990). Once these beliefs and values are established, they tend to persist over time as the organization shapes and molds its members in its image (Baron & Greenberg, 1990). For example, can you recall how different all of the freshmen looked the first week of classes? Some were "punk," others appeared "preppy," and others "earthy." By senior year, many of these same students looked more similar because other students pres-sured them to conform to the organization's image. Those students who most deviated from the norm of the campus often left rather than change.

Besides influencing conformity, the prevailing organizational culture guides the organization's structure. How decisions are made in the organization relates to its structure. For instance, whether decisions originate from the bottom, as when average organizational citizens participate in decisions, or from the top, when a centralized management makes the decisions, is part of the organization's structure.

The organizational structure, including the decision-making system, also determines class distinctions within organizations, such as status differences between executives and middle managers. The distribution of power in the organization is likely to be affected by the organization's culture, too. If lower-level members make decisions, they will have more power than if they are not allowed to participate in decision making. Finally, organizational culture affects the ideology of the organization. If the organization views human nature as good, it will tend to allow subordinate participation (Tosi, Rizzo, & Carroll, 1986). If the organizational culture emphasizes the development of human potential, then the members are more likely to be allowed to develop and create new ideas without much interference from the organization.

An **open culture,** one appreciative of human dignity and one that enhances human growth, is preferred by most organizational members and by most community psychologists. Open cultures foster a sense of community, which can exist in an organization just as in neighborhoods (Klein & D'Aunno, 1986; Pretty & McCarthy, 1991). However, when the culture is **repressive** in that it inhibits human growth or when there are huge gaps in what the organization professes to be (e.g., professing to have a positive culture that is negative in reality), then high levels of member cynicism develop, performance deteriorates (Baron & Greenberg, 1990), and cohesiveness drops. Perhaps this is what happened to Sarah as she felt the disregard of her new supervisor flood over her.

Community psychologists are presently studying a phenomenon related to organizational culture: the sense of community within an organization. Chapter 1 discussed sense of community in some detail. *Sense of community* pertains to an individual's feeling that he or she is similar to others and that the individual and the other individuals in the setting belong there. There is a sense of "we-ness" and belongingness coinciding with a sense of community.

Pretty and McCarthy (1991) explored the sense of community in men and women in corporations. They found that for different employees, the sense of community was predicted by different features of the organization. For instance, men and women differed, as did managers and nonmanagers, in the characteristics that determined a sense of community for them. Male managers' sense of community was predicted best by their perceptions of peer cohesion and involvement, whereas female managers' sense of community was predicted by their perceptions of supervisor support, involvement, and amount of work pressure.

Environmental Conditions

Have you ever driven by an old factory that has weeds growing up around it and has had its windows smashed? When some of these factories were operating, the work conditions were dreadful. The factories were dark, polluted, noisy, and drafty. Today, people know that physical conditions in organizations affect what goes on in them, so the health of the national workforce has become one of the most significant issues of modern time (Ilgen, 1990). Temperature and humidity are known to affect performance, and excessive noise creates hearing loss (Smithers, 1994).

The size of organizations is important, too. Large organizations create negative conditions. For instance, Hellman, Greene, Morrison, and Abramowitz (1985) examined residential mental health treatment programs by measuring staff and client perceptions. Not surprisingly, the larger the program, the more the members experienced anxiety, held negative views of the psychosocial aspects of the organization, and perceived greater psychological distance from the organization. Beyond that, though, even the use of space in organizations affects comfort level; when the space is crowded, individuals in it feel most uncomfortable (Baron & Greenberg, 1990). Organizations that care about their members will create safe and comfortable environments for them.

Poor Human Resource Management

What used to be called *personnel administration* is today called **human resource management (HRM).** HRM involves a series of decisions designed to influence the effectiveness of organizations and their members (Milkovich & Boudreau, 1991). HRM decisions include recruiting, selecting, training, and appraising staff, as well as other aspects of maintaining organizational membership. Some members of organizations may feel that their expertise is mismatched to what they are asked to do; others feel that poor decisions are being made about them without input from them. These situations often lead to poor morale, absenteeism, stress, and unpleasant feelings that can be vented on or affect client services. If organizational members are poorly trained or if they feel their contributions are undervalued, they become disgruntled with their organizational affiliation and perhaps resign. Sarah probably felt relatively unappreciated by her new supervisor, especially in contrast with the treatment afforded her by Jan Hayes. This contrast in how Sarah was "managed" contributed, in part, to her resignation.

TRADITIONAL TECHNIQUES FOR MANAGING ORGANIZATIONS

When Sarah left Harmony House, she was a discontented employee. Sarah wasn't the only one hurt by her decision to leave, though. The organization also would suffer. Harmony House would now have to recruit and select a replacement for Sarah as well as train and indoctrinate the new individual. Clients might perhaps feel disoriented when they came looking for Sarah but could not find her. What do organizations traditionally do to attract and retain good members and to manage poor members? Are these strategies helpful?

Compensation Packages

Many of the traditional attempts by organizations to treat employees well or to terminate them focus on the individual. An age-old method of motivating employees to work hard and work well is to manipulate compensation levels. In fact, setting compensation levels is often considered the primary function of many HRM staff (Milkovich & Boudreau, 1991). Interestingly, organizational members rarely mention pay as the job facet most related to their job satisfaction (Schultz & Schultz, 1990). Nonetheless, one of the common ways organizations attempt to motivate their members is by tampering with compensation and benefits packages. One study showed that raising wage and salary levels was the most common response to reducing quitting in organizations (Bureau of National Affairs, 1981). However, in reality, pay adjustments only partially increase job satisfaction (Sarata, 1984).

Rules and Regulations

Organizations also attempt to control member behavior by means of policies and regulations. Policy manuals and codes of ethics for employees have become quite common (Lewin, 1983). Some policies are specific: "No gambling on company property." Others are less so: "Employees are expected to be loyal to the company." Add to this the multitude of public policies or federal and state legislation intended to regulate organizations and the individuals in them, and the total number of regulations is overwhelming. Federal Equal Employment Opportunity Guidelines and the Occupational Safety and Health Regulations alone would create a stack of policies higher than the average person is tall!

The extent to which employees follow organizational policies is unclear, but some classic studies of employee behavior indicate that not all organizational members appreciate regulations. In the bank wiring room study of the classic Hawthorne research at the Western Electric Plant in Hawthorne, Illinois, the men of the bank wiring room purposely worked *below* the production standard set by their supervisors. Why? The men believed that if they worked up to standard, their superiors would simply raise the standard (Roethlisberger & Dickson, 1939), thereby forcing the men to work even harder. It is known today that in professional bureaucracies such as hospitals, universities, and other human services agencies, the professionals prefer to operate according to their *own* codes rather than the formal policies of their organizations (Cheng, 1990; Mintzberg, 1979). Most organizational members have little say in the policies or regulations of their organization; that may be the primary reason they are discontented with the guidelines and violate the rules, as is often found in studies of organizational rules.

A sample study of rules and rule violating behavior in college dormitories can illustrate the above point. Triplet, Cohn, and White (1988) examined rules and rule violations in a variety of dormitories on a particular campus. The researchers found that stronger compliance to dormitory rules was achieved when students living in the dormitories participated in the regulatory system than when the rules were set by a strong external authority such as the dormitory director or other administrator. From the Hawthorne study and this dormitory study, one can infer that efforts at governing individuals in organizations are somewhat futile if the organizational members are not involved in policy setting. Organizational members need to be empowered to govern their own organizations.

Discipline

Another traditional treatment, this time for a problem member of an organization, is to discipline him or her. **Discipline** is the systematic administration of punishment in organizations (Baron & Greenberg, 1990). Discipline typically commences with warnings and/or counseling about the problem behavior and how to correct it and then progresses to dismissal for subsequent infractions. Approximately 95% of the managers discuss the problem with their subordinates first (Beyer & Trice, 1984). If the problematic behavior results in damages, the amount is usually deducted from the paycheck (Milkovich & Boudreau, 1991). Negative side effects of discipline can be aggression (as in vandalism) and withdrawal of the worker (as in **working to rule** or working to minimal standards as set by policy) (Baron & Greenberg, 1990).

As just mentioned, one other customary method of managing organizational behavior is via **discharging,** or **terminating,** the problem employee. Employees are often terminated for attendance (60% of the terminations), performance (17%), drug or alcohol abuse (9%), and other problems (14%) (Bureau of National Affairs, 1985).

Both discipline and termination are, of course, costly to the individual—and not just in lost wages but in lost esteem as well. They are also costly to the organization in terms of its human resource investments (recruiting, training, etc.) and effects on other watchful organizational members (Milkovich & Boudreau, 1991). When an organizational decision or action has an impact on more than the intended individual or targeted part of the organization, this is called a **systems impact**.

In summary, then, these traditional methods of regulating individuals in organizations are typically the antithesis of what community psychologists would recommend. First, most are aimed at the individual level of the organization. They do not address nor acknowledge the role that the context or the organization itself plays in producing and influencing individual behavior. Second, most of these methods are not particularly humanizing, especially discipline and discharge. Community psychologists value strategies that benefit the individual and speak to the individual's worthiness. On the contrary, in most of these traditional techniques, it is the organization that benefits, if at all. Third, community psychologists emphasize prevention over treatment. In these solutions to organizational situations, the solution often comes *after*, not before, the problem has occurred. Finally, community psychologists believe that individuals should actively engage in—indeed, be empowered to—create their own environments and design the solutions to their problems. In none of these traditional approaches to organizational problems is there much room for that.

We now turn to changes in organizations that encompass some of the values of community psychology. Although much of the progressive work in the fields of organizational behavior and organizational psychology has been conducted in and for industrial settings, you will see that what follows can also generally apply to any community organization.

OVERVIEW OF ORGANIZATIONAL CHANGE

Reasons for Change

Organizations require change for a number of reasons, a few of which will be mentioned briefly here. Pressures for change may be internal or external. **Internal pressures to change** come from within and include pressures from clients, staff, supervisors, or all three. As in the case of Harmony House, internal budget pressures can force change. Organizations also sometimes change their focus or offer new or different services, which leads to further change.

Forces outside of the organization create **external pressures to change**. Government regulations, external competition, political and social trends, and other factors create the need for organizations to change in order to adapt. For example, the move to deinstitutionalize people who are mentally disabled has forced communities to provide alternative services such as group homes. Both the availability of homes and the conditions in the institutions have been affected by this trend. Case in Point 11.1 demonstrates how one organization coped with change.

Issues Related to Organizational Change

We have already mentioned in Chapters 3 and 4 that change is difficult. Organizational change is no different; it, too, is not easy (Barney, 1986). One reason organizational change is complex is because many organizational members resist change. They feel threatened by the changes, perhaps because they do not feel competent to handle the changes or they do not want to put forth the effort to adapt to them.

There are other reasons change in organizations is complicated. Organizations are interdependent systems (Tosi, Rizzo, & Carroll, 1986). The people in the organization influence the organization and the organization influences the people. One cannot be changed without changes occurring in the other. For example, suppose in his budget cuts, the Harmony House supervisor decided also to cut staff to save money. Fewer staff mean less attention to each youth; fewer staff also mean more work for the remaining staff. Hence, the services of the organization may start to decline; therefore, its reputation might also decline, and it would perhaps attract fewer clients and fewer qualified job applicants because of the budget cuts.

Glidewell (1987) offered a second example of the interdependence of people and organizations from the community psychology literature. Glidewell worked with a group of citizens who hoped to change a school board, which desired instead to change the citizens' attitudes. Specifically, the citizens had voted down a tax referendum three times in one year; the board hoped the citizens would pass the referendum. Glidewell tracked the changes in the citizens and the school board over several years. His data clearly showed a mutually causative, sequential, yet circular system of influence. An increase in citizen negotiation skills were followed by changes in influence on board decisions as well as changes in self-esteem of the participants. Changes in self-esteem and changes in attendance at

❖ *CASE IN POINT 11.1*

Inside Employee Assistance Programs (EAPs): A Coping Organization Copes with Change

Jim Sipe, program manager for the New York state government employee assistance program (EAP), knew change was in the wind. The state's budget was in bad shape, several of his staff had resigned because of their uncertain future, and staff morale was sliding downhill. Jim's primary staff consisted of the field representatives who consult by region to the more than 350 local, public-sector EAPs run by volunteer counselors. In EAPs, the counselor provides advice, assistance, and referrals to other helping agencies for government employees whose personal problems may interfere with their work life. Because of colleagues' resignations, the remaining field staff territories were about to grow very large, as the budget did not allow replacements to be hired.

Organizational development came to the rescue. Jim arranged for consultants to institute two techniques: team building and quality circles. The field representatives first were introduced to team building to develop a sense of cohesiveness and team spirit. After the initial training, the staff met regularly to discuss issues and concerns within their own ranks. Continual group assessment is essential to team building, as it is an *ongoing* process of group development.

At another training, the staff divided into smaller groups, known as quality circles, to discuss current problems and how to solve them. Before these circles began developing solutions, staff were inspired to think creatively. One of us (Duffy), acting as a consultant, took the staff through **brainstorming**, a technique that induces creative problem solving by encouraging "hitch-hiking" on other peoples' ideas and by separating idea evaluation (which can be threatening and therefore stifling) from idea generation. Once the groups were comfortable with brainstorming, they were able to more easily generate creative approaches to the budget problems, the shrinking staff size, and the morale issues.

To adapt to the smaller number of field representatives and a shrinking budget, the field staff and central headquarters were **reorganized**. Field staff, who had formerly been isolated in their own offices around the state, soon shared more centralized offices. Not only did this reduce costs but it also allowed field staff to regularly interact with and provide social support and consultation to each other. The staff at headquarters, which now housed some of the field representatives, also provided telephone back-up to the volunteer counselors whose field representative might be on the road in the enlarged territory and therefore unavailable.

One final problem that Jim and his staff, as well as the volunteer counselors, perpetually face is burnout. Caregivers often need care themselves. In recognition of this, one of the field representatives suggested that at trainings for the New York state EAP professionals a module entitled Take Care of Yourself be incorporated. The segment outlines how the staff can provide better service to others *only if* they, themselves, are well. One of the key elements to taking care of themselves is to seek social support from other EAP professionals. Social support and OD maintained this helping agency's health.

board meetings were followed by changes in risk taking. Changes in risk taking were followed by further changes in negotiation skills. Changes in negotiation skills attracted the attention of the board; thus, the board was more likely to listen to the citizens, whose esteem was further enhanced.

Another reason organizations are difficult to change lies in the fact that the intervention or change must fit the organizational paradigm (Cheng, 1990). What does this mean? Organizations are diverse in terms of their staffing, functions, structures, and other parameters. By using two dimensions from organizational theory, Schubert and Borkman (1991) found not one but *five* different types of self-help groups. The two dimensions were "dependence on external funds" and "extent of internal experiential authority" (or self-determination). Therefore, even in organizations with similar purposes—in this case self-help groups—there are diverse types of organizations varying on several dimensions. Changing organizations requires customizing the intervention or fitting the change to the organizational model (Constantine, 1991) and to the organizational constituencies.

To ensure that change is indeed needed, change should commence with action research. The research can also address whether the organization is ready for change. Both need and readiness are generally prompted by dissatisfaction with the organization by its members (Baron & Greenberg, 1990). The age of the organization is also important, as there exist different stages of development of community organizations (Bartunek & Betters-Reed, 1987). Some preliminary plan for change should also be in place, although a long-range plan may be better (Taber, Cooke, & Walsh, 1990). Such planning should involve staff and perhaps clients in all phases. Staff participation has a significant effect on both job satisfaction and self-esteem (Roberts, 1991; Sarata, 1984).

Change in organizations can occur at the organizational level, the group level, or the individual level. Although community psychologists might prefer to change the whole organization, the whole community so to speak, often it is the subparts of the organization that are easiest to change. We will look at all levels of organizational change and a few techniques at each level. For a complete review of methods of organizational change, see Head and Sorenson (1988).

CHANGING THE WHOLE ORGANIZATION

Reorganization

Several techniques may be employed for changing the whole organization or system; two will be examined here. One change strategy is reorganization of the organization. **Reorganization** means that a structural change takes place; that is, the tasks, interpersonal relationships, reward system or decision-making techniques are rearranged (Beer & Walton, 1990). For example, Hellman, Greene, Morrison, and Abramowitz (1985) studied residential mental health treatment programs and found that both staff and client perceptions of the program were more negative in the larger organizations. These authors suggested that the change from three small homes to one large facility may have exacerbated the schizophrenic clients' fears about loss of self. Hellman and colleagues recommended careful review and related research by policy makers before commencing any other similar reorganizations.

Organizations can also be reorganized by becoming linked, affiliated with, or networked with other organizations. **Networks, enabling systems,** and **umbrella organizations** have been discussed in an earlier chapter. Suffice it to say here that these "master" organizations help ensure the survival and success of their member organizations. However, competition, lack of coordinating mechanisms, and other factors can diminish the effectiveness of such organizational federations.

Quality of Work Life Programs

Another change that can be made throughout an organization is to introduce quality of work life (QWL) programs, mentioned earlier. Recall that these programs include **participatory decision making,** designed to encourage democracy and staff motivation, satisfaction, and commitment. Such programs also foster career development and leadership by empowering or fostering decision making in others besides the leaders or managers already designated on the organizational chart (Hollander & Offerman, 1990). In QWl programs, the staff and possibly the clients design programs and action plans that they think will be effective and that are well reasoned. The programs are then implemented and perhaps funded by higher levels in the organization. Such programs have been shown to be fairly effective in improving organizational productivity as well as employee satisfaction in various settings (Baron & Greenberg, 1990).

Bennis (1989) has accused most of today's organizational leaders of being too self-absorbed and therefore causing some of the country's economic and social problems as well as organizational misery. He recommended that if managers do not allow participation by others within organizations, they should at least learn more humanistic leadership styles. One means by which to achieve sensitivity to others, authenticity in interpersonal relationships, and a renewed spirit of inquiry among organizational leaders, or any organizational members for that matter, is **sensitivity or T-group training** (Schein & Bennis, 1965). This training generally involves lectures and experiential exercises in which group members learn about interpersonal relations, conflict and its management, openness of feelings, self and others' motivations, and a respect for self-disclosure.

Do QWL programs work in community settings? The literature in community psychology suggests that empowering individuals to create self-generated change, whether the individuals be staff or clients, seems to work. One such study is interesting. Hamilton, Basseches, and Richards (1985) studied the link between participatory-democratic work and adolescents' mental health. In this study, working adolescents were encouraged to make their own decisions, to increase the complexity of their work, and to take on more responsibility as they felt ready.

Between pre- and posttests, the adolescents showed significant growth, as measured by moral and social reasoning.

Hamilton and associates (1985) have suggested that the number of programs in communities that promote participatory decision making is steadily increasing, but several studies suggest that simply allowing participation in community organizations is hollow and therefore not beneficial. Prestby, Wandersman, Florin, Rich, and Chavis (1990) found that in order for individuals to continue to participate in block or neighborhood booster associations, benefits such as getting to know ones neighbors better or learning a new skill like public speaking have to exceed costs (such as feeling the association never gets anything done or finding less time to spend with friends and family). Community organizations need to manage their incentive efforts well so that participation by others results in satisfaction.

GROUP CHANGE WITHIN THE ORGANIZATION

In the Hawthorne studies mentioned earlier, one group of men in a bank wiring room developed their own group norms and standards that were well outside of those of the company. Groups in organizations often do that. You might have noticed this phenomenon in some of the groups to which you belong. For example, you may be taking classes outside of the psychology department. The psychology department perhaps has its own culture that is casual, personable, and informal. Students are called by their first names, class discussions are frequent, and students are allowed full representation and voting privileges within the department. On the other hand, a different department, say mathematics, might be more formal and less personable. Students are called Miss Smith or Mister Jones, there are few class discussions, and the department meetings are closed to students. Groups exist as mini-organizations within organizations, and as the next two studies demonstrate, groups in community organizations are no exception.

Maton (1988) examined social support as well as organizational variables in self-help groups such as Overeaters Anonymous. He found that self-help alone was not the only condition that facilitated well-being. Group variables also were related to individual progress, as measured by such variables as weight loss. Specifically, groups with higher levels of role differentiation, greater organization or order, and leaders who were perceived as capable resulted in the group members' reporting more positive well-being and more liking for their groups. In a similar study, Luke, Rappaport, and Seidman (1991) found that type of group or group phenotype (e.g., groups that did "small talk" versus "advising") was related to reported change of members in mutual help groups. Groups, then, are just as important, complex, and relevant to their members' well-being as are large organizations.

Several techniques for group change exist; we will mention only two, which have been targeted in the community psychology literature as important. Both team building and quality circles can result in better functioning of groups in community organizations and therefore result in better services to the community.

Team Building

One technique for improving groups in organizations is team building. **Team building** is an ongoing group method in which group members are encouraged to work together in the spirit of cooperation that contributes to the group's sense of community. The purpose of team building is to *accomplish* goals and to *analyze* tasks, member relations, and processes such as decision making in the group. In other words, the group is simultaneously the object of and a participant in the process (Moorehead & Griffin, 1992). Team building is probably the most frequently used OD method (Covin & Kilmann, 1991). Team building has been examined using a sophisticated technique called **meta-analysis**, which is utilized to statistically examine the literature on a particular process and to draw implications for policy and practice (Durlak & Lipsey, 1991). By means of meta-analysis, team building has been shown to be quite effective (Neuman, Edwards, & Raju, 1989).

Team building—or **team development,** as it is also known (Sundstrom, DeMeuse, & Futrell, 1990)—has been used to improve staff services to clients at mental health agencies (Bendicsen & Carlton, 1990); Cohen et al., 1991; Olson & Cohen, 1986) as well as to improve the performance of both the corrections officers and staff at forensic (psychiatric) prisons (Miller, Maier, & Kaye, 1988), patients at methadone maintenance clinics (Magura, Goldmith, Casriel, & Lipton, 1988), teachers (Thatcher & Howard, 1989), nurses at an eating disorders clinic (Sansone et al., 1988), physicians (Bair & Greenspan, 1986), and staff at other types of service agencies (Davis & Luthans, 1988). Team building also has been successfully used to sensitize multiculturally staffed agencies to the needs of their diverse members (Ratiau, 1986).

Quality Circles

Quality circles as change techniques have also been mentioned earlier in this chapter. Quality circles are small groups of volunteer employees who meet regularly to identify and solve problems related to organizational conditions. These solutions, then need to be implemented if the quality circle's participants are to feel that their input has been useful. Implementation motivates the circle's members to continue their deliberations from meeting to meeting. These group solutions, when implemented, should result in higher member satisfaction and better service to clients.

Although apparently less extensively used in community agencies than team building, quality circles have been used recently and successfully with teachers (Long, 1986; Sherman, 1990; Schofield, 1986), college student services personnel (Steele, Rue, Clement, & Zamostny, 197), and government employees (Bowman, 1989).

HELPING INDIVIDUALS WITHIN THE ORGANIZATION CHANGE

It has already been stated that community psychologists prefer the ecological approach where the whole system rather than the individual is examined and changed; however, the literature has emphasized the individual in community psychology. In line with this, the next section will discuss how individuals can change, especially in coping with everyday problems instigated by their organizations.

Burnout and Stress

Burnout and stress are problems in contemporary organizations, as already noted. Today's organizations need to recognize that burnout and stress are related to organizational conditions rather than merely to an individual's makeup (McCulloch & O'Brien, 1986) or poor coping strategies (Shinn, Morch, Robinson, & Neuer, 1993). Some organizations, though, do little to help their staff cope with organizational stress (Shinn, Lehmann, & Wong, 1984). Organizations need to be involved in interventions, and community psychologists offer a growing literature on what can be done to alleviate these problems in organizations. Traditional organizational interventions for stress in individuals include meditation and relaxation training as well as exercise programs (Ivancevich, Matteson, Freedman, & Phillips, 1990). Such interventions treat the individual and ignore the context in which that individual works. Community psychologists have developed alternative programs, which will be showcased next.

Social support from coworkers in the form of modeling various strategies for coping, showing empathy, and giving advice has been demonstrated to be useful in ameliorating the effects of stress and burnout in various community agencies (Shinn et al., 1993). For instance, Kirmeyer and Dougherty (1988) demonstrated that social support for police dispatchers favorably reduces the officers' anxiety. Olson's (1991) research showed that appropriate support provides teachers with acculturation experiences and encourages them to make autonomous decisions. Hirsch and David (1983) and McIntosh (1991) found that social support from other nurses enables nurses to reduce general stress levels and cope better with patient death. Human services workers (Shinn et al., 1984), and more specifically social workers (Himle, Jayertne, & Thyness, 1991; Melamed, Kushnir, & Meir, 1991), also benefit from the social support of coworkers. Broman, Hamilton, and Hoffman (1990), Caplan, Vinokur, Price, and van Ryn (1989), Turner, Kessler, and House (1991), and Zippay (1990–91) have shown that social support also alleviates the effects of unemployment for terminated employees.

Cautions are needed here, however. Social support often operates in complex ways in organizational settings (Schwarzer & Leppin, 1991,) just as it does elsewhere; for example, group coping and support is often but not always better than individual coping strategies. And, in some instances, social support can actually worsen the individual's situation (Grossi & Berg, 1991). Similarly, regard must be given to each person's cultural background and what kind of support is most appropriate for that person (Jay & D'Augelli, 1991).

Another organizational method for managing stress is to provide constructive feedback. **Constructive feedback**—providing information about how to do the job or how well the individual is doing his or her job—can sometimes help to alleviate stress. In organizations, there are usually formal reviews of an employee's performance; these are called **performance appraisals**. However, informal feedback that is constructive—in that it is meant to help the individual perform better or develop a sense of confidence or satisfaction—is also useful *before* formal appraisals are completed. Digman, Barrera, and West (1986) found that prison corrections officers who have more opportunity for receiving goal clarification from both supervisors and coworkers experienced less role ambiguity and therefore less burnout and stress. Likewise, Eisenstat and Felner (1984) found that staff *and* client feedback to human service workers was important in abating workers' burnout.

Finally, mass education programs on stress management can help employees and community citizens cope with stress. Jason and colleagues (1989) produced a series of television programs on stress and coping. Many viewers reported that they tried the coping methods. Measures of viewer adjustment and well-being showed significant improvement, especially among the most distressed viewers. Organizations can also provide mass education about stress and coping through newsletters, workshops, and trainings.

Other Personal Problems

In modern society, personal problems also plague members of organizations. In human service settings, it is not just the clients who experience the myriad problems that the organization is designed to address. Chemical dependency, family strife, financial problems, mental health, and other issues also affect the staff and can lessen their enthusiasm and perhaps productivity while at work. People do not leave their personal problems outside the organization when they enter it each working day. Avant-garde organizations recognize that by assisting employees with personal problems, they are inspiring loyalty to the organization and thus helping the organization. Health insurance rates, turnover, and absenteeism are probably reduced when organizations help individuals cope with personal problems. We will sample here two different personal problems that can, but need not, interfere with an individual's working life: smoking and role conflict in working parents. Both of these issues have received recent attention in the community psychology literature.

Smoking

Smoking by employees is troublesome for many reasons, among which are the health-related problems of the smokers, consequent health insurance costs to the organization, and complaints by other employees affected by secondhand smoke

(Milkovich & Boudreau, 1991). In one study, psychologists hoping to reduce workplace smoking enlisted participants from 43 different corporations. The smokers participated in a televised smoking cessation program combined with self-help abstinence groups. Compared to other smokers, those in the smoking cessation program most reduced their smoking (Jason et al., 1987). However, in this first study, **recidivism,** or return to the problem behavior—in this case, smoking—remained a dilemma. The conjectured reason for relapse was that worksites can be stressful and thus create the return to smoking.

In a second study, after an introduction to the smoking cessation program, some participants were provided with follow-up support groups and other incentives to remain abstinent. At the 12-month follow-up period, the strongest predictor of abstinence was the availability of group meetings (Jason et al., 1989). Therefore, when an organization provides assistance as simple as encouraging support groups, it encourages the well-being of its employees.

Family Issues

The second example of personal circumstance that can cause problems for employees of organizations is their family situation. There are more parents either from single- or dual-parent families who work today than in the past. Finding child care, coordinating different family members' schedules, and so on can be a burden for these parents (Zedeck & Mosier, 1990). Some organizations remain unresponsive to the conflict created by work and family responsibilities, but there is much that can be done. We have already addressed day-care issues in Chapter 8. In that chapter, Zigler's idea to link early childhood day-care with public school systems was reviewed. This solution coupled with work site day care might provide ample day care for children of harried parents. We will turn here to other possible solutions that are in line with community psychology's philosophies.

Work schedule adaptations are one possibility. In **work schedule adaptations,** employees' work-site time is not the standard 9-to-5 day. Instead, employees are usually given the freedom to select *when* and sometimes *where* they would like to work. One such system is flexitime. In most **flexitime** systems, there are core hours during which all employees must be present. However, the employee can often select the total number of hours worked, the length of the work week, or other variations. A wider variety of service hours might also be attractive to clients, too. Research has not always demonstrated strong, positive effects of flexitime and other work schedule adaptations. For example, in one study (Shinn, Wong, Simko, & Ortiz-Torres, 1989), perceived time flexibility was only weakly related to positive outcomes and formal flexitime was unrelated. Other program dimensions such as social support were more strongly related to coping.

Compressed workweeks offer another alternative. The compressed workweek is not the standard five-day, Monday-through-Friday week. In the typical scheme, all employees work four 10-hour days with either Friday or Monday off, which ensures a longer weekend and therefore more concentrated time with the family. Some organizations are even allowing **home work** in which the individual works at home for all or a portion of the week. These individuals are usually linked to their work site via computer or some other form of technology yet are also home with young children (Milkovich & Boudreau, 1991).

Some programs of work schedule alteration have been found to reduce organizational problems (Zedeck & Mosier, 1990) and perhaps improve family members' home and work lives. Greenberger, Goldberg, Hamill, O'Neill, and Payne (1989) found that organizational policies that are family responsive best assist women in coping with role strain, because it is women who still have greater responsibility than men for adjusting work life to meet the demands of their families.

Today, a variety of programs in organizations exist that are designed to help an individual cope with personal problems as well as financial, legal, emotional, drug, and other problems. **Employee assistance programs (EAPs)** are designed to assist employees with personal problems that may interfere with their organizational behaviors. EAPS in industrial settings have existed from as early as 1917 (New York State Employees Assistance Program Manual, 1990) and have grown rapidly in the last two decades (Bureau of National Affairs, 1986). When such programs are designed and maintained by the employees themselves (rather than, say, managers), are on-site, and are voluntary rather than coercive, the programs fit the ideals of community psychology. Moreover, when EAPs are linked with **wellness programs** designed to prevent health problems before they begin and designed to change norms away from stress and unproductive coping, then these programs certainly are aligned with the philosophy of community psychology (Shinn, 1987; Shinn & Perkins, in press). Wellness programs include but are not limited to education about diet, weight loss, and exercise as well as lifestyle modification programs (Gebhardt & Crump, 1990). Profile 11.1 will introduce you to Elise Everett, EAP coordinator.

CHANGING WHAT PEOPLE DO: ALTERING JOBS

As you now know from your reading, the context of work creates problems. The **job context**—that is, the jobs people do and how and where they do them—can also be a factor in organizational and individual well-being. There are a number of recently developed strategies for changing jobs that are important, but we will mention only a few.

Job Expansion

Individuals can become frustrated by what they do in organizations. The jobs might be too demanding, too boring, too complex, or too difficult. Suppose that Sarah Anderson, the individual in the opening story, had become disenchanted with her job not because of budget cuts but because the job was not challenging enough. What could she and her supervisor have done about this? Two possible and seemingly similar strategies are job enlargement and job enrichment. **Job enlargement** involves adding more to the job, but what is added usually requires

◆ **PROFILE 11.1**
Elise Everett

Elise Everett is indeed a determined woman—determined to better her own life as well as the lives of others.

Everett was born in Brooklyn but was raised by her aunt in the West Indies because both her parents worked. She did not return to the United States and to her parents until she was 5 years of age. In the United States, she completed high school and was referred upon graduation to a developmental disabilities center for employment. Developmental disabilities centers in New York generally serve learning disabled and retarded clients in a residential or day treatment setting. The one in Brooklyn at which Everett works is a large, self-maintained facility with its own physical plants, kitchens, and residences.

Everett worked first as a stenographer, but she was determined to educate herself and move up the organizational ladder. She therefore started her college education, which was soon interrupted by the birth of her daughter. She found working, raising a daughter as a single parent, and attending college to be too arduous, so she had to drop out of college for a while. She did, however, better her employment position by taking the examination for developmental therapy aides, where she was excited to have direct client contact. Everett liked the contact very much, which made her all the more determined to pursue an education and to continue moving up the career ladder.

Eventually, Everett took the examination for recreation and rehabilitation assistants and passed. She next worked in the education and training department to train other staff about interacting with their clients—the disabled residents. At this present position, Everett instructs staff on first aid, crisis intervention techniques, and cardiopulmonary resuscitation. She enjoys the wide range of responsibilities, the multiculturalism of the people with whom she works, and the opportunities provided for more training and education. The agency also wisely provides a much-needed day-care center for staff.

In her training interactions with other staff, Everett recognized that the organization was not without problems. High stress levels, a lack of consideration for family problems, inconsistency in enforcement of rules and regulations, and favoritism by supervisors sometimes creates poor morale. Unequal workloads and little advance notice of job changes (e.g., in shift hours) cause staff turnover.

Recently, Elverett discovered a job-posting for an EAP coordinator position and realized that she could be the solution to some of these organizational problems if she applied for and received the EAP position. EAP coordinators are sounding boards for employees with personal problems and make suggestions for solutions to the problems to assist the employees. She succeeded in landing this part-time assignment, enthusiastically trained for her new position, and, in fact, started in the job the day after the training. Elise Everett has successfully scaled the organizational ladder and benefited others in the process by her determination and dedication to service.

about the same level of responsibility and skill. Suppose that Sarah led therapy groups at Harmony House. If she did not find this challenging enough, perhaps she could have developed wellness, exercise and nutrition or diet classes for interested youths, or perhaps she could have done outreach to other at-risk youths in the community.

Job enrichment involves adding higher-level responsibilities to an individual's repertoire. Perhaps Sarah felt she had accomplished all she could in her current position at Harmony House and was bored. She and her supervisor could have decided that Sarah had sufficient experience to train and mentor all new case managers who were hired. In this way, Sarah would have been further challenged by managerial responsibilities but also would have used all of the skills that she had already attained in supervising the new caseworkers.

Is there evidence to support the notion that task interest is an important aspect of work life quality? Using interviews and questionnaires with the nursing staff at a psychiatric hospital, Zautra, Eblen, and Reynolds (1986) found that task interest was an important variable. Specifically, task interest combined with job stress predicted turnover in this study. Furthermore, employees tended to stay at work *even if the job was stressful* as long as the tasks were interesting. In a second study, Lindquist and Whitehead (1986) surveyed corrections officers in traditional roles in the prisons as well as officers whose jobs were expanded to provide additional community supervision to inmates. Those with expanded jobs reported increased feelings of accomplishment and higher job satisfaction. These studies demonstrate that making jobs richer or more challenging creates happier staff members.

Management by Objectives

Altering staff perceptions of the job is also important, and there are at least two interesting methods for accomplishing this. In **management by objectives (MBO)**, the staff person and his or her supervisor jointly discuss the tasks at hand and how goals related to them will be accomplished. The two then jointly set goals for the employee and, during a later review, decide whether the goals were accomplished or too over-or underambitious. MBO, therefore, is a sort of participative negotiation (Katzell & Thompson, 1990). Although the individual employee is not solely empowered to make his or her own decisions, the method is popular because some of the fear is taken out of traditional performance appraisal in that the employee knows in advance what is expected. The staff member is also motivated to accomplish the goals because he or she has had a role in designing them.

Participation in goal setting and decision making in organizations has been shown to be highly effective. Using **meta-analysis**, which is a sophisticated statistical technique for reviewing relevant literature and deducing the overall utility of a practice, Rodgers and Hunter (1991) found MBO to be effective in 68 of 70 studies. Of the studies related to community services Rodgers and Hunter reviewed, MBO was used successfully to improve municipal governments (Poister

& Streib, 1989), hospitals (Sloan & Schreiber, 1971; Stoelwinder & Clayton, 1978), the Equal Employment Opportunity Commission (Taylor & Tao, 1980), college faculty (Terpstra, Olson, & Lockeman, 1982), and a police diversion agency for youths (Williams, 1984).

Realistic Job Preview

Another method for altering perceptions of jobs is to provide a **realistic job preview (RJP)** to the individual *before* she or he takes the job. When we discussed burnout, we made clear that the most ideal or naive individual often burns out first. Why? The reason is simple. Idealistic individuals are not in touch with the realities of the job. Their expectations of the job are higher than reality, and thus they have the furthest to "fall." Providing a realistic sample of what the job entails, its glamorous as well as its gloomy side, enables individuals who are not appropriate for the job to select themselves out of the search. Perhaps Sarah was a little too idealistic for the realities of Harmony House. Had she been informed that budget problems were predicted and that some services had to be cut *before* she took the job, she might never have become so disillusioned.

Many human services workers often heroically hope to "save the world." They frequently pin their high expectations on their clients' levels of progress. When they do, they burn out when the reality strikes that they are not going to "save" everyone. Case after case materializes and the workers do not see much progress. An *expectation shift* can help avoid this type of burnout. As noted earlier, if human services workers can shift their focus to other facets of their jobs, such as progress in their own learning or competence, then they are less likely to burnout (Stevens & O'Neill, 1983). The majority of studies on RJPs found no adverse effects of the employer being candid with the prospective employee about the realities of the job (Shinn & Perkins, in press).

DOES ORGANIZATIONAL INTERVENTION WORK?

We have reviewed many strategies for changing parts of or whole organizations. We have also provided at least one or two studies for each strategy that suggest that these techniques are viable. The field of organizational development is old enough at this point that several large-scale reviews of OD have been conducted in order to draw general conclusions about OD's efficacy. We would like briefly to share one representative review with you.

Porras, Robertson, and Goldman (in press) compared almost 50 different OD studies conducted between 1975 and 1986. Many of the different techniques described in this chapter were utilized in the studies: MBO, quality circles, survey feedback, team building, and others. These outcome studies examined either individual, organizational, or both types of outcomes. Overall, the studies demonstrated that OD is beneficial. The results, however, were more beneficial to the organization than to the individual, and benefits were more likely to be obtained when a number of methods were used rather than just one. This last finding is not surprising in that most studies in community psychology show that multipronged efforts are more successful. One might conclude then, that OD shows promise; however, it merits more research.

Anyone considering organizational change must also consider that changes need to be made in a coherent, systematic fashion. Hit-or-miss and one-shot approaches probably will not be productive in the long run. Bennis (1969) also suggested that organizations need to become **organic systems**. That is, organizations need to replace mechanistic methods (such as adherence to rules and regulations) with transactional methods such that *mutual* trust, *shared* control and responsibility, and *multigroup* membership are enhanced. In fact, procedural rigidity (strict adherence to rules) is the most frequent, single constraint against change, especially in public sector organizations (Golembiewski, 1985).

SUMMARY

Organizations are communities. Just like any community, organizations are comprised of various individuals and groups. Many of today's organizations need humanizing, as do many communities, if they are to enhance the well-being of the individuals in them.

By making today's community agencies and organizations better places to work for their staffs, organizations can deliver better services to clients. The problems facing human services workers today include but are not limited to stress, burnout, workaholism or Type-A personality, repressive organizational cultures, poor environmental conditions, and human resources mismanagement.

Historically, organizations have considered individual employee's characteristics rather than anything organizational to be the root of the problems. Traditional techniques for managing problem individuals have been to alter compensation packages such as pay, institute rules and regulations, or discipline or discharge the individual.

Community organizations need to undergo change if they are to continue to provide quality services and become more humane. That is, they need to adopt more avant-garde methods for coping with change and with problems inside the organizations. The whole organization can change or, within the organization, groups or individuals can change.

Methods for changing the whole organization include reorganization—for example, creating smaller, friendlier agencies from one large one. Another organizational strategy for change is to institute quality of work life programs (QWL) programs. These are programs where staff members and perhaps clients participate in planning and designing the changes the organization needs.

Groups within organizations can also change in order that they become more effective. Two methods for group change include team building, or ongoing team development, and quality circles, where small groups of volunteer organizational members meet to address problems within the organization.

Finally, individuals inside the organization bring with them an array of problems that can diminish the effectiveness of the organization. Burnout and stress are two examples. The use of social support from others within the organization is effective in assisting distressed individuals. Employee assistance programs (EAPs) and wellness programs are also useful for addressing a variety of personal problems individuals bring to work with them that decrease their ability to serve the agency's clients. These and other organizational development techniques have been proven effective according to recent research.

12

THE FUTURE OF COMMUNITY PSYCHOLOGY

"So that's the face that goes with the voice I hear on the phone all the time,"
Rita said to John. John is in charge of a meal program for people living with
acquired immune deficiency syndrome (AIDS). Rita is the head of the Meals on
Wheels program for the elderly in the same semi-rural county. "Glad to finally
meet you in person," replied John.

Rita and John had spoken to each other many times in the past but always
by phone. Their conversations revolved around buying food in bulk at low cost,
finding volunteers, and the toll rural roads and the weather take on getting
clients the multiple services they need. The two agency heads had never met
until an important conference was sponsored by the only college in the county.

In speaking to both John and Rita, as well as other agency heads, it became
apparent to the volunteer coordinator at the college that volunteer services to
these agencies was anything but coordinated. In fact, none of the services was
coordinated with any other service. The volunteer coordinator, in consultation
with the agency heads, planned a conference on the campus for all the agencies.
Although they knew each other's names, and some had communicated with
each other by phone and mail for years, many of the agency directors met each
other for the first time at the conference.

The conference was successful in that agency directors could now better
coordinate with each other in providing needed services. The directors also established formal communication channels (e.g., a conference every six months)
and discussed mechanisms for moving service delivery forward (e.g., a part-
time rural mass transit system so clients without cars could access services). The
agency directors also discussed the problems with overlapping services, how to
better utilize volunteers, and how they could share information about available
grants and other funding sources. Some of the agency directors had never heard
about private foundations and the grants they offered, and were excited to hear
of them. The volunteer coordinator at the college agreed to make her office a
clearinghouse for funding opportunities, communication, and other coordinated
endeavors among the agencies.

INTRODUCTION

Perhaps a paradoxical but good starting point for concluding this book would be for us to return to the beginning of the book. In Chapter 1 and elsewhere, we reviewed some political and social history that influenced community psychology. Such ideologies are also used to frame and shape a sense of community (Humphreys & Rappaport, 1993; Linney, 1990). This chapter will discuss the political and social agendas of the 1980s.

RECENT SOCIAL AND POLITICAL AGENDAS AFFECTING COMMUNITY PSYCHOLOGY

After the oil and hostage crises of the 1970s, Americans wanted a President such as Ronald Reagan who could tell them that "things are fine," a leader who was thought to be able to heal the wounded collective psyche. Reagan's charismatic leadership was also able to impress upon the American people that they have the determination to fix almost any problems that might arise. For example, Reagan did not hesitate to fire all the air traffic controllers as part of his deregulation of the airline industry. This action, however, indirectly sent a message to the American public that "survival of the fitness" was the norm. Thus, people who were recipients of social programs or welfare tended to be viewed as nonproductive or lazy (i.e., victim blaming), and programs such as public assistance were often viewed as wasteful. As a consequence, more than $700 million was cut from various social programs during Ronald Reagan's first year in the presidency.

Meanwhile, AIDS, crack abuse, economic downturn, educational crisis and reform, homelessness, and urban violence and other social ills were looming, and many reached epidemic proportion. Reacting to these problems, George Bush, the successor to Ronald Reagan, plotted a course of action, the emphasis of which was on volunteerism, or Bush's "thousand points of light." Bush reasoned that rehabilitation of a community depended on volunteer and cooperative efforts, especially because of dwindling federal support. Certainly, this was not a new idea; similar ideology was evidenced during the administration of John F. Kennedy. However, unlike Kennedy, Bush was practicing the ideology of **individualism,** in which people are ultimately responsible for their *own* actions, rather than **collectivism,** where everyone in the community shares the responsibility for addressing social problems.

This redefinition of responsibility for the community has become more evident with President Clinton. Clinton has attempted to project himself and his administration as "new democrats," those who are socially conscious (e.g., who want universal health care) yet who are also fiscally conservative and responsible. Clinton wanted to "reinvent government," as he called it. For example, he proposed that college students who receive loans from the government pay back some of their money by performing community service. This concept is similar to the GI Bill of World War II; it has a similar flavor to the Peace Corps and the Job Training Partnership Act (JTPA). Table 12.1 presents other historic social issues.

Given the ideologies or slogans used recently by politicians, Linney (1990) argued that this country has observed a "shifting responsibility from federal to state government" (p. 4). That is, for one reason or another (and economic downturn is an important one), "the federal government has reduced its level of involvement in many realms of service delivery" (p. 4). There are others who agree with Linney (Snowden, 1993), including us, that there are major shifts in responsibility taking place. Most levels of governments are also cutting costs because of economic problems; cost cutting may indeed conflict with quality of care (Snowden, 1993). Government commitment to services, especially preventive ones, and funding has never been very consistent nor very strong (Gesten & Jason, 1987).

In our opinion, the shifting of responsibility is both good news and bad news. We concur with Linney (1990) that the shifting responsibility has created an unprecedented opportunity for many state and local communities to be flexible and innovative in their approaches to handling social agendas or problems. Linney reviewed a number of innovative programs at the state and local levels, including such notable programs as the Citizens Clearinghouse for Hazardous Wastes and the National Alliance for the Mentally Ill. The Citizens Clearinghouse for Hazardous Wastes was founded by Lois Gibbs, President of the Homeowners Association at Love Canal. As you may recall, Love Canal (near Buffalo, New York) was a housing development built clandestinely on a hazardous waste dump. The residents became ill and their homes became relatively worthless because of seepage of waste into them. The Clearinghouse monitors illegal or irresponsible dumping of hazardous wastes.

Many similar programs have been inspired by citizen participation or grass-roots activism. Empowerment (including prevention and intervention) and social change can be achieved in local communities even under limited resources. The opening vignette about the agency heads and the volunteer coordinator is a good example. As governments slough off responsibility for social ills, we anticipate that more grass-roots citizens groups will evolve.

Perhaps another resource for community development in times of government cutbacks lies in disseminating information about possible funds available through private foundations. Money is sometimes available either for community research or community program development or both. Many community agencies do not know about these funding possibilities, as demonstrated in the opening vignette. Just as likely is that many agencies do not employ a grants writer. Community psychologists with grant-writing experience might enable and empower community programs to access this money by educating agency directors about such resources as well as about grant-writing skills.

So, what is the bad news as a result of this shifting responsibility from federal to state government? In our analysis, social agendas and problems such as AIDS, crack use, homelessness, and urban violence are often construed and treated as separate and somewhat unrelated issues (cf. Final Report of Task Force on Home-

TABLE 12.1   Some Social Issues in the Last Four Decades

Years	President	Presidential Issue	Social Issues
1960s	Kennedy	Civil Rights	"Happy Mythical Kingdom"
	Johnson	Civil Rights	Desegregation
			Deinstitutionalization
1970s	Nixon	Pornography	Deinstitutionalization
			Illegal Immigration
			Teenage Pregnancy
	Ford	(N/A)	(N/A)
	Carter	Human Rights	Deinstitutionalization
			Illegal Immigration
			Teenage Pregnancy
1980s	Reagan	Drug Abuse	AIDS
			Crack
			Economic Downturn
			Educational Crisis
			Environmental Crisis
			Health Care
			Homeless
			Illegal Immigration
			Teenage Pregnancy
			Urban Violence
	Bush	Education	AIDS
			Crack
			Economic Downturn
			Educational Crisis
			Environmental Crisis
			Health Care
			Homeless
			Illegal Immigration
			Teenage Pregnancy
			Urban Violence
1990s	Clinton	Government Downsizing	AIDS
		Health Care	Crack
			Economic Downturn
			Educational Crisis
			Environmental Crisis
			Health Care
			Homeless
			Illegal Immigration
			Teenage Pregnancy
			Urban Violence

less Women, Children, and Families, Society for Community Research and Action, 1994; Speer, Dey, Griggs, Gibson, Lubin, & Hughey, 1992).

Recall all that has be learned about interventions for the mentally ill after deinstitutionalization. Studies have consistently demonstrated that some homeless mentally ill also have alcohol and other drug-abuse problems (e.g. Diamond & Schnee, 1990). Furthermore, many of these individuals are at risk for contracting HIV, which is responsible for AIDS (Susser, Valencia, & Conover, 1993; Dennehy, Wong, Meyer, Colson, & Susser, 1994). However, funding agencies such as the National Institute on Drug Abuse and the National Institute of Mental Health often do not fund research that investigates the mentally ill *who also have* alcohol and other substance-abuse problems. Instead, research dollars are often designated for mental disorders *or* alcohol and other drug abuse problems, *but not both.* Funding therefore is often fragmented, and the constant shifting of responsibility is likely to result in more fragmentation, because states and local governments have less money for funding large, multifocused programs.

In the opening vignette, it became apparent that some agencies in this rural country were providing overlapping services. Such overlap is wasteful of resources and money in tight economic times. Moreoever, fragmentation is an obstacle to effective service delivery (Snowden, 1993). Clients, for example, are likely to fall through service system "cracks" created by fragmentation. Coordination of funding and services rather than fragmentation of funding and services is crucial for the future. In fact, some see the integration and coordination of services possible only when there is interagency collaboration so that existing services can monitor the movement of clients between programs, thereby facilitating the delivery of services (Snowden, 1993). The conference described in the opening vignette was a good start to the integration and coordination of services in Jack and Rita's county.

Unfortunately, the perspective that social problems merit attention, intervention, and priority funding is not shared by all people, including the average community citizen. For example, more than 30 years ago, one of the first reports made by the surgeon general warned about the danger of tobacco use (including smokeless tobacco). One of every six deaths in the United States is still attributable to tobacco use, even though it is the single most preventable cause of death. The average citizen continues to smoke, and does not always share the same social agenda as research scientists or government officials.

Private sector enterprises do not necessarily share the same social agenda as the government or social scientists, which further complicates progressive social change. Not all companies and industries are as socially conscious as Ben and Jerry's Ice Cream, about which you read in Chapter 3. For example, despite concerted antitobacco efforts, each year the tobacco industry spends millions of dollars advertising and promoting tobacco.

In constant dollars, money spent by the tobacco industry on advertising and promotion has tripled since 1975. The total expenditure for cigarette advertising and promotion in 1988 was $3.3 billion, a 27% increase over 1987 (Johnson, 1990).

In sum, government spending on social programs is declining. Given this situation and the fact that citizens are often indifferent to and private industry is sometimes hostile to scientists' agendas, social interventions and community research are needed more than ever. However, community experimenters will encounter more obstacles in the future. Social research and community intervention indeed require more resourcefulness, a special tenacity, and perhaps a larger research team than ever before (Gersten & Jason, 1987). We might surmise at the expense of sounding trite that community psychologists have their work cut out for them in the future.

GENERAL RECOMMENDATIONS ABOUT SOCIAL CHANGE FOR THE COMING YEARS

We cannot review here all the issues raised in previous chapters, so we will examine an important few: social change, action research, and diversity.

Social change will be difficult to accomplish, but this is no reason for community activists to give up. Community intervention still holds more promise than individual intervention (e.g., face-to-face psychotherapy). One means by which community change can be accelerated is to avoid repeatedly reinventing change. Sorely needed in community psychology is more program replication and refinement for other settings (Gesten & Jason, 1987). Only when good ideas are disseminated through journals, conferences, and books will ideas be utilized by community activists elsewhere. Dissemination is also of utmost importance if citizen acceptance is to occur. In the future, community psychologists may have to turn to the mass media as much as to their own literature. We have reviewed elsewhere in this book interventions that have successfully utilized the mass media for inducing social and individual change.

In a similar vein, most community psychologists recognize that interventions are more easily implemented when they are consistent with community beliefs and values. It is important to recognize, though, that the more an intervention fits a community, the more minor it is likely to be and the less likely it is to produce substantial change (Heller, 1990).

One mechanism by which to promote large-scale, significant change is through public policy and other legislative action. Many community psychologists are contented to "think small" (Heller, 1990) and therefore have pretty much ignored this possibility. On the other hand, public policy also presents a paradox in that a sweeping policy at the state or federal level sometimes ignores or is insensitive to local values and concerns. One of us (Duffy) lives in Rochester, New York, a city that President Clinton has identified as having an exemplary health care system. Citizens in the Rochester area want to know if and when universal health care is achieved at the federal level, whether it will diminish their own exemplary health care coverage. At press time for this book, the question remains unanswered. Citizens of Rochester have requested assistance from their legislators. Senator

Daniel Patrick Moynihan of New York, a key player in the health reform debate, has promised that this model plan will remain as is. Community psychologists pay lip service to the advantages of using public policy and lobbying efforts to create sweeping social change, but few have made either one a predominant theme in their published work.

Heller (1990) proposed another interesting social change solution that offers sensitivity to local concerns yet affords more power to individuals in local communities to influence public policy: **regionalization of community building**. These coalitions are loose-knit, large-scale confederations of local groups with common interests, which can, when called upon, act in unison. This country is currently witnessing some very effective confederated associations at the national level that were built from local grass-roots groups. These coalitions of groups with similar interests provide the large-scale leverage to address important concerns. Heller offered MADD (Mothers Against Drunk Driving) as an example of a local group that developed national constituencies and therefore successfully influenced policy makers on a wide scale. All of this was done through regional and ultimately national coalition building. Case in Point 12.1 offers a second example of the success of coalition building. Coalition building is another vehicle for creating social change that needs more investigation and dissemination effort in community psychology.

In summary, planned social change is becoming more complicated and difficult. Communities would be well served if community psychologists would attend more to information dissemination outside of and within their own media,

❖ *CASE IN POINT 12.1*

Coalition Building: The Massachusetts Tobacco Control Program

Another less familiar example of local groups coming together to form a coalition was the establishment of the Massachusetts Tobacco Control Program (MTCP), now the largest tobacco control and prevention program in the world. Its funding was $96 million for fiscal year 1993–1994, which amounts to $10 per capita.

In 1992, the Massachusetts division of the American Cancer Society, which in the past had little political experience, successfully built a statewide, grass-roots network of over 200 organizations. Together they sought approval of a ballot question to raise the Massachusetts state cigarette excise tax 25 cents and to allocate these funds to tobacco control programs, comprehensive school health education, and health services. These organizations were able to convince state legislators to earmark these funds specifically for tobacco control and prevention activities, which is a rarity. The legislation and subsequent funding led to the MTCP.

The program is evidently successful. Since 1993, there has been a 10% decline in smoking, the largest single decline in the history of the Commonwealth of Massachusetts and three times higher than the U.S. average.

concerted and well-researched public policy and legislative endeavors, and bottom-up coalition building of grass-roots groups within large regions or at the national level.

PROMOTING THE VALUES AND GOALS
OF COMMUNITY PSYCHOLOGY

In Chapter 1, we discussed some of the values and goals of community psychology. Some of these may need rethinking or added emphasis in the future. For example, Riger's (1994) contention that empowerment is primarily a masculine concept speaks to the possible need to reframe some of the values, goals, and processes of community psychology. Likewise, some concepts are discussed in the literature either as conceptual frameworks *or* as distinct interventions (Gesten & Jason, 1987) but not both. Stated another way,

> *In the main, theories [and concepts] in community psychology are less well grounded [than in traditional psychology]. They are more likely to represent attempts to grapple with issues associated with how psychological phenomena are best conceptualized (e.g., ecological models and systems analyses), sprinkled with a healthy mixture of skepticism and social conscience. (Heller, 1990, p. 159)*

Further elaboration on these constructs, especially on the specific variables used to assess outcomes, will benefit the field in the future (Gesten & Jason, 1987).

Among the most important concepts mentioned in Chapter 1 were prevention, action research, and respect for diversity. Because much has been written about these concepts and their relationship to the past, present, and future of community psychology, it is to these concepts that we will turn next.

Prevention

Primary prevention is one of the guiding principals in community psychology. By 1985, Buckner and others found over 1,000 references on primary prevention alone. Recall that **primary prevention** attempts to block a problem from occurring altogether. Primary prevention refers most generally to activities that can be undertaken with a healthy population to maintain or enhance their physical or emotional health (Bloom & Hodges, 1988).

We agree with Gesten and Jason (1987) that modest but significant progress has been made in the understanding and implementation of primary preventive efforts, but no major disorder nor any social problem has thus far been eliminated nor prevented altogether. For example, while teenage pregnancy remains an important social issue and the number of teen parents is still high, the overall rate of teenage births is slowing down, and more teens who are having babies are completing high school than at any earlier date (Levine, Toro, & Perkins, 1993). However, the truly disadvantaged still have high rates of out-of-wedlock births

(Wilson, 1987). It perhaps is to this group, the truly disadvantaged and those with multiple disorders, that more attention and preventive efforts should turn in community psychology, and not just in the realm of teen pregnancy.

Despite advances in prevention, controversy still swirls around this concept. For example, Gesten and Jason (1987) suggested that controversy exists over whether primary prevention needs to be disorder specific and whether the disorder needs to be part of the *Diagnostic and Statistical Manual*. Similarly, there remains controversy over what preventive strategy is most effective: modifying the environment, eliminating the agent or cause of the problem, or strengthening the competence of the affected individual(s).

Complicating *how* to intervene is the knowledge held by community psychologists that **comorbidity of psychiatric disorders** usually exists. *Comorbidity* means that often an individual who manifests one disorder manifests other disorders. Using an earlier example, you know that some individuals who have a mental disorder are also substance abusers. Many community psychologists would agree that multiple approaches are probably best *if* they can be offered, given funding and other problems. But how in prevention research can we intervene successfully with multiple disorders and tease out the effects of which intervention components are most efficacious with what disorders (Kessler & Price, 1993)? This is a very complex challenge for the future.

There are other issues related to *how* research on prevention is accomplished. If multiple preventive strategies are utilized, how can one tease out the effects of individual components of the prevention strategy? For example, through what processes are the components of the intervention achieving their effects and is each component contributing equally to success (West, Aiken, & Todd, 1993)?

Controversy in and of itself is not bad, but it should not impede or halt research nor weigh down the journals, especially in the spirit of "publish or perish." Crucial research needs to continue on concepts of paramount importance to the field so that people can fine-tune their understanding of them. Profile 12.1 introduces David Chavis, a psychologist who empowers community groups to conduct their own research by educating them about *how* to conduct research.

Action Research

We have already detailed in Chapter 2 how community psychologists conduct research and we have also disclosed how research in other areas of psychology often differs from research in community psychology. One consideration for the future involves community research participants. As Cook and Shadish (1994) and Jansen and Johnson (1993) have noted, one is better able to draw causal inferences in experiments, field or laboratory, when one uses a random sample. A **random sample** was defined in Chapter 2 as a sample in which every member of a population has an equal chance of being selected. In much **action research** (research designed to resolve social problems), community participants from real community settings are under study. The participants commonly are volunteers

◆ PROFILE 12.1
David M. Chavis

In 1992, David Chavis was justifiably honored with the Society for Community Research and Action Distinguished Practice in Community Psychology Award. Chavis finished his graduate work in the mid-1970s, which means he was receiving his training in the middle of much political and social chaos. The protests against the Vietnam War were winding down, and the riots at Attica Prison in western New York had also just occurred. The political and social events of that era are, in part, what attracted Chavis to community psychology.

Ever the activist and change specialist, while in graduate school, Chavis was insistent at Peabody College of Vanderbilt University that he wanted to major in community psychology, *not* in clinical, counseling, or school psychology with only a minor in community psychology (Newbrough, 1993). In fact, he was the first "pure" community psychology student at that university.

After graduating, Chavis went to New York City, where he completed a postdoctoral fellowship in environmental psychology and became Director of Research and Evaluation for the Citizens Committee of New York. In a few years, he landed a position at the Center for Social and Community Development in the School of Social Work at Rutgers University. As you can see, his career combined research and community service as well as collaboration in a variety of disciplines related to community psychology—the epitome of achievement in community psychology.

With Paul Florin, who had been a fellow student with him, Chavis designed an approach called **Social Reconnaissance**, a way of getting citizens actively involved in their locality through self-study research and evaluation strategies. In this approach, Chavis attempts to "give research skills away in a friendly manner," a seemingly excellent idea, since few community citizens nor agency directors have the requisite research skills to evaluate their own programs (Chavis, 1993). This technique has been applied to drug-abuse prevention, AIDS prevention, Indian tribal settings, Latino neighborhoods, community-based policing, smoking prevention, and health promotion, to name a few (Chavis, 1993; Newbrough, 1993).

In his address to the American Psychological Association upon accepting his award, Chavis stated that the future goal of community practice should be to

> strengthen the capacity of institutions to meet the needs and dreams of their constituencies or members and therefore improve their quality of life....I believe that the knowledge base for this practice of community psychology will come not only from within our field but we must vigorously study the knowledge available in community organization and development as well as public health. Some skills will come from these disciplines, some must be borrowed and adapted from others....The settings for this future practice are available today. Almost every major social institution has its own programs of reform underway....Each of these programs addresses the issues I presented here and are looking for people with the skills to meet the challenge....The opportunities are there, the need is there, what is missing are enough of us willing to pursue those dreams we have now and had as students. We must bring back the dreams that brought us to community psychology. (pp. 179–180)

With those thoughts in mind, Chavis dedicated his award and remarks to the future of community psychology and to his students. In his words, "I have faith in community psychology....I believe in the future of the field....I believe most of all in the true guardians of [the] future, our students"(p. 171).

and thus have not been randomly assigned to conditions. Random assignment, then, can be complicated at best and impossible at worst when evaluating social programs.

Causal inferences—such as about what interventions are most effective—are more difficult given the type of research usually conducted by community psychologists. It is incumbent upon community psychologists in the future to find statistic analyses and other methods that will allow participants to volunteer for interventions, yet allow scientists to draw meaningful conclusions. For more discussion of this issue, see Cook and Shadish (1994), who dedicate a whole chapter to these and other issues related to community experimentation and action research.

A second solution to assessing action research and community interventions where studies vary in terms of samples and methods is meta-analysis, a method mentioned infrequently in this text. **Meta-analysis** emphasizes the robustness of a particular causal connection across a wide range of persons, settings, times, and cause-and-effect constructs (Heller, 1990). As studies accumulate about a particular concept, such as empowerment, or about a particular intervention, such as interpersonal cognitive problem solving, meta-analysis will allow community psychologists to make assessments that can guide the field in the future. We hope to see more meta-analytic research in the future as the field matures and its potential scientific contributions unfold.

Another problem for action researchers is that their studies often demonstrate effectiveness or discover cause and effect in small samples only. Heller (1990) reminded us in his chapter in the *Annual Review of Psychology* that the effectiveness of a school intervention when administered to a sample of 100 students in a particular school may look effective on a large scale. However, at the group or community level, this is only a sample size of one. As stated earlier, replications in other samples and across other groups and communities is essential. This can happen only when dissemination of information occurs.

Finally, many research-related journal articles that concern community intervention are program evaluations. As a result, most of the data are outcome data. Because *the process by which an outcome is achieved is as important as the outcome,* more **process analysis** of underlying mechanisms by which change occurred is needed. The history of change is as important as the outcome of the change if other affected groups with similar or different histories are to benefit from the research by adapting it to their locales.

In his contribution to the special issue of the *American Journal of Community Psychology* on methodological issues in community research, Sechrest (1993) concluded that the problems of our "research are not altogether intractable; they simply require the best of our thinking and the firmest of our commitments" (p. 665).

Diversity Issues

Community psychologists understand well the richness of ideas and experiences that diverse ethnic, racial, and life-style groups can bring to a community. Community psychologists, in fact, suggest that they actively *promote* appreciation of diversity. Again, this appreciation is not always shared by everyone in the community.

As more varied groups arrive in American communities (e.g., Haitian refugees), are community psychologists, themselves, making progress in promoting diversity and examining diversity issues in their literature? In Chapter 1, we reviewed the research of Loo, Fong, and Iwamasca (1988), who reviewed the top journals in community psychology and found that about 11% of the articles pertain to ethnic minorities. They concluded that progress toward understanding this nation's diverse population is being made but more needs to be done. At about the same time, Snowden (1987) reviewed the journals and found that community mental health services were improving for minorities as presented in the journals.

Where is the field today, though, on this issue of diversity? For the purposes of writing this book, we examined the top American journal in the field of community psychology for the publication year 1993, five years after Loo and his colleagues published their review of the percent of diversity issues in the community psychology literature. We used a somewhat generous definition of articles containing information related to diversity. The articles either pertained in the main to diverse ethnic, racial, or religious groups or at least reported the ethnic and racial background of participants. In the *American Journal of Community Psychology* from December 1992 to October 1993, we found that of the 45 articles published, 17 of them reported information about diverse groups in U.S. population. In other words, almost 38% of the articles pertained to groups other than White Americans. Given that most of the articles intensively studied diverse groups, we feel that this historic increase is substantial. However, community psychologists need to continue work with various groups so that interventions are sensitive to the needs and cultures of diverse groups. Snowden (1993) reminded readers that equal benefits and an equal avoidance of harm cannot be taken for granted for minorities.

SUMMARY

The field of community psychology has grown in leaps and bounds since its founding at the Swampscott Conference in the 1960s. The growth has been witnessed in the number of journals, conferences, and graduate programs. There is also an ever-increasing interest in community psychology at the undergraduate level—hence, the need for this book.

We agree, however, with Altman (1987) that the field is only in its adolescence. Although community psychology perhaps does not have serious growing pains, it could use a few midcourse adjustments. We do believe, however, that the field can look forward to a healthy adulthood.

REFERENCES

Abella, R. (1991). *Evaluation of the satellite learning centers program.* Paper presented at the Annual Convention of the American Psychological Association, San Francisco, CA.

Abrahams, R. B., & Patterson, R. D. (1978–1979). Psychological distress among the community elderly: Prevalence, characteristics and implications for service. *International Journal of Aging and Human Development, 9,* 1–18.

Adams, R. E. (1992). Is happiness a home in the suburbs? The influence of urban versus suburban neighborhoods on psychological health. *Journal of Community Psychology, 20,* 353–371.

Agopian, M. W. (1989). Targeting juvenile gang offenders for community service. *Community Alternatives International Journal of Family Care, 1,* 99–108.

Albee, G. W., & Gullotta, T. P. (1986). Facts and fallacies about primary prevention. *Journal of Primary Prevention, 6,* 207–218.

Alderson, G., & Sentman, E. (1979). *How you can influence Congress: The complete handbook for the citizen lobbyist.* New York: Dutton.

Aldwin, C., & Greenberger, E. (1987). Cultural differences in predictors of depression. *American Journal of Community Psychology,* 789–812.

Alinsky, S. (1971). *Rules for radicals: A practical primer for realistic radicals.* New York: Random House.

Allen, H., & Simonsen, C. E. (1992). *Corrections in America: An introduction.* New York: Macmillan.

Allen, J. P., Philliber, S., & Hoggson, N. (1990). School-based prevention of teen-age pregnancy and school dropout: Process evaluation of the national replication of the Teen Outreach Program. *American Journal of Community Psychology, 18,* 505–524.

Allen, L. (1990). A developmental perspective on multiple levels of analysis in community research. In P. Tolan, C. Keys, F. Chertok, & L. Jason (Eds.), *Researching community psychology: Issues of theory and methods.* Washington, DC: American Psychological Association.

Allen-Meares, P., & Shore, D. A. (1986). A transactional framework for working with adolescents and their sexualities. Special issue: Adolescent sexualities: Overview and principles of intervention. *Journal of Social Work and Human Sexuality, 5,* 71–80.

Allison, D. B., Faith, M. S., & Franklin, R. D. (1994). *Antecedent exercise in the treatment of disruptive behavior: A meta–analytic review.* Manuscript under review.

Allport, G. W. (1954). *The nature of prejudice.* Reading, MA: Addison-Wesley.

Alpert, G. P., & Dunham, R. G. (1986). Community policing. *Journal of Police Science and Administration, 14,* 212–222.

Altman, I. (1987). Community psychology twenty years later: Still another crisis in psychology? *American Journal of Community Psychology, 15*, 613–627.

Altman, I., Wohlwill, J. F., & Werner, C. (Eds.). (1985). *Home environments.* New York: Plenum.

American Association for Protecting Children. (1987, October 23). *National estimates of child abuse and neglect reports, 1976–1986.* Denver: American Humane Association.

American Psychological Association. (1985). *Standards for educational and psychological testing* (3rd ed.). Washington, DC: Author.

American Psychological Society. (1991). The importance of the citizen scientist in national science policy. *The APS Observer, 4,* 10, 12, 23.

Anderson, C. A., & Anderson, D.C. (1984). Ambient temperature and violent crime: Tests of the linear and curvilinear hypothesis. *Journal of Personality and Social Psychology, 46,* 91–97.

Another round for the homeless. (1982, June 15). *The New York Times,* A28.

Aronson, E., Blaney, N., Stephan, C., Sikes, J., & Snapp, M. (1978). *The jigsaw classroom.* Beverly Hills, CA: Sage.

Aubrey, T., Tefft, B., & Kingsbury, N. (1990). Behavioral and psychological consequences of unemployment in blue-collar couples. *Journal of Community Psychology, 18,* 99–109.

Baba, Y., & Austin, D. M. (1989). Neighborhood environmental satisfaction, victimization, and social participation as determinants of perceived neighborhood safety. *Environment and Behavior, 21,* 763–780.

Bachrach, L. L. (1989). Deinstitutionalization: A semantic analysis. *Journal of Social Issues, 45,* 161–171.

Bagby, W. (1981). *Contemporary American social problems.* Chicago: Nelson Hall.

Bair, J. P., & Greenspan, B. K. (1986). Teamwork training for interns, residents, and nurses. *Hospital and Community Psychiatry, 37,* 633–635.

Baker, J., & Sansone, J. (1990). Interventions with students at risk for dropping out of school: A high school responds. *Journal of Educational Research, 83,* 181–186.

Baker, R. A. (1991). Modeling the school dropout phenomenon: School policies and prevention program strategies. *High School Journal, 74,* 203–210.

Baltes, M. M., & Baltes, P. B. (Eds.). (1986). *The psychology of control and aging.* Hillsdale, NJ: Erlbaum.

Bandura, A. (1977). Self-efficacy: Toward a unifying theory of behavior change. *Psychological Review, 84,* 191–215.

Bandura, A. (1986). *Social foundations of thought and action.* Englewood Cliffs, NJ: Prentice Hall.

Bank, L., Hicks, R., Marlowe, J., Reid, J. B., Patterson, G. R., & Weinrott, M. R. (1991). A comparative evaluation of parent-training interventions for families of chronic delinquents. *Journal of Abnormal Child Psychology, 19,* 15–33.

Banks, J. K., & Gannon, L. R. (1988). The influence of hardiness on the relationship between stressors and psychosomatic symptomology. *American Journal of Community Psychology, 16,* 25–37.

Banziger, G., & Foos, D. (1983). The relationship of personal financial status to the utilization of community mental health centers in rural Appalachia. *American Journal of Community Psychology, 11,* 543–552.

Barak, G. (1991). *Gimme Shelter: A social history of homelessness in contemporary America.* New York: Praeger.

Barney J. B. (1986). Organizational culture: Can it be a source of sustained competitive advantage? *Academy of Management Review,* 656–665.

Baron, R., & Byrne, D. (1994). *Social psychology: Understanding human interaction* (7th ed.). Boston: Allyn and Bacon.

Baron, R., & Greenburg, J. (1990). *Behavior in organizations: Understanding and managing the human side of work.* Boston: Allyn and Bacon.

Barrera, M. (1986). Distinctions between social support concepts, measures, and models. *American Journal of Community Psychology, 14,* 413–445.

Barrera, M., Sandler, I. N., & Ramsay, T. B. (1981). Preliminary development of a scale of social support: Studies on college students. *American Journal of Community Psychology, 9,* 435–448.

Barth, R. P. (1988). Social shell and social support among young mothers. *Journal of Community Psychology, 16,* 132–143.

Barth, R. P., Fetro, J. V., Leland, N., & Volkan, K. (1992). Preventing adolescent pregnancy with social and cognitive skills. *Journal of Adolescent Research, 7,* 208–232.

Bartunek, J. M., & Betters-Reed, B. L. (1987). The stages of organizational creation. Special issue: Organizational perspectives in community psychology. *American Journal of Community Psychology, 15,* 287–303.

Bassuk, E. L., & Rosenberg, L. (1988). Why does family homelessness occur? A case-control study. *American Journal of Public Health, 78,* 783–788.

Baum, A., Singer, J. E., & Baum, C. S. (1981). Stress and the environment. *Journal of Social Issues, 37,* 4–35.

Baumann, D. J., Schultz, D. F., Brown, C., Paredes, R., & Hepeworth, J. (1987). Citizen participation in police crisis intervention activities. *American Journal of Community Psychology, 15,* 459–472.

Beach, S. R., Greenberg, M. S., & Yee, J. (1992). *Predicting the perceived seriousness of property crimes.* Paper presented at the annual meeting of the Eastern Psychological Association, Boston, MA, April.

Beardon, L. J., Spencer, W. A., & Morroco, J. C. (1989). A study of high school dropouts. *School Counselor, 37,* 112–120.

Becker, F., & Zarit, S. H. (1978). Training older adults as peer counselors. *Educational Gerontologist, 3,* 241–250.

Becker, M. H. (1974). The health belief model and personal health behavior. *Health Education Monographs, 2,* 220–243.

Beer, M., & Walton, E. (1990). Developing the competitive organization. *American Psychologist, 45,* 154–161.

Belcher, J. R. (1988). Are jails replacing the mental health care system for the homeless mentally ill? *Community Mental Health Journal, 24,* 185–195.

Belle, D. (Ed.). (1982). Lives in stress: Women and depression. Beverly Hills, CA: Sage.

Bendicsen, H., & Carlton, S. (1990). Clinical team building: A neglected ingredient in the therapeutic milieu. *Residential Treatment for Children and Youth, 8,* 5–21.

Bennett, C. C., Anderson, L. S., Cooper, S., Hassol, L., Klein, D. C., & Rosenblum, G. (Eds.). (1966). *Community psychology: A report of the Boston conference of the education of psychologists for community mental health.* Boston: Boston University Press.

Bennett, T. (1989). Factors related to participation in neighborhood watch schemes. *British Journal of Criminology, 29,* 207–218.

Bennett, T. (1991). The effectiveness of a police-initiated fear-reducing strategy. *British Journal of Criminology, 31,* 1–14.

Benviente, G. (1989). *Mastering the politics of planning: Crafting credible plans and policies.* San Francisco: Jossey-Bass.

Bernal, G., & Marin, B. (1985). Community psychology in Cuba: An introduction. *Journal of Community Psychology, 13,* 103–104.

Berry, T. D., & Geller, E. S. (1991). A single-subject approach to evaluating vehicle safety belt reminders: Back to basics. *Journal of Applied Behavior Analysis, 24,* 13–22.

Beyer, J. M., & Trice, II. M. (1984). A field study of the use and perceived effects of discipline in controlling work performance. *Academy of Management Journal, 27,* 743–764.

Biegel, D. (1984). Help seeking and receiving in urban ethnic neighborhoods: Strategies for improvement. In J. Rapport, C. Swift, & R. Hess (Eds.), *Studies in empowerment: Steps toward understanding and action.* New York: Haworth.

Bingham, J., & Piotrowski, C. (1989). House arrest: A viable alternative for sex offenders. *Psychological Reports, 65,* 559–562.

Blakely, C. H. (1991). *Maternal cocaine use during pregnancy: Implications for public health intervention.* Unpublished manuscript. Public Policy Resources Laboratory, Texas A&M University, College Station, TX.

Blakely, C. H., Mayer, J. P., Gottschalk, R. G., Schmidt, N., Davidson, W. S., Roitman, D. B., & Emshoff, J. G. (1987). The fidelity-adaptation debate: Implications of the implementation of public sector social programs.

American Journal of Community Psychology, *15,* 253–268.

Blaney, N. T., Stephan, C., Rosenfield, D., Aronson, E., & Sikes, J. (1977). Interdependence in the classroom: A field study. *Journal of Educational Psychology, 69,* 139–146.

Blom, G. E. (1986). A school disaster: Intervention and research aspects. *Journal of the American Academy of Child Psychiatry, 25,* 336–345.

Blonsksy, L. E. (1973). An innovative service for the elderly. *Gerontologist, 13,* 189–196.

Bloom, B. L. (1988). *Health psychology: A psychosocial perspective.* Englewood Cliffs, NJ: Prentice Hall.

Bloom, B. L., & Hodges, W. F. (1988). The Colorado Separation and Divorce Program: A preventive intervention program for newly separated persons. In R. Price, E. W. Cowen, R. P. Lorion, & J. Ramos-McKay (Eds.), *14 ounces of prevention,* Washington, DC: American Psychological.

Bloom, M. (1987). Toward a technology in primary prevention: Educational strategies and tactics. *Journal of Primary Prevention, 8,* 25–48.

Bobo, B. F. (1984). *A report to the secretary on the homeless and emergency shelters.* Washington, DC: Department of Housing and Urban Development.

Boggiano, A. K., & Katz, P. (1991). Maladaptive patterns in students: The role of teachers' controlling strategies. *Journal of Social Issues, 47,* 35–52.

Bond, G. R., Miller, L. D., & Krumweid, R. D. (1988). Assertive case management in three CMHCs: A controlled study. *Hospital Community Psychiatry, 39,* 411–417.

Bond, G. R., Witheridge, T. F., Dincin, J., & Wasmer, D. (1991). Assertive community treatment: Correcting some misconceptions. *American Journal of Community Psychology, 19,* 41–51.

Bond, G. R., Witheridge, T. F., Dincin, J., Wasmer, D., Webb, J., & DeGraaf-Kaser, R. (1990). Assertive community treatment for frequent users of psychiatric hospitals in a large city: A controlled study. *American Journal of Community Psychology, 18,* 865–891.

Bond, M. A. (1990). Defining the research relationship: Maximizing participation in an unequal world. In P. Jolan, C. Keep, F. Chertok, & L. Jason (Eds.), *Resarch community psychology: Issues of theory and methods* (pp. 183–184). Washington, DC: American Psychological Association.

Booth, W. (July 22, 1991). Most elderly go gently. *Washington Post, 3.*

Bootzin, R. R., Shadish, W. R., & McSweeney, A. J. (1989). Longitudinal outcomes of nursing home care for severely mentally ill patients. *Journal of Social Issues, 45,* 31–48.

Botvin, G. J., & Wills, T. A. (1985). Personal and social skills training: Cognitive-behavioral approaches to substance abuse prevention. In C. S. Bell & R. Battjes (Eds.), *Prevention research: Deterring drug abuse among children and adolescents.* National Institute on Drug Abuse Research Monograph Number 63. DHHS publication number (ADM) 87–1334. Washington, DC: Superintendent of Documents, U.S. Government Printing Office.

Bowen, G. L., & Richman, J. M. (1991). The willingness of spouses to seek marriage and family counseling services. *Journal of Primary Prevention, 11,* 277–293.

Bowers, C. A., & Getsen, E. L. (1986). Social support as a buffer of anxiety: An experimental analog. *American Journal of Community Psychology, 14,* 447–451.

Bowers, L. B. (1990). Traumas precipitating female delinquency: Implications for assessment, practice, and policy. *Child and Adolescent Social Work Journal, 7,* 389–402.

Bowman, J. S. (1989). Quality circles: Promise, problems, and prospects in Florida. *Public Personnel Management, 18,* 375–403.

Bowman, L. S., Stein, R. E. K., & Ireys, H. T. (1991). Reinventing fidelity: The transfer of social technology among settings. *American Journal of Community Psychology, 19,* 619–639.

Braddock, J. H., II. (1985). School desegregation and black assimilation. *Journal of Social Issues, 41,* 9–22.

Braver, S. (1990). *Selection issues in children of divorce interventions.* Paper presented at the meeting of the American Psychological Association, Boston, MA.

Bravo, M., Rubio-Stipec, M., Canino, G. J., Woodbury, M. A., & Ribera, J. C. (1990). The psychological sequelae of disaster stress prospectively and retrospectively evaluated. *American Journal of Community Psychology, 18*, 661–680.

Breakey, W. R., & Fischer, P. J. (1990). Homelessness: The extent of the problem. *Journal of Social Issues, 46*, 31–47.

Brenner, G. F., Norvell, N. K., & Limacher, M. (1989). Supportive and problematic social interactions: A social network analysis. *American Journal of Community Psychology, 17*, 831–836.

Broman, C. L., Hamilton, V. L., & Hoffman, W. S. (1990). Unemployment and its effects on families: Evidence from a plant closing study. *American Journal of Community Psychology, 18*, 643–659.

Bronfenbrenner, U. (1979). *The ecology of human development: Experiments by nature and design.* Cambridge, MA: Harvard University Press.

Bronfenbrenner, U. (1986, February). Alienation and the four worlds of childhood. *Phi Delta Kappan*, 430–436.

Bronzaft, A. L. (1981). The effect of a noise abatement program on reading ability. *Journal of Environmental Psychology, 1*, 215–222.

Brown, J. D. (1991). Staying fit and staying well: Physical fitness as a moderator of life stress. *Journal of Personality and Social Psychology, 60*, 555–561.

Brown, L. P., & Cowen, E. L. (1988). Children's judgments of event upsettingness and personal experiencing of stressful events. *American Journal of Community Psychology, 16*, 123–136.

Brown, M. K. (Ed.). (1988). *Remaking the welfare state: Retrenchment and social policy in America and Europe.* Philadelphia: Temple University Press.

Brownell, A., & Shumaker, S. A. (1984). Social support: An introduction to a complex phenomenon. *Journal of Social Issues, 40*, 1–9.

Bruce, M. L., Takeuchi, D. T., & Leaf, P. J. (1991). Poverty and psychiatric status: Longitudeinal evidence from the New Haven Epidemiologic Catchment Area Study. *Aarchives of General Psychiatry, 48*, 470–474.

Buchanon, D. R., & Chasnoff, P. (1986). Family crisis intervention programs: What works and what doesn't. *Journal of Police Science and Administration, 14*, 161–168.

Buckner, J. C. (1988). The development of an instrument to measure neighborhood cohesion. *American Journal of Community Psychology, 16*, 771–791.

Buckner, J. C., Trickett, E. J., & Corse, S. J. (1985). *Primary prevention in mental health: An annotated bibliography.* DHHS Publication (ADM) 85–1405. Washington, DC: Government Printing Office.

Bui, K., & Takeuchi, D. T. (1992). Ethnic minority adolescents and the use of community mental health care services. *American Journal of Community Psychology, 20*, 403–417.

Buie, J. (1989a). Psychology confronts efforts to limit practice. *The APA Monitor, 20*, 1, 21.

Buie, J. (1989b). Turf battle heats up on many fronts. *The APA Monitor, 20*, 7, 15–16.

Burden, D. S., & Klerman, L. V. (1984). Teenage parenthood: Factors that lessen economic dependence. *Social Work, 29*, 11–16.

Bureau of Justice Statistics. (1993). *Highlights from 20 years of surveying crime victims.* Washington, DC: U.S. Department of Justice.

Bureau of National Affairs. (1981). Job absence and turnover control. *Personnel Forum Survey Number 132.* Washington, DC: Author.

Bureau of National Affairs. (1985). Employee discipline and discharge in the 20th century. *Personnel Policies Forum Survey Number 139.* Washington, DC: Author.

Bureau of National Affairs. (1986). *Work and family: A changing dynamic.* Washington, DC: Author.

Burke, M. J., & Hayes, R. L. (1986). Peer counseling for elderly victims of crime and violence. Special issue: Support groups. *Journal for Specialists in Group Work, 11*, 107–113.

Caplan, G. (1964). *Principles of preventive psychiatry.* New York: Basic Books.

Caplan G. (1974). *Support systems and community mental health.* New York: Behavioral Publications.

Caplan G. (1989). Recent developments in crisis intervention and the promotion of support service. *Journal of Primary Prevention, 10,* 3–25.

Caplan, N., Morrison, A., & Stambaugh, R. J. (1975). *The use of social science knowledge in policy decisions at the national level: A report to respondents.* Ann Arbor: Institute for Social Research, University of Michigan.

Caplan, R. D., Vinokur, A. D., Price, R. H., & van Ryn, M. (1989). Job seeking, reemployment, and mental health. Journal of Applied Psychology, 74, 759–769.

Carnevale, P. J., & Pruitt, D. G. (1992). Negotiation and mediation. *Annual Review of Psychology, 43,* 531–582.

Cassel, J. (1974). Psychosocial processes and "stress": Theoretical formulations. *International Journal of Health Services, 4,* 471–482.

Catterall, J. S., & Stern, D. (1986). The effects of alternative school programs on high school completions and labor market outcomes. *Educational Evaluation and Policy Analysis, 8,* 77–86.

Cauce, A. M. (1986). Social networks and social competence: Exploring the effects on early adolescent friendships. *American Journal of Community Psychology, 14,* 607–628.

Centers for Disease Control. (1990). Cigarette advertising—United States, 1988. *Morbidity and Mortality Weekly Report, 39,* 261–265.

Chamberlain, P. (1990). Comparative evaluation of specialized foster care for seriously delinquent youths: A first step. *Community Alternatives International Journal of Family Care, 2,* 21–36.

Chan, K. B. (1977). Individual differences in reactions to stress and their personality and situational determinants: Some implications for community mental health. *Social Science and Medicine, 11,* 89–103.

Chandler, L. A., Million, M. E., & Shermis, M. D. (1985). The incidence of stressful life events of elementary school-aged children. *American Journal of Community Psychology, 13,* 743–746.

Chapman, N. J., & Pancoast, D. L. (1985). Working with the informal helping networks of the elderly: The experiences of three programs. *American Journal of Community Psychology, 41,* 47–63.

Chasnoff, I. J., Landress, H. J., & Barrett, M. E. (1990). The prevalence of illicit-drug and alcohol use during pregnancy and discrepancies in mandatory reporting in Pinellas county. *New England Journal of Medicine, 322,* 1202–1206.

Chattoraj, B. N. (1985). The social, psychological and economic consequences of imprisonment. *Social Defence, 20,* 19–24.

Chavis, D. M. (1993). A future for community psychology practice. *American Journal of Community Psychology, 21,* 171–183.

Chavis, D. M., & Florin, P. (1990). *Sustaining voluntary community organizations through action research.* Unpublished manuscript. Center for Community Education, New Brunswick, NJ.

Chavis, D. M., Florin, P., & Felix, M. R. J. (1992). Nurturing grass roots initiatives for community development: The role of enabling systems. In T. Mizrahi & J. Morrison (Eds.), *Community organization and social administration: Advances, trends, and emerging principles.* Binghamton, NY: Haworth.

Chavis, D. M., Stucky, P. E., & Wandersman, A. (1983). Returning research to the community: A relationship between scientist and citizen. *American Psychologist, 38,* 424–434.

Chavis, D. M., & Wandersman, A. W. (1990). Sense of community in the urban environment: A catalyst for participation and community development. *American Journal of Community Psychology, 18,* 55–82.

Chemers, M. M., Hays, R. B., Rhodewalt, F., & Wysocki, J. (1985). A person-environment analysis of job stress: A contingency model explanation. *Journal of Personality and Social Psychology, 49,* 628–635.

Cheng, S. (1990). Change processes in the professional bureaucracy. *Journal of Community Psychology, 18,* 183–193.

Chesler, M. A., & Barbarin, O. A. (1984). Difficulties of providing help in a crisis: Relationships between parents of children with cancer and their friends. *American Journal of Community Psychology, 40,* 113–134.

Cheung, F. M. (1988). Surveys of community attitudes toward mental health facilities: Reflections or provocations? *American Journal of Community Psychology, 16,* 877–822.

Cheung, F. M. C. (1986). Psychopathology among Chinese people. In M. H. Bond (Ed.), *The psychology of the Chinese people.* New York: Oxford University Press.

Chidester, T. R. (1986). Problems in the study of interracial aggression: Pseudo-interracial dyad paradigm. *Journal of Personality and Social Psychology, 50,* 74–79.

Children's Defense Fund. (1991). *The state of American children.* Washington, DC: Author.

Chipperfield, J. (1993). Perceived barriers in coping with health problems: A twelve-year longitudinal study of survival among elderly individuals. *Journal of Aging and Health, 5,* 123–139.

Christensen, J. A., & Robinson, J. W. (1989). *Community development in perspective.* Ames, IA: Iowa State University Press.

Christensen, L. (1988). Deception in psychological research. *Personality and Social Psychology Bulletin, 14,* 664–675.

Christian, T. F. (1986). A resource for all seasons: A state-wide network of community dispute resolution centers. In J. Palenski & H. Launer (Eds.), *Mediation: Contexts and challenges.* Springfield, IL: Charles C. Thomas.

Clark, K. B., & Clark, M. P. (1947). Racial identification and preference in Negro Children. In T. M. Newcomb & E. L. Hartley (Eds.), *Readings in social psychology.* New York: Holt.

Coates, R. (1981). Community-based services for juvenile delinquents: Concept and implications for practice. *Journal of Social Issues, 37,* 87–101.

Coates, R., & Gehm, J. (1989). An empirical assessment. In M. Wright & B. Galaway (Eds.), *Mediation and criminal justice.* London: Sage.

Coates, T. J. (1990). Strategies for modifying sexual behavior for primary and secondary prevention of HIV disease. *Journal of Consulting and Clinical Psychology, 58,* 57–69.

Cohen, C. I., Teresi, J., & Holmes, D. (1986). Assessment of stress-buffering effects of social networks on psychological symptoms in an inner-city elderly population. *American Journal of Community Psychology, 14,* 75–91.

Cohen, M. A. (1988). Pain, suffering, and jury awards: A study of the cost of crime to victims. *Law and Society Review, 22,* 538–555.

Cohen, M. D., Shore, M. F., & Mazda, N. A. (1991). Development of a management training program for state mental health program directors. Special issue: Education in mental health administration. *Administration and Policy in Mental Health, 18,* 247–256.

Cohen, S. A., Evans, G. W., Stokols, D., & Krantz, D. (1986). *Behavior, health, and environmental stress.* New York: Plenum.

Colson, P., et al. (1993). *HIV among homeless, mentally ill men.* Paper presented at the 9th Annual Northeast Community Psychology Conference, New York, NY.

Compas, B. E., Wagner, B. M., Slavin, L. A., & Vannatta, K. (1986). A prospective study of life events, social support, and psychological symptomatology during the transition from high school to college. *American Journal of Community Psychology, 14,* 241–257.

Constantine, L. L. (1991). Fitting intervention to organizational paradigm. *Organization Development Journal, 9,* 41–50.

Cook, S. W. (1984). The 1954 social science statement and school desegregation: A reply to Gerard. *American Psychologist, 39,* 819–832.

Cook, S. W. (1985). Experimenting on social issues: The case of school desegregation. *American Psychologist, 47,* 452–460.

Cook, T. D., & Shadish, W. R. (1994). Social experiments: Some developments over the past fifteen years. In L. W. Porter & M. R. Rosenzweig (Eds.), *Annual review of psychology.* Palo Alto, CA: Annual Reviews.

Cottingham, P. H., & Ellwood, D. T. (Eds.). (1989). *Welfare policy for the 1990s.* Cambridge, MA: Harvard University Press.

Covin, T. J., & Kilmann, R. H. (1991). Profiling large-scale change efforts. *Organization Development Journal, 9,* 1–8.

Cowen, E. L. (1980). The wooing of primary prevention. *American Journal of Community Psychology, 8,* 258–284.

Cox, V. C., Paulus, P. B., & McCain, G. (1984). Prison crowding research: The relevance for prison housing standards and a general crowding phenomena. *American Psychologist, 39,* 1148–1160.

Crawford, I., & Jason, L. A. (1990). Strategies for implementing a media-based AIDS prevention program. *Professional Psychology Research and Practice, 21,* 219–221.

Crawford, I., Jason, L. A., Riordan, N., & Kaufman, J. (1990). A multimedia-based approach to increasing communication and the level of knowledge within families. Special Issue: AIDS and the community. *Journal of Community Psychology, 18,* 361–373.

Crittenden, P. M., & Snell, M. E. (1983). Intervention to improve mother-infant interaction and infant development. *Infant Mental Health Journal, 4,* 23–31.

Crosson, M. T., & Christian, T. F. (1990). *The Community Dispute Resolution Centers Program annual report.* Albany, New York: Office of Court Administration.

Crouch, B. M. (1988). Women guards. *Law and Society Review, 21,* 835–836.

Cummins, R. C. (1988). Perceptions of social support, receipt of supportive behaviors, and locus of control as moderators of the effects of chronic stress. *American Journal of Community Psychology, 16,* 685–700.

D'Alessio, S., & Stolzenberg, L. (1990). A crime of convenience: The environment and convenience store robbery. *Environment and Behavior, 22,* 255–271.

Danish, S. J. (1983). Musings about personal competence: The contributions of sport, health, and fitness. *American Journal of Community Psychology, 11,* 221–240.

Darity, W., Jr., & Myers, S., Jr. (1987). *Transfer programs and the economic well-beings of minorities.* Mimeo.

Darity, W., Jr., & Myers, S., Jr. (1988). Distress versus dependency: Changing income support programs. In M. K. Brown (Ed.), *Remaking the welfare state: Retrenchment and social policy in America and Europe.* Philadelpha: Temple University Press.

Davidson, W. B., & Cotter, P. R. (1989). Sense of community and political participation. *Journal of Community Psychology, 17,* 119–125.

Davidson, W. B., & Cotter, P. R. (1991). The relationship between sense of community and

subjective well-being: A first look. *Journal of Community Psychology, 19,* 246–253.

Davidson, W. S., & Redner, R. (1988). The prevention of juvenile delinquency: Diversion from the juvenile justice system. In R. Price, E. L. Cowen, R. P. Lorion, & J. Ramos-McKay (Eds.), *14 ounces of prevention,* Washington, DC: American Psychological Associaton.

Davis, R., Tichane, M., & Grayson, D. (1980). *Mediation and arbitration as alternatives to criminal prosecution in felony arrest cases: An evaluation of the Brooklyn Dispute Resolution Center (first year).* New York: Vera Institute of Justice.

Davis, T. R., & Luthans, F. (1988). Service OD: Techniques for improving the delivery of quality service. *Organization Development Journal, 6,* 76–80.

Delgado, G. (1986). *Organizing the movement: The roots and growth of ACORN.* Philadelphia: Temple University Press.

Denham, S. A., & Almeida, M. C. (1987). Children's social problem-solving skills, behavioral adjustment, and interventions: A meta-analysis evaluating theory and practice. *Journal of Applied Developmental Psychology, 8,* 391–409.

Dennehy, E. B., Wong, F. Y., Meyer, I., Colson, P., & Susser, E. (1994). *Predictors of condom use in homeless, mentally ill men.* Paper presented to the American Psychological Association, Los Angeles, CA.

Depner, C., Wethington, E., & Ingersoll-Dayton, B. (1984). Social support: Methodological issues in design and measurement. *Journal of Social Issues, 40,* 37–54.

D'Ercole, A., Milburn, N. G., Wong, F. Y., & Beatty, L. (1992). *Identifying effectiveness of alcohol/drug programs.* Unpublished grant application. Manhattan Bowery Corporation, New York.

D'Ercole, A., Skodol, A. E., Struening, E., Curtis, J., & Millman, J. (1991). Diagnosis of physical illness in psychiatric patients using Axis III and a standardized medical history. *Hospital and Community Psychiatry, 42,* 395–400.

Des Jarles, C. D., Wish, F., Friedman, S. R., Stoneburner, R., Wildvan, D. E., El Sadr, W.,

Brady, E., & Cuadrado, M. (1987). Intravenous drug use and the hetersexual transmission of the human immunodeficiency virus: Current trends in New York City. *New York State Journal of Medicine, 20*, 283–296.

Deutsch, M., & Hornstein, H. A. (Eds.). (1975). *Applying social psychology: Implications for research, practice, and training.* Hillsdale, NJ: Erlbaum.

Diamond, P. M., & Schnee, S. B. (1990). *Tracking the costs of chronicity: Towards a redirection of resources.* Presented to the Annual Meeting of the American Psychological Association, Boston, MA, August.

DiFranza, J. R., et al. (1991). RJR Nabisco's cartoon camel promotes Camel cigarettes to children. *Journal of the American medical Association, 266*, 3149–3154.

Digman J. T., Barrera, M., & West, S. G. (1986). Occupational stress, social support, and burnout among correctional officers. *American Journal of Community Psychology, 14*, 177–193.

Dobmeyer, T. W., McKee, P. A., Miller, R. D., & Wescott, J. S. (1990). The effect of enrollment in a prepaid health plan on utilization of a community crisis intervention center by chronically mentally ill individuals. *Community Mental Health Journal, 26*, 129–137.

Dohrenwend, B. S. (1978). Social stress and community psychology. *American Journal of Community Psychology, 6*, 1–14.

Dorian, B. J., Keystone, E., Garfinkel, P. E., & Brown, J. M. (1982). Aberrations in lymphocyte subpopulations and function during psychological stress. *Clinical and Experimental Immunology, 50*, 132–138.

Dovidio, J. F. (1984). Helping behavior and altruism: An empirical and conceptual overview. In L. Berkowitz (Ed.), *Advances in experimental social psychology* (Vol. 17). New York: Academic Press.

Dovidio, J. F., & Gaertner, S. L. (1986). *Prejudice, discrimination, and racism: Theory and research.* Orlando, FL: Academic Press.

Dowell, D. A., & Farmer, G. (1992). Community respone to homelessness: Social change and constraint in local intervention. *Journal of Community Psychology, 20*, 72–83.

Downing, J., & Harrison, T. C. (1990). Dropout prevention: A practical approach. *School Counselor, 38*, 67–74.

Duffy, K. G. (1991). Introduction to community mediation programs: Past, present and future. In K. G. Duffy, J. W. Grosch, & P. V. Olczak (Eds.), *Community mediation: A handbook for practitioners and researchers.* New York: Guilford.

Duffy, K. G., Grosch, J. W., & Olczak, P. V. (1991). *Community mediation: A handbook for practitioners and researchers.* New York: Guilford.

Duffy, K. G., & Olczak, P. V. (1989). Perceptions of mediated disputes: Some characteristics affecting use. *Journal of Social Behavior and Personality, 4*, 541–554.

Duffy, K. G., Olczak, P. V., & Grosch, J. W. (1993). *The influence of minority status on mediation outcome.* Paper presented to the International Association for Conflict Management, Henglehoef, Belgium.

Duffy, K. G., & Thompson, J. (1992). Community mediation centers: Humanistic alternatives to the court system, a pilot study. *Journal of Humanistic Psychology, 32*, 101–114.

Dumont, M. P. (1982). Review of private lives/public spaces, by E. Baxter & K. Hopper, and shopping bag ladies, by A. M. Rousseau. *American Journal of Orthopsychiatry, 52*, 367–369.

Dunham, R. G., & Alpert, G. P. (1987). Keeping juvenile delinquents in school: A prediction model. *Adolescence, 22*, 45–57.

Dunkel-Schetter, C. (1984). Social support and cancer: Findings based on patient interviews and their implications. *American Journal of Community Psychology, 40*, 77–98.

Durlak, J. A. (1983). Social problem-solving as a primary prevention strategy. In R. D. Felner, L. A. Jason, J. N. Moritsugu, & S. S. Farber (Eds.), *Prevention psychology: Theory, research, and practice.* New York: Pergamon.

Durlak, J. A., & Lipsey, M. W. (1991). A practitioner's guide to meta-analysis. *American Journal of Community Psychology, 19*, 291–332.

Earls, M., & Nelson, G. (1988). The relationship between long-term psychiatric clients' psychological well-being and their perceptions of housing and social support. *American Journal of Community Psychology, 16,* 279–293.

Ebert-Flattau, P. (1980). *A legislative guide.* Washington, DC: Association for the Advancement of Psychology.

Echterling, L. G., & Hartsough, D. M. (1989). Phases of helping in successful crisis telephone calls. *Journal of Community Psychology, 17,* 249–257.

Educational Conference on Psychiatry, Psychology and the Law. (1990). Dangerousness and discharge. *American Journal of Forensic Psychology, 8,* 19–58.

Egeland, B., Breitenbucher, M., & Rosenberg, D. (1980). Prospective study of the significance of life stress in the etiology of child abuse. *Journal of Consulting and Clinical Psychology, 48,* 195–205.

Eigen, M. (1993). Viral quasispecies. *Scientific American, 269,* 42–49.

Eisdorfer, C. (1983). Conceptual models of aging. *American Psychologist, 2,* 197–202.

Eisenstat, R. A., & Felner, R. D. (1984). Toward a differentiated view of burnout: Personal and organizational mediators of job satisfaction and stress. *American Journal of Community Psychology, 12,* 411–430.

Elias, M. J. (1987). Improving the continuity between undergraduate psychology and graduate community psychology: Analysis and case study. *Journal of Community Psychology, 15,* 376–386.

Elias, M. J., Gara, M., Ubriaco, M., Rothbaum, P. A., Clabby, J. F., & Schuyler, T. (1986). Impact of a preventative social problem solving intervention on children's coping with middle-school stressors. *American Journal of Community Psychology, 14,* 259–275.

Ellis, R. T. (1991). Perceptions, attitudes and beliefs of police recruits. *Canadian Police College Journal, 15,* 95–117.

Ellison, K. (1985). Community involvement in police selection. *Social Action and the Law, 11,* 77–78.

Ellwein, M. C., Walsh, D. J., Eades, G. M., & Miller, A. (1991). Using readiness tests to route kindergarten students: The snarled intersection of psychometrics, policy, and practice. *Educational Evaluation and Policy Analysis, 13,* 159–175.

Emery, R. E., & Wyer, M. M. (1987). Divorce mediation. *American Psychologist, 42,* 472–480.

Evans, I. M., & DiBenedetto, A. (1990). Pathways to school dropout: A conceptual model for early prevention. *Special Services in the School, 6,* 63–80.

Eysenck, H. J. (1952). The effects of psychotherapy: An evaluation. *Journal of Consulting Psychology, 16,* 319–324.

Eysenck, H. J. (1961). The effects of psychotherapy. In H. J. Eysenck (Ed.), *Handbook of abnormal psychology.* New York: Basic Books.

Fagan, J. (1991). Community-based treatment for mentally disordered juvenile offenders. Special issue: Child Advocacy. *Journal of Clinical Child Psychology, 20,* 42–50.

Fairweather, G. W. (1986). The need for uniqueness. *American Journal of Community Psychology, 14,* 128–137.

Fairweather, G. W., & Davidson, W. S. (1986). *An introduction to community experimentation.* New York: McGraw Hill.

Fairweather, G. W., Sanders, D. H., Maynard, H., & Cressler, D. L. (1969). *Community life for the mentally ill.* Chicago: Aldine.

Fairweather, G. W., & Tornatzky, L. G. (1977). *Experimental methods for social policy research.* New York: Pergamon.

Faith, M. S., Wong, F. Y., & Carpenter, K. M. (1994). *Sensitivity training groups: Updates, meta-analysis, and recommendation.* Manuscript under review.

Falkenberg, I. E. (1987). Employee fitness programs: Their impact on the employee and the organization. *Academy of Management Review, 12,* 511–522.

Farber, S. S., Felner, R. D., & Primavera, J. (1985). Parental separation/divorce and adolescents: An examination of factors mediating adaptation. *American Journal of Community Psychology, 13,* 171–186.

Fawcett, S. B. (1990). Some emerging standards for community research and action: Aid from a behavioral perspective. In P. Tolan, C. Kelp, F. Chertak, & L. Jason (Eds.), *Researching community psychology: Issues of theory and methods.* Washington, DC: American Psychology Association.

Fawcett, S. B., Seekins, T., & Silber, L. (1988). Low-income voter registration: A small-scale evaluation of an agency-based registration strategy. *American Journal of Community Psychology, 16,* 751–758.

Federal Mediation and Conciliation Service. (1984). *Thirty-sixth annual report, fiscal year 1983.* Washington, DC: U.S. Government Printing Office.

Feldheusen, J. F. (1989, March). Synthesis of research on gifted youth. *Educational Leadership,* 6–11.

Felner, R. D., Ginter, M., & Primavera, J. (1982). Primary prevention during school transitions: Social support and environmental structure. *American Journal of Community Psychology, 10,* 277–290.

Felton, B. J., & Shinn, M. (1992). Social integration and social support. Moving "social support" beyond the individual level. *Journal of Community Psychology, 20,* 103–115.

Fendrich, M. (1991). Institutionalization and parole behavior: Assessing the influence of individual and family characteristics. *Journal of Community Psychology, 19,* 109–122.

Fielding, J. C., & Williams, C. A. (1991). Adolescent pregnancy in the United States: A review and recommendations for clinicians and research needs. *American Journal of Preventative Medicine, 7,* 47–52.

Fielding, N. G. (1986). Evaluating the role of training in police socialization: A British example. *Journal of Community Psychology, 14,* 319–330.

Finch, J. F., Okun, M. A., Barrera, M., Zautra, A. J., & Reich, J. W. (1989). Positive and negative ties among older adults: Measurement modes and the prediction of psychological distress and well-being. *American Journal of Community Psychology, 17,* 585–605.

Fine, M. (1986). Why urban adolescents drop into and out of public high school. *Teachers College Record, 87,* 393–409.

Finn, P., & Lee, B. N. W. (1988). *Establishing and expanding victim-witness assistance programs.* Washington, DC: U.S. Department of Justice.

Fiore, J., Coppel, D. B., Becker, J., & Cox, G. B. (1986). Social support as a multifaceted concept: Examination of important dimensions for adjustment. *American Journal of Community Psychology, 14,* 93–111.

Fischer, C. S., Jackson, R. M., Stueve, C. A., Gerson, G., & McAllister-Jones, L. (1977). *Networks and places.* New York: Free Press.

Fisher, J. D., & Fisher, W. A. (1992). Changing AIDS-risk behavior. *Psychological Bulletin, 111,* 455–474.

Fiske, S. T., Bersoff, D. N., Borgida, E., Deaux, K., & Heilman, M. E. (1991). Social science research on trial: Use of sex stereotyping research in Price Waterhouse V. Hopkins. *American Psychologist, 46,* 1049–1060.

Flay, B. R., & Petraitis, J. (1991). Methodological issues in drug use prevention research: Theoretical foundation. In C. G. Leukefeld & W. J. Buoski (Eds.), *Drug abuse prevention intervention research methology.* National Institute on Drug Abuse Research Monograph 107. DHHS publication number (ADM) 91–1761. Washington, DC: Superintendent of Docments, U.S. Government Print Office.

Flick, L. H. (1986). Paths to adolescent parenthood: Implications for prevention. *Public Health Reports, 101,* 132–147.

Florin, P. (1989). *Nurturing the grassroots: Neighborhood volunteer organizations and American cities.* New York: Citizen's Committee for New York City.

Florin, P., & Wandersman, A. (1990). An introduction to citizen participation, voluntary organizations, and community development: Insights for improvement through research. *American Journal of Community Psychology, 18,* 41–54.

Ford Foundation Report. (1983). *Child survival/fair start.* New York: Ford Foundation.

Forer, L. G. (1980). *Criminals and victims: A trial judge reflects on crime and punishment.* New York: Norton.

Forlenza, S. G. (1991). Mediation and psychotherapy: Parallel processes. In K. G. Duffy, T. W. Grosch, & P. V. Olczak (Eds.), *Community mediation: A handbook for practitioners and researchers.* New York: Guilford.

Fortune, J. C., Bruce, A., Williams, J., & Jones, M. (1991). What does evaluation of your dropout prevention program show about its success?... Maybe not enough. *High School Journal, 74,* 225–231.

Foster, H. W., Greene, L. W., & Smith, M. S. (1990). A model for increasing access: Teenage pregnancy prevention. *Journal of Health Care for the Poor and Underserved, 1,* 136–146.

Fowler, R. (1990). Psychology: The core discipline. *American Psychologist, 45,* 1–6.

Frank, J. D. (1983). Galloping technology, a new social disease. *Journal of Social Issues, 39,* 193–206.

Fraser, B. J., Williamson, J. C., & Tobin, K. G. (1987). Use of classroom and school climate scales in evaluating alternative high schools. *Teaching and Teacher Education,* 219–231.

Freedman, A. M. (1989). Mental health programs in the United States: Idiosyncratic roots. *International Journal of Mental Health, 18,* 81–98.

Freedman, E. (1974). Their sisters' keepers: An historical perspective on female correctional institutions in the United States: 1870–1900. *Feminist Studies, 2,* 77–95.

Freeman, R. J., & Roesch, R. (1989). Mental disorder and the criminal justice system. *International Journal of Law and Psychiatry, 12,* 105–115.

French, W. L. & Bell, C. H. (1990). *Organizational development: Behavioral science interventions for organization improvement.* Englewood Cliffs, NJ: Prentice Hall.

Friedman, M., & Rosenman, R. (1974). *Type A behavior and your heart.* New York: Knopf.

Galaway, B. (1985). Victim participation in the penal-corrective process. *Victimology, 10,* 617–630.

Gamble, T. J., & Zigler, E. F. (1986). Effects of infant day care: Another look at the evidence. *American Journal of Orthopsychology, 56,* 26–42.

Garbarino, J., & Abramowitz R. H. (1992). Sociocultural risk and opportunity. In J. Garbarino (Ed.), *Children and families in the social environment.* Hawthorne, NY: Aldine de Gruyter.

Garbarino, J., & Benn, J. L. (1992). The ecology of childbearing and child rearing. In J. Garbarino (Ed.), *Children and families in the social environment.* Hawthorne, NY: Aldine de Gruyter.

Garbarino, J., & Kostelny, K. (1992). Child maltreatment as a community problem. *Child Abuse and Neglect, 16,* 455–464.

Garn, S. M., & Petzold, A. S. (1983). Characteristics of the mother and child in teenage pregnancy. *American Journal of Diseases of Children, 137,* 365–368.

Gebhardt, D. L., & Crump, E. (1990). Employee fitness and wellness programs in the workplace. *American Psychologist, 45,* 262–272.

Geen, R. G. (1981). Behavioral and physiological reactions to observed violence: Effects of prior exposure to aggressive stimuli. *Journal of Personality and Social Psychology, 40,* 868–875.

Geen, R. G., & Thomas, S. L. (1986). The immediate effects of media violence on behavior. In L. R. Huesmann & N. M. Malamuth (Eds.), *Journal of Social Issues, 42,* 7–27.

Gehm, J., & Umbreit, M. (1986). *Victim-offender reconciliation and mediation program directory.* Valparaiso, IN: Prisoner and Community Together Institute.

Geller, E. S. (1988). A behavioral science approach to transportation safety. *Bulletin of the New York Academy of Medicine, 64,* 632–661.

Geller, E. S. (1991). War on the highways: An international tragedy. *Journal of Applied Behavior Analysis, 24,* 3–7.

Geller, E. S., Berry, T. D., Ludwig, T. D., Evans, R. E., Gilmore, M. R., & Clarke, S. W. (1990). A conceptual framework for developing and evaluating behavior change interventions for injury control. *Health Education Research, 5,* 125–137.

Geller, E. S., & Lehman, G. R. (1988). Drinking-driving intervention strategies: A person-situation-behavior framework. In M. D. Laurence, J. R. Snortum, & F. E. Zimring (Eds.), *The social control of drinking and driving.* Chicago: University of Chicago Press.

Geller, J. L. (1986). Rights, wrongs, and the dilemma of coerced community treatment. *American Journal of Psychiatry, 143,* 1259–1264.

Gendrau, P., & Ross, R. R. (1987). Revivification of rehabilitation: Evidence from the 1980s. *Justice Quarterly, 4,* 349–406.

Gerard, H. B., & Miller, N. (1975). *School desegregation: A long–term study.* New York: Plenum.

Gergen, K. J., Morse, S. J., & Kristeller, J. L. (1973). The manner of giving: Cross-national continuities in reactions to aid. *Psychologia, 16,* 121–131.

Gesten, E. L., & Jason, L. A. (1987). Social and community interventions. In L. W. Porter & M. R. Rosenzweig (Eds.). Annual review of psychology. Palo Alto, CA: Annual Reviews.

Giamartino, G. A., & Wandersman, A. (1983). Organizational climate correlates of viable urban block organizations. *American Journal of Community Psychology, 11,* 529–542.

Gidron, B., Chesler, M. A., & Chesney, B. K. (1991). Cross-cultural perspectives on self-help groups: Comparisons between participants and nonparticipants in Israel and the United States. *American Journal of Community Psychology, 19,* 667–682.

Gil, D. G. (Ed.). (1979). *Child abuse and violence.* New York: AMS Press.

Gilbert, M. J., & Cervantex, R. C. (1986). Patterns and practices of alcohol use among Mexican Americans: A comprehensive review. *Hispanic Journal of Behavioral Sciences, 8,* 1–87.

Gillespie, J. F., Durlak, J., & Sherman, D. (1982). Relationship between kindergarten children's interpersonal problem solving skills and other indices of school adjustment: A cautionary note. *American Journal of Community Psychology, 10,* 149–153.

Glaberson, W. (1990, February 19). Mean streets teach New Yorkers to just walk on by. *The New York Times,* B1–B2.

Glenwick, D. S., Heller, K., Linney, J. A., & Pargament, K. I. (1990). Criteria of excellence I. Models for adventuresome research in community psychology: Commonalties, dilemmas, and future direction. In P. Tolan, C. Keys, F. Chertok, & L. Jason (Eds.), *Researching community psychology: Issues of theory and methods.* Washington, DC: American Psychological Association.

Glidewell, J. C. (1976). A theory of induced social change. *American Journal of Community Psychology, 4,* 227–239.

Glidewell, J. C. (1987). Induce change and stability in psychological and social systems. *American Journal of Community Psychology, 15,* 741–772.

Glynn, T. J. (1986). Neighborhood and sense of community. *Journal of Community Psychology, 14,* 341–352.

Goelman, H. (1988). The relationship between structure and process variables in home and day care settings on children's language development. In A. R. Pence (Ed.), *Ecological research with children and families.* New York: Teachers College Press.

Goffman, E. (1961). *Asylums.* Garden City, NJ: Doubleday.

Golding, J. M., Potts, M. K., & Aneshensel, C. S. (1991). Stress exposure among Mexican Americans and non-Hispanic whites. *Journal of Community Psychology, 19,* 37–59.

Golding, J. M., Siegel, J. M., Sorenson, S. B., Burnam, M. A., & Stein, J. A. (1989). Social support sources following sexual assault. *Journal of Community Psychology, 17,* 92–107.

Goleman, D. (1989, January 24). Sad legacy of abuse: The search for remedies. *The New York Times, C1,* C6.

Golembiewski, R. T. (1985). *Humanizing public organizations.* Mt. Airy, MD: Lomond.

Goodman, A. M. (1990). A model for police officer burnout. *Journal of Business and Psychology, 5,* 85–99.

Gore, A. (1990). Public policy and the homeless. *American Psychologist, 45,* 960–962.

Gottfried, A. E., & Gottfried, A. W. (1988). Maternal employment and children's development. In A. E. Gottfried & A. W. Gottfried (Eds.), *Maternal employment and children's development.* New York: Plenum Press.

Gottlieb, B. H. (1981). Social networks and social support in community mental health. In B. H. Gottlieb (Ed.), *Social networks and social support.* Beverly Hills: Sage.

Gottlieb, B. H. (1987). Using social support to protect and promote health. *Journal of Primary Prevention, 8,* 49–70.

Gottlieb, B. H., & Peters, L. (1991). A national demographic portrait of mutual aid group participants in Canada. *American Journal of Community Psychology, 19,* 651–666.

Grace, J., I-Chin Tu, J., Rochman, B., & Woodbury, R. (1994, July 25). Out of the line of fire. *Time,* 25–29.

Graue, M. E. (1992). Social interpretations of readiness for kindergarten. *Early Childhood Research Quarterly, 7,* 225–243.

Gray, D. O., & Braddy, B. A. (1988). Experimental social innovation and client-centered job seeking programs. *American Journal of Community Psychology, 16,* 325–343.

Gray, P., & Chanoff, D. (1986). Democratic schooling: What happens to young people who have charge of their own education? *American Journal of Community Psychology, 94,* 182–213.

Greatbatch, D., & Dingwall, R. (1989). Selective facilitation: Some preliminary observations on a strategy used by divorce mediators. *Law and Society Review, 23,* 613–641.

Greenberger, E., Goldberg, W. A., Hamill, S., O'Neill, R., & Payne, C. K. (1989). Contributions of a supportive work environment to parents' well-being and orientation to work. *American Journal of Community Psychology, 17,* 755–783.

Greene, V. L., & Monahan, D. J. (1989). The effect of a support and education program on stress and burden among family caregivers to frail elderly persons. *Gerontologist, 29,* 472–477.

Grob, G. N. (1991). *From asylum to community: Mental health policy in modern America.* Princeton, NJ: Princeton University Press.

Grossi, E. L., & Berg, B. L. (1991). Stress and job dissatisfaction among correctional officers: An unexpected finding. *International Journal of Offender Therapy and Comparative Criminology, 35,* 73–81.

Grotberg, E. (1969). *Project Head Start: Review of research 1965–1969.* Washington, DC: Office of Economic Opportunity.

Gruber, J., & Trickett, E. J. (1987), Can we empower others? The paradox of empowerment in the governing of an alternative public school. *American Journal of Community Psychology, 15,* 353–371.

Hagborg, W. J. (1988). A study of the intensity and frequency of crisis intervention for students enrolled in a school for the severely emotionally disturbed. *Adolescence, 23,* 825–836.

Halpern, R. (1991). Supportive services for families in poverty: Dilemmas of reforms. *Social Science Review, 65.*

Halpert, H. P. (1985). Surveys of public opinions and attitudes about mental illness. *Public Health Report, 80,* 589–597.

Hamilton, S. F., Basseches, M., & Richards, F. A. (1985). Participatory-democratic work and adolescents' mental health. *American Journal of Community Psychology, 13,* 467–486.

Handel, G. (1982). *Social welfare in western society.* New York: Random House.

Haney, C., Banks, C., & Zimbardo, P. (1973). Interpersonal dynamics in a simulated prison. *International Journal of Criminology and Penology, 1,* 69–97.

Haney, C., & Pettigrew, T. F. (1986). Civil rights and institutional law: The role of social psychology in judicial implementation. *Journal of Community Psychology, 14,* 267–277.

Harpin, P., & Sandler, I. (1985). Relevance of social climate: An improved approach to assessing person-environment interactions in the classroom. *American Journal of Community Psychlgy, 13,* 329–352.

Harrington, C. (1985). *Shadow justice: The ideology and institutionalization of alternatives to court.* Westport, CT: Greenwood Press.

Harris, L. (1985, March, 21). *Crime fear decreasing: Harris survey.* Orlando, FL: Tribune News Service.

Harrison, D. P. (1976). *Social forecasting methodology: Suggestions for research.* New York: Russell Sage Foundation.

Hart, N. (1985). *The sociology of health and medicine.* Lancashire: Causeway Press.

Hawkins, J. D., & Weis, J. G. (1985). The social development model: An integrated approach to delinquency prevention. *Journal of Primary Prevention, 6,* 73–97.

Hayden, R. M. (1989). Cultural context and the impact of traffic safety legislation: The reception of mandatory seatbelt laws in Yugoslavia and Illinois. *Law and Society, 23,* 283–294.

Head, T. C., & Sorenson, P. F. (1988). Contemporary trends in OD. *Organizational Development Journal, 7,* 13–24.

Hellem, D. M. (1990). Sixth grade transition groups: An approach to primary prevention. *Journal of Primary Prevention, 10*, 303–311.

Heller, K. (1989). Return to community. *American Journal of Community Psychology, 17*, 1–15.

Heller, K. (1989). Ethical dilemmas in community intervention. *American Journal of Community Psychology, 17*, 367–378.

Heller, K. (1990). Social and community intervention. In L. W. Porter & M. R. Rosenzweig (Eds.), *Annual Review of Psychology.* Palo Alto, CA: Annual Reviews.

Heller, K., & Mansbach, W. E. (1984). The multifaceted nature of social support in a community sample of elderly women. *American Journal of Community Psychology, 40*, 99–112.

Heller, K., Price, R. H., Reinharz, S., Riger, S., & Wandersman, A. (1984). *Psychology and community change.* Homewood, IL: Dorsey.

Heller, K., Thompson, M. G., Trueba, P. E., Hogg, J. R., & Vlachos-Weber, I. (1991). Peer support telephone dyads for elderly women: Was this the wrong intervention? *American Journal of Community Psychology, 19*, 53–74.

Hellman, I. D., Greene, L. R., Morrison, T. L., & Abramowitz, S. I. (1985). Organizational size and perceptions in a residential treatment program. *American Journal of Community Psychology, 13*, 99–110.

Henderson, J., & Taylor, J. (1985, November 17). Study finds bias in death sentences: Killers of whites risk execution. *Albany Times Union,* A19.

Hendrix, W. H., Steel, R. P., & Schultz, S. A. (1987). Job stress and life stress: Their causes and consequences. *Journal of Social Behavior and Personality, 2*, 291–302.

Hersch, C. (1969). From mental health to social action: Clinical psychology in historical perspective. *American Psychologist, 24*, 906–916.

Hersey, J. C., Klibanoff, L. S., Lam, D. J., & Taylor, R. L. (1984). Promoting social support: The impact of California's "Friends Can Be Good Medicine" campaign. *Health Education Quarterly, 11*, 293–311.

Hersey, J. C., Klibanoff, L. S., Lam, D. J., & Taylor, R. L. (1984). Promoting social support: The impact of California's "Friends Can Be Good Medicine" campaign. *Health Education Quarterly, 11*, 293–311.

Hess, B. B., Markson, E. W., & Stein, P. J. (1991). *Sociology.* New York: MacMillan.

Heyman, S. R. (1986). Toward the development of rural community psychology. *American Journal of Community Psychology, 14*, 453–456.

Himle, D. P., Jayertne, S., & Thyness, P. (1991). Buffering effects of four social support types on burnout among social workers. *Social Work Research and Abstracts, 27*, 22–27.

Hinrichsen, G. A., Revenson, T. A., & Shinn, M. (1985). Does self-help help? An empirical investigation of scoliosis peer support groups. *American Journal of Community Psychology, 41*, 65–87.

Hirsch, B. J., & David, T. G. (1983). Social networks and work/nonwork life: Action research with nurse managers. *American Journal of Community Psychology, 11*, 493–508.

Hochstedler, E. (1986). Criminal prosecution of the mentally disordered. *Law and Society Review, 20*, 279–292.

Hofferth, S. L. (1991). Programs for high risk adolescents: What works? Special issue: Service to teenage parents. *Evaluation and Program Planning, 14*, 3–16.

Hoffnung, R. J., Morris, M., & Jex, S. (1986). Training community psychologists at the master's level: A case study of outcomes. *American Journal of Community Psychology, 14*, 339–349.

Holahan, C. J., Betak, J. F., Spearly, J. L., & Chance, B. J. (1983). Social integration and mental health in a biracial community. *American Journal of Community Psychology, 11*, 301–311.

Holcomb, W. B., & Ahr, P. R. (1986). Clinicians' assessments of the service needs of young adult patients in public mental health care. *Hospital and Community Psychiatry, 37*, 908–913.

Hollander, E. P., & Offerman, L. (1990). Power and leadership in organizations. *American Psychologist, 45*, 179–189.

Hollin, C. R., Huff, G. J., Clarkson, F., & Edmondson, A. C. (1986). Social skills training with young offenders in a Borstal: An evaluative study. *Journal of Community Psychology, 14,* 289–299.

Holmes, T. H., & Masuda, M. (1974). Life changes and illness susceptibility. In B. S. Dohrenwend & B. P. Dohrenwend (Eds.), *Stressful life events: Their nature and effects.* New York: Wiley.

Holmes, T. H., & Rahe, R. H. (1967). The social readjustment rating scale. *Journal of Psychosomatic Research, 11,* 213–218.

Honing, A. (1988). *Parent involvement in early childhood education.* Washington, DC: National Association for the Education of Young Children.

Horgan, J. (1992). Profile: Karl R. Popper: The intellectual warrior. *Scientific American, 267,* 38, 40, 42, 44.

Horowitz, M., Schaefer, C., Hiroto, D., Wilner, N., & Levin, B. (1977). Life event questionnaires for measuring presumptive stress. *Psychosomatic Medicine, 39,* 413–431.

Hoshino, K. (1989). Community programs for preventing delinquency and internalization of the bond to conventional society. *Reports of National Research Institute of Police Science, 30,* 131–150.

Huesmann, L. R., & Eron, L. D. (Eds.). (1986). *Television and the aggressive child: A cross-national comparison.* Hillsdale, NJ: Erlbaum.

Huhn, R. P., & Zimpfer, D. G. (1988). Effects of a parent education program on parents and their preadolescent children. *Journal of Community Psychology, 17,* 311–318.

Humphreys, K., & Rappaport, J. (1993). From the community mental health movement to war on drugs: A study in the defintion of social problems. *American Psychologist, 48,* 892–901.

Hunt, J. M. (1961). *Intelligence and experience.* New York: Ronald Press.

Ilgen, D. R. (1990). Health issues at work. *American Psychologist, 45,* 273–283.

Inciardi, J. A. (1980). Problems in the measurement of criminal behavior. In D. H. Kelley (Ed.), *Criminal behavior: Readings in criminology.* New York: St. Martin's Press.

Irwin, J. (1980). The contemporary prison. In D. H. Kelley (Ed.), *Criminal behavior: Readings in criminology.* New York: St. Martin's Press.

Iscoe, I. (1990). The 1989 Division 27 Award for distinguished contributions to community psychology and community mental health: Edward Zigler. *American Journal of Community Psychology, 18,* 179–182.

Ivancevich, J. M., Matteson, M. T., Freedman, J. M., & Phillips, J. S. (1990). Worksite stress management interventions. *American Psychologist, 45,* 252–261.

Iverson, D. C., Fielding, J. E., Crow, R. S., & Christenson, G. M. (1985). The promotion of physical activity in the United States population: The status of programs in medical, worksite, community, and school settings. *Public Health Reports, 100,* 212–224.

Jackson, S. E., Schwab, R. L., & Schuler, R. S. (1986). Toward an understanding of the burnout phenomenon. *Journal of Applied Psychology, 71,* 630–640.

Jacobs, J. B. (1980). The prisoners' rights movement and its impacts, 1960–1980. In N. Morris & M. Tonry (Eds.), *Crime and justice: An annual review of research.* Chicago: University of Chicago Press.

Jansen, M. A., & Johnson, E. M. (1993). Methodological issues in prevention research: An introduction to the special issue. *American Journal of Community Psychology, 21,* 561–569.

Jason, L. A. (1991). Participation in social change: A fundamental value of our discipline. *American Journal of Community Psychology, 19,* 1–16.

Jason, L. A., Curran, T., Goodman, D., & Smith, M. (1989). A media-based stress management intervention. *Journal of Community Psychology, 17,* 155–165.

Jason, L. A., Gruder, C. L., Martins, S., Flay, B. R., Warnecke, R., & Thomas N. (1987). Work site group meeting and the effectiveness of a televised smoking cessation intervention. *American Journal of Community Psychology, 15,* 57–72.

Jason, L. A., La Pointe, P., & Bellingham, S. (1986). The media and self-help: A preventive community intervention. *Journal of Primary Prevention, 6,* 156–167.

Jason, L. A., Lesovitz, T., Michaels, M., Blitz, C., Victors, L., Dean, L., & Yeager, E. (1989). A worksite smoking cessation intervention involving the media and incentives. *American Journal of Community Psychology, 17,* 785–800.

Jay, G. M., & D'Augelli, A. R. (1991). Social support and adjustment to university life: A comparison of African-American and White freshman. *Journal of Community Psychology, 19,* 95–100.

Jemelka, R., Trupin, E., & Chiles, J. A. (1989). The mentally ill in prisons: A review. *Hospital and Community Psychiatry, 40,* 481–491.

Jemmett, J. B., III, & Magloire, K. (1988). Academic stress, social support, and secretory immuniglobin. *Journal of Personality and Social Psychology, 55,* 803–810.

Johnson, D. (1991). Psychology in Washington: Why should government support science now that the Russians aren't competing? *Psychological Science, 2,* 133–134.

Johnson, F., Lay, P., & Wilbrandt, M. (1988). Teenage pregnancy: Issues, intervention, and direction. *Journal of the National Medical Association, 80,* 145–152.

Johnson, L. D. (February 13, 1990). University of Michigan press release. Ann Arbor, MI: University of Michigan News Information Services.

Johnston, D. F. (1980). *The handbook of social indicators: Success, characteristics, and analysis.* New York: Garland STPM Press.

Johnston, L. D., O'Malley, P. M., & Bachman, J. G. (1993). *National survey results on drug use from monitoring the future study, 1975–1992.* Rockville, MD: National Institute on Drug Abuse.

Jones, E. E., & Nisbett, R. E. (1971). *The actor and the observer: Divergent perceptors of the causes of behavior.* Morristown, NJ: General Learning Press.

Jones, J. W., & DuBois, D. (1987). A review of organizational stress assessment instruments. In L. R. Murphy and J. F. Schoenborn (Eds.), *Stress management in work settings.* Washington DC: National Institution for Occupational Safety and Health.

Jordan, T. J., Grallo, R., Deutsch, M., & Deutsch, C. P. (1985). Long-term effects of early enrichment: A 20 year perspective on persistence and change. *American Journal of Community Psychology, 13,* 393–415.

Jung, R. S., & Jason, L. A. (1988). Firearm violence and the effects of gun control legislation. *American Journal of Community Psychology, 16,* 515–524.

Kagan, S. L. (1990). Readiness 2000: Rethinking rhetoric and responsibility. *Phi Delta Kappan, 71,* 272–279.

Kale, W. L., & Stenmark, D. E. (1983). A comparison of four life event scales. *American Journal of Community Psychology, 11,* 441–458.

Kamerman, S., & Kahn, A. (1987). *Child care: Facing the hard choices.* Boston: Auburn House.

Kaniasty, K., & Norris, F. H. (1992). Social support and victims of crime: Matching event, support, and outcome. *American Journal of Community Psychology, 20,* 211–241.

Kanigsberg, J. S., & Levant, R. F. (1988) Parental attitudes and children's self concept and behavior following parent's participation in training groups. *Journal of Community Psychology, 16,* 152–160.

Kanner, A. D., Coyne, J. C., Schaefer, C., & Fayarus, R. S. (1981). Comparison of two models of stress management: Daily hassles and uplifts versus major life events. *Journal of Behavioral Medicine, 4,* 1–39.

Kaplan, M. (1983). A woman's view of DSM-III. *American Psychologist, 7,* 786–792.

Katz, D. (1983). Factors affecting social change: A social psychological interpretation. *Journal of Social Issues, 39,* 25–44.

Katzell, R. A., & Thompson, D. E. (1990). Work motivation. *American Psychologist, 45,* 144–153.

Kaufman, J., & Zigler, E. (1987). Do abused children become abusive parents? *American Journal of Orthopsychology, 57,* 186–192.

Kazarean, S. S., & McCabe, S. B. (1991). Dimensions of social support in the MSPSS: Factorial structure, reliability, and theoretical implications. *Journal of Community Psychology, 19,* 150–160.

Kazden, A. E. (1980). *Research design in community psychology.* New York: Harper and Row.

Kelly, G. W. R., & Ekland-Olson, S. (1991). The response of the criminal justice system to prison overcrowding: Recidivism patterns among four successive parolee courts. *Law and Society Review, 25,* 601–620.

Kelly, H. H. (1973). The process of causal attribution. *American Psychologist, 28,* 107–128.

Kelly, J. A., Murphy, D. A., Sikkema, K. L., & Kalichman, S. C. (1993). Psychological intervention to prevent HIV infection are urgently needed: New priorities for behavioral research in the second decade of AIDS. *American Psychologist, 48,* 1023–1034.

Kelly, J. A., St. Lawrence, J. S., Diaz, Y. E., Stevenson, L. Y., Hauth, A. C., Brasfield, T. L., Kalichman, S. C., Smith, J. E., & Andrew, M. E. (1991). HIV risk behavior reduction following intervention with key opinion leaders of population: An experimental analysis. *American Journal of Public Health, 81,* 168–171.

Kelly, J. G. (1986a). An ecological paradigm: Defining mental health consultation as a preventative service. *Prevention in the Human Services, 4,* 1–36.

Kelly, J. G. (1986b). Context and process: An ecological view of the interdependence of practice and research. *American Journal of Community Psychology, 14,* 581–589.

Kelly, J. G. (1990). Changing contexts and the field of community psychology. *American Journal of Community Psychology, 18,* 769–792.

Kelsey, J. L., Thompson, W. D., & Evans, A. S. (1986). *Methods in observational epidemiology.* New York: Oxford University.

Kennedy, C. (1989). Community integration and well-being: Toward the goals of community care. *Journal of Social Issues, 45,* 65–78.

Kerlinger, F. N. (1973). *Foundations of behavioral research.* New York: Holt, Rinehart, and Winston.

Kessler, R. C., & Price, R. H. (1993). Primary prevention of secondary disorders: A proposal and agenda. *American Journal of Community Psychology, 21,* 607–633.

Kessler, R. C., Turner, J. B., & House, R. H. (1988). Effects of unemployment on health in a community survey: Main, mediating, and modifying effects. *Journal of Social Issues, 44,* 69–86.

Kessler, R. C., Turner, J. B., & House, R. H. (1989). Unemployment, reemployment, and emo-

tional Functioning in a community sample. *American Sociological Review, 54,* 648–657.

Ketterer, R. E. (1981) *Consultation and education in mental health: Problems and prospects.* Beverly Hills, CA.

Kettner, P. M., Daley, J. M., & Nichols, A. W. (1985). *Initiating change in organizations of communities: A macro practice model.* Monterey, CA: Brooks Cole.

Keys, C. B., & Frank, S. (1987). *Organizational perspectives in community psychology* (Special issue). *American Journal of Community Psychology, 15.*

Keys, C. B., & Fuehrer, A. (1987). Law enforcement in court: Role identity and interpersonal relations training of deputy sheriffs. *Journal of Community Psychology, 15,* 35–42.

Kiernan, M., Toro, P. A., Rappaport, J., & Seidman, E. (1989). Economic predictors of mental health service utilization: A time-series analysis. *American Journal of Community Psychology, 17,* 801–820.

Kiesler, C. A. (1980). Mental health policy as a field of inquiry for psychology. *American Psychologist, 35,* 1066–1080.

Kiesler, C. A. (1992). Mental health policy: Doomed to fail. *American Psychologist, 47,* 1077–1082.

Killias, M. (1993). Gun ownership, suicide, and homicide: An international perspective. In *understanding crime: Experiences of crime and crime control.* Rome, Italy: United Nations Interregional Crime and Justice Research Institute.

Kilmann, P. (1984). *Human sexuality in contemporary life.* Boston: Allyn and Bacon.

King, C. A., & Kirschenbaum, D. S. (1990). An experimental evaluation of a school-based program for children at risk: Wisconsin early intervention. *American Journal of Community Psychology, 18,* 167–178.

Kirmeyer, S. L., & Dougherty, T. W. (1988). Workload, tension, and coping: Moderating effects of supervisor support. *Personnel Psychology, 41,* 125–139.

Kitchen, C. D. (1991). Crisis intervention using reality therapy for adult sexual abuse victims. *Journal of Reality Therapy, 10,* 34–39.

Kleck, G. (1991). *Point blank: Guns and violence in America*. New York: De Gruyter.

Klein, A. G. (1992). *The debate over child care 1969–1990*. Albany, NY: SUNY Press.

Klein, K. J., & D'Aunno, T. A. (1986). Psychological sense of community in the workplace. *Journal of Community Psychology, 14*, 365–377.

Klein, L., Luxenburg, J., & King, M. (1989). Perceived neighborhood crime and the impact of private security. Special issue: Controlling crime in the community: Citizen-based efforts and initiatives. *Crime and Delinquency, 35*, 365–377.

Kleinman, J. C., & Madanas, J. H. (1985). The effects of maternal smoking, physical stature, and educational attainment on the incidence of low birthweight. *American Journal of Epidemiology, 121*, 843–855.

Klingman, A. (1985). Mass inoculation in a community: The effect of primary prevention of stress reactions. *American Journal of Community Psychology, 13*, 323–332.

Kobasa, S. C. (1979). Stressful life events and health: An inquiry into hardiness. *Journal of Personality and Social Psychology, 37*, 1–11.

Koegel, P., Burnam, M. A., & Farr, R. K. (1990). Substance adaptation among homeless adults in the inner city of Los Angeles. *Journal of Social Issues, 46*, 83–107.

Kofkin, J. A., & Repucci, N. D. (1991). A reconceptualization of life events and its application to parental divorce. *American Journal of Community Psychology, 19*, 227–250.

Kohlberg, L. (1984). *Essays on moral development (Vol. 2). The nature and validity of moral stages*. San Francisco: Harper and Row.

Koslowsky, M., Caspy, T., & Lazar, M. (1988). Are volunteers more committed than nonvolunteers? *Journal of Applied Social Psychology, 18*, 985–991.

Kotch, J. B., Blakely, C. H., Brown, S. S., & Wong, F. Y. (1992). *A pound of prevention: The case of universal maternity care in the U.S.* Washington, DC: American Public Health Associaton.

Kozol, J. (1990, Winter/Spring). The new untouchables (special edition). *Newsweek*, 48–49, 52–53.

Kruzich, J. M. (1985). Community integration of the mentally ill in residential facilities. *American Journal of Community Psychology, 13*, 553–564.

Kuhn, T. S. (1970). *The structure of scientific revolutions*. Chicago: University of Chicago Press.

Lamb, M. E., Hwang, C., Bookstein, F. L., Broberg, A., Hult, G., & Frodi, M. (1988). Determinants of social competence in Swedish preschoolers. *Developmental Psychology, 24*, 58–70.

Lamb-Parker, F., Piotrkowski, C. S., & Peay, L. (1987). Head Start as a social support for mothers: The psychological benefits of involvement. *American Journal of Orthopsychiatry, 57*, 220–223.

Landers, S. (1989). Homeless children lose childhood. *The APA Monitor, 20* (12), 1, 33.

Langer, L. J., & Rodin, J. (1976). The effects of choice and enhanced personal responsibility for the aged: A field experiment in an institutional setting. *Journal of Personality and Social Psychology, 34*, 191–198.

Lanza, M. L. (1986). Victims of international terrorism. *Issues in Mental Health Nursing, 8*, 95–107.

La Piere, R. T. (1934). Attitudes and actions. *Social Forces, 13*, 230–237.

Latane, B., & Darley, J., M. (1970). *The irresponsive bystander: Why doesn't he help?* New York: Appleton-Century-Crofts.

Launay, G., & Murray, P. (1989). Victim/offender groups. In M. Wright & B. Galoway (Eds.), *Mediation and criminal justice*. London: Sage.

Lawson, A., & Rhode, D. L. (1993). *The politics of pregnancy: Adolescent sexuality and public policy*. New Haven, CT: Yale University Press.

Lazarus, R. S. (1984). Puzzles in the study of daily hassles. *Journal of Behavioral Medicine, 7*, 375–389.

Lazarus, R. S., & Folkman, S. (1984). *Stress, appraisal, and coping*. New York: Springer-Verlag.

LeFebvre, R. C., Lasater, T. M., Carleton, R. A., & Peterson, G. (1987). Theory and delivery health programming in the community: The

Pawtuckett Heart Health Program. *Preventive Medicine, 16,* 80–95.

Leitenberg, H. (1987). Primary prevention of delinquency. In J. D. Burchard & S. N. Burchard (Eds.), *Prevention of delinquent behavior.* Newbury Park, CA: Sage.

Lempert, R., & Sanders, J. (1986). *An invitation to law and social science.* New York: Longman Press.

Leonard, P. A., Dolbeare, C. N., & Lazere, E. B. (1989). *A place to call home: The crisis in housing for the poor.* Washington, DC: Center on Budget and Policy Priorities and Low Income Housing Information Service.

Lester, D. (1987). The police as victims: The role of guns in the murder of police. *Psychological Reports, 60,* 366.

Lester, D., & Murrell, M. E. (1986). The influence of gun control laws and personal violence. *Journal of Community Psychology, 14,* 315–318.

Lettieri, D. J., Sayers, M., & Pearson, H. W. (Eds.). (1984). *Theories on drug abuse: Selected contemporary perspectives.* National Institute on Drug Abuse Research Monograph 30. Washington, DC: Superintendent of Documents, U.S. Government printing Office.

Levenson, D. (1977, October). Whatever happened to early childhood education? *Instructor, 71.*

Levi, Y., & Litwin, H. (1986). *Communities and cooperatives in participatory development.* Brookfield, VT: Gower Press.

Levin, M. (1985). Unwanted intercourse: The difficulty of saying no. *Psychology of Women Quarterly, 9,* 184–266.

Levin, T. (1983, December 11). Business ethics' new appeal. *The New York Times,* 4F.

Levine, I. S., & Huebner, R. D. (1991). Homeless persons with alcohol, drug, and mental disorders. *American Psychologist, 46,* 1113–1114.

Levine, M. (1988). An analysis of mutual assistance. *American Journal of Community Psychology, 16,* 167–188.

Levine, M. (1989). Community psychology in Asia. *American Journal of Community Psychology, 17,* 67–71.

Levine, M., & Perkins, D. V. (1987). *Principles of community psychology: Perspectives and application.* New York: Oxford University Press.

Levine, M., Toro, P. A., & Perkins, D. V. (1993). Social and community interventions. In L. W. Porter & M. R. Rosenzweig (Eds.), *Annual review of psychology.* Palo Alto, CA: Annual Reviews.

Levine, M. D. (1986). Working it out: A community re-creation approach to crime prevention. *Journal of Community Psychology, 14,* 378–390.

Levine, N., Wachs, M., & Shirazi, E. (1986). Crime at bus stops: A study of environmental factors. *Journal of Architectural and Planning Research, 3,* 339–361.

Levine, R. V., Miyake, K., & Lee, M. (1989). Places rated revisited: Psycho-social pathology in metropolitan areas. *Environment and Behavior, 21,* 531–553.

Lewin, K. (1948). *Resolving social conflict.* New York: Harper.

Lewin, K. (1951). *Field theory in social science.* New York: Harper and Row.

Lewis, D. A., & Salem, G. (1981). Community crime prevention: An analysis of a development strategy. *Crime and Delinquency, 27,* 405–421.

Liebert, R. M., & Sprafkin, J. (1988). *The early window* (3rd ed.). New York: Pergamon Press.

Liem, R., & Liem, J. H. (1988). Psychological effects of unemployment on workers and their families. *Journal of Social Issues, 44,* 87–105.

Light, D., & Keller, S. (1985). *Sociology.* New York: Knopf.

Lindquist, C. A., & Whitehead, J. T. (1986). Guards released from prison: A natural experiment in job enlargement. *Journal of Criminal Justice, 14,* 283–294.

Link, B. G., & Cullen, F. T. (1983). Reconsidering the social injection of ex-mental patients: Levels of attitudinal response. *American Journal of Community Psychology, 11,* 261–273.

Linney, J. A. (1990). Community psychology into the 1990's: Capitalizing opportunity and promoting innovation. *American Journal of Community Psychology, 18,* 1–17.

Lippa, R. A. (1990). *Introduction to social psychology.* Belmont, CA: Wadsworth.

Lippett, R., Watson, J., & Westley, B. (1958). *The dynamics of planned change.* New York: Harcourt, Brace, and World.

Lombana, J. H. (1976). Counseling the elderly: Remediation plus prevention. *Personnel and guidance Journal, 55,* 143–144.

Long, B. B. (1992). Developing a constituency for prevention. *American Journal of Community Psychology, 20,* 169–178.

Long, C. K. (1986). Quality circles in the schools: Problems and solutions. *Education, 107,* 55–57.

Loo, C., Fong, K. T., & Iwamasca, G. (1988). Ethnicity and cultural diversity: An analysis of work published in community psychology journals, 1965–1985. *Journal of Community Psychology, 16,* 332–349.

Lorion, R. P. (1991). Targeting preventive interventions: Enhancing risk estimates through theory. *American Journal of Community Psychology, 19,* 859–865.

Lounsbury, J. W., Leader, D. S., Meares, E. P., & Cook, M. P. (1980). An analytic review of research in community psychology. *American Journal of Community Psychology, 8,* 415–441.

Lovell, A. M. (1990). Managed cases, drop-ins, drop-outs, and other by-products of mental health care. *American Journal of Community Psychology, 18,* 917–921.

Lowenthal, M. F., & Haven, C. (1968). Interaction and adaptation: Intimacy as a cultural variable. *American Sociological Review, 33,* 20–30.

Ludwig, T. D., & Geller, E. S. (1991). Improving the driving practices of pizza deliverers: Response generalization and moderating effects of driving history. *Journal of Applied Behavior Analysis, 24,* 31–44.

Luke, D. A., Rappaport, J., & Seidman, E. (1991). Setting phenotypes in a mutual help organization. Expanding behavior setting theory. *American Journal of Community Psychology, 19,* 147–167.

Lundman, R. J. (1986). Beyond probation: Assessing the generalizability of the delinquency suppression effect measures reported by Murray and Cox. *Crime and Delinquency, 32,* 134–147.

Lustig, J. L., Wolchik, S. A., & Braver, S. L. (1992). Social support in chumships and adjustment in children of divorce. *American Journal of Community Psychology, 20,* 391–393.

MacDonald, J. E., & Gifford, R. (1989). Territorial cues and defensible spaces theory: The burglar's point of view. *Journal of Environmental Psychology, 9,* 193–205.

Madera, E. J. (1986). A comprehensive approach to promoting mutual AIDS self-help groups: The New Jersey Self-Help Clearinghouse model. *Journal of Voluntary Action Research, 15,* 57–63.

Magura, S., Goldsmith, D. S., Casriel, C., & Lipton, D. S. (1988). Patient-staff governance in methadone maintenance treatment: A study in participative decision making. *Narcotic and Drug Research, 23,* 253–278.

Maier, G. J., Morrow, B. R., & Miller, R. (1989). Security safeguards in community rehabilitation of forensic patients. *Hospital and Community Psychiatry, 40,* 529–531.

Marin, B. V., Marin, G., Perez-Stable, E. J., Otero-Sabogal, R., & Sabogal, F. (1990). Cultural differences in attitudes toward smoking: Developing messages using the theory of reasoned action. *Journal of Applied Social Psychology, 20,* 478–493.

Marin, G. (1993). Defining culturally appropriate community interventions: Hispanics as a case study. *Journal of Community Psychology, 21,* 149–161.

Marin, G., Marin, B. V., Perez-Stable, E. J., Sabogal, F., & Otero-Sabogal, R. (1990). Changes in information as a function of a culturally appropriate smoking cessation community intervention for Hispanics. *American Journal of Community Psychology, 18,* 847–864.

Marlatt, G. A., & Gordon, J. R. (1985). *Relapse prevention: Maintenance strategies in the treatment of addictive behaviors.* New York: Guilford.

Marlowe. (1971). *Social psychology: An interdisciplinary approach to human behavior.* Boston: Hollbrook.

Marquart, J. W., & Crouch, B. M. (1985). Judicial reform and prisoner control: The impact of

Ruiz v. Estille on Texas penitentiary. *Law and Society Review, 19,* 557–586.

Marquart, J. W., Ekland-Olson, S., & Sorensen, J. R. (1989). Gazing into the crystal ball: Can jurors accurately predict dangerousness in capital cases. *Law and Society Review, 23,* 449–468.

Martin, F. P., & Osgood, D. W. (1987). Autonomy as a source of pro-social influence among incarcerated adolescents. *Journal of Applied Social Psychology, 17,* 97–107.

Martinson, R. (1980). What works? Questions and answers about prison reform. In D. H. Kelley (Ed.), *Criminal behavior: Readings in criminology.* New York: St. Martin's Press.

Maslach, C., & Jackson, D. (1981). *Maslach burn-out inventory manual.* Palo Alto, CA: Consulting Psychologist Press.

Massachusetts Department of Public Health. (1991). *Handbook on smoking laws and regulations for Massachusetts Communities.* Boston: Massachusetts Department of Public Health.

Mathias, R. E., & Sindberg, R. M. (1986). Time limited group therapy in minimum security. *Journal of Offender Counseling, Services and Rehabilitation, 11,* 7–17.

Maton, K. I. (1988). Social support, organizational characteristics, psychological well being, and group appraisal in three self-help group populations. *American Journal of Community Psychology, 16,* 53–78.

Maton, K. I., Levanthal, G. S., Madara, E. J., & Julien, M. (1989). Factors affecting the birth and death of mutual help groups: The role of national affiliation, professional involvement, and member focal point. *American Journal of Community Psychology, 17,* 643–671.

Maton, K. I., & Zimmerman, M. A. (1992). Psychosocial predictors of substance use among urban black male adolescents. In J. E. Trimble, C. S. Boleck, & S. J. Niemcryk (Eds.), Current perspectives in ethnic-minority drug abuse research. Special edition of *Drugs and Society, 6,* 79–113.

Matthews, D. B. (1991). The effects of school environment on intrinsic motivation of middle-school children. *Journal of Humanistic Education and Development, 30,* 30–38.

Mawby, R. I. (1986). Fear of crime and concern over the crime problem among the elderly. *Journal of Community Psychology, 14,* 300–306.

Mawby, R. I., & Brown, J. (1984). Newspaper images of the victim: A British study. *Victimology, 9,* 82–94

May, R. L., II, Peters, R. H., & Kearns, W. D. (1990, September/October). The extent of drug treatment programs in jail: A summary report. *American Jails,* 32–34.

Maynard, D. W. (1984). *Inside plea bargaining: The language of negotiation.* New York: Plenum.

McCartney, K., Scarr, S., Phillips, D. A., & Grajek, S. (1985). Day care as intervention: Comparisons of varying quality programs. *Journal of Applied Developmental Psychology, 6,* 247–260.

McCaughey, B. G. (1987). U.S. Navy special psychiatric rapid and intervention team (SPRINT). *Military Medicine, 152,* 133–135.

McClure, L., Cannon, D., Belton, E., D'Ascio, C., Sullivan, B., Allen, S., Connor, P., Stone, P., & McClure, G. (1980). Community psychology concepts and research base: Promise and product. *American Psychologist, 12,* 1000–1011.

McCulloch, A., & O'Brien, L. (1986). The organizational determinants of worker burnout. *Children and Youth Services Review, 8,* 175–190.

McDonald, D. C. (1986). *Punishment without walls: Community service sentences in New York City.* New Brunswick, NJ: Rutgers University Press.

McGillis, D. (1980). Neighborhood centers as mechanisms for dispute resolution. In P. D. Lipsett & B. D. Sales (Eds.), *New directions in psychological research.* New York: Van Nostrand Reinhold.

McGonagle, K. A., & Kessler, R. C. (1990). Chronic stress, acute stress, and depressive symptoms. *American Journal of Community Psychology, 18,* 681–706.

McGrath, J. E. (1983). Looking ahead by looking backwards: Some recurrent themes about social change. *Journal of Social Issues, 39,* 225–239.

McIntosh, N. J. (1991). Identification of properties of social support. *Journal of Organizational Behavior, 12,* 201–217.

McLoyd, V. (1989). Socialization and development in a changing economy: The effects of paternal job and income loss on children. Special issue: Children and their development: Knowledge base, research agenda, and social policy application. *American Psychologist, 44,* 293–302.

McLoyd, V. (1990). The impact of economic hardship on Black families and children: Psychological distress, parenting, and socioemotional development. Special issue: Minority children. *Child Development. 61,* 311–346.

McMillan, D. W., & Chavis, D. M. (1986). Sense of community: A definition and theory. *Journal of Community Psychology, 14,* 6–23.

McVeigh, J. S., Davidson, W. S., & Redner, R. (1984). The long term impact of nonprofessional service experience on college students. *American Journal of Community Psychology, 12,* 725–729.

Meade, J. (1991). Turning on the bright lights. *Teacher Magazine,* 36–42.

Medway, F. J. (1979). How effective is school consultation? A review of recent research. *Journal of School Psychology, 17,* 275–282.

Medway, F. J., & Updyke, J. F. (1985). Meta-analysis of consultation outcome studies. *American Journal of Community Psychology, 13,* 489–505.

Meehan, T. (1986). Alternatives to lawsuits. *Alternatives to Legal Reform, 6,* 9–12.

Meehl, P. E. (1954). *Clinical versus statistical prediction.* Minneapolis: University of Minnesota Press.

Meehl, P. E. (1960). The cognitive activity of the clinician. *American Psychologist, 15,* 19–27.

Melamed, S., Kushnir, T., & Meir, E. I. (1991). Attenuating the impact of job demands: Addictive and interactive effects of perceived control and social support. *Journal of Vocational Behavior, 39,* 40–53.

Meyer, V. F. (1991). A critique of adolescent pregnancy prevention research: The invisible white male. *Adolescence, 26,* 217–222.

Milburn, N. G., Gary, L. E., Booth, J. A., & Brown, D. R. (1991). Conducting research in a minority community: Methodological consid-erations. *Journal of Community Psychology, 19,* 3–12

Milkovich, G. T., & Boudreau, J. W. (1991). *Human resource management.* Homewood, IL: Irwin.

Miller, N., Brewer, M. B., & Edwards, K. (1985). Cooperative interaction in desegregated settings: A laboratory analogue. *Journal of Social Issues, 41,* 63–79.

Miller, R. D., Maier, G. J., & Kaye, M. S. (1988). Orienting the staff of a new maximum security forensic facility. *Hospital and Community Psychiatry, 39,* 780–781.

Miller, R. L., & Klotz, D. (1993). HIV prevention with Latino hustlers. *The Community Psychologist, 27,* 43.

Milne, A. (1985). Mediation or therapy—Which is it? In S. C. Grebe (Ed.), *Divorce and family mediation.* Rockville, MD: Aspen.

Minde, K. K., Shosenburg, N. E., & Marton, P. L. (1982). The effects of self-help groups in a premature nursery on maternal autonomy and caretaking style one year later. In I. A. Bond & J. M. Jaffe (Eds.), *Facilitating infant and early childhood development.* Hanover: University Press of New England.

Mintzberg, H. (1979). *The structuring of organizations.* Englewood Cliffs, NJ: Prentice Hall.

Mitchell, R. E. (1982). Social networks and psychiatric clients: The personal and environmental context. *American Journal of Community Psychology, 10,* 387–402.

Molnar, J. (1988). *Home is where the heart is: The crisis of homeless children and families in New York City.* New York: Bank Street College of Education.

Molnar, J. M., Rath, W. R., & Klein, T. P. (1990). Constantly compromised: The impact of homelessness on children. *Journal of Social Issues, 46,* 109–124.

Molnar, J. M., Rath, W. R., Klein, T. P., Lowe, C., & Hartmann, A. H. (1991). *Ill fares the land: The consequences of homelessness and chronic poverty for children and families in New York City.* New York: Bank Street College of Education.

Montgomery, R. J. V., Gonyea, J. G., & Hooyman, N. R. (1985). Caregiving and the experience of subjective and objective burden. *Family Relations, 34*, 19–26.

Moore, E. (1982). *Day care: Scientific and social policy issues.* Boston: Auburn House.

Moore, S. M. (1977). The effects of Head Start Programs with different curricular and teaching strategies. *Young Children, 32*, 54–60.

Moorehead, G., & Griffin, R. W. (1992). *Organizational behavior: Managing people and organizations.* Boston: Houghton Mifflin.

Moos, R. H. (1979). *Evaluating educational environments.* San Francisco: Jossey-Bass.

Moos, R. H., Finney, J. W., & Cronkite, R. C. (1990). *Alcoholism treatment: Context, process, and outcome.* Oxford, England: Oxford University Press.

Morgan, G. (1983). Child day care policy in chaos. In E. F. Zeigler, S. L. Kagan, & E. Klugman (Eds.), *Children, families, and government: Perspectives on American social policy.* Cambridge, England: Cambridge University Press.

Morrison, J. K. (1980). The public's current beliefs about mental illness: Serious obstacle to effective community psychology. *American Journal of Community Psychology, 8*, 697–707.

Morse, G. H., Calsyn, R. J., & Burger, G. K. (1992). Development and cross-validation of a system for classifying homeless persons. *Journal of Community Psychology, 20*, 228–242.

Morton, S. E. (1990). Commentary: Reconsidering education. *Journal of Primary Prevention, 11*, 239–241.

Moser, C. G., & Dyck, D. G. (1989). Type A behavior, uncontrollability, and the activation of hostile self-schema responding. *Journal of Research in Personality, 23*, 248–267.

Moss, L. (1981). *Management stress.* Reading, MA: Addison-Wesley.

Mowbray, C. T. (1979). A study of patients treated as incompetent to stand trial. *Social Psychiatry, 14*, 31–39.

Mowbray, C. T. (1990). Community treatment for the seriously mentally ill: Is this community psychology? *American Journal of Community Psychology, 18*, 893–902.

Mowbray, C. T., Bybee, D., & Cohen, E. (1993). Describing the homeless mentally ill: Cluster analysis results. *American Journal of Community Psychology, 21*, 67–94.

Mowbray, C. T., Herman, S. E., & Hazel, K. (1992). Subgroups and differential treatment needs of young adults with long-term severe mental illness. *Psychosocial Rehabilitation Journal, 16*, 45–62.

Muha, D. G., & Cole, C. (1990). Dropout prevention and group counseling: A review of the literature. *High School Journal, 74*, 76–80.

Muller, C. F. (1990). *Health care and gender.* New York: Russell Sage Foundation.

Mulvey, E. P., & Reppucci, N. D. (1988). The context of clinical judgments of amenability to treatment in juvenile offenders. *American Journal of Community Psychology, 16*, 525–545.

Muñoz, R. F., Glish, M., Soo-Hoo, T., & Robertson, J. (1982). The San Francisco Mood Survey project: Preliminary work toward the prevention of depression. *American Journal of Community Psychology, 10*, 317–329.

Murray, J. D. (1984). Training community psychologists for work in rural areas. *American Journal of Community Psychology, 12*, 227–232.

Myers, H. F., Taylor, S., Alvy, A., Arrington, & Richardson, M. A. (1992). Parental and family predictors of behavior problems in inner-city Black children. *American Journal of Community Psychology, 20*, 557–575.

Myers, J. K., et al. (1984). Six month prevalence of psychiatric disorders in three communities. *Archives of General Psychiatry, 41*, 959–967.

Nadler, A., & Fisher, J. D. (1984). Effects of donor-recipient relationships on recipients' reactions to aid. In E. Staub, D. Bar-Tal, J. Karylowski, & J. Reylowski (Eds.), *Development and maintenance of prosocial behavior: International perspectives on positive morality.* New York: Plenum.

Naisbitt, J., & Aburdene, P. (1990). *Megatrends 2000.* New York: William Morrow and Company.

Nakell, B., & Hardy, K. A. (1987). *The arbitrariness of the death penalty.* Philadelphia: Temple University Press.

National Association of State Boards of Education. (1988). *Right from the start.* Alexandria, VA: Author.

National Cancer Institute. (1991). *Strategies to control tobacco use in the United States: A blueprint for public health action in the 1990s.* HIH Publication Number 92–3316. Washington, DC: U.S. Department of Health and Human Services.

National Center for Health Statistics. (1989). *Smoking and other tobacco use: United States, 1987,* by Schoenborn, C. A., & Boyd, G. Vital and health statistics. Series 10, No. 169. DHHS Publication Number (PHS) 89–1597. Hysttsville, MD: U.S. Department of Health and Human Services.

National Coalition for the Homeless. (1988). *Precious resources: Government owned housing and the needs of the homeless.* New York: Author.

National Commission on AIDS. (1993). *Behavioral and social sciences and the HIV/AIDS epidemic.* Washington, DC: Author.

National Commission on Working Women. (1989, Winter). Women, work, and the future. *Women at work.* Washington, DC: Author.

National Crime Prevention Council. (1989). The success of community crime prevention. *Canadian Journal of Criminology, 31,* 487–506.

National Crime Survey. (1991). *National crime survey preliminary press release.* March 24.

Nelson, D. W., & Cohen, L. H. (1983). Locus of control and control perceptions and the relationship between life stress and psychological disorder. *American Journal of Community Psychology, 11,* 705–722.

Nelson, G. (1990). Women's life strains, social support, coping, and positive and negative affect: Cross-sectional and longitudinal tests of the two-factor theory of emotional well-being. *Journal of Community Psychology, 18,* 239–263.

Nettler, G. (1980). Definition of crime. In D. H. Kelly (Ed.), *Criminal behavior: Readings in criminology.* New York: St. Martin's Press.

Neuman, G. A., Edwards, J. E., & Raju, N. S. (1989). Organizational development interventions: A meta-analysis of their effects on satisfaction and other attitudes. *Personnel Psychology, 42,* 461–489.

Newbrough, J. R. (1973). Community psychology: A new holism. *American Journal of Community Psychology, 1,* 201–211.

Newbrough, J. R. (1993). David Chavis—Community action psychologist: The troublesome artist. *American Journal of Community Psychology, 21,* 166–170.

Newbrough, J. R., & Chavis, D. M. (Eds.). (1986). Psychological sense of community, I: Forward. *American Journal of Community Psychology, 14,* 3–5.

New York State Employee Assistance Program Manual. (1990). Albany, NY: Governor's Office of Employee Relations.

Nikelly, A. G. (1990, August). *Political activism: A new dimension for community psychology.* Paper presented to the Annual Convention of the American Psychological Association, Boston, MA.

Nimmer, J. G., & Geller, E. S. (1988). Motivating safety belt use at a community hospital: An effective integration of incentive and commitment strategies. *American Journal of Community Psychology, 16,* 381–394.

Nishimura, H., & Suzuki, S. (1986). Citizen-helping role of the police and inhabitants of the community. *Reports of National Research Institute of Police Science, 27,* 64–74.

Norris, F. H., & Kaniasty, K. (1992). A longitudinal study of the effects of various crime prevention strategies on criminal victimization, fear of crime, and psychological distress. *American Journal of Community Psychology, 20,* 625–648.

O'Barr, W. M., & Conley, J. M. (1985). Litigant satisfaction versus legal adequacy in small claims court narratives. *Law and Society Review, 19,* 660–701.

Office on Smoking and Health. (1989). *Reducing the health consequences of smoking: 25 years of progress. A report of the Surgeon General.* DHHS Publication Number (CDC) 89–8411. Washington, DC: U.S. Department of Health and Human Services.

Okun, M. A., Sandler, I. N., & Bauman, D. J. (1988). Buffer and booster effects as event-support transactions. *American Journal of Community Psychology, 16,* 435–449.

Olds, D., Henderson, C., Chamberlin, R., & Tatelbaum, R. (1986). Preventing child abuse and neglect: A randomized trial of nurse home visitation. *Pediatrics, 78,* 65–78.

Olfson, M. (1990). Assertive community treatment: An evaluation of experimental evidence. *Hospital Community Psychiatry, 41,* 634–641.

Olson, M., & Cohen, A. A. (1986). An alternative approach to the training of residential treatment. *Residential Group Care and Treatment, 3,* 65–88.

Olson, M. R. (1991). Supportive growth experiences of beginning teachers. *Alberta Journal of Educational Research, 37,* 19–30.

O'Neill, P. (1989). Responsible to whom? Responsible for what? Some ethical issues in community intervention. *American Journal of Community Psychology, 17,* 379–383.

O'Neill, P., Duffy, C., Enman, M., Blackmer, E., & Goodwin, J. (1988). Cognition and citizen participation in social action. *Journal of Applied Sociology, 18,* 1067–1083.

Oskamp, S. (1984). *Applied social psychology.* Englewood Cliffs, NJ: Prentice Hall.

Ostermeyer, M. (1991). Conducting the mediation. In K. G. Duffy, J. W. Grosch, & P. V. Olczak (Eds.), *Community mediation: A handbook for practitioners and researchers.* New York: Guilford.

O'Sullivan, R. G. (1990). Validating a method to identify at-risk middle school students for participation in a dropout prevention program. *Journal of Early Adolescence, 10,* 209–220.

Palmer, T., & Wedge, R. (1989). California's juvenile probation camps: Findings and implications. *Crime and Delinquency, 35,* 234–253.

Palmore, E. (1976). Total change of institution among the aged. *The Gerontologist, 16,* 504–507.

Pargament, K. I. (1986). Refining fit: Conceptual and methodological challenges. *American Journal of Community Psychology, 14,* 677–684.

Paternoster, R. (1989). Decisions to participate in and desist from four types of delinquency: Deterrence and the national choice perspective. *Law and Society Review, 23,* 7–40.

Patterson, D. (1990). Gaining access to community resources: Breaking the cycle of adolescent pregnancy. *Journal of Health Care for the Poor and Undeserved, 1,* 147–149.

Patteson, D. M., & Barnard, K. E. (1990). Parenting of low birth weight infants: A review of issues and interventions. *Infant Mental Health Journal, 11,* 37–56.

Paulus, P. B. (1988). *Prison crowding: A psychological perspective.* New York: Springer-Verlag.

Paulus, P. B., McCain, G., & Cox, V. C. (1978). Death rates, psychiatric commitments, blood pressure, and perceived crowding as a function of institutional crowding. *Environmental Psychology and Nonverbal Behavior, 3,* 107–116.

Pedro-Carroll, J. L., Cowen, E. L., Hightower, A. D., & Guare, J. C. (1986). Preventative intervention with latency-aged children of divorce: A replication study. *American Journal of Community Psychology, 14,* 277–290.

Pennell, S., Curtis, C., Henderson, J., & Tayman, J. (1989). Guardian angels: A unique approach to Crime Prevention. Special issue: Controlling crime in the community: Citizen-based alternatives. *Crime and Delinquency, 35,* 378–400.

Perkins, D. D. (1988). The use of social science in public interest litigation: A role for community psychologists. *American Journal of Community Psychology, 16,* 465–485.

Perkins, D. D., Florin, P., Rich, R. C., Wandersman, A., & Chavis, D. M. (1990). Participation and the social and physical environment of residential blocks: Crime and community context. *American Journal of Community Psychology, 18,* 83–115.

Peters, R. H., May, R. L., Alaimo, C. J., Dolente, A. S., & Hecht, F. R. (1990, August). *In-jail drug treatment: A national demonstration program.* Paper presented at the Annual Meeting of the American Psychological Association, Boston, MA.

Phares, E. J. (1991). *Introduction to personality.* New York: Harper Collins.

Phillips, D. A., Howes, C., & Whitebook, M. (1992). The social policy context of child care: Effects on quality. *Journal of Community Psychology, 20,* 25–50.

Phillips, D. P. (1983). The impact of mass media violence on U.S. homicides. *American Sociological Review, 48,* 560–561.

Pilisuk, M., & Acredolo, C. (1988). Fear of technological hazards: One concern or many? *Social Behavior, 3,* 17–24.

Pittman, R. (1986). Importance of personal social factors as potential means for reducing high school dropout. *High School Journal, 70,* 7–13.

Plisko, V. W., & Stern, J. D. (1985). *The condition of education: 1985 edition.* Washington, DC: U.S. Government Printing Office.

Pogrebin, M. R. (1986–1987). Police responses for mental health assistance. *Psychiatric Quarterly, 58,* 66–73.

Pogrebin, M. R., & Poole, E. D. (1987). Deinstitutionalization and increased arrest rates among the mentally disordered. *Journal of Psychiatry and Law, 15,* 117–127.

Pogrebin, M. R., & Regoli, R. M. (1985). Editorial. Mentally disordered persons in jail. *Journal of Community Psychology, 13,* 409–412.

Poister, T. H., & Streib, G. (1989). Management tools in municipal government: Trends over the past decade. *Public Administration Review, 49,* 240–248.

Popper, K. R. (1968). *The logic of scientific discovery.* New York: Harper Torchbooks.

Porras, J. L., & Robertson, P. J. (1992). Organization development: Theory, practice, and research. In M. D. Dunnette & L. M. Hough (Eds.), *Handbook of industrial and organizational psychology* (2nd ed.). Palo Alto, CA: Consulting Psychologists Press.

Porras, J. L., Robertson, P. J., & Goldman, L. (in press). Organization development: Theory, practice and research. In M. D. Dunnette (Ed.), *Handbook of industrial/organinzational psychology* (2nd) ed.). Palo Alto, CA: Consulting Psychologists Press.

Prestby, J., & Wandersman, A. (1985). An empirical exploration of a framework of organizational viability: Maintaining block organization. *Journal of Applied Behavioral Sciences, 21,* 287–305.

Prestby, J., Wandersman, A., Florin, P., Rich, R., & Chavis, D. (1990). Benefits, costs, incentive management and participation in volunteer organizations: A means to understanding and promoting empowerment. *American Journal of Community Psychology, 18,* 117–150.

Pretty, G. M. H., & McCarthy, M. (1991). Exploring the psychological sense of community among women and men of the corporation. *Journal of Community Psychology, 19,* 351–361.

Price, R. H. (1985). Work and community. *American Journal of Community Psychology, 13,* 1–12.

Price, R. H. (1990). Wither participation and empowerment? *American Journal of Community Psychology, 18,* 163–167.

Price, R. H., Cowen, E. L., Lorion, R. P., & Ramos-McKay, J. (1988). *14 ounces of prevention.* Washington, DC: American Psychological Association.

Priddy, J. M., & Knisely, J. S. (1982). Older adults as peer counselors: Considerations in counselor training with the elderly. *Educational Gerontology, 8,* 53–62.

Prince-Embury, S. (1992, April). *Information attributes as related to psychological symptoms and perceived control among information seekers in the aftermath of technological disaster.* Paper Presented at the Eastern Psychological Association Convention, Boston, MA.

Public Agenda Foundation. (1992). *The health care crisis: Containing costs, expanding coverage.* New York: McGraw-Hill.

Public Health Service. (1980). *Toward a national plan for the chronic mentally ill.* Washington, DC: U.S. Department of Health and Human Services.

Putman, R. B. (1986). Important personal, social factors as potential means for reducing high school dropout rates. *High School Journal, 70,* 7–13.

Quinn, J. F., & Holman, J. E. (1991). Intrafamilial conflict among felons under community supervison: An examination of the co-habitants of electronically monitored offenders. *Journal of Offender Rehabilitation, 16,* 177–192.

Radelet, M. L., & Pierce, G. L. (1985). Race and prosecutorial discretion in homicide cases. *Law and Society Review, 19,* 587–621.

Rafferty, Y. (1990). Testimony on behalf of Advocates for Children of New York and the American Psychological Asssociation to the oversight hearings on homelessness. House of Representatives, Washington, DC.

Rafferty, Y., & Shinn, M. (1991). The impact of homelessness on children. *American Psychologist, 46,* 1170–1179.

Rapkin, B. D., & Fischer, K. (1992). Personal goals of older adults: Issues in assessment and prediction. *Psychology and Aging, 7,* 127–137.

Rappaport, J. (1977). *Community psychology: Values, research, and action.* New York: Holt, Rinehart, and Winston.

Rappaport, J. (1981). In praise of paradox: A social policy of empowerment over prevention. *American Journal of Community Psychology, 9,* 1–25.

Rappaport, J. (1987). Terms of empowerment/Exemplars of prevention: Toward a theory for community psychology. *American Journal of Community Psychology, 15,* 121–148.

Rappaport, J. (1990). Research methods and the empowerment social agenda. In P. Tolan, C. Keys, F. Chertok, & L. Jason (Eds.), *Researching community psychology: Issues of theory and methods.* Washington, DC: American Psychological Association.

Rappaport, J., Seidman, E., Toro, P., McFadden, L. S. , Reischl, T. M., Roberts, L. J. , Salem, D. A., Stein, C. H. , & Yimmerman, M. (1985). Collaborative research of a mutual help organization. *Social Policy, 15,* 12–24.

Rappaport, J., Swift, C., & Hess, P. (Eds.). (1984). *Studies in empowerment: Steps toward understanding and action.* New York: Haworth.

Ratiu, I. S. (1986). A workshop on managing in a multicultural environment. Special issue: International management and development. *Management Education and Development, 17,* 252–256.

Redeinstituionalization. (1986, August 25). *The New York Times,* A18.

Redman, W. K., Cullari, S., & Farris, H. E. (1985). An analysis of some important tasks and phases in consultation. *Journal of Community Psychology, 13,* 375–386.

Reed, R. (1988). Education and achievement of young black males. In J. T. Gibbs (Ed.), *Young, Black, and male in America: An endangered species.* Dover, MA: Auburn House.

Reeves, H. (1989). The victim support perspective. In M. Wright & B. Gallaway (Eds.), *Mediation and criminal justice.* London: Sage.

Reich, J. W., & Zautra, A. J. (1991). Experimental and measurement approaches to internal control in at-risk older adults. *Journal of Social Issues, 47,* 143–158.

Rein, M., & Schon, D. A. (1977). Problem setting in policy research. In C. H. Weiss (Ed.), *Using social research in public policy making.* Lexington, MA: Lexington Books.

Reissman, F. (1990). Restructuring help: A human services paradigm for the 1990s. *American Journal of Community Psychology, 18,* 221–230.

Reppucci, N. D. (1987). Prevention and ecology: Teen-age pregnancy, child sexual abuse, and organized youth sports. *American Journal of Community Psychology, 15,* 1–22.

Reuss-Ianni, E. (1983). *Two cultures of policing: Street cops and management cops.* New Brunswick, NJ: Transaction Books.

Reyes, O., & Jason, L. A. (1991). An evaluation of a high school dropout prevention program. *Journal of Community Psychology, 19,* 221–230.

Reynolds, A. J. (1991). Early schooling of children at risk. *American Educational Research Journal, 28,* 392–422.

Richey, C. A., Lovell, M. L., & Reid, K. (1991). Interpersonal skill training to enhance social support among women at risk for child maltreatment. *Children and Youth Services Review, 13,* 41–59.

Rickel, A. U. (1986). Prescriptions for a new generation: Early life interventions. *American Journal of Community Psychology, 14,* 1–15.

Rickel, A. U. (1989) *Teen pregnancy and parenting.* New York: Hemisphere/Taylor & Francis.

Rickel, A. U., & Burgio, J. C. (1982). Assessing social competencies in lower income preschool children. *American Journal of Community Psychology, 10,* 635–647.

Riga, J., & Morganti, J. B. (1992). *Rated differences in territorial barriers and exterior maintenance in owner-occupied vs. rental-only housing.* Paper presented at the meeting of the Eastern Psychological Association, Boston, MA.

Riger, S. (1985). Crime as an environmental stressor. *Journal of Community Psychology, 13,* 270–280.

Riger, S. (1989). The politics of community intervention. *American Journal of Community Psychology, 17,* 379–383.

Riger, S. (1990). Ways of knowing and organizational approaches to community psychology. In P. Tolan, C. Keys, F. Chertak, & L. Jason (Eds.), *Researching community psychology.* Washington, DC: American Psychological Association.

Riger, S. (1993). What's wrong with empowerment. *American Journal of Community Psychology, 21,* 279–292.

Rivlin, L. G., & Imbimbo, J. E. (1989). Self-help efforts in a squatter community. *American Journal of Community Psychology, 17,* 705–728.

Roak, K. S. (1991). Facilitating friendship formation in late life: Puzzles and challenges. *American Journal of Community Psychology, 19,* 103–110.

Roberts, D. G. (1991). "I don't get no respect." *Organization Development Journal, 9,* 55–60.

Roberts, M. C., Fanurik, D., & Wilson, D. R. (1988). A community program to reward children's use of seat belts. *American Journal of Community Psychology,* 395–407.

Robins, L. N. et al. (1984). Lifetime prevalence rates of DIS/DSM-III disorders. *Archives of General Psychiatry, 41,* 952–958.

Robinson, C. D., & Scaglion, R. (1987). The origin and evolution of the police function in society. Notes toward a theory. *Law and Society Review, 21,* 109–153.

Robinson, W. L. (1990). Data feedback and communication to the host setting. In P. Tolan, C. Keys, F. Chertak, & L. Jason (Eds.), *Researching community psychology: Issues of theory and methods.* Washington, DC: American Psychological Association.

Rodgers, R., & Hunter, J. E. (1991). Impact of management by objectives on organizational productivity. *Journal of Applied Psychology, 76,* 332–336.

Rodin, J., & Langer, E. J. (1977). Long-term effects of a control-relevant intervention with the institutionalized aged. *Journal of Personality and Social Psychology, 35,* 897–902.

Rodin, J., Timko, C., & Harris, S. (1986). The construct of control: Biological and psychological correlates. In C. Eisdorfer, M. P. Lawson, & G. I. Maddoy (Eds.), *Annual review of gerentology and geriatics.* New York: Springer.

Roehl, J. A. (1986). *The Multi-Door Courthouse Project of the American Bar Association Special Committee on Dispute Resolution: Phase I. Intake and referral assessment.* (National Institute of Justice Grant Executive Summary). Washington, DC: National Institute of Justice.

Roesch, R. (1988). Community psychology and the law. *American Journal of Community Psychology, 14,* 451–463.

Roethlisberger, F. J., & Dickson, W. J. (1939). *Management and the worker: An account of a research program conducted by the Western Electric Company, Chicago.* Cambridge, MA: Harvard University Press.

Rogers, E. M. (1982). *Diffusion of innovations.* New York: Free Press.

Rogler, L. H., Cortes, D. E., & Malgady, R. G. (1991). Acculturation and mental health status among Hispanics. *American Psychology, 46,* 585–597.

Rokeach, M. (1960). *The open and closed mind.* New York: Basic Books.

Roll, J. M., & Habemeier, W. (1991, April). *Gender differences in coping with potential victimization.* Paper presented at the Annual Meeting of the Eastern Psychological Association, New York.

Rose-Gold, M. S. (1992). Intervention strategies for counseling at-risk adolescents in rural school districts. *School Counselor, 39,* 122–126.

Rosenfeld, S. (1991). Homelessness and rehospitalization: The importance of housing for the chronic mentally ill. *Journal of Community Psychology, 19,* 60–69.

Rosenhan, D. L. (1973). On being sane in insane places. *Science, 179,* 250–258.

Rosenman, R. H., & Chesney, M. A. (1982). Stress, type A behavior, and coronary disease. In L. Goldberger & S. Breznitz (Eds.), *Handbook of stress.* New York: The Free Press.

Rosenthal, J. A., & Glass, G. V. (1990). Comparative impacts of alternatives to adolescent placement. *Journal of Social Services Research, 13,* 19–37.

Rosenthal, R., & Jacobson, L. V. (1968). *Pygmalion in the classroom: Teacher expectation and pupils' intellectual development.* New York: Holt.

Rosentock, I. M. (1986). Why people use health services. *Milburn Memorial Fund Quarterly, 44,* 94–127.

Rosenzweig, S. (1954). A trans-valuation of psychotherapy: A reply to Hans Eysenck. *Journal of Abnormal and Social Psychology, 49,* 298–304.

Ross, I. (1966). Heard Start is a banner project. *The PTA Magazine, 60,* 3.

Ross, R. R., Altmaier, E. M., & Russell, D. W. (1989). Job stress, social support, and burnout among counseling center staff. *Journal of Counseling Psychology, 36,* 464–470.

Rossell, C. H. (1988). How effective are voluntary plans with magnet schools? *Educational Evaluation and Policy Analysis, 10,* 325–342.

Rossi, P. H. (1989). *Down and out in America: The origins of homelessness.* Chicago: University of Chicago Press.

Rossi, P. H. (1990). The old homeless and the new homelessness in historical perspective. *American Psychologist, 45,* 954–959.

Rossi, P. H., Fisher, G. A., & Willis, G. (1986). *The condition of the homeless of Chicago.* Amherst: University of Massachusetts.

Rossi, P. H., Fisher, G. A., & Willis, G. (1987). The urban homeless: Estimating composition and size. *Science, 235,* 1336–1341.

Rotheram-Borus, M. J., Koopman, C., & Haignere, C. (1991). Reducing HIV sex risk behaviors among runaway adolescents. *Journal of the American Medical Association, 266,* 1237–1241.

Rotter, J. B. (1966). Generalized expectancies for internal versus external control of reinforcement. *Psychological Monographs,* 80 (Whole No. 609).

Ruddick, R. (1989). A court-referred scheme. In M. Wright & B. Galaway (Eds.), *Mediation and criminal justice.* London: Sage.

Ruehlman, L. S., & Karoly, P. (1991). With a little flak from my friends: Development and preliminary validation of the Test of Negative Social Exchange (TENSE). *Psychological Assessment, 3,* 97–104.

Ruffini, J. L., & Todd, H. F. (1979). A network model for leadership development among the elderly. *Gerontologist, 17,* 158–162.

Rumberger, R. W. (1987). High school dropouts: A review of issues and evidence. *Review of Educational Research, 57,* 101–121.

Sahjpaul, S., & Renner, K. E. (1988). The new sexual assault law: The victim's experience in court. *American Journal of Community Psychology, 16,* 503–513.

Salazar, J. M. (1988, August). *Psychology and so-cial change in Latin America.* Paper presented to the Annual Convention of the American Psychological Association, Atlanta, GA.

Salem, D. A. (1990). Community-based services and resources: The significance of choice and diversity. *American Journal of Community Psychology, 18,* 909–915.

Sampson, R. J., & Cohen, J. (1988). Deterrent effects of the police on crime: A replication and theoretical expansion. *Law and Society Review, 22,* 163–189.

Sandhu, H. S., Dodder, R. A., & Davis, S. P. (1990). Community adjustment of offenders supervised under residential vs. non-residential programs. *Journal of Offended Rehabilitation, 16,* 139–162.

Sandler, I. N., & Keller, P. A. (1984). Trends observed in community psychology training descriptions. *American Journal of Community Psychology, 12,* 157–164.

Sandler, I. N., Wolchik, S. A., & Braver, S. L. (1988). The stressors of children's post divorce environments. In S. Wolchik & P. Karoly (Eds.), *Children of divorce: Empirical perspectives on adjustment.* New York: Gardner.

Sansone, R. A., Fine, M.A., & Chew, R. (1988). A longitudinal analysis of the experiences of nursing staff on an inpatient eating disorder unit. *International Journal of Eating Disorders, 7,* 125–131.

Sarason, I. G. (1980). Life stress, self-preoccupation and social supports. In I. G. Sarason & C. D. Speelberger (Eds.), *Stress and anxiety* (Vol. 7). Washington, DC: Halstead.

Sarason, S. B. (1972). *The creation of settings & the future societies.* San Francisco: Jossey-Bass.

Sarason, S. B. (1974). *The psychological sense of community: Prospects for a community psychology.* San Francisco: Jossey-Bass.

Sarason, S. B. (1976). Community psychology and the anarchist insight. *American Journal of Community Psychology, 4,* 246–259.

Sarason, S. B. (1976). Community psychology, networks, and Mr. Everyman. *American Journal of Community Psychology, 18,* 317–328.

Sarason, S. B. (1978). The nature of problem solving in social action. *American Psychologist, 33,* 370–380.

Sarason, S. B. (1983). *Schooling in America: Scapegoat and salvation.* New York: Free Press.

Sarason, S. B., Carroll, C. F., Maton, K., Cohen, S., & Lorentz, E. (1977). *Human services and resource networks.* San Francisco: Jossey-Bass.

Sarason, S. B., & Klaber, M. (1985). The school as a social situation. *Annual Review of Psychology, 36,* 115–140.

Sarata, B. P. V. (1984). Changes in staff satisfactions after increases in pay, autonomy, and participation. *American Journal of Community Psychology, 12,* 431–445.

Saunder, F. (1976). The multi-door courthouse: Settling disputes in the year 2000. *The Barrister, 3,* 18–21, 40–42.

Scales, P. (1990). Developing capable young people: An alternative strategy for prevention programs. *American Journal of Community Psychology, 10,* 420–438.

Scales, P. C. (1987). How we can prevent teen pregnancy (and why it's not the real problem). *Journal of Sex Education and Therapy, 13,* 12–15.

Scarr, S. (1984). *Mother care/Other care.* New York: Basic Books.

Scarr, S., & Eisenberg, M. (1993). Child care research: Issues, perspectives, and results. *Annual Review of Psychology, 44,* 613–644.

Schein, E. H. (1985). How culture, forms, develops and changes. In R. H. Kilmann, M. J. Saxton, & R. Serpa (Eds.), *Gaining control of the corporate culture.* San Francisco: Jossey-Bass.

Schein, E. H. (1990). Organizational culture. *American Psychologist, 45,* 109–119.

Schiaffino, K. M. (1991). Fine-tuning theory to the needs of the world: Responding to Heller et al. *American Journal of Community Psychology, 19,* 99–102.

Schmidt, G., & Weiner, B. (1988). An attributional-affect-action theory of behavior. Replications of judgments of helping. *Personality and Social Psychology Bulletin, 14,* 610–621.

Schmolling, P., Jr., Youkeles, M., & Burger, W. R. (1989). *Human services in contemporary America.* Pacific Grove, CA: Brooks Cole.

Schneider, A. L. (1986). Restitution and recidivism rates of juvenile offenders: Results from four experimental studies. *Criminology, 24,* 533–552.

Schoenrade, P. A., Batson, C. D., Brandt, J. R., & Toud, R. E. (1986). Attachment, accountability, and maturation to benefit another not in distress. *Journal of Personality and Social Psychology, 51,* 557–563.

Schofield, R. G. (1986). Quality circles: Introducing change in educational systems. *Social Work in Education, 8,* 220–230.

Schubert, M. A., & Borkman, T. J. (1991). An organizational typology for self-help groups. *American Journal of Community Psychology, 19,* 769–788.

Schultz, D., & Schultz, S. (1990). *Psychology and industry today.* New York: MacMillan.

Schutt, R. K., & Dannefer, D. (1988). Detention decisions in juvenile cases: JINS, JDs, and gender. *Law and Society Review, 22,* 509–520.

Schwarzer, R., & Leppin, A. (1991). Social support and health: A theoretical and empirical overview. *Journal of Social and Personal Relations, 8,* 99–127.

Schweinhart, L. J., & Weikart, D. P. (1988). The High/Scope Perry Preschool Program. In R. H. Price, E. L. Cowen, R. P. Lorion, & J. R. McKay (Eds.), *14 ounces of prevention.* Washington, DC: American Psychological Association.

Scott, R. R., Balch, P., & Flynn, T. C. (1983). A comparison of community attitudes toward CMHC services and clients with those of mental hospitals. *American Journal of Community Psychology, 11,* 741–749.

Searight, H. R., Oliver, J. M., & Grisso, J. T. (1986). The community competence scale in the placement of the deinstitutionalized mentally ill. *American Journal of Community Psychology, 14,* 291–301.

Sechrest, D. K. (1989). Prison "boot camps" do not measure up. *Federal Probation, 53,* 15–20.

Sechrest, L. (1993). Preventing problems in prevention research. *American Journal of Community Psychology, 21,* 665–672.

Seekins, T., & Fawcett, S. B. (1987). Effects of a poverty-clients agenda on resource allocations by community decision-makers. *American Journal of Community Psychology, 15,* 305–322.

Segal, S. P., Silverman, C., & Baumohl, J. (1989). Seeking person-environment fit in community care placement. *Journal of Social Issues, 45,* 49–64.

Seidman, E. (1983). Unexamined premises of social problem solving. In E. Seidman (Ed.), *Handbook of social intervention.* Beverly Hills: Sage.

Seidman, E. (1990). Pursuing the meaning and utility of social regularities for community psychology. In P. Tolan, C. Keys, F. Chertak, & L. Jason (Eds.), *Researching community psychology: Issues of theory and methods.* Washington, DC.: American Psychological Association.

Seigel, J. M., & Kuykendall, D. H. (1990). Loss, widowhood, and psychological distress among the elderly. *Journal of Consulting and Clinical Psychology, 58,* 519–524.

Seitz, V., Apfel, N., & Efron, C. (1977). *Long-term effects of early intervention: A longitudinal investigation.* Paper presented at the Annual Meeting of the American Association for the Advancement of Science. Denver, CO.

Seitz, V., Apfel, N. H., & Rosenbaum, L. K. (1991). Effects of an intervention program for pregnant adolescents: Educational outcomes at two years postpartum. *American Journal of Community Psychology, 19,* 911–930.

Seligman, M. E. P. (1975). *Helplessness: On depression, development, and death.* San Francisco: W. H. Freeman.

Selye, H. (1956). *The stress of life.* New York: McGraw-Hill.

Selye, H. (1974). *Stress without distress.* Philadelphia: J. B. Lippincott.

Seranno-Garcia, I. (1990). Implementing research: Putting our values to work. In P. Tolan, C. Keys, F. Chertak, & L. Jason (Eds.), *Researching community psychology: Issues of theory and methods.* Washington, DC: American Psychology Association.

Serrano-Garcia, I., Lopez, M. M., & Rivera-Medena, E. (1987). Toward a social-community psychology. *Journal of Community Psychology, 15,* 431–446.

Seybold, J., Fretz, J., & MacPhee, D. (1991). Relation of social support to the self-perception of mothers with delayed children. *Journal of Community Psychology, 19,* 29–36.

Shadish, W. R., Jr. (1990). Defining excellence criteria in community research. In P. Tolan, C. Keys, F. Chertak, & L. Jason (Eds.), *Researching community psychology: Issues of theory and methods.* Washington, DC: American Psychological Association.

Shadish, W. R., Cook, T. D., & Leviton, L. C. (1991). *Foundations of program evaluation: Theories of practice.* Newbury Park, CA: Sage.

Shadish, W. R., Lurigio, S. J., & Lewis, D. A. (1989a). After deinstitutionalization: The present and future of mental health long-term care policy. *Journal of Social Issues, 45,* 1–15.

Shadish, W. R., Lurigio, S. J., & Lewis, D. A. (Eds.). (1989b). After deinstitutionalization. *Journal of Social Issues, 45.*

Shadish, W. R., Thomas, S., & Bootzin, R. R. (1982). Criteria for success in deinstitutionalization: Perceptions of nursing homes by different interest groups. *American Journal of Community Psychology, 10,* 553–566.

Shepard, L. A., Graue, M. E., & Catto, S. (1989). *Delayed entry into kindergarten and escalation of academic demands.* Paper presented at the annual meeting of the American Educational Research Association, San Francisco, CA.

Shephard, R. J., Cox, M., & Corey, P. (1981). Fitness program: Its effect on workers' performance. *Journal of Occupational Medicine, 23,* 359–363.

Sherif, M., Harvey, O., White, B., Hood, W., & Sherif, C. (1961). *Intergroup conflict and cooperation: The Robber's Cave experiment.* Norman, OK: Institute of Group Relations, University of Oklahoma.

Sherman, R. (1990). The relationship between quality circles and teacher satisfaction. *Educational Research Quarterly, 14,* 53–56.

Shernock, S. K. (1988). An empirical examination of the relationship between police solidarity and community orientation. *Journal of Police Science and Administration, 16,* 182–194.

Shinn, M. (1987). Expanding community psychology's domain. *American Journal of Community Psychology, 15,* 555–574.

Shinn, M. (1990). Mixing and matching: Levels of conceptualization, measurement, and statistical analysis in community research. In P. Tolan, C. Keys, F. Chertok, & L. Jason (Eds.), *Research community psychology*. Washington, DC: American Psychological Association.

Shinn, M. (1992). Homelessness: What is a psychologist to do? *American Journal of Community Psychology, 20*, 1–24.

Shinn, M., & Gillespie, C. (1993). *Structural vs. individual explanation for homelessness: Implications for intervention*. Paper presented at the ninth annual Northeast Community Psychology Conference, New York, NY.

Shinn, M., Knickman, J. R., Ward, D., Petrovi, N. L., & Muth, B. J. (1990). Alternative models for sheltering homeless families. *Journal of Social Issues, 46*, 175–190.

Shinn, M., Lehmann, S., & Wong, N. W. (1984). Social interaction and social support. *American Journal of Community Psychology, 40*, 55–76.

Shinn, M., Morch, H., Robinson, P. E., & Neuer, R. A. (1993). Individual, group, and agency strategies for coping with job stressors in residential child care programmes. *Journal of Community and Applied Social Psychology, 3*, 313–324.

Shinn, M., & Perkins, D. N. T. (1994). Contributions from organization psychology. In J. Rappaport & E. Seidman (Eds.), *Handbook of community psychology* (2nd ed.) New York: Wiley.

Shinn, M., Rosario, M., Morch, H., & Chestnut, D. E. (1984). Coping with job stress and burnout in the human services. *Journal of Personality and Social Psychology, 46*, 864–876.

Shinn, M., & Weitzman, B. C. (1990). Research on homelessness: An introduction. *Journal of Social Issues, 46*, 1–11.

Shinn, M., Wong, N., Simko, P. & Ortiz-Torres, B. (1989). Promoting the well-being of working parents: Coping, social support, and flexible job schedules. *American Journal of Community Psychology, 17*, 31–55.

Shumaker, S. A., & Brownell, A. (1984). Toward a theory of social support: Closing conceptual gaps. *Journal of Social Issues, 40*, 11–36.

Shumaker, S. A., & Brownell, A. (1985). Introduction: Social support interventions. *Journal of Social Issues, 41*, 1–4.

Shure, M. B., & Spivack, G. (1988). Interpersonal cognitive problem solving. In R. H. Price, E. L. Cowan, R. P. Lorion, & J. Ramos-McKay (Eds.), *14 ounces of prevention: A casebook for practitioners*. Washington, DC: American Psychological Association.

Siegel, J., & Kuykendall, D. A. (1990). Loss, widowhood, and psychological distress among the elderly. *Journal of Consulting and Clinical Psychology, 58*, 519–524.

Silberman, C. E. (1980). Race, culture, and crime. In B. H. Kelly (Ed.), *Criminal behavior: Readings in criminology*. New York: St. Martin's Press.

Sime, W. E. (1984). Psychological benefits of exercise training in the healthy individual. In J. D. Matarazzo, S. M. Weiss, J. A. Herd, N. E. Miller, & S. M. Weiss (Eds.), *Behavioral health: A handbook of health enhancement and disease prevention*. New York: Wiley.

Singer, S. I., & McDowall, D. (1988). Criminalizing delinquency: The deterrent effects of the New York juvenile offender law. *Law and Society Review, 22*, 519–535.

Slaikeu, K. A., & Leff-Simon, S. I. (1984). Crisis intervention by telephone. In K. A. Slaikeu (Ed.), *Crisis intervention: A handbook for practice and research*. Boston: Allyn and Bacon.

Slavin, R. E. (1985). Cooperative learning: Applying contact theory in desegregated schools. *Journal of Social Issues, 41*, 45–62.

Sloan, H. A., & Schrieber, D. E. (1971). *Hospital management: An evaluation* (Monograph 4). Madison, WI: Bureau of Business.

Smith, D. B. (1986). The effect of intermediate treatment on a local juvenile criminal justice system. *Journal of Community Psychology, 14*, 278–288.

Smith, J. J. (1992). Humiliation, degradation and the criminal justice system. *Journal of Primary Prevention, 12*, 209–222.

Smith, M. L., & Shepard, L. A. (1988). Kindergarten readiness and retention: A qualitative study of teachers' beliefs and practices. *American Education Research Journal, 25*, 307–333.

Smither, R. D. (1994). *The psychology of work and human performance.* New York: Harper-Collins.

Snowden, L. R. (1987). The peculiar successes of community psychology: Service delivery to ethnic minorities and the poor. *American Journal of Community Psychology, 15,* 575–586.

Snowden, L. R. (1992). Community psychology and the "severely mentally ill." *The Community Psychologist, 25,* 3.

Snowden, L. R. (1993). Emerging trends in organizing and financing human services: Unexamined consequences for ethnic minority populations. *American Journal of Community Psychology, 21,* 1–13.

Snyder, M., & Omoto, A. M. (1992). Volunteerism and society's response to the HIV epidemic. *Current Directions in Psychological Science, 1,* 113–116.

Society for Community Research and Action. (1994). *Final report of the task force on homeless women, children, and families.* Washington, DC: American Psychological Associaton.

Solarz, A., & Bogat, G. A. (1990). When social support fails: The homeless. *Journal of Community Psychology, 18,* 79–96.

Sosin, M., Piliavin, I., & Westerfelt, H. (1990). Toward a longitudinal analysis of homelessness. *Journal of Social Issues, 46,* 157–174.

Sosin, M. R., Colson, P., & Grossman, S. (1990). *Homelessness in Chicago: Poverty and pathology, social institutions, and social change.* Chicago: University of Chicago, School of Social Service Adminisration.

Speer, P., Dey, A., Griggs, P., Gibson, C., Lubin, B., & Hughey, J. (1992). In search of community: An analysis of community psychology research from 1984–1988. *American Journal of Community Psychology, 20,* 195–209.

Speigel, H. (1987). Coproduction in the context of neighborhood development. *Journal of Voluntary Research, 16,* 54–61.

Spivack, G., & Marcus, J. (1987). Marks and classroom adjustment as early indicators of mental health at age twenty. *American Journal of Community Psychology, 15,* 35–56.

Sprafkin, J. N., Liebert, R. M., & Poulous, R. W. (1975). Effects of a prosocial televised ex-ample on children's helping. *Journal of Personality and Social Psychology, 48,* 35–46.

St. Lawrence, J. S. (1993). African-American adolescents' knowledge, health-related attitudes, sexual behavior, and contraceptive decisions: Implications for the prevention of adolescent HIV infection. *Journal of Consulting and Clinical Psychology, 61,* 104–112.

Stack, L. C., Lannon, P. B., & Miley, A. D. (1983). Accuracy of clinicians' expectancies for psychiatric rehospitalization. *American Journal of Community Psychology, 11,* 99–113.

Starfield, B. (1982). Family income, ill health, and medical care of U.S. children. *Journal of Public Health Policy, 3,* 244–259.

Steele, B. H., Rue, P., Clement, L., & Zamostny, K. (1987). Quality circles: A corporate strategy applied in a student sevices setting. *Journal of College Student Personnel, 28,* 146–151.

Stein, C. H. (1992). The power of a place: Opening the college classroom to people with serious mental illness. *American Journal of Community Psychology, 20,* 523–547.

Stein, L. I., & Test, M. A. (1980). An alternative to mental hospital treatment. I: Conceptual model, treatment program, and clinical evaluation. *Archives of General Psychiatry, 37,* 392–397.

Stein, L. I., & Test, M. A. (1985). The training in community living model: A decade of experience. In *New directions for mental health services* (Vol. 26). San Francisco: Jossey-Bass.

Stevens, G. B., & O'Neill, P. (1983). Expectation and burnout in the developmental disabilities field. *American Journal of Community Psychology, 11,* 615–628.

Stevenson, H. W., & Lee, S. (1990). Contexts of achievement. *Monographs of the Society for Research in Child Development,* Serial 221, 55.

Stewart, J. E. (1980). Defendant's attractiveness as a factor in the outcome of criminal trials: An observational study. *Journal of Applied Social Psychology, 10,* 348–361.

Stoelwinder, J. U., & Clayton, P. S. (1978). Hospital organization development: Changing the focus from "better management" to "better patient care." *Journal of Applied Behavioral Science, 14,* 400–414.

Stolberg, A. L., & Garrison, K. M. (1985). Evaluating a primary prevention program for children of divorce. *American Journal of Community Psychology, 13,* 111–124.

Stone, D. A. (1994). Making the poor count. *The American Prospect, 17,* 84–88.

Streeter, C. L., & Franklin, C. (1991). Psychological and family differences between middle class and low income dropouts: A discriminant analysis. *High School Journal, 74,* 211–219.

Strother, C. R. (1987). Reflections on the Stanford Conference and Subsequent events. *American Journal of Community Journal, 15,* 519–522.

Struening, E. L., & Padgett, D. K. (1990). Physical health status, substance use and abuse, and mental disorders among homeless adults. *Journal of Social Issues, 46,* 65–81.

Sue, S., Fujino, D., Hu, L., Takechui, D., & Zane, N. (1991). Community mental health services for ethnic minority groups: A test of the cultural responsiveness hypothesis. *Journal of Consulting and Clinical Psychology, 59,* 533–540.

Suffering in the streets. (1984, September 15). *The New York Times,* A20.

Sundberg, N. D. (1985). The use of future studies in training for prevention and promotion in mental health. *Journal of Primary Prevention, 6,* 98–114.

Sundel, M., & Schanie, C. E. (1978). Community mental health and mass media preventive education: The alternatives project. *Social Service Review, 52,* 297–306.

Sundstrom, E., DeMeuse, K. P., & Futrell, D. (1990). Work teams. *American Psychologist, 45,* 120–133.

Susser, E., Moore, R., & Link, B. (1993). Risk factors for homelessness. In H. K. Armenian, L. Gordis, J. L. Kelsey, M. Levine, & S. B. Thacker (Eds.), *Epidemiologic reviews* (Vol. 15). Baltimore, MD: The Johns Hopkins University School of Hygiene and Public Health.

Susser, E., Valencia, E., & Conover, S. (1993). Prevalence of HIV infection among pscyhiatric patients in a New York City men's shelter. *American Journal of Public Health, 83,* 55–57.

Svec, H. (1987). Youth advocacy and high school dropout. *High School Journal, 70,* 185–192.

Swift, C., & Levin, G. (1987). Empowerment: An emerging mental health technology. *Journal of Primary Prevention, 8,* 71–94.

Szasz, T. S. (1961). *The myth of mental Illness.* New York: Dell.

Taber, T. D., Cooke, R. A., & Walsh, J. T. (1990). A joint business-community approach to improve problem solving by workers displaced in a plant shutdown. *Journal of Commuity Psychology, 18,* 19–33.

Talbott, J. A. (1975). Current cliches and platitudes in vogue in psychiatric vocabularies. *Hospital and Community Psychiatry, 26,* 530.

Tarantola, D., & Mann, J. (1993). Coming to terms with the AIDS epidemic. *Issues: In Science and Technology, 9,* 41–48.

Tausig, M. (1987). Detecting "cracks" in mental health service systems: Application of Network Analytic Techniques. *American Journal of Community Psychology, 15,* 337–351.

Taylor, L. W., & Tao, L. S. (1980). E.E.O.C.'s improved case management system. *Management, 1,* 14–16.

Taylor, R. B., & Shumaker, S. A. (1990). Local crime as a natural disaster: Implications for understanding the relationship between disorder and fear of crime. *American Journal of Community Psychology, 18,* 619–641.

Taylor, R. L., Lam, D. J., Roppel, C. E., & Barter, J. J. (1984). Friends can be good medicine: An excursion into mental health promotion. *Community Mental Health Journal, 20,* 294–303.

Taylor, S. E. (1986–87). The impact of an alternative high school program on students labeled "deviant." *Educational Research Quarterly, 11,* 8–12.

Taylor, S. E., Helgeson, V. S., Reed, G. M., & Skokan, L. A. (1991). Self-generated feelings of control and adjustment to physical illness. *Journal of Social Issues, 47,* 91–110.

Tebes, J. K., & Kraemer, D. T. (1991). Quantitative and qualitative knowing in mutual support research: Some lessons from the recent history of scientific psychology. *American Journal of Community Psychology, 19,* 739–756.

Terpstra, D. E., Olson, P. D., & Lockeman, B. (1982). The effects of MBO on levels of performance and satisfaction among university faculty. *Group and Organization Studies, 7,* 356–366.

Terris, M., & Terris, L. D. (1990). Confusion worse confounded: Health promotion and prevention (editorial). *Journal of Public Health Policy, 11,* 144–145.

Tetzloff, C. E., & Barrera, M. (1987). Divorcing mothers and social support: Testing the specificity of buffering effects. *American Journal of Community Psychology, 15,* 419–434.

Thatcher, J., & Howard, M. (1989). Enhancing professional effectiveness: Management training for the head teacher. *Educational and Child Psychology, 6,* 45–50.

Thoits, P. A. (1983). Multiple identities and psychological well-being: A reformulation and test of the social hypothesis. *American Sociological Review, 48,* 174–187.

Thomas, E., Rickel, A. U., Butler, C., & Montgomery, E. (1990). Adolescent pregnancy and parenting. *Journal of Primary Prevention, 10,* 195–206.

Thompson, D. W., & Jason, L. A. (1988). Street gangs and preventive interventions. Special issue: Community psychology perspectives of delinquency. *Criminal Justice and Behavior, 15,* 323–333.

Thompson, M. P., & Norris, F. H. (1992). Crime, social status and alienation. *American Journal of Community Psychology, 20,* 97–119.

Thompson, S. C., & Spacespan, S. (1991). Perceptions of control in vulnerable populations. *Journal of Social Issues, 47,* 1–21.

Tice, C. H. (1991). Developing informal networks of caring through intergenerational connections in school settings. *Marriage and Family Review, 16,* 377–389.

Tobin, S. S. (1988). Preservation of the self in old age. Special issue: Life transitions in the elderly. *Social Casework, 69,* 550–555.

Toch, H., & Adams, K. (1987). The person as dumping ground: Mainlining disturbed offenders. *Journal of Psychiatry and Law, 15,* 539–553.

Tolan, P., Keys, C., Chertak, F., & Jason, L. (1990). *Researching community psychology.* Washington, DC: American Psychological Association.

Tolan, P. H., & Lorion, R. P. (1988). Multivariate approaches to the identification of delinquency proneness in adolescent males. *American Journal of Community Psychology, 16,* 547–561.

Tolan, P. H., Perry, M. S., & Jones, T. (1987). Delinquency prevention: An example of consultation in rural commuity mental health. *Journal of Community Psychology, 15,* 43–50.

Toro, P. A. (1986). A comparison of natural and professional help. *American Journal of Community Psychology, 14,* 147–159.

Toro, P. A. (1990). Evaluating professionally operated and self-help programs for the seriously mentally ill. *American Journal of Community Psychology, 18,* 903–907.

Toro, P. A., Cowen, E. L., Gesten, E. L., Weissberg, R. P., Rapkin, B. D., & Davidson, E. (1985). Social environmental predictors of children's adjustment in elementary school classrooms. *American Journal of Community Psychology, 13,* 353–364.

Tosi, H. L., Rizzo, J. R., & Carroll, S. J. (1986). *Managing organizational behavior.* Marshfield, MA: Pitman.

Tracey, T. J., Sherry, P., & Keitel, M. (1986). Distress and help-seeking as a function of person-environment fit and self-efficacy: A causal model. *American Journal of Community Psychology, 14,* 657–676.

Tramontana, M. G., Hooper, S. R., & Selzer, S. C. (1988). Research on the preschool prediction of later academic achievement: A review. *Developmental Review, 8,* 89–146.

Traynor, M. P., Begay, M. E., & Glantz, S. A. (1993). New tobacco industry strategy to prevent local tobacco control. *Journal of the American Medical Association, 270,* 479–486.

Trickett, E. J., McConahay, J. B., Phillips, D., & Ginter, M. A. (1985). Natural experiments and the educational context: The environment and effects of an alternative inner-city public school on adolescents. *American Journal of Community Psychology, 13,* 617–643.

Trimble, J. E., Bolek, C. S., & Niemcryk, S. J. (Eds.). (1992). *Ethnic and multicultural drug abuse: Perspectives on current research.* New York: Harrington Park Press.

Triplet, R. G., Cohn, E. S., & White, S. O. (1988). The effect of residence hall judicial policies on attitudes toward rule-violation behaviors. *Journal of Applied Social Psychology, 18,* 1288–1294.

Turner, D. N., & Saunders, D. (1990). Medical relabeling in gamblers anonymous: The construction of an ideal member. *Small Group Research : An International Journal of Theory, Investigation and Application, 21,* 59–78.

Turner, J. B., Kessler, R. C., & House, J. S. (1991). Factors facilitating adjustment to unemployment: Implications for intervention. *American Journal of Community Psychology, 19,* 521–524.

Turner, J. S., & Robinson, L. (1993). *Contemporary human sexuality.* Englewood Cliffs, NJ: Prentice Hall.

Tziner, A., & Vardi, Y. (1982). Effects of command style and group cohesiveness on the performance effectiveness of self-selected crews. *Journal of Applied Psychology, 67,* 769–775.

Unger, D. G., & Wandersman, A. (1985a). The importance of neighbors: The social, cognitive and affective components of neighboring. *American Journal of Community Psychology, 13,* 139–170.

Unger, D. G., & Wandersman, L. P. (1985b). Social support and adolescent mothers: Action research contributions to theory and application. *American Journal of Community Psychology, 41,* 29–45.

USA Today. (March 9, 1993). Atlanta success story. *USA Today,* 10A.

U.S. Bureau of the Census. (1985). *Statistical abstract of the United States, 1986* (196th ed.). Washington, DC: U.S. Government Printing Office.

U.S. Bureau of the Census. (1987). *Statistical abstract of the United States, 1988* (108th ed.). Washington, DC: U.S. Department of Commerce.

U.S. Bureau of the Census. (1989). *Statistical abstract of the United States, 1989.* Washington, DC: U.S. Department of Commerce.

U.S. Bureau of Labor Statistics. (1992, June). *Current labor statistics: Employment data. Monthly labor review.* Washington, DC: Author.

U.S. Department of Health and Human Services. (1991). *Healthy people 2000: National health promotion and disease prevention objectives.* DHHS publication number (PHS) 91–50212. Washington, DC: Superintendent of Documents, U.S. Government Printing Office.

U.S. Department of Justice. (Crime File Study Guide). *Families and crime.* Washington DC: U.S. Department of Justice.

U.S. Department of Justice. (1988). *Criminal victimization in the United States, 1986: A national crime survey report.* Washington, DC: U.S. Department of Justice, Bureau of Justice Statistics.

U.S. Deparment of Justice. (1991). National update. *Bureau of Justice Statistics Bulletin, 1,* 1–10.

U.S. Department of Justice. (1992). National update. *Bureau of justice Statistics Bulletin, 1, 7.*

U.S. Department of Justice (1991). *Violent crime in the United States.* Washington, DC: U.S. Deparment of Justice, Bureau of Justice Statistics Bulletin.

U.S. Government Printing Office. (1970). *Project Head Start. A child development program.* Washington, DC: Author.

Van Fleet, D. D. (1991). *Behavior in organizations.* Boston: Houghton Mifflin.

Van Koppen, P. J., & Malsch, M. (1991). Defendants and one-shotters win after all: Compliance with court decisions in civil cases. *Law and Society Review, 25,* 803–820.

van Ryn, M., & Vinokur, A. D. (1992). How did it work? An examination of the mechanisms through an intervention for the unemployed promoted job-search behavior. *American Journal of Community Psychology, 20,* 577–597.

Vaux, A. (1991). Let's hang up and try again: Lessons learned from a social support intervention. *American Journal of Community Psychology, 19,* 85–90.

Vaux, A., & Harrison, D. (1985). Support network characteristics associated with support satisfaction and perceived support. *American Journal of Community Psychology, 13,* 245–268.

Vaux, A., Riedel, S., & Stewart, D. (1987). Modes of social support: The Social Support Behaviors (SS-B) Scale. *American Journal of Community Psychology, 15,* 209– 237.

Veiel, H. O. F., Brill, G., Hafner, H., & Welz, R. (1988). The social supports of suicide attempters. The different roles of family and friends. *American Journal of Community Psychology, 16,* 839–862.

Vidal, A. P. C., Howitt, A. M., & Foster, K. P. (1986). *Stimulating community report? An assessment of the local initiative support corporation.* Cambridge, MA: John F. Kennedy School of Government.

Vidmar, N. (1992). Procedural justice and alternative dispute resolution. *Psychological Science, 3,* 224–228.

Vincent, T. A. (1990). A view from the hill: The human element in policy making on capitol hill. *American Psychologist, 45,* 61–64.

Viney, L. L. (1985). They call you a Dole Bludger. *Journal of Community Psychology, 13,* 31–45.

Vinokur, A., & Caplan, R. D. (1986). Cognitive and affective components of life events: Their relations and effects on well-being. *American Journal of Community Psychology, 14,* 351–370.

Vogelman, L. (1990). Psychology, mental health care and the future: Is appropriate transformation in post-Apartheid South Africa possible? *Social Science and Medicine, 31,* 501–505.

Wahl, O. F., & Lefkowits, J. Y. (1989). Impact of a television film on attitudes toward mental illness. *American Journal of Community Psychology, 17,* 521–528.

Walfish, S., Polifka, J. A., & Stenmark, D. E. (1984). An evaluation of skill acquisition in community psychology training. *American Journal of Community Psychology, 12,* 165–174.

Walfish, S., Polifka, J. A., & Stenmark, D. E. (1986). The job search in community psychology: A survey of recent graduates. *American Journal of Community Psychology, 14,* 237–240.

Walker, B. S. (1992, December 8). Good-humored activist back to the fray. *USA Today,* B1-B2.

Walker, C. R., & Walker, S. G. (1990). The citizen and the police: A partnership in crime prevention. *Canadian Journal of Criminology, 32,* 125–135.

Walklate, S. (1986). Reparation: A Messeyside view. *British Journal of Criminology, 26,* 287–298.

Wallander, J. L., & Varni, J. W. (1989). Social support and adjustment in chronically ill and handicapped children. *American Journal of Community Psychology, 17,* 185– 202.

Walsh, R. T. (1987). A social historical note on the formal emergence of community psychology. *American Journal of Community Psychology, 15,* 523–529.

Wandersman, A. (1990). Dissemination. In P. Tolan, C. Keys, F. Cherntak, & L. Jason (Eds.). *Researching community psychology: Issues of theory and methods.* Washington, DC: American Psycholoical Association.

Wandersman, A., Hallman, W., & Berman, S. (1989). How residents cope with living near a hazardous waste landfill: An example of substantive theorizing. *American Journal of Community Psychology, 17,* 575–584.

Warner, R. (1989). Deinstitutionalization: How did we get where we are? *Journal of Social Issues, 45,* 17–30.

Wasik, B. H., Ramey, C. T., Bryant, D. M., & Sparling, J. J. (1990). A longitudinal study of two early intervention strategies: Project CARE. *Child Development, 61,* 1682–1696.

Watson, R. E. L. (1986). The effectiveness of increased police enforcement as a general deterrent. *Law and Society Review, 20,* 293–299.

Watters, J. K., Downing, M., Case, P., Lorvick, J., Cheng, Y., & Fergusson, B. (1990). AIDS prevention for intravenous drug users in the community: Street-based education and risk behavior. *American Journal of Community Psychology, 18,* 587–596.

Watts, R. J. (1992). Elements of a psychology of human diversity. *Journal of Commuity Psychology, 20,* 116–131.

Weaver, J. Therapeutic implications of divorce mediation. *Mediation Quarterly, 12,* 75– 90.

Webb, D. H. (1989). PBB: An environment contaminant in Michigan. *Journal of Community Psychology, 17,* 30–46.

Weber, E. M. (1992). Alcohol- and drug-dependent pregnant women: Laws and public policies that promote and inhibit research and the delivery of services. In M. M. Kibey & K. Asghar (Eds.), *Methological issues in epidemiological, prevention, and treatment research on drug-exposed women and their children.* National Institute on Drug Abuse Research Monograph 117. DHHS publication number (ADM) 92–1881. Washington, DC: Superintendent of Docments, U.S. Government Printing Office.

Weed, D. S. (1990, August). *Providing consultation to primary prevention programs: Applying the technology of community psychology.* Paper presented to the Annual Convention of the American Psychological Association, Boston, MA.

Weigel, R. H., Wiser, P. L., & Cook, S. W. (1975). The impact of cooperative learning experiments on cross-ethnic relations and attitudes. *Journal of Social Issues, 31,* 219–244.

Weikert, D. P., Bond, J. T., & McNeil, J. T. (1978). *The Ypsilanti Perry Preschool Project: Preschool years and longitudinal results through the fourth grade.* Ypsilanti, MI: High/Scope Press.

Weinberg, R. B. (1990). Serving large numbers of adolescent victim-survivors: Group interventions following trauma at school. *Professional psychology Research and Practice, 21,* 271–278.

Weinstein, R. S. (1990). The universe of alternatives in schooling: The contributions of Seymour B. Sarason to education. *American Journal of Community Psychology, 18,* 359–369.

Weinstein, R. S., Soule, C. R., Collins, F., Cone, J., Mehlhorn, M., & Simontacchi, K. (1991). Expectations and high school change: Teacher-researcher collaboration to prevent school failure. *American Journal of Community Psychology, 19,* 333–362.

Weissberg, R. P. (1985). Developing effective social problem-solving programs for the classroom. In B. Schneider, K. H. Rubin, & J. Ledingham (Eds.), *Peer relationships and social skills in childhood.* New York: Spring-Verlag.

Weissberg, R. P. (1990). Fidelity and adaptation: Combining the best of both perspectives. In P. Tolan, C. Keys, F. Cherntak, & L. Jason (Eds.), *Researching community psychology: Issues of theory and methods.* Washington, DC: American Psychological Association

Weissberg, R. P., Cowen, E. L., Lotyczewski, B. S., Boike, M. F., Orara, N. A., Stalonas, P., Sterling, S., & Gesten, E. L. (1987). Teacher ratings of children's problem and competence behaviors: Normative and parametric characteristics. *American Journal of Community Psychology, 15,* 387–402.

Weitzman, B. C., Knickman, J. R., & Shinn, M. (1990). Pathways to homelessness among New York City families. *Journal of Social Issues, 46,* 125–140.

Wener, R. E., & Keys, C. (1988). The effects of changes in jail population densities on crowding sick call, and spatial behavior. *Journal of Applied Psychology, 18,* 852–866.

Wenzel, S. L. (1992). Length of time spent homeless: Implications for employment of homeless persons. *Journal of Community Psychology, 20,* 57–71.

West, S. G., Aiken, L. S., & Todd, M. (1993). Probing the effects of individual components in multiple component prevention programs. *American Journal of Community Psychology, 5,* 571–605.

Wheeler, S., Cartwright, B., Kagan, R. A., & Friedman, L. M. (1987). Do the "haves" come out ahead? Winning and losing in state supreme courts, 1870 1970: *Law and Society Review, 21,* 403–445.

White, R. W. (1959). Motivation reconsidered: The concept of competence. *Psychological Review, 66,* 297–333.

Wilcox, W. B. (1983). An historian looks at social change. *Journal of Social Issues, 39,* 9–24.

Williams, L. (1984, February). A police diversion alternative for juvenile offenders. *Police Chief,* 54–56.

Willis, T. A. (1991). Comments on Heller, Thompson, Trueba, Hogg and Vlachos-Weber, "Peer support telephone dyads for elderly women." *American Journal of Community Psychology, 19,* 75–83.

Willowbrook plan worked. (1982, September 4). *The New York Times,* 20.

Wilson, G. T., O'Leary, K. D., & Nathan, P. (1992). *Abnormal psychology.* Englewood Cliffs, NJ: Prentic-Hall.

Wilson, W. J. (1987). *The truly disadvantaged: The inner city, the underclass, and public policy.* Chicago: University of Chicago Press.

Winch, C. L., McCarthy, P., & Reese, R. G. (1993). Factors predicting successful completion of a welfare to work program. Paper presented at the annual meeting of the *American Psychological Association,* Toronto, Canada.

Winget, W. G. (1982). The dilemma of affordable child care. In E. F. Zigler & E. W. Gordon (Eds.), *Day care: Scientific and social policy issues.* Boston: Auburn House.

Winkel, F. W., & Vrij, A. (1993). Facilitating problem- and emotion-focused coping in victims of burglary: Evaluating a police crisis intervention program. *Journal of Community Psychology, 21,* 97–122.

Wolchik, S. A., Ruehlman, L. S., Braver, S. L., & Sandler, I. N. (1989). Social support of children of divorce: Direct and stress buffering effects. *American Journal of Community Psychology, 17,* 485–501.

Wolchik, S. A., Sandler, I. N., Braver, S. L., & Fogas, B. S. (1985). Events of parental divorce: Stressfulness ratings by children, parents, and clinicians. *American Journal of Community Psychology, 14,* 59–74.

Wolff, T. (1987) Community psychology and empowerment: An activist's insights. *American Journal of Community Psychology, 15,* 151–166.

Wollert, R. The Self-Help Research Team. (1987). The self-help clearinghouse concept: An evaluation of one program and its implications for policy and practice. *American Journal of Community Psychology, 15,* 491–508.

Wong, F. Y., Blakely, C. H., & Worsham, S. (1991). Techniques and pitfalls of applied behavioral science research: The case of community mediation. In K. G. Duffy, J. W. Grosch, & P. V. Olczak (Eds.), *Community mediation: A handbook for practitioners and researchers.* New York: Guilford.

Wood, W., Wong, F. Y., & Chachere, J. G. (1991).

Effects of media violence on viewer's aggression in unconstrained social interaction. *Psychological Bulletin, 109,* 371–383.

Woolpert, S. (1991). Victim-offender reconciliation programs. In K. G. Duffy, J. W. Grosch, & P. V. Olczak (Eds.), *Community mediation: A handbook for practitioners and researchers.* New York: Guilford.

Worcester, M. I. (1990). Family coping: Caring for the elderly in home care. Special issue: Facilitating self care practices in the elderly. *Home Health Care Services Quarterly, 11,* 121–185.

Worchel, S. (1986). The role of cooperation in reducing intergroup conflict. In S. Worchel & W. G. Austin (Eds.), *Psychology of intergroup relations.* Chicago: Nelson Hall.

Worchel, S., Cooper, J., & Goethals, G. R. (1991). *Understanding social psychology.* Pacific Grove, CA: Brooks/Cole.

Worchel, S., & Lundgren, S. (1991). The nature of conflict and conflict resoluton. In K. G. Duffy, J. W. Grosch, & P. V. Olczak (Eds.), *Community mediation: A handbook for practitioners and researchers.* New York: Guilford.

Worchel, S., Wong, F. Y., & Scheltema, K. E. (1989). Improving intergroup relations: Comparative effects of anticipated cooperation and helping in attraction for an aidgiver. *Social Psychology Quarterly, 52,* 213–219.

Work, W. C., Cowen, E., Parker, G. R., & Wyman, P. A. (1990). Stress resilient children in an urban setting. *Journal of Primary Prevention, 11,* 3–17.

Work, W. C., & Olsen, K. H. (1990). Evaluation of a revised fourth grade social problem solving curriculum: Empathy as a moderator of adjustive gain. *Journal of Primary Prevention, 11,* 143–157.

Wright, J. D. (1987). Testimony presented before the U.S. House of Representatives Select Committee on Children, Youth, and Families. *The crisis in homelessness: Effect on children and families.* Washington, DC: U.S. Government Printing Office.

Wright, S., & Cowen, E. L. (1985). The effects of peer teaching on student perceptions of class environment, adjustment, and academic performance. *American Journal of Community Psychology, 13,* 417–432.

Wurstein, A., & Sales B. (1988). Community psychology in state legislative decision making. *American Journal of Community Psychology, 16,* 487–502.

Youngstram, N. (1991). Psychology helps curb cigarette smoking. *The American Psychological Association Monitor, 22,* 1.

Zabin, L. S., Hirsch, M. B., Smith, E. A., Streett, R., & Hardy, J. B. (1986). Adolescent pregnancy-prevention program: A model for research and evaluation. *Journal of Adolescent Health Care, 7,* 77–87.

Zander, A. (1990). *Social psychology as social action.* San Francisco: Jossey Bass.

Zautra, A. J., Eblen, C., & Reynolds, K. D. (1986). Job stress and task interest: Two factors in work life quality. *American Journal of Community Psychology, 14,* 377–394.

Zax, M., & Specter, G. A. (1974). *An introduction to community psychology.* New York: Wiley.

Zedick, S., & Mosier, K. L. (1990). Work in the family and employing organization. *American Psychologist, 45,* 240–251.

Zigler, E. (1990). Shaping child care policies and programs in America. *American Journal of Community Psychology, 18,* 183–216.

Zigler, E. F., & Goodman, J. (1982). The battle for day care in America: A view from the trenches. In E. F. Zigler & E. W. Gordon (Eds.), *Day care: Scientific and social policy issues.* Boston: Auburn House.

Zigler, E. F., & Muenchow, S. (1992). *Head start: The inside story of America's most successful educational experiment.* New York: Basic Books.

Zigler, E. F., & Stevenson, M. F. (1993). *Children in a changing world: Development and social issues.* Pacific Grove, CA: Brooks/Cole.

Zigler, E. F., & Turner, P. (1982). Parents, and day care workers: A failed partnership? In E. F. Zigler & E. W. Gordon (Eds.), *Day care: Scientific and social policy issues.* Boston: Auburn House.

Zigler, E., & Valentine, J. (1979). *Project Head Start: A legacy of the war on poverty.* New York: Free Press.

Zimmer, L. E. (1986). *Women guarding men.* Chicago: University of Chicago Press.

Zimmerman, M. A., & Rappaport, J. (1988). Citizen participation, perceived control, and empowerment. *American Journal of Community Psychology, 16,* 725–750.

Zimmerman, M. A., Reischl, T. M., Seidman, E., Rappaport, J., Toro, P., & Salem, D. A. (1991). Expansion strategies of a mutual help organization. *American Journal of Community Psychology, 19,* 251–278.

Zinobar, J. W., & Dinkel, N. R. (Eds.). (1981). *A trust of evaluation: A guide for involving citizens in community mental health program evaluation.* Tampa, FL: The Florida Consortuum for Research and Evaluation.

Zippay, A. (1990–91). The limits of intimates: Social networks and economic status among industrial workers. Special issue: Applications of social support and social network interventions in direct practice. *Journal of Applied Social Sciences, 15,* 75–95.

AUTHOR INDEX

SUBJECT INDEX